COL...BIA

Marc Lessard

ULYSSES
TRAVEL PUBLICATIONS
Travel better... enjoy more

Editorial *Series Director:* Claude Morneau; *Production Director:* Pascale Couture; *Editor:* Daniel Desjardins.

Research and Composition *Author:* Marc Lessard.

Production *Design:* Patrick Farei (Atoll Direction); *Proofreading:* Tara Salman, Stephanie Heidenreich; *Translation:* Troy Davidson, Tracy Kendrick, Sarah Kresh, Danielle Gauthier, Janet Logan, Stéphanie Lemire, Suzanne Murray, Peter Nicholl, Josée Olivier, Christina Poole, *Cartography:* André Duchesne, Patrick Thivièrge (Assistant); *Layout:* Tara Salman, Stéphanie Heidenreich.

Illustrations *Cover and Interior Photos:* Carlos Pineda; *Drawings:* Sophie Matteau, Lorette Pierson, Marie-Annick Viatour.

Thanks to This guide could never have been written without the help of several organizations and individuals in the various stages. I cannot express enough thanks to my brother Serge Lessard at the National Research Council of Canada, to whom I sent my texts by Internet. In Colombia, special thanks go to Murry Esselmont from the Canadian Embassy, Jairo Alfredo González Izquierdo, Director Estrategia Turística, Ministero de Desarrolo Económico in Santafé de Bogotá, Enrique Arcienegas, president of COTELCO, Associación Hotelera de Colombia, also in Santafé de Bogotá, and Pedro Luis Mogollón V., director of the Centro de Convenciones de Cartagena de Indias. I would also like to mention the helpful and always forthcoming assistance of Avianca and Air Canada.
The following individuals have made invaluable contributions to this project, directly and indirectly: Abedda Abdelkader, Richard Barabé, Jacques Bazinet, Élise Labelle, Louise L'Andriaut, Claude Robert and Patrick Ropars in Montréal; Patricia Puccetti Carvajal in Cartagena de Indias; Joaquím Romero Díaz, Ferbabdo E. Muños S. and María Liria Ortega B. in Medellín; Luisa Liliana Velásquez R. and Ximena Dávila Mejía in Manizales; Edgar Omar Garzón G. in Armenia; José Gómez in Tuluá; Jeff Benoît in Cali; la señoraYolanda Mosquera T. and guides Ramiro and Lucio Marino Bravo Muños in Popayán; John Jairo Benjumea in San Agustín; Jaime Calderón Devia in Tierradentro; and other people in Colombia.

DISTRIBUTORS

AUSTRALIA: Little Hills Press, 11/37-43 Alexander St., Crows Nest NSW 2065, ☎ (612) 437-6995, Fax: (612) 438-5762

BELGIUM AND LUXEMBOURG: Vander, Vrijwilligerlaan 321, B-1150 Brussel, ☎ (02) 762 98 04, Fax: (02) 762 06 62

CANADA: Ulysses Books & Maps, 4176 Saint-Denis, Montréal, Québec, H2W 2M5, ☎ (514) 843-9882, ext.2232, 800-748-9171, Fax: 514-843-9448, www.ulysses.ca

GERMANY AND AUSTRIA: Brettschneider, Fernreisebedarf, Feldfirchner Strasse 2, D-85551 Heimstetten, München, ☎ 89-99 02 03 30, Fax: 89-99 02 03 31, brettschneider_fernreisebedarf@t-online.de

GREAT BRITAIN AND IRELAND: World Leisure Marketing, Unit 11, Newmartket Court, Newmartket Drive, Derby DE24 8NW, ☎ 1 332 57 37 37, Fax: 1 332 57 33 99, office@wlmsales.co.uk

ITALY: Centro Cartografico del Riccio, Via di Soffiano 164/A, 50143 Firenze, ☎ (055) 71 33 33, Fax: (055) 71 63 50

NETHERLANDS: Nilsson & Lamm, Pampuslaan 212-214, 1380 AD Weesp (NL), ☎ 0294-494949, Fax: 0294-494455, E-mail: nilam@euronet.nl

PORTUGAL: Dinapress, Lg. Dr. Antonio de Sousa de Macedo, 2, Lisboa 1200, ☎ (1) 395 52 70, Fax: (1) 395 03 90

SCANDINAVIA: Scanvik, Esplanaden 8B, 1263 Copenhagen K, DK, ☎ (45) 33.12.77.66, Fax: (45) 33.91.28.82

SPAIN: Altaïr, Balmes 69, E-08007 Barcelona, ☎ 454 29 66, Fax: 451 25 59, altair@globalcom.es

SWITZERLAND: OLF, P.O. Box 1061, CH-1701 Fribourg, ☎ (026) 467.51.11, Fax: (026) 467.54.66

U.S.A.: The Globe Pequot Press, 6 Business Park Road, P.O. Box 833, Old Saybrook, CT 06475, ☎ 1-800-243-0495, Fax: 800-820-2329, sales@globe-pequot.com

Other countries, contact Ulysses Books & Maps (Montréal), Fax: (514) 843-9448

© May 1999, Ulysses Travel Publications.
All rights reserved
Printed in Canada   ISBN 2-89464-089-7

We are neither Europeans nor Indians, but rather belong to a people situated between the indigenous and the Spanish.

Simon Bolívar, *El Libertador*

TABLE OF CONTENTS

"We acknowledge the financial support of the Government of Canada through the Book
Publishing Industry Development Program (BPIDP) for our publishing activities." We would also
like to thank SODEC for their financial support.

Canadä

WRITE TO US

Canadian Cataloguing in Publication Data

Main entry under title :

    Colombia

    (Ulysses Travel Guide)
    Translation of: Colombie
    Includes index.

    ISBN 2-89464-089-7

    1. Colombia - Guidebooks. I. Title II. Series

F2259.5.L4713 1999   918.6104'635   C98-941546-5

MAP SYMBOLS

🛈	Tourist Information	♧	Park
🚌	Bus Station	▲	Mountain
🚋	Funicular	∴	Archaeological Site
✈	Airport	◔	Beach
🛄	Train Station	✉	Post Office

SYMBOLS

🌴	Ulysses' favourite
☎	Telephone number
⇄	Fax number
≡	Air conditioning
⊗	Fan
≈	Pool
ℜ	Restaurant
⊛	Whirlpool
ℝ	Refrigerator
K	Kitchenette
△	Sauna
⊘	Exercise room
◙	Safe
𝒫	Parking
tv	Television
pb	Private bathroom
sb	Shared bathroom
bkfst	Breakfast
mb	Minibar
hw	Hot water

ATTRACTION CLASSIFICATION

★	Interesting
★★	Worth a visit
★★★	Not to be missed

HOTEL CLASSIFICATION

$	less than 30,000 pesos
$$	30,000 to 50,000 pesos
$$$	50,000 to 70,000 pesos
$$$$	70,000 to 100,000 pesos
$$$$$	more than 100,000 pesos

RESTAURANT CLASSIFICATION

$	less than 5,000 pesos
$$	5,000 to 10,000 pesos
$$$	10,000 to 20,000 pesos
$$$$	20,000 to 30,000 pesos
$$$$$	more than 30,000 pesos

The prices in the guide are for a meal for one person, not including taxes, drinks and tip.

All prices in this guide are in Colombian Pesos.

LIST OF MAPS

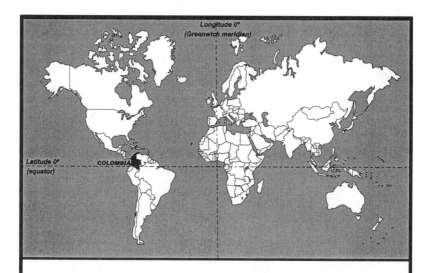

Where is Colombia?

Colombia

Capital: Santafé de Bogotá
Area: 1,141,740 km²
Population: 38,000,000 inhab.
Official language: Spanish
Currency: peso

PORTRAIT

Like a *morrión* (metal war helmet) at the top of South America, protecting the head of an arrogant, young, half-soused conquistador, Colombia crowns its continent and seems to stand watch over it. Its geographic location, linking the north of the continent to the isthmus of Panamá, has many advantages. Colombia is the only South American country with shores on both oceans: the Atlantic lies beyond the Caribbean Sea to the northeast, and the Pacific to the southwest. The country is transected by the equator, which runs through its Amazonian territory.

Morrión

GEOGRAPHY

Colombia has a surface area of 1,141,748 km², twice that of France, and is home to a population two thirds the size of the latter country's: about 38 million inhabitants (0-14 years, 32%; 15-64 years, 64%; 65 years and over, 4%). It is bordered to the north by the Caribbean Sea (1,600 km), to the west by Panamá (266 km) and the Pacific (1,300 km), to the east by Venezuela (2,219 km) and Brazil (1,645 km), and to the south by Perù (1,626 km) and Ecuador (586 km). Its national flag is made up of three horizontal stripes: the upper half is yellow, followed by a narrower blue stripe representing the sky and the sea, and a red stripe the same size as the blue one, representing the blood of Colombian heroes. July 20 is the national holiday, and the condor, the *Cattleya trianae* orchid, and the Quindío palm are the national emblems.

Three mountain chains in the western part of the country render the landscape a living sculpture. As it enters Colombia from Ecuador in the south, the Andean Cordillera branches off into three tines like a trident. The Cordillera Occidental is the shortest of the three chains with its highest peak reaching 4,250 metres and stretches along the Pacific coast into Central America where it is truncated by the Panamá Canal. The middle tine is the Cordillera Central, the country's "spine", which dominates the entire massif with its volcanoes, inselbergs and snow-covered peaks of more than 5,000 metres. Finally, the right-hand branch is the Cordillera Oriental, dotted with high plateaus including Santafé de Bogotá. It forms the Sierra Nevada de Santa Marta to the north and narrows to points jutting into the Caribbean Sea. Spur-like Cristobál Colón, one of the highest summits in South America, culminates at 5,800 metres (in comparison, Kilimanjaro, in northern Tanganyika, Africa, reaches 5,895 metres; while Mont Blanc, the highest peak in the Alps, on the French-Italian border, rises a mere 4,807 metres). Geologists believe that the Andean Cordillera is a young mountain chain, which would explain why it is regularly shaken by earthquakes.

The branches of the Cordilleras enclose two fertile valleys, Valle del Cauca and Valle de la Magdalena, named for the rivers that run through them. The *llanos* (plains) and the Amazon jungle lie in the eastern part of the country, while the west coast is covered by an impenetrable tropical forests: the primitive forest of the Chocó. The population is concentrated on the high plateaus, in the valleys and near the Caribbean coast, so a significant proportion of Colombia's territory remains uninhabited. The famous and controversial Pan-American Highway, or Carretera Panamericana, still does not traverse the entire country. It is interrupted at the Chocó forest, where environmental groups demonstrate regularly for the preservation of the region's unique ecosystem and so far have succeeded to the extent that it is still impossible to reach Colombia by road (or rail) from North America.

Colombia's territory also comprises the San Andrés y Providencia Archipelago in the Caribbean Sea, as well as many Pacific islands, including Malpedo and Gorgona.

Colombia is home to mighty rivers including Río Orinoco and Río Amazonas. The latter is the second-longest waterway in the world at 6,520 kilometres, slightly shorter than the 6,670-kilometre Nile River. However, it runs along Colombia's border with Perù for only 130 kilometres, according to a treaty signed by Colombia, Brazil and Perù following numerous border conflicts in 1930. Colombia is also washed by the waters of the Ríos Magdalena, Atrato, Cauca, Meta, Río Guaviare, Caquetá and Putumayo. All of these great rivers originate in the Cordilleras and, along with their many tributaries, generously irrigate Colombia's soil, which in turn nourishes its inhabitants.

FAUNA AND FLORA

Fauna

The variety of Colombia's fauna is only equalled by the variability of its climate and the diversity of its geography, which includes plains, mountains, rivers and jungles. In the Amazon forest for example, 1,500 flowering plant species, 750 types of trees, 450 species of birds, 150 kinds of butterflies, 100 reptile species, 60 amphibians and more than 8,000 different insects (many of which sting) can be found in an area of less than 10 hectares. Because of the diversity of life found in the country, much of which is specific to the country, Colombia is recognized internationally as the "world's gene bank". Animals frequently spotted in various parts of the country include llamas, alpacas, iguanas, crested quetzals, Ara parrots and, of course, the whole gamut of common domestic animals.

The equatorial forest is teeming with jaguars, alligators, bears, deer, poisonous snakes and constrictors, wolves, foxes, hares, monkeys, tapirs, ocelots, anteaters, wildcats and wild turkeys. The country is also populated by an impressive number of land and water birds including pelicans, pink flamingoes, condors, falcons, storks, parrots, toucans, peacocks, hummingbirds and mockingbirds.

One hundred and fifty aquatic species have been counted in Río Magdalena and more than 250 have been surveyed in Río Orinoco alone, not to mention the two species of freshwater dolphins that inhabit Río Amazonas (see p 284).

The two oceans rival each other both in quantity and quality of fish, mammals and crustaceans, from the humpback whales near Buenaventura to the entire dolphin family (*Delphinidae*). Shark, swordfish, tuna, shrimp, mullet and ray are among the game fish that are captured, and a whole range of small, exotic species are caught for aquariums.

Jaguar

Flora

Since Colombia can boast of enjoying subsequently, or even simultaneously, all of the climates of the planet, its flora presents an astonishing variety. It includes desert vegetation on the Atlantic coast, the flora of mountain plateaus in the cordilleras, of savannas near Santafé de Bogotá, and even tundra in the perpetually snow-capped mountains. The country also possesses dense, misty tropical forests like the Chocó and the Amazon, whose foliage, some of the most varied in the world, conceals all sorts of fascinating animals.

In this area too, Colombia distinguishes itself. In fact, close to 20,000 of its 55,000 plant species are considered unique to the region. The wax palm found in the department of Quindío, the tallest palm tree in the world, is just one of these indigenous species.

HISTORY

Anthropologists and ethnographers are still perplexed by the difficult task of unravelling the interwoven threads of evidence about the ancient civilizations of South America, which include innumerable legends passed down orally from generation to generation along with archaeological relics. Because so much information is lacking, they can only make informed guesses as to the pre-Columbian population. An additional obstacle is the fact that the conquistadors melted down and destroyed a great number of artifacts, and *huaqueros*, or tomb raiders, have kept up this nefarious tradition, so researchers must base their conclusions on the information they can draw from rare architectural fragments and minimal remains of pottery, textiles, jewels, and gold objects. Through critical examinations of texts written by chroniclers of the period and by a few more erudite Spaniards, they are at the very best able to trace the rough outlines of the indigenous populations of pre-Columbian Colombia.

Migrants from Asia

Specialists have established that the New World was populated long ago through massive waves of migration from northeast Asia. Nomads crossed northern Europe and Alaska about 50,000 years ago in small tribes, either by way of the Bering Strait or the Aleutian Islands, which formed a land bridge during the Ice Age.

These tribes lived in isolated groups, hunting herds of reindeer, deer and wild bison for survival, following them, unaware of their whereabouts and their destinations. The Lapps, the nomadic people of the northern steppes of Sweden, the Kola Peninsula in northern Finland, and Siberia still travel in this manner, following the reindeer that provide meat, milk, fur and transportation (the animals are semi-domesticated) as they search for pasturage.

The first palaeolithic tribes advanced into this new territory, naked and weakly armed with roughly hewn stone clubs which they used for hunting and building. In addition to herds of reindeer, they followed mammoths and other mastodons that have since become extinct. These large animals were adept at finding trails that led to water. While using the gregarious species as a sort of larder, the nomads gradually populated the whole northern hemisphere, then penetrated the central isthmus and finally reached the southern continent, migrating all the way to Tierra del Fuego. Probably because of the extremely hot climate, the uneven terrain, the dense, humid tropical forest, and the absence of adequate pastureland, the large groups of wanderers never entered México, ending their own journey in the lush plains of the southern United States.

The last major glacial period ended about 10,000 BC when the ice bridge between northern Eurasia and America dissolved under the warming sun. Europeans would not set foot on the isolated continent again until they built the tall ships that would carry them to the "discovery" of this ancient population, which not only survived but also developed several original, often sophisticated civilizations. These cultures mastered agriculture, weaving, pottery and metalworking even earlier than some "Old World" nations. In the meantime, Southeast Asian navigators, who had colonized the Pacific islands, reached the shores of the Americas in ballasted dugout canoes and injected new life into the indigenous populations of these lands. Many native legends make reference to giants who came from the west in woven cane vessels. This would account for these early Americans' knowledge of certain technologies, including perhaps the bow and arrow and the dugout canoe, which was used on the Pacific coast when the European explorers arrived.

Members of the camel family (Camelidae) – llamas, alpacas, vicunas, and guanacos – inhabit the Andes, especially in Perù, and these animals allowed early peoples to develop a more sedentary pastoral lifestyle. Nonetheless, horses, donkeys and hogs, along with livestock farming, would not be seen until the conquest. The first inhabitants of the southern continent were thus mainly nomadic and left behind very few traces of their existence. Constant roaming did not allow the development of arts such as writing or painting which contemporary, sedentary peoples had already cultivated in Europe. (Cave paintings discovered at Altamira, Spain, dating from 30,000 BC, depict primitive life with astonishing realism.) However, pottery was produced in southern Colombia some 4,000 years BC, and some archaeological artifacts exhibit striking similarities with those of ancient Chinese civilizations. Other phenomena further perplex researchers. In San Agustín, for example, funerary monuments and giant

monoliths carved in stone dating from more than 3,000 years BC were found to bear similarities to the megaliths (moai) on Easter Island in the Pacific, 900 kilometres west of Chili. Although Easter Island belongs to Chile, geographically it is part of Polynesia.

For lack of a better alternative, archaeologists and historians have frequently used the names of South American archaeological sites to designate the tribes that inhabited them. For example, the San Agustín dominated the region of San Agustín in southern Colombia; the main city of the Mochicas in Perù was Moché; and the capital of Nazca artisans was Nazca. Conversely, Nicaragua, the Central American country, is named after Nicaragua, a cacique (chief or king) whose remarkable intelligence impressed the Spanish.

The First Colombian Nations

Colombia was first inhabited by several separate nations (see p 40). They were spread throughout the territory, which they entered by two different routes: some landed on the Caribbean coast and settled there, while others crossed the Andes to settle in the low plains of Río Orinoco and Río Amazonas. The Arawaks and the hostile, warlike Caribs, ancestors of the Sierra Nevada Tayrona and the Cartagena Sinú, colonized the islands of the Caribbean Sea a few millennia later. Other groups spread along the Pacific coast to form villages in riverside oases. They colonized western Colombia and then went on to Ecuador, Perù, Chili and the southern tip of Tierra del Fuego in Argentina.

Because of the country's geography, the first Colombians were isolated from one another and did not develop the extensive cultural and political system that characterized the Incas of Perù, the Aztecs of México and the Maya of Central America. However, they were descended from two major groups and shared the same language, Quechua, the most common language in the Andes, or dialects derived from it. When the Spanish arrived, the groups descended from these two cultures still dominated the Colombian territory.

Except for a few isolated groups, most of the inhabitants of the new continent were completely self-sufficient at the time of the conquest. They were talented metalworkers, ceramists, potters, hydraulic engineers and architects, and certainly did not need the instruction of missionaries to grow cotton, corn, tomatoes, potatoes, cocoa, tobacco, calabash, peppers, peas, beans, peanuts, pineapples, guava and other crops that were once unknown or unused in Europe. In fact, they introduced these newcomers to many of the crops that are now strongly associated with certain European countries: the tomato in Italy, the potato in Belgium and cocoa in Switzerland, for example. They were more advanced in the fields of botany, zoology (Moctezuma had his very own zoo in México) and surgery than Europeans were, and their pharmaceutics included stimulants, anaesthetics, purgatives, anti-haemorrhagic agents, vulneraries, and remedies such as quinine. Archaeologists have discovered the vestiges of a medicine ball game practised by most of the pre-Columbian cultures, specifically in México.

Although most indigenous groups did not have knowledge of writing – exceptionally, the Maya developed an alphabet and a calendar – they used currency for trade, so they did have a system of mathematics. In addition, they had been building palaces, monuments, temples and public buildings using solid masonry for centuries, and on a scale that rightfully impressed the Spanish. If the Spanish were often victims of famine, it was not for lack of resources. The natives refused to feed the conquistadors, however, because of the revolting, aberrant behaviour of these brutal, murderous gods from beyond the seas.

The Pre-Columbian Era

It is impossible to understand modern Colombia without reexamining the context of the "discovery" of the New World by Christopher Columbus in 1492, that much more so because the country bears his name – although the man himself never set foot in it. In addition to the discovery of Colombia (1499), this great epic includes the conquests of the other nations of Latin America, particularly Venezuela in 1498, Panamá in 1501, Perù in 1532 and Ecuador in 1533, all of which were united in 1819 under the banner of Gran Colombia. The United States (1513), México (1519), Tierra del Fuego (1520) and Canada (1534) were also discovered by Europeans in this era, the last two being situated at opposite ends of the Americas, which stretch about 20,000 kilometres from one end of the Earth to the other and cover close to 5,000 kilometres at their widest point.

Cartographers had to rechart their maps of the planet every day in this period. This discovery of the New World was the most revolutionary advancement humanity had made to that point: in less than 50 years the known limits of the world were shattered and the surface area of the planet doubled.

Try to imagine the excitement that would be provoked by the discovery of a distant planet with a surface area equivalent to that of our Earth. At the twilight of the Middle Ages (476-1453), at a time when communication and travel were extremely restricted by today's standards, humanity was bestowed an immense new territory that included North, Central and South America and the Caribbean islands. Of course, they were far away. They were also astonishingly beautiful, wealthy, and sparsely populated. The few inhabitants who did occupy the land were seen as gullible savages, ignorant of the value of and uses for their gold, so the Europeans sent a bunch of misfits who acted more like criminals than ambassadors.

The highly developed civilizations (the Aztecs, the Maya, the Incas, the Chibcha) that had ruled these lands for millennia, not to mention their various offshoots, were decimated, if not exterminated, in the brief period of the conquest. They were systematically cheated, robbed, violated and ultimately crushed in the course of unjustified wars fought with unequal arms, and then they were condemned to forced labour (*mita*). To worsen matters, new epidemics from Europe, to which the natives had no immunity, were introduced by the new arrivals: smallpox, measles, influenza, typhus, diphtheria and other scourges. The indigenous civilizations' borders, circumscribed by geographical features, by their subsistence needs and by their own conquests, were permanently distorted by the European intruders, who established their own boundaries, based on their criteria, to suit their own needs, but especially their greed.

When the conquistadors invaded the New World in 1492, they were motivated by three main objectives. The wealthy lands of the Far East discovered by Marco Polo in 1271 had become inaccessible by land, since the Muslim Turks had cut off traditional caravan routes when they conquered Constantinople (formerly Byzantium, now Istanbul) in 1453. Thus, European merchants had to find an ocean route to the East if their flourishing trade with exotic China and Japan was to carry on. The Portuguese were the first to make a serious effort in this pursuit. Although ignorant of the size and contour of Africa, Bartholomew Díaz took up the challenge of sailing around the southern tip of the continent in 1487 and reached the Cape of Good Hope.

Secondly, wars had been raging for a long time in Europe, and each kingdom – France, England, Portugal, Spain, the Italian principalities and Austria, among others – was vying to expand its own territory and reign over new subjects who could be converted into soldiers.

Despite the cynicism of their second motive for exploration, the Europeans also hoped to bring the gospel to the New World. Every expedition and conquest was sanctioned by the Holy Church, which allowed the conquistadors to rob and murder infidels without the least bit of remorse, "for the greater glory of God". Even if most of the men initially thought of murder as loathsome, they never hesitated to resort to it when it came to the souls of the infidels. And even if we still pretend that the missionaries – particularly the mendicant orders such as the Franciscans, Dominicans, Augustinians and other Jesuits – helped the subjugated populations of Africa and the New World by bringing them knowledge acquired in the monasteries of Europe, the truth is that more often than not they behaved like common soldiers schooled in warfare by the Crusades. The Templars (119- 1312), for example, were an order of banker monks whose responsibilities included management of the Treasury of the Kingdom of France. Their primary role, however, was that of a military force of knighted soldiers recognized by Pope Honorius II in 1128 and ordered to protect crusaders and pilgrims on their way to Palestine. The Hospitallers of St. John of Jerusalem and the Teutonic Knights were other military orders with the same mission. Furthermore, the Jesuits, a Catholic "militia" founded in 1540 by Spaniard Ignatius of Loyola, who was more of a "general" than a priest.

Once in the New World, the coarsest peasant or servant, the lowest ranking officer in the army rabble, and the humblest monk could achieve "nobility" from one day to the next. These commoners saw themselves favoured with a superiority from which their modest origins completely excluded them in Europe. In the New World they lived as aristocrats, as arrogant kinglets, housed and fed by servants and slaves whom they subjugated, reduced to the rank of animals or annihilated if the need arose. They stole the conquered peoples'

wealth and women and girls were forced into concubinage, even if they were high-ranking princesses in a sophisticated civilization. Contrary to the strict mores imposed in Spain, passing affairs, concubinage and polygamy with native women soon became the norm in the New World – as spoils of war, women were as coveted as gold. Promiscuity was so prevalent that when Columbus returned from his first voyage to the Americas in 1493, syphilis was introduced to Europe, and then spread like wildfire across the globe.

In addition to being lured by the adventure, glory and wealth that awaited them in this faraway land, most of the conquistadors were desperate to flee a Europe ravaged by famine, the inevitable result of interminable, ruinous wars that prevented farmers from cultivating the land. As well, a series of epidemics devastated the population, including the Black Death, an outbreak of bubonic plague that killed an estimated quarter of Europe's population in the 14th century, and countless other diseases.

Portugal

Portugal was a nascent nation in the pre-Columbian era. In fact, Terra Portucalense, a Roman province in Antiquity inhabited by Iberians and Celts, only became known as Portugal in the middle of the 12th century when Alfonso Henriques proclaimed himself king. It was an eminently dynamic country from the outset, mainly because navigation was the easiest means to rapid economic development at that time, and it had direct access to the sea.

Spain

Religious fanaticism was the watchword of the day, especially in Spain, which expelled Jews and persecuted Moors. Under the leadership of Dominican Tomás de Torquemada, the Spanish Inquisition initiated in 1477 fiercely attacked heretics (anyone who displeased the monarchy or the clergy) and caused many sleepless nights! It was said at the time that travellers could cross the whole of Spain at night by listening for the screams and moans of the tortured and watching for the light of the bonfires that were then used to burn them, "for the greater glory of God". It was not unusual for the cadavers of these victims of the Inquisition to have disappeared by morning, so severe was the famine in Spain.

In the late 15th century, Spain was divided between Catholics and Moors. The Moors were North Africans who entered southern Spain in 711 by way of Gibraltar, named in honour of the Berber chief Jabal al-Táriq. They then conquered Spain completely and were only stopped at Moussais-la Bataille, near Poitiers, in southwestern France, by Charles Martel in 732. Following centuries of constant conflict, the Catholic monarchies of Castile and Aragon amalgamated in 1479 following the marriage of Queen Isabella I and Ferdinand of Aragon, forming an alliance that permitted the intensification of the effort to dislodge the highly advanced Moors from Granada, a city that was reputedly impregnable. The Moors raised the white flag on January 2, 1492, unable to withstand the new force of the united monarchies. Spain reigned again – ¡Viva España!

A few years later, in 1519, Charles V, ruler of Spain and its possessions across the Atlantic, was crowned Holy Roman Emperor and became the most powerful sovereign in Europe. He reigned over several German states, Belgium and Holland, as well as Austria, which he inherited from his father. He was also King of Naples, Sicily and Sardinia by inheritance from his mother. He led four wars against France over the course of 30 years and his forces even succeeded in imprisoning Francis I in Pavie in 1525. Francis I was obliged to sign the Treaty of Madrid on January 13, 1526, by which he ceded Burgundy to Spain and renounced his suzerainty over Artois and Picardy. From this point on Spain was the greatest power in the world and it continued to dominate the globe for nearly 200 years with the help of its invincible Armada.

France

Late 15th-century France was in ruins from hundreds of years of wars. The army, the cross and the banner were raised early in the new millennium, in the course of eight successive crusades to the Holy Land from 1095 to 1270 to liberate Palestine from the hands of the Muslims. There was also the Albigensian Crusade against the heretics in southern France from 1207 to 1213, from which was born the French Inquisition, created by Pope Gregory IX in 1233. At the same time, France threw itself into 300 years of near-constant conflict with England, including two Hundred Years' Wars – from 1152 to 1259 and from 1337 to 1453 – against Henry Plantagenet and his descendants Richard the Lion-Heart and John Lackland.

Wars with Italy (1494) and Spain (1516) followed, along with civil and religious wars that did not end until Henry IV signed the Edict of Nantes in 1598.

Despite these preoccupations, there was a sense in France – and in the other western European monarchies as well – of ambivalent curiosity about the Spanish conquests. The successful return of Columbus from his fruitful first voyage was announced, and tales of his exploits passed quickly from court to court. The English, despite their reputation as excellent navigators thanks to their island geography, appeared indifferent to these stories, but Jacques Cartier left Saint-Malo in search of new territory "for the greater glory of France". Cartier was an experienced sailor who had already fished on the Grand Banks of Newfoundland, which were discovered in 1496 by Giovanni Cabotto (John Cabot), a Genovese explorer in the service of England. Cartier headed out with an expedition of two ships and 60 men financed by Francis I. In 1534, after passing through a beautiful bay he named Baie des Chaleurs, he disembarked in Canada and founded New France in the name of his king by planting a 10-metre-tall wooden cross at Gaspé.

The Columbian Era

The name Christopher Columbus is famous around the world. The man himself was known as Cristoforo Colombo in his native Italian and as Cristóbal Colón by the Spanish who took him in. The sailing son of Genovese weaver Domenico Colombo and Susanna Fontanarosa, herself a weaver's daughter, obtained for the Spanish one of the richest lands outside Europe when he "discovered" the Americas. He opened the way for conquistadors to develop an empire twice the size of all of the kingdoms of Europe put together. And if we still marvel at the courage of Neil Armstrong and Edwin "Buzz" Aldrin, the men who walked on the moon on July 16, 1969 (Michael Collins stayed in the cabin), what should we say about those who braved the unknown to sail precariously on an ocean they called the Sea of Darkness to unravel the mysteries of this Earth? At the end of the 15th century, no one had yet confirmed that the Earth was round. Science in this era had to gibe with religious dogma and was subject to the Inquisition, and the prevailing cosmology of the day was that of Egyptian astronomer and mathematician Ptolemy (85-

160). In his *Almagest* (Arabic for "mathematical composition"), Ptolemy described an astronomical system in which the Earth was the centre of the universe, although he did not specify its contours or dimensions. It was not until 1530 that this theory was challenged by Polish astronomer Copernicus. Later, Galileo Galilei was accused of heresy by Pope Urban VIII (Maffeo Barberini) and condemned to denounce his own theories about the Earth's spherical shape and rotational movement. "Nevertheless, it does move!" he answered with unconcealed contempt for the uneducated pope. This was in 1633, some 150 years after Columbus's first suicide missions.

The epic of the discovery of the new continent was not the product of chance nor the effect of a fortuitous alignment of the stars. It was the logical evolution of countless maritime adventures and fishing expeditions in a period when Breton, Basque and English cod fishers were making regular trips to the Grand Banks of Newfoundland, then abundant with fish. Long before Christopher Columbus, these fishermen had described rich, fertile lands, inhabited by strange, naked beings, far beyond the archipelagos of Madeira, the Azores, the Canary Islands and the islands of Cape Verde. In fact, some 500 years before Columbus, the Vikings of Scandinavia, also known as Norsemen or Northmen, had already sailed to Labrador and Newfoundland aboard their *drakkars* – square-rigged galleys with prows sculpted in dragon shapes (*drakkar* is a Scandinavian word for "dragon") – and established trading posts there. Vestiges of their many passages have been found as far south as Boston, Massachusetts.

The search for new territories was made possible by the circumstances of the era, which included a few crucial technological advancements. Two key developments were the perfection of the stern-post rudder and the construction of a new type of vessel, the caravel, by Portuguese naval architects in Henry the Navigator's Sagres shipyards in 1440. Based on a revolutionary design, these slender 50-ton boats were more solid, easier to manoeuvre and faster than any other vessels of the era. They had three masts and triangular, lengthwise, lateen sails that set them apart from square-rigged ships, which were only efficient when the wind blew at their backs. These were the first boats specifically built for high-seas navigation. They opened up the exploration of Africa by freeing captains from perilous coastal navigation in uncharted estuaries, and because

of their size, they were substantially better for transporting slaves from the "Dark Continent".

Time is an essential factor in calculating position, so another new technology, the spiral spring clock invented at the beginning of the 15th century, along with the appearance of the minute hand (the second hand would only come into use toward 1560), allowed navigators to take their bearings much more accurately. The suspended weight clock that had been used before was not very efficient on the high seas, especially over long periods, while neither the oil clock – which measured time according to the decrease in the level of oil that feeds a candle – nor the sand hourglass had hour or minute hands. As for the compass, a rudimentary version appeared in China around AD 1000. Although it allows navigators to gauge where they are headed thanks to its needle pointed north, it does not allow for a calculation of one's current location, essential information for navigation on the high seas, without knowledge of the precise time.

Preparation

When he began to talk about reaching the countries of Asia by sailing west, Christopher Columbus had already completed several voyages as a sailor and captain to England, Iceland and the Azores, hired by different shipowners whose countries were at war. He even had occasion to make a deal and dipped his finger into the lucrative slave trade in Portuguese Guinea. He was a controversial figure when he presented himself to the various courts to request ships with which to discover new lands containing enough gold to liberate the Holy Land from the juggernaut of the Turks of Constantinople, a task he earnestly felt was his personal mission.

To some he was a power-hungry, greedy slave trader cashing in on all sides. Obsequious before the powerful, he was arrogant with his subordinates and critical of his intimates. To others, Columbus was nothing more than a crazy poet, a dreamer who was disconnected from reality, a perpetual adolescent infatuated with the adventures of Marco Polo detailed in *The Book of Marco Polo,* published in Genoa in 1299. Today we might even say he was a schizophrenic, incapable of choosing between his messianic vocation in service of the Holy Church, his military role, and his thirst for personal glory. Nonetheless, he was the quintessential conquistador: courageous, audacious,

Caravel

proud, and devout. He was also the archetype of the mercenary adventurer who would not be thwarted by any obstacle – he lied unabashedly to his suppliers, captains and crew about the distance of the first voyage, endangering the three ships of the former and the lives of the latter.

According to the admittedly exultant accounts of his son Fernando and of an author during his time, Las Casas, it seems Columbus did not head off searching for the Indies, as is commonly assumed. According to these two biographers, his first aim was to find islands where he could replenish his supplies of water and food, like the Azores for example, to facilitate his long voyage toward Cypango, the islands of Japan. As stopover points, these new ports would allow him to reach the exotic lands of the Far East, full of fabulous riches, by sea.

In 1483, Christopher Columbus asked King John II of Portugal for three caravels well-equipped to sail for at least one year. Columbus requested that the sailing be loaded with worthless trinkets like mirrors, necklaces of cheap stones, little knives and small bells. These baubles would not have paid for the gold objects, the silk and the spices that he would have been expected to return with if he had been able to land in the Indies without making any stops, according to Fernando Colombo. He did not expect to reach the Far East on his first voyage. He already suspected that the people he would meet in the new lands he was actually heading for were far from civilized. Two

sailors, Fernão D'Ulmo, a Fleming whose real name was Ferdinand Van Olmen, and the Portuguese João Estreito, had already raised anchor in search of the mythical island of Antilia – probably the Antilles – in 1487. They were never heard from again. In his *Timaeus*, Plato described an island called Atlantis that was so beautiful it was the home of the gods. Columbus had also consulted an ancient marine chart that outlined the contour of this mysterious island, along with routes to the known ports of the era, by Marinus of Tyre, an eminent first-century astronomer and the founder of mathematical geography. In the beginning, Columbus was not at all interested in colonization. (Although Latin America and the United States were subjected to three successive invasions – by conquistadores, by colonists, and by the clergy – Canada experienced only two because Cartier and his sailors were not military men.) The establishment of settlements only became a preoccupation on his third voyage. To him, the goal of these journeys was to come back richer. To ensure this end, as the businessman that he was, he claimed the dignified titles of admiral, governor and viceroy as payment for a successful voyage, along with remuneration equal to 10 percent of the value of any merchandise he brought back. The Portuguese king judged these demands preposterous. His proposal was rejected.

Still convinced of the feasibility of his project, Columbus left Portugal for Spain were he presented himself to the royal court. However, in this period, Spain had committed its entire treasury to the fight against the Moors in the southern province of Andalusia ("Andalusia" is derived from Vandalitia, the name given to the territory by the Vandals, a Germanic people who invaded Gaul and Spain in 406), so Christopher Columbus had to patiently wait out almost five years before receiving a first humiliating refusal from a royal commission that found the adventure farfetched. Given the generally accepted scientific theories of the day, how could anybody imagine that the east could be reached by heading west?

Columbus then decided to try his luck with the king of France. Just as he was about to leave Spain, Queen Isabella summoned him anew. He suffered a second rebuff, this one even more mortifying than the first, from an ad hoc committee. However, after Spain's unexpected victory on January 2, 1492, at the Moorish towers of the Alhambra (in Arabic al-Hamra' means "red", the colour of the adobe with which the Moors had built these towers, the same material used to construct the red earth ramparts that protected Marrakech in Morocco, their country of origin) and the capture of the Moorish leader, Sultan Boabdil, the Crown changed its priorities. After the Reconquista, Spain was ready for fresh challenges and a new destiny. Columbus was granted all that he requested from the court, except remuneration if his mission failed. Spain's war against the Moors would be continued against other infidels in new lands. The guerra de Moros was transformed into the Guerra de Indias. To the term matamoros, "killer of Moors", was added mataindios, "killer of Indians". So had Isabella decided, and her royal banners would from then on fly over the Atlantic "for the greater glory of Spain and of the Holy Church".

Departure

That same year, at eight o'clock on the morning of Friday, August 3, 1492, some 90 crewmen and thirty others of various occupations set sail. They left the port of Palos de la Frontera in the province of Huelva, at the mouth of Río Tinto in Andalusia, on three lateen-rigged caravels. Columbus, then 39 years old, commanded the largest and slowest of the three ships, the Santa María, a bridged, 100-ton ship piloted by a Cantabrian captain, Juan de la Cosa. Martín Alonzo Pinzón, another experienced sailor, was in charge of the Pinta, a 50-ton ship, with his brother Francisco as captain. The other caravel, the 40-ton Niña, was commanded by the third Pinzón brother,

Vicente Yañes, and piloted by Pedro Alonzo Niño, who named the boat after himself since he was also the ship's owner. The three caravels, sailing in convoy, headed to the Canary Islands where Columbus stopped on August 12 to modify the rigging of his boats, switching from lateen sails to square sails to take fuller advantage of the trade winds at their backs. Modern sailboats that participate in the annual transatlantic race called the Transat des Alizés follow basically the same route, leaving France in early November and skirting the Azores before mooring in the waters of Guadeloupe in early December. They raise their spinnakers from the outset to take advantage of tail winds.

On September 9, the three ships left the Canary Islands heading due west and, on October 12, 1492, some 70 days after their departure from Palos, Juan Rodríguez Bermejo, a sailor perched in the Pinta's crow's-nest, finally exclaimed "Land! Land!", becoming the first person to discover America. (However, it was Christopher Columbus who pocketed the reward of 1,000 maravedis, the equivalent of one month's salary, offered by the Queen to the first sailor to see a new land.) A few hours later, the boats moored in the Bay of Guanahani, now thought to be Watling Island in the Bahamas. Christopher Columbus took possession of the island in the name of the Court of Spain in the presence of a group of Arawak islanders: naked, beardless, powerless and peaceful natives who were constantly surrounded by clouds of smoke from the cigars that they smoked.

On December 6, Columbus landed on the western edge of a large island which he named Isla Española (Hispaniola, now shared by Haiti and the Dominican Republic). There he met other islanders who, this time, offered him masks and primitive gold ornaments in exchange for little bells and other trinkets. Although Columbus did not speak their language, he did remark that the indigenous men and women did not understand each other any more than he understood them. It was only on his second voyage that he came to understand this enigma. The men were Caribs, aggressive, cannibalistic natives (the English word "cannibal" is derived from the native word caribal) who terrorized all of the southern Antilles. According to a millennia-old ritual, they devoured their vanquished enemies and appropriated their wives as concubines. The Arawak women were not eager to understand the language of men who had recently been picking their teeth with the bones of their former husbands.

Return

Using wood and materials recuperated from the shipwrecked *Santa María*, Columbus built a fort, Navidad, and left a garrison of 40 men behind when he left for Spain on January 4, 1493. He arrived at the port of Palos on March 15. Although he only brought back a tiny amount of gold, his exploits prompted much enthusiasm and he was received by the court with all of the honours due his success. Confirmed in his titles of admiral and viceroy of Spain, he had no difficulty financing his second expedition, this one undertaken in 1493 with 17 boats stuffed with more than 1,500 men armed with swords, lances, crossbows and blunderbusses (primitive muskets with short, flared barrels). He also brought along horses and a few priests.

During this period, to avoid a war between Spain and Portugal (the latter had title to all discoveries beyond the Azores, including those across the Atlantic – although sovereignty over the Azores themselves fell to Spain when the Treaty of Alcaçovas was signed in 1479 – and was clamorously laying claim to all of Columbus's discoveries) Spanish Pope Alexander VI, the patriarch of the Borgias, drew up four bulls in 1493 which accorded authority over all new territories 100 leagues west of the Azores to Spain. Again to avoid war, Spain signed the Treaty of Tordesillas in 1494 with King Manuel the Fortunate of Portugal, which moved the border dictated by the Pope to 370 leagues west of the Azores, giving Portugal authority over the territory of present-day Brazil – to the great displeasure of France and England who were excluded altogether from this division of the booty. Brazil thereby became a Portuguese colony six year before the first Portuguese explorer, Pedro Álvarez Cabral, who was on his way to Calcutta, India, first set foot on it on April 21, 1500.

Between November 12 and 25, 1493, during the course of his second voyage, Columbus landed on an island he named Guadalupe. Then he navigated toward Dominica, Marie-Galante (named for his ship), the Virgin Islands, the Saintes, Monserrat, Santa María la Redonda, Antigua and La Désirade before finally arriving at Navidad on Hispaniola. His fort had been razed to the ground, and there were no survivors from the garrison he had left behind. With horror, Columbus discovered that his men had been killed and eaten by the natives.

Rather than seek vengeance, he appealed to the goodwill of the Carib cacique and asked him for the help of the natives to build the town of Isabela (more of a fort to defend against the cannibals than a proper town). Unused to forced labour, they took little time to revolt and attack the Spanish, who, this time, were fully inclined to subdue them. Although they were better armed than the Arawaks, the Caribs were easily slaughtered. The Spanish on horseback, with firearms and swords in hand, set their war dogs on the natives and their poison arrows that could not penetrate the iron of armour. The battle was even shorter because the Caribs were completely panic-stricken. They were utterly convinced that these iron-armoured men who could spit fire and iron from their hands, and the immense, similarly shielded beasts upon which they rode, were a single giant creature and none other than demons directly from the depths of hell.

The natives suffered great losses; the survivors were distributed as slaves for the Spanish in a custom called *repartimiento*. Nevertheless, there was a shortage of labour so desperate that, at the suggestion of a monk, Fray Bartolomé de Las Casas, the Spanish decided to bring black slaves over from Africa to complete the construction of Isabela's church. It is not certain whether Columbus made that decision himself, but it is incontestable that he had contacts in this business in Portuguese Guinea and that he could easily arrange the transportation of the human "cargo".

Rebellion soon began to brew in the hearts of the members of the Spanish colony, who were weakened by hunger and fevers that caused many fatalities. Columbus imposed rations on nobles and priests and even obliged them to work, which provoked their ire even further since in Europe their social status automatically exempted them from the abjections of all forms of labour. The Catalan Maragrit escaped, stole a ship and reached Spain accompanied by a rebel priest, Fray Boyl. They delivered a damning report to the Queen and claimed that Columbus treated priests and her majesty's noble subjects like slaves. Queen Isabella was forced to delegate a royal administrator to assume authority over the colonies. She even specified that none of her loyal subjects, neither old nor new, would be a slave, since slaves did not pay taxes. The conquistadors contemptuously dismissed the Spanish court's admonitions

El Dorado

According to legend, the region about 50 kilometres from Bogotá, near the shores of the magnificent Laguna de Guatavita (see p 98), was once inhabited by the peaceful cacique Guatavita and his harem of uncommonly beautiful women. One day, his favourite, whose beauty surpassed that of the others, had an affair with a mere commoner, offending the ruler's royal dignity as well as his masculine pride (Colombian machismo has a long tradition!). The cacique had the traitor executed on the spot, subjecting him to cruelties in keeping with his crime, and publicly denounced his former beloved who had cuckolded him.

From then on, the latter lived as a pariah in a society that was profoundly loyal to its cacique. The young woman was subjected to insults from all sides, without the least regard for her lovely appearance. Driven to despair by these humiliations, she threw herself into the lake, along with her child. The cacique was utterly astounded when he heard what she had done. He had certainly intended to punish her harshly, but he never imagined that he would lose her entirely.

He ordered the lake to be searched. A high priest dived into the depths of the water, but returned empty-handed. However, he informed the cacique that his wife and son were alive and well, living happily at the bottom of the lake, in an immense palace guarded by a demon who respected her. She had no intention of returning to shore only to suffer from the injustices to which Guatavita had subjected her. "I wish to see my wife and my child," the cacique cried when he heard this news, and ordered the high priest to return to the bottom of the lake. The latter plunged into the water, and resurfaced several moments later, carrying the lifeless body of the child whom the demon had murdered. Before killing him, the monster had gouged out his eyes to demonstrate the extent of his anger.

In order to appease the demon, Guatavita decided to bring him gifts. He arranged grand ceremonies and made his followers pray for the return of his beautiful wife. Once a month, the cacique set out onto the lake at sunrise, accompanied by the dignitaries of his court as well as musicians and pilgrims, and threw emeralds and gold into the middle of the lake. Servants then covered his naked body in sticky terebinth resin and dusted him with fine gold powder. The cacique then delivered a sad but powerful lament, which the waves carried to the shore where the kneeling masses responded in chorus. At the break of dawn, the cacique's gilded body gleamed beneath the rising sun, and he threw the cargo of emeralds, gold artifacts and devotional items with which the raft was laden into the water, in the hopes that the demon would return his beloved. He then washed himself in the lake with a saponin so that the gold that had covered his body might cover the walls of the underwater palace.

The demon, however, refused to return the woman, who did not want to come back ashore herself. Had she found true love in the arms of the underwater monster? The legend does not say. At any rate, she set off a frenzy among the conquistadors and colonial adventurers looking for gold. In fact, the native people of the area claimed that the tradition of bathing in gold had been passed down from cacique to cacique, ever since the tragedy of the unhappy ruler, and that it would only cease when the two former lovers were reunited.

Although the Spanish never found the Guatavita's treasure, they pillaged vast amounts of gold from the Chibcha and other groups in the region. They sent a veritable armada of galleons (large, heavily armed ships weighing 600 tons which replaced the caravels) back to Spain. The ships were often attacked by pirates, including the famous privateer Jean Fleury (Juan Florín to the Spanish) who was ordered by King Francis I to avenge the honour of France, which had been damaged through the division of the southern colonies. The gold from the galleons that actually reached their destination was transported to Torro del Oro, the tower of gold in Seville, which still stands today, to be made into currency. After Colombia gained independence, Simón Bolívar also melted down some of the indigenous treasures to be made into coins bearing his likeness.

Today, all jewellery and gold objects discovered at archaeological sites are systematically bought by the Colombian government at standardized prices and bequeathed to the Museo del Oro de Bogotá. The *huaqueros* have no problems selling the gold objects they recuperate to the government. However, they do not bother with other types of archeological artifacts since they are ignorant of both their commercial and historic value. These pieces are often destroyed at the sites before they can be analysed by specialists.

regarding the treatment of the indigenous people. They continued to distribute natives to *encomenderos*, who became the natives' masters and guardians, throughout the entire period of the conquest.

When the Queen's emissary arrived, he found the town of Isabela abandoned and overgrown with tropical vegetation. Nueva Isabela was founded, later to be renamed Santo Domingo, and would serve as the seat of government of the Spanish Indies for more than 50 years.

In 1499, nobleman Alonzo de Ojeda set off on an expedition to Hispaniola accompanied by Juan de la Cosa and a then-unknown Italian called Amerigo Vespucci, a grocer turned sailor by chance. He navigated into the interior of the continent on Lake Maracaibo and landed in Venezuela, "little Venice", a slightly derisive name inspired by the natives' huts built on stilts. He then disembarked at Cabo de la Vela, on the Guajira Peninsula, and "discovered" Colombia. It was not until two years later, in 1501, that a first reconnaissance expedition into this new land was organized, under the leadership of Juan de la Cosa. The crew included a simple, ambitious soldier who would later go on to conquer Perù – Francisco Pizarro.

Christopher Columbus did not actually see the continent proper (*tierra firme*) until his third voyage, when he skirted the shores of Venezuela, at the mouth of Río Orinoco, which he mistook for the river to paradise. On his fourth and final voyage, in 1502, Columbus landed in Central America and learned from the natives of the existence of another ocean. Vasco Núñez de Balboa discovered the Pacific when he spotted this other sea for the first time on September 25, 1513, from the heights of a Panaménian mountaintop. By this time the New World was known as America, a name derived from Amerigo Vespucci. Geographer and monk Martin Waldseemüller, who had sailed with Vespucci and was a personal friend of his, was the first to make use of this appellation in an atlas published in 1507 in the paper-mill town of Saint-Dié-des-Vosges, France. Despite the namesake, historians unanimously attribute the

discovery of America to Christopher Columbus, who died in 1506 at the age of 55 years. Some even consider Vespucci a vulgar usurper. However, Vespucci was the first to grasp that the newly discovered territories were in fact a new continent, while Columbus persisted in believing that he had reached the eastern edge of Asia. Vespucci died of malaria in Seville in 1512.

The Post-Columbian Era

Despite a betrayal by some of his companions in arms, Núñez de Balboa was granted the title of governor of two Pacific provinces, where he built four brigs (two-masted ships with single decks and square topsails) and set off to discover new lands on the new ocean. Denounced again, this time for treason against Governor Pedro Arias ("Pedrarias") de Ávila, he was arrested by Francisco Pizarro, brought before the court on a charge of high treason, and condemned to decapitation in 1517. Pizarro then took charge of the brand-new ships and set out on the Pacific. This foray into the Pacific was a first for the conquistadors. It was also a failure, since the ships came across inhospitable coasts lined with swamps and primal forests that offered no means of replenishing their supplies. But Pizzaro would try again a few years later, as we will see further on.

Hernán Cortés

In 1519, Hernán Cortés y Pizarro, born in Trujillo, Extremadura, a region of western Spain, cousin of Francisco Pizarro, left Cuba and landed on the island of Cozumel. There he reviewed his troops before heading to the continental coast of México, which had been discovered in 1517 by Francisco Hernández de Córdoba.

With some 600 men armed with muskets and about 20 horses, he planned to invade the land of the Mexica, which would later become New

Spain (México). To force his reluctant men to continue into the interior, he landed his own ships on the coast of the Yucatán Peninsula south of the Mexica territory. He visited the Toltec-Maya pyramids of the Yucatán, also "discovered" in 1517 by Hernández de Córdoba. There, he was informed that the Aztecs had been terrorizing the other Mexica tribes, including the Toltecs, the Maya, the Tlaxcalans, and the Cempoalans, among others, for a long time. The powerful Aztec civilization had in fact established its domination centuries ago over the Mexica land all the way to Guatemala.

Hernán Cortés soon understood the benefit he could gain from this explosive situation. In fact, it was his duty to ally himself with some native groups in order to fight others, as prescribed in the sixth *requerimiento* (see p 27). At that time, the Aztecs controlled an empire of several million subjects. They knew how to read and write, and Moctezuma, the Aztec ruler, literally walked on gold since the soles of his shoes were made of the precious metal. A courier informed the emperor that strange, white, bearded beings covered in iron had landed on the coast and undertaken a voyage into the interior of the continent over the high plateaus of present-day México City. The Aztecs occupied Tenochtitlán-México, a high valley 2,270 metres above sea level protected by mountains. They were spread over about ten cities, most of which were built on islands in salt-water lakes and connected to shore by pivot bridges. The cities had ramparts, towers, temples, fabulous palaces, public buildings, esplanades and even aqueducts to transport freshwater into houses and remove wastewater.

All of the buildings were constructed with well-cut stone and mortar and entirely covered with lime. They were often decorated with woodwork in fragrant cedar or other exotic trees. They were separated by broad, straight, level, paved roads that crossed each other at right angles (although no civilization of North or South America, no matter how advanced it was, knew about the wheel). According to the earliest Spanish chroniclers, some of the cities were larger and more magnificent than Granada or Seville while others rivalled waterside cities like Geneva, Pisa or even Venice, in beauty. Abundance was evident everywhere. The public markets were larger than those of most of the great cities of Spain, more goods were available in larger quantities, and the stalls were organized by product, like Arab markets.

In 1520, Cortés built brigs so that he could attack the Aztecs simultaneously by land and water and thereby avoid the trap of the pivot bridges. During a supposedly peaceful meeting, Cortés had the *requerimiento* read to Moctezuma by one of his captains. Through the intervention of Cortés' native translator and concubine, Doña Marina, Moctezuma asked who this firebrand of a king was who, in this faraway country, permitted himself to distribute lands that did not belong to him.

Cortés took Moctezuma hostage and made himself master of the entire Aztec civilization easily enough. For one thing, the Aztec people thought that the bearded white man was the incarnation of one of their gods, Quetzalcóatl, the plumed serpent. As well, Cortés had united under his command most of the other indigenous groups, who saw him as their liberator from the yoke of Aztec domination. Moreover, he was the master of thunder: he fired the cannon. Although his first confrontation with the Aztecs went smoothly and quickly, it took three long years for him to establish his domination over of this part of the New World. He confronted rebellion after rebellion on the part of the natives, who fought him with uncommon courage, now that they realized that he was human and in no way related to their gods. Cortés was even forced to abandon México City on June 30, 1520, as a result of a nighttime battle, the *Noche Triste*, in which all of his boats were destroyed and close to two thirds of his men were killed or captured.

Cortés received reinforcements from Cuba to relieve his weary troops. He began the campaign anew and, this time, emerged victorious once and for all. The Aztecs, the people and their culture, were completely obliterated. Cortés shamelessly razed to the ground all of the cities that he himself had described as marvellous. He ordered the demolition of temples and buildings by pickax. The Spanish then used any materials they could recuperate to construct their own churches, palaces, public buildings, and houses, in the Hispano-Islamic Mudéjar style that was popular in Spain at that time – and on the exact sites of the structures that they had just demolished.

Ferdinand Magellan

In addition to the Italians Cristoforo Colombo, Amerigo Vespucci and Giovanni Cabotto, Spain had also adopted another decorated navigator, Fernão de Maghalhães from Portugal, who took the name Fernando de Magallanes. On November 28, 1519, while Cortés was busy conquering México, Magellan discovered the famous, much-sought passage that linked the Atlantic and Pacific Oceans. It was a dangerous but navigable route south of Argentina, appropriately named the Strait of Magellan, and it was one of the most fantastic geographic discoveries of the time. Upon reaching the new ocean, at Cape Deseado, Chile, he named it El Mar Pacífico, the Pacific Ocean, because of the beautiful, calm weather he observed there, which, as it turned out, is particular to this latitude. Although Núñez de Balboa had sighted the Pacific a few years earlier, in 1513, from Panamá, the name chosen by Magellan would be the one used in contemporary and future atlases.

Magellan died in the Philippines on April 27, 1521, killed by a native's *assegai* (spear), but one of his lieutenants, Elcano, pursued his course on the *Victoria*, one of Magellan's five original vessels, and ultimately reached Spain, completing the first ever successful circumnavigation of the globe, a trip that took over three years.

Francisco Pizarro

Francisco Pizarro could neither read nor write. He was a pig keeper in his native Extremadura. But what real importance is literacy to a conquistador who is expected to master the sword and be able to count gold? In these two departments, Pizarro was a competent man – he was a soldier who could count. He was also required to lead men, and in that area as well he had little difficulty. His troops were actually as afraid of him as they were of the enemies they encountered. The illegitimate son of a ruined gentleman from Trujillo, a town in the region of Extremadura, Spain, Pizarro was a simple soldier in Juan de la Cosa's 1499 reconnaissance expedition to the Caribbean coast of Colombia. His personal ambition and his total lack of consideration for anyone else propelled him up the ladder of military rank. For this reason, he was put in charge of arresting Núñez de Balboa, whose ships he captained along the Pacific shores of Central America.

In 1524 Pizarro was joined in Panamà by Diego de Almagro, another illustrious illiterate who identified himself by the name of his village, Almagro, also in Extremadura. (Later, in 1538, Pizarro had Almagro strangled in prison. In turn, supporters of Almagro's son assassinated

Pizarro in 1541.) He also enlisted a priest, Fernando de Luque, whom the Panamánians had nicknamed Fernando el Loco ("the Crazy"). Together, the three men chartered a ship and Pizarro headed back south with a crew of about 100. Finding that it was difficult to restock his supplies on the swampy Pacific coast, he landed at a more hospitable spot, Isla Gorgona, and then at a village on the mainland, south of Buenaventura, thereby becoming the only conquistador to explore both the Atlantic and Pacific coasts of Colombia.

Natives provided Pizarro with supplies and offered him small quantities of gold. This was enough to pique his curiosity. He began to hear rumours of a fascinating people who had a hierarchical social order that was expanding northward into Colombia. In fact, the Incas had established their domination of Ecuador, Birú (Perù), Bolivia, Chile and probably parts of Uruguay and Argentina hundreds of years earlier and were just beginning to take over southern Colombia. The natives described to Pizarro astonishingly advanced Inca cities of houses, temples and palaces brimming with gold (Cuzco and Cajamarca, undoubtedly). Enthralled by these tales, which he heard again every time he stopped for provisions, Pizarro sailed further and further south.

He founded the town of San Miguel in Ecuador, in a protected harbour at the mouth of the Chira, which would serve as a safe base from which he could set off to conquer Perù and where he could receive reinforcements from Panamá or New Spain if necessary. He left the fort under the command of Sebastián Moyano de Belalcázar.

To the great surprise of Pizarro himself, all of the Inca territory was traversed by cobbled roads to facilitate trade – though by other means of transportation than the wheel, which the Incas were no more aware of than any other Native American culture. One road, for example, linked Santiago, Chile, to Quito, Ecuador, covering a distance of more than 5,000 kilometres. All of these arteries were equipped with supply stations judiciously placed at regular intervals where travellers would find silos full of corn and other rations and even fresh clothing for their use on the road. So it was with surprising ease, thanks to the assistance of these facilities graciously put at his disposal by the very people he was preparing to attack, that Pizarro penetrated the Inca land in 1525.

PORTRAIT

During this period, two brothers were disputing the throne of the Inca Empire and civil war was ravaging the countryside. (In Quechua, the word *inca* means "chief"; its use to designate the culture as a whole implies that the civilization was highly advanced and organized around a nobility.) The 11th Inca of a dynasty, Huayna Cápac, had died seven years earlier. In his will, Huayna Cápac had divided the empire. He willed the government of Cuzco, Perù (the site of Inti-Huasi, the Temple of the Sun, famous for its solid gold walls), to his legitimate heir and son, Huascár and he gave the province of Quito, Ecuador, to Atahualpa, a more aggressive son born to a mother in his harem. Atahualpa came out the victor of a fratricidal war that projected him onto the throne and the people worshipped him as a veritable sun-god.

Atahualpa had established his residence at Cajamarca in northern Perù, which is where Pizzaro requested an audience with him. Atahualpa received the explorer with great generosity – like a brother, one might say – and settled him and his men in a sumptuous residence reserved for distinguished guests. He even offered him *coca*, the sacred drug that the Incas used in religious ceremonies and civil festivities. Too bad he accepted, because Pizzaro felt strange suddenly. He may even have hallucinated, since the drug produced different effects in different people. He was struck with panic and suddenly felt trapped. He realized that he had walked with his eyes shut tight right into the lion's den, along with his entire contingent of 170 men and 62 horses. They were surrounded by more than 40,000 natives, who, although weakly armed, were skilful with the bow, poison arrows and the slingshot. He realized he had to attempt a first strike if he wanted to survive this impasse. In accord with his men, he hatched a plan to grab Atahualpa. He knew very well that his own cousin Hernán Cortés had used this ruse in México a few years earlier and taken Moctezuma hostage. He also knew from experience that because of their centralized political system, if the Inca were captured, the people would put up little resistance.

On the pretext of a casual conversation between "brothers", he invited Atahualpa to an informal meeting early the next day. Equipped with horses, war dogs, culverins (cannons with long, tapering barrels), and muskets and crossbows, weapons and animals never seen here before, it took Pizzaro less than an hour to force the Inca Empire to its knees and turn it into a vassal province of the kingdom of Spain.

Pizzaro and his band of lunatics fired in every direction – into the crowd – without aiming. The result? The capture of Atahualpa, more than 4,000 dead Incas, and no losses for the Spanish.

During the detention of the Inca, which lasted over six months, Pizzaro had the decency to treat him with the dignity due to a man of his rank, letting him keep his court and his harem. He invited him to eat at his own table and even taught him to play chess. In the meantime, his soldiers were given free rein and took advantage of the situation to pillage the Inca's sumptuous palace, which could have been part of the enchanted kingdoms described in the chivalric novels popular at that time in Spain like *Amadis of Gaul* (1508) and *The Labours of the Very Brave Knight Esplandian* (1521), by Ordóñez Montalvo. Pizzaro may not have been able to read, but he could appreciate sheer splendour. Long ago, the Incas had defeated the Chimú and stolen their treasure, and before that the Chimú had helped themselves to the gold of their ancestors, the Mochicas. Atahualpa's palace was brimming with exquisite objects made of solid gold, jewellery, vases, implements and precious gems.

Atahualpa offered to fill a four- by five-metre room shoulder-high with gold as a ransom for his liberty, and he fulfilled this promise within two months by sending his *chasquis* (messengers) to the far reaches of the kingdom to collect all the gold, silver and emeralds, in the form of statuettes, jars, ornaments and jewellery, that they could. And these riches represented only an infinitesimal part of the immense royal fortune that had been secreted away in a still undiscovered hiding place (treasure hunters take note!).

Prompted by their own avarice, the Spanish pounced on the emeralds and tested their value like diamonds by hitting them with a blacksmith's hammer. They shattered most of the gems before realizing their blunder.

Instead of setting the Inca free, Pizzaro broke his word and had the chief baptized – a brilliantly underhanded manoeuvre – at the instigation of an ill-willed ecclesiastic, Fray Vicente de Valverde. Then, in a stunning turn, he used Catholicism as a pretext to accuse Atahualpa of incest with his sisters, to whom the Inca actually was married. He also accused the native king of polygamy, because he had many wives; fratricide (did he not kill his own brother Huascár?); and idolatry, because he was wor-

Requerimiento

During the conquest, the Spanish reduced all of the civilizations of the New World to servitude, treating the natives with generosity at times, but more often with cruelty, and always according to their whim. The armed conquistadors would have a clerk read the *requerimiento* to the cacique and his followers, which was a formal demand that they recognize only one God and the authority, conferred by the pope, of the king of Spain over their lands. The natives never understood the content of this document, and to the conquistadors their indifference justified open war and capturing slaves.

In this regard, the conquistadors adhered precisely to the following principles described by Vittoria and later published in Salamanque in the *Relectiones de Indis* (1539):

1- The conquistadors had the right of passage and trade. Resistance to these rights justified war.

2- The conquistadors had the right to preach the gospel everywhere. Resistance to the gospel justified war.

3- If the newly converted were forced to return to their old divinities by their princes, this justified war.

4- The pope could replace a pagan prince by a Christian one if a sufficient number of the subjects were converted.

5- War was justified if the majority of subjects of a prince wanted to become subjects of the king of Spain.

6- If two pagan princes were at war, the Spanish could ally themselves with one against the other and share the spoils of victory.

7- The natives were incapable of governing themselves. Armed intervention by the Spanish to impose their own government was therefore justified.

shipped as a sun-god. According to Catholic laws of the day, each of these crimes was punishable by death.

Atahualpa was garotted and quartered, the punishment imposed in Spain by the Inquisition, and then burned, with no form of trial. The natives viewed this murder as unforgivable and it sparked an uprising that was savagely put down. Some 50 years after Pizzaro's arrival in Perù, barely 30 percent of the indigenous population survived, decimated as it was in the course of confrontations and skirmishes, and by the spread of imported European diseases like smallpox. Condemned to forced labour as punishment for rebellion against the Spanish detachments, millions of natives died in the silver mines of Potosí, Bolivia, the richest mines in the world, discovered by accident in 1545 by an indigenous *yanacona* (servant) and his master, a Spaniard called Villarroël. The natives died of exposure, famine or fatigue in the mines. Most often they were buried alive by cave-ins caused by digging techniques that did not employ supports. All this, with the tacit blessing of the Church, or at least without its condemnation. In cases of premeditated murder and systematic genocides like these, there is no keeping silent. If we do not express our indignation loudly and clearly, we approve. Some ecclesiastics were opposed to slavery and forced labour, among them the Dominicans Fray Bartolomé de Las Casas and Fray Antonio de Montesinos, but rarely did these monks protest the unacceptable cruelty, even by the morals of the period, of the Spanish toward the natives directly to those in power.

It may be small consolation, but if the Aztecs and the Incas had known of the wheel and firearms, if they had been able to fight their enemies on horseback with equal weapons, they may have very well triumphed.

The Conquest of Colombia

In 1536, Pizzaro's right-hand man in San Miguel, Sebastián Moyano de Belalcázar, was preparing to invade Colombia from the Pacific. With his command firmly entrenched in San Miguel and Quito, Ecuador, over which he also had authority as governor, he gathered together all of the Spaniards he could and almost one thousand natives. He penetrated deep into the province of Popayán, and his expedition brought him to the edge of the territory previously dominated by the Incas, whose own forays into Colombia, which local natives thought inescapable, were stopped dead by Pizzaro's occupation.

Colombia was at that time populated by indigenous people, the majority of whom were cannibals, under the authority of petty regional kings who were continually at war – and who were thus too pre-occupied to put up much resistance to a detachment of foot soldiers well armed with cannons and muskets and a cavalry complemented by packs of war dogs.

Conquistadors from the North, the East and the West

It was evident from the beginning of the Conquest of Colombia that the conquistadors would not encounter very much, if any, resistance on the part of the indigenous people, who in the Europeans' eyes were barely more advanced than the natives of the Antillean archipelagos. The Spanish already had experience fighting the latter and were aware of their weaknesses. The ferocious man-eating Caribs, Tumacos, Pijaos and Panches did not put up a fight. Nonetheless, despite their successive and relatively easy victories in the Caribbean (Ponce de León completed the occupation of Hispaniola in 1493 and went on to take Puerto Rico in 1508; Jamaica was conquered May 5, 1509, by Juan de Esquivel; Cuba in 1511 by Diego Velázquez), the Spanish were truly terrorized by the thought of doing battle with these groups to the south. According to Bernal Díaz del Castillo, a contemporary chronicler, the cannibals actually ate their prisoners right on the battlefield, before their very eyes, stewed in pots with salt, peppers and tomatoes, or even raw, if there were no means of cooking them. Throughout the ages and across cultures, tired, injured, starving soldiers have not always adequately supplied with provisions, and have

had to resort to cannibalism. As well, many mythologies include the belief that warriors acquire the souls and courage of their enemies by devouring them. The natives often allied themselves with the Spanish when they were preparing to invade the territory of a tyrant. They knew that the defeated would make a valuable feast and replenish their mettle. Some groups went further and practised sybaritism in homage to the gods. They fattened up child prisoners like farmyard animals, strictly for the purpose of eating them during religious ceremonies. Other groups even organized raids on their neighbours solely to replenish their stock of human flesh.

Although the Quimbayá did not offer any resistance, the same did not apply in the case of the native peoples of the Andean plateaus, who fought fiercely before retreating into the mountains to escape the imperialist manoeuvres of Charles V, whose troops were invading their territory on three fronts. These civilizations, which numbered close to one million people, were almost completely wiped out.

In search of gold (the natives were endlessly boasting of countless veins of the precious metal) many explorers and picaresque dreamers crisscrossed the country, despite its reputed impenetrability. A first survey of the Colombian territory was organized in 1501, under the leadership of Juan de la Cosa, a member of Rodrigo de Bastidas' expedition. He explored the Caribbean coast and founded the first Colombian city, Santa Marta, in 1525, at the tip of Cape Aguja, with Bastidas as its governor. A few years later, in 1533, Pedro de Heredia (Pedredia), a Madrid aristocrat, laid the first stones of Cartagena, the second permanent settlement in the country, at the very northeastern end of the mouth of the Gulf of Darien (Golfo de Darién).

Gonzalo Jiménez de Quesada

Gonzalo Jiménez de Quesada is credited with founding Ciudad Nueva de Granada, which became Santafé de Bogotá, the capital of Colombia.

Descended from a noble Spanish family, a lawyer by profession, Gonzalo de Quesada landed in Colombia on the Caribbean coast with about 160 of the 800 men that had left Spain with him, the others having died on route from falling overboard during heavy storms, among other reasons. In 1538, at the age of 34 years,

Quesada travelled up Río Magdalena from Santa Marta accompanied by don Pedro Fernández de Lungo. He survived the loss of his boats, several skirmishes with natives, fever, and famine, and saw his men die of exhaustion and devoured by alligators, before he finally arrived at a cultivated Andean valley. He was surprised to discover many villages of pretty wooden houses, the doors of which were adorned with softly ringing, solid gold chimes. Further on he came to cities full of imposing buildings and fortresses that were difficult take: the land of the Chibcha. The Chibcha had conquered this territory and established their civilization here one millennia prior to Quesada's arrival. Terrified at the sight of horses, the first natives he met offered him children to eat, believing him to be a member of the Panches, their cannibal rivals.

Quesada made quick work of enslaving one of the two reigning kings, Tunja, and looting his palace, since the natives had hidden most of the cacique's riches. He then set off to find the second king, Bogotá, whose refuge had been revealed to him by tortured Chibchas. Following a short battle – more of a scattering of the natives, who were terrified by the horses and guns – the king was found dead before the Spanish could take hold of the second royal treasury. Suspecting that Bogotá's successor, Sagipa, knew of the treasure's whereabouts, Quesada helped him accede to the throne. When he tired of the cacique's hemming and hawing, Quesada subjected him to torture. Sagipa kept mum. He and his secret died together one month later.

Quesada took advantage of this respite in the treasure hunt to found Santafé de Bogotá in 1538 on the site of Bacatá, the Chibcha capital. Then, in 1539, he created the Audiencia of New Granada, under the administration of the Viceroyalty of Perù, based in Lima.

The conquistador Belalcázar continued his march from the Pacific toward the centre of Colombia and along the way he established the towns of Popayán, in 1536, and Cali, in the Cauca Valley, in 1537.

In the meantime, Charles V had pledged his crown to reimburse German loans and was forced to concede Venezuela to the Welser bankers and shipowners of the Hanseatic town of Augsburg. Several expeditions left the Venezuelan coast for the interior of the country. One of these even reached *las sabanas*, the savannahs of Bogotá, after a voyage of more than three years, to find that the Spanish were already well established in the area. The mostly Spanish and native troop was under the command of a German called Klaús Federmann.

Simultaneously, the Spanish coming from the Pacific for the first time met men who spoke their language, to the astonishment of both groups, south of Bogotá. Colombia became the first American country "discovered" from both the Atlantic and the Pacific at the same time, from 1501 to 1537, from three different departure points – and the conquistadors themselves had no idea. (The United States, discovered March 27, 1513, by Juan Ponce de León, who was killed in Florida, were crossed from east to west by Pánfilo de Narváez and his men in 1536). This coincidence actually provoked rivalry among the three groups, each of whose leader claimed for himself the title of commander of the Order of Saint James, a sort of legion of honour responsible for granting large rewards and *adelantados*, or governorships, to the conquerors of newly discovered regions. The riches the Order allotted finally permitted the conquistador to pay his men, who would do well for their trouble.

In 1717, all of these territories were united as a viceroyalty independent of Lima, Perù, still called New Granada, roughly corresponding to modern Panamá and Colombia, to which were later annexed Venezuela and part of Ecuador. Abolished in 1724, New Granada was reconstituted in 1739.

Independence

The first jolts of anti-Spanish activity shook Soccoro, in the Department of Santander, in 1781. These took the form of a quickly aborted uprising of *comuneros* against an increase of market taxes. In addition to this tax, the Spanish had adopted a series of offensive, discriminatory policies including the prohibition of traditional native clothing, the expropriation of their collective lands, which in any case belonged to the State, and their outright deportation to Spain for any reason whatsoever.

The decline of Spanish domination over *criollos* (people born of Spanish parents in the Americas) was also precipitated by the American War of Independence and the French Revolution. In 1794, Antonio Nariño translated the Declaration of the Rights of Man and of the Citizen, which had been written in France in

1789 by Marie Joseph, Marquis de Lafayette, among others, and inspired by the United States Declaration of Independence, drafted July 4, 1776, by Thomas Jefferson. This explosive text planted the idea that Colombia could also reach independence and liberate itself from the now too oppressive yoke of the motherland.

Between 1809 and 1815, several cities rebelled against colonial authority and joined together to form *cabildos*, independent provinces, giving rise to three major factions: royalists, who were loyal to the colonial administration; centralists based in Bogotá, who wanted a state independent of Spain; and federalists gathered in Cartagena, who were in favour of a union of relatively independent provinces within a federated state. The many quarrels and conflicts among these contingents ruined their respective leaders financially and sapped their spirit. The Spanish easily retook possession of the territories from 1815 to 1819, a period mainly marked by cruel and massive repression by the colonial military administration, which ultimately provoked a unanimous upheaval supported even by the most fervent royalists.

Simón Bolívar

General Simón José Antonio de la Santísima Trinidad Bolívar y Palacios is still thought of as the saviour of South America. *El Libertador*, one of the greatest strategists of his day, succeeded in expelling the Spanish from South America and granting its people their independence.

Bolivar was born in Venezuela to an aristocratic Caracas family. After partially liberating his own country, he invaded Colombia with 2,500 supporters and the backing of Colombian Francisco de Paula Santander, and beat the 5,000-strong Spanish who met them at the Boyacá bridge on August 7, 1819. On December 17 of that same year in Angostura (now called Ciudad Bolívar), Venezuela, the representatives of the former viceroyalty of Santafé de Bogotá proclaimed independence. Simón Bolívar was named president by acclamation of Gran Colombia, which then included Cundinamarca (another name for New Granada), Bolivia, Panamá, Venezuela and part of Perù. Simón Bolívar took the opportunity to grant equal rights to the indigenous people. He helped Perù win its independence and became that country's president in 1824.

His dream of a united nation like the United States, however, did not live long. In 1830, Venezuela seceded, soon followed by Ecuador. Unfortunately, authorities were in a hurry to reinstate the old regime and equal rights for indigenous people were abolished simultaneously. People of mixed lineage were given the right to hold slaves, and they showed themselves, if it can be believed, to be crueler and more beastly than the Spanish. Bitter, war-weary, worn out by tuberculosis, Simón Bolívar perished in Santa Marta on December 17 of that same year.

Francisco Santander returned to Colombia, from which he had been exiled the day after independence, and governed the nation until 1837. During his and his successor's presidencies, two large political parties were born: the federalist Liberal Party and the centralist Conservative Party. The chasm between the two grew deep and wide, and while the parties were preoccupied with their own quarrels, the provinces became almost totally autonomous. The creation in 1863 of Los Estados Unidos de Colombia quelled that trend, but the union was ravaged for several years by civil wars among the federated states. In 1886, a government commission comprised of members of both parties drafted the texts on which the 1894 constitution of the Republic of Colombia was based. This constitution would govern the nation until 1991.

In 1894 the Republic still included the territory of Panamà, but in 1903 Panamà broke away from Colombia following a territorial dispute over the inter-oceanic Panamá Canal, the construction of which was begun by French engineer Ferdinand de Lesseps in 1881 and completed by the United States in 1914. Colombia did not recognize Panamá's secession until 1921, after the former received an indemnity payment of 25 million dollars from the United States. Colombia's borders were now set as we know them today, and this heir to a tumultuous past set off into its even stormier future, with guerrilla warfare, military coups and riots on the horizon.

Contemporary Colombia: Land of Political Upheaval

Colombia, in the final century of this millennium, has witnessed a veritable maelstrom of atrocities. The violence of confrontations between the nation's two main political parties erupted in no fewer than 19 civil wars, including the bloody War of a Thousand Days, from 1899 to 1902, which ruined the country's economy and led to the secession of Panamá.

The Conservatives held power until 1930, when they were replaced by the Liberals, headed by Rafael Uribe. Another Liberal, Alfonso López Pumarejo, succeeded Uribe as president from 1934 to 1938. From 1938 to 1946, the Liberals stayed in power for two consecutive mandates led first by Eduardo Santos and then by Alfonso López Pumarejo. The latter resigned midterm in 1945 and his position was filled by Alberto Lleras Camargo.

An internal struggle had been eating away at the Liberal Party for several years, and in 1946 an especially charismatic Marxist lawyer, Jorge Eliécer Gaitán, decided to run in the elections against his own party's candidate. Conservative Mariano Ospina Pérez took power in those elections, and the Liberals regrouped around Gaitán. Threatened by the "Gaitanism" that became popular in every stratum of society, irrespective of political trends, the Conservatives used violence to coerce electors but did not prevent the signing in 1948 of a tripartite agreement to open up trade between Venezuela, Ecuador and Colombia.

The same year also marked the beginning of one of the darkest periods in Colombia's recent history. Gaitán was assassinated, provoking the spontaneous sacking of Bogotá by a populace utterly disgusted by this act. Ten years of terror and more than 300,000 deaths ensued. Some have named this period *La Violencia*, others call it *El Bogotazo*. The two parties sponsored assassinations and unprecedented acts of violence, from the elimination of entire families to physical tortures of all sorts. Here, death no longer took centre stage – the process of killing was more important. Eyes were ripped out of their sockets. Ears were sliced off. Pregnant women were disembowelled. Men were castrated. Parents were murdered in front of children, children under the noses of their parents. No one was excluded from the horror. All of the nation's institutions including the Church participated in this frenzy. The countryside was especially hard-hit and became the main setting for this real-life theatre of cruelty, precipitating an unprecedented exodus to the cities. Destitute, hungry newcomers found the cities absolutely unprepared to accommodate them and had no recourse but to settle in shantytowns on the outskirts of existing neighbourhoods.

La Violencia finally subsided under the dictatorship of army commander-in-chief General Gustavo Rojas Pinilla, who took power in 1953 following a *pronunciamento* (a coup d'etat), and held it until 1957. Exhausted by their bloody confrontations, the two parties joined together under the insignia of the National Front and drew up an agreement to alternate terms in government and share administrative duties. Pinilla was forced into exile in Spain, while the "Benidorm pact" gave Colombia a period of relative stability. From 1958 to 1962, Liberal Alberto Lleras Camargo headed the government, replaced from 1962 to 1966 by Conservative Guillermo León Valencia, followed from 1966 to 1970 by Liberal Carlos Lleras Restrepo.

Despite the relatively calm political climate, these administrations' impotence in the face of the nation's economic problems (agriculture, unemployment, taxation, and education, among other sectors) prompted the emergence of several guerrilla groups. Among these were the communist Revolutionary Armed Forces of Colombia (FARC), the Maoist Popular Liberation Army (Ejército de Liberación Popular, ELP), and the coalition of populist and nationalist elements called M-19, or April 19 Movement, whose name commemorates the death of Jorge Eliécer Gaitán. The sensational actions of these groups succeeded in hindering the government, although they never destabilized it completely.

The fraudulent elections of 1970 brought to power Conservative Misael Pastrana Borrero, who would remain in office until 1974, even though most Colombians voted for his adversary, Rojas. In 1974, Liberal Alfonzo López Michelsen took over leadership of the country, followed by Liberal Julio César Turbay Ayala from 1978 to 1982 and Conservative Belisario Betancur from 1982 to 1986. In a period when over 60 percent of the populace abstained from voting in elections they considered phoney, social stratification and the even more dramatic polarization of political trends gave way to another wave of violence. Betancur wanted at all costs to establish a socialist Christian program and a rational peace with the guerrillas. After several deceptions, breaches of agreements and the assassination by secret forces of guerrillas who had been pardoned by the government, the revolutionary groups returned to the underground.

In 1985, shortly after an attack on the Bogotá courthouse that ended in a bloodbath, Betancur decided to focus his attention on international

Jorge Eliécer Gaitán

Born into a relatively modest family, Liberal Jorge Eliécer Gaitán Ayala soon became a hero for many Colombians because of his passionate speeches denouncing the injustices of the elites of his era. Abandoning the political norm whereby identification with a party constitutes an unequivocal acceptance of its philosophy, Gaitán was the first true Colombian champion who rose above partisanship to deal with the demands of the people.

Held in contempt by his rivals and even by members of his own party, he was nonetheless extremely popular with the majority of the population, which admired him for his direct public addresses. His assassination during a parade in 1948 provoked the same horror in Colombia as did that of John F. Kennedy in the United States in 1963. Gaitán is still considered a national hero all over Colombia, even by Conservatives.

politics. He played a preponderant role in the creation of the Contadora group, which worked to end the conflicts in Central America, with México, Panamá and Venezuela. Among other achievements, Contadora averted a direct armed intervention by the United States in the war in Nicaragua. Although Ronald Reagan saw the situation in Nicaragua as an attempt to expand international communism, Contadora succeeded in re-framing it in a local perspective. Contadora also formulated a sort of *modus vivendi* for social peace among the different political groups in the majority of Latin American countries. During the years that followed, most of the guerrilla groups in Colombia left the mountains to participate in the official political arena. They played the role of a true opposition by denouncing the material greed, social inequality and poverty caused by the privileges that most large landowners still enjoyed.

Liberal Virgilio Barco took power from 1986 to 1990 and led an active fight against drug traffickers, which culminated in August 1989 with the assassination of the Liberal presidential candidate, Luis Carlos Galán. Conservative César Gaviria was the leader of the government from 1990 to 1994, and it was during his term that a new constitution was ratified on July 5, 1991, and the nation witnessed the birth of a government with authentically pluralistic inclinations. In 1992, however, the economic situation took a turn for the worse and the guerrilla movement reemerged. This was one of the main problems, along with the ever-present drug issue, that confronted the controversial Liberal government of Ernesto Samper Pizano during his term from 1994 to 1998. As well, in 1996 Samper faced strong pressure to resign midterm because of accusations that he had received over five million dollars from the Cali cartel to finance his election campaign. Conser-

vative former mayor of Bogotá Andrés Pastrana Arango came into power on August 7, 1998, winning on the second ballot in the elections of the preceding June, and now steers Colombia toward its destiny. He defeated Horacio Serpa, Ernesto Samper's successor at the helm of the Liberal Party. Since he took office, and with the help of Nobel prize winner Gabriel García Márquez, Pastrana has initiated talks with the major guerrilla groups in the hope of establishing the lasting peace loudly demanded by the entire Colombian populace. Since Pastrana came into power and thanks to his credibility, relations with the United States have greatly improved, while the American State Department has let it be known that they would like to turn the page and establish bilateral relations based on an agenda that includes much more than the drug issue.

POLITICS

Colombia is a decentralized unitarian republic that elects a president and chief of state every four years by means of direct, universal suffrage. Conservative Andrés Pastrana Arango has led Colombia since the change of government of August 7, 1998, after winning the second ballot of the elections of the previous June. He beat Horacio Serpa Uribe, the successor to Liberal Ernesto Samper Pizano, who served as president from 1994 to 1998. The results of the election of June 22, 1998, were as follows: 6,065,342, or 50.45 percent, for the Conservative Party of Andrés Pastrana Arango; 5,585,627, or 46.46 percent for the Liberal Party of Horacio Serpa Uribe; 371,927, or 3.09 percent, of unmarked ballots; 107,729, or 1 percent, of ballots rejected (spoiled).

The Departments

The president exercises his executive power through ministers that he appoints himself. Legislative power belongs to the Congress, made up of two houses, the members of which are also directly elected by universal suffrage. These are the 112-member Senate and the 199-member House of Representatives.

Every two years, the congress elects a vice-president in a joint session. Should the president be unable to remain in office, the vice-president assumes his duties and position and looks after the institutions of government in the interim.

The organization of the judiciary includes a Supreme Court of 24 judges elected for life. It intervenes in four distinct areas: civil, penal, labour and constitutional law. In questions of major importance, the criminal, civil and labour courts meet in plenary sessions.

There are county and appellate courts in the provinces and departments of each region. Magisterial courts sit in smaller communities.

At the administrative level, Colombia is divided into 32 departments according to the revised Constitution of 1991, each with its own capital, under the authority of a governor. These are Amazonas, Antioquia, Arauca, Atlántico, Bolívar, Boyacá, Caldas, Caquetá, Casanare, Cauca, Valle del Cauca, Cesar, Chocó, Córdova, Cundinamarca, Guainía, Guajira, Guaviare, Huila, Magdalena, Meta, Nariño, Norte de Santander, Santander, Putumayo, Quindío, Risaralda, San Andrés y Providencia, Sucre, Tolima, Vaupés, and Vichada. There are also the capital district, Santafé de Bogotá, and four metropolitan cities (Santiago de Cali, Medellín, Barranquilla and Bucaramanga), as well as five administrative divisions called *Commissarías*, four *Intendencias*, or intendancies, and even a special district, Cartagena de Indias.

On the international level, Colombia is a member of the movement of Nonaligned Nations, which now includes 113 members. Instituted about 40 years ago in Bandung, Indonesia, by about 30 African and Asian countries, the nonalignment movement ensures political consensus by organizing meetings of the leaders of participating nations every three years to raise their common standard of living and offer a solid platform for discussion with the other countries of the world. In 1995, in Cartagena, Colombia was elected to hold the presidency of the Movement until 1998. This demonstrated that Colombia had the acknowledgement and support from its partners for its enthusiastic participation during the course of the previous years in international organizations such as the United Nations Security Council.

Since 1968 Colombia has also been a member of the Latin American Free Trade Association, which promotes the development of foreign trade among signatory nations including Argentina, Brazil, Chile, México, Paraguay, Perù, Uruguay, Bolivia, Ecuador and Venezuela. Colombia was one of the countries responsible for the creation of the Andean Pact, a treaty that allows the countries involved to institute regional economic initiatives and to sign agreements of limited impact without the participation of the other members. This accord gave rise to Mercosur, (Mercado Comun del Sur, literally "Common Market of the South"), in 1991. It is possible that Mercosur will join NAFTA (North American Free Trade Agreement) in the near future, as Canada has already concluded talks on a similar accord with Chile.

THE ECONOMY

In addition to gold and emeralds, Colombia possesses large deposits of bauxite, potash, coal (in Cerrejón), nickel and copper. The country produces oil; the wells on the coastal plains of the Caribbean pump more than 500,000 barrels per day. Agriculture is also an important sector and provides employment for more than 30% of the workforce. While rice and corn are grown for local markets, bananas, cotton, cocoa, tobacco, coffee and sugar are exported. Colombia recently became the second-ranking flower-producing country in the world, and the nation's blossoms can now be found in every international market. Crustaceans are also exported, but fishing remains an under-exploited area, and the livestock industry could easily be doubled. Recently, Colombia has found some lucrative openings on international markets for its crafts and light-industry products.

Tourism

Colombia has suffered many setbacks in the tourism industry, which it blames on its bad reputation from terrorism. Despite this fact, the country's facilities are not only adequate on every level, but often surpass international norms. Tourist destinations in Colombia are astonishingly beautiful and diverse, and some of them could easily and incontrovertibly claim the title of eighth wonder of the world. The salt cathedral of Zipaquirá, near Santafé de Bogotá (see p 97), and the ruins of San Agustín (see p 274) and Tierradentro (see p 276) are just a few examples of the country's world-class attractions.

Emeralds

Colombia is the world's top producer of emeralds, furnishing close to 80% of global production of these gems. The emerald (*esmeraldas*) market is controlled by the government through two mining companies, Techminas and Coexminas. However, people can buy these precious gems at low prices from street resellers, especially in Bogotá, provided they know enough about them not to be duped.

In Muzo, for example, reputedly a very violent town in a zone that can only be entered with a special permit, emeralds can be bought at ridiculously low prices directly from men, women and children who scavenge the debris of an open-pit mine.

The owner of this mine, himself a former miner and scavenger, has his bulldozers dispose of waste debris at streams. Independent rummagers swarm to this debris. His actions permit an entire population of between 10,000 and 15,000 to recuperate stones that they can sell at specialized counters. The debris still contains close to 30 percent of the entire find of precious stones, but because the pieces are so small it would be too expensive to separate them with industrial techniques.

Living in board barracks, these sedentary adventurers generally spend all of their gem-trade income in the proliferation of neighbouring bars and brothels. It is easy to imagine the particularly fiery atmosphere of this eerie city where frequent clashes between individuals go unnoticed except by those close enough to the brawl to stake their day's income on one of the combatants.

People also come to this town from all over the country and from every walk of life and live in tents. These are generally vacationing families, who swell the ranks of the scroungers for a few weeks, looking for the big stone that will someday make them rich. Not everyone rum-

mages in the same place, and the *tambre* (mine waste) is reserved for a privileged set: police officers and the disabled. An imaginary line separates this section from the others and is constantly watched by armed guards. Well, the line may be imaginary, but the guards are not. They are liable to fire without warning in the direction of anyone who dares set foot on the reserved area.

Gold

Colombia is ranked ninth in the world for the gold production, supplying 20% of the global market. Nationalized companies exploit the mines and veins, but foreign companies also lease concessions. These last include Frontino Gold Mines, Consolidated Gulf Fields, Anglo-Colombian Development, South American Gold and Platinum, and International Mining.

Aside from these corporate miners, independent gold washers live in villages like Las Peñas, Los Barzos, and El Venero on rivers that flow into the Pacific, especially Río Guelmambi, Río Pimbi, Río Guapípi and Río Ragui. These foragers search for bits of gold by filtering water and mud in a pan and then collecting anything that shines. Gold collected this way garners laughable prices from middlemen, often not enough to pay for a day's work, and gold washers who have bad weeks must supplement their incomes with agricultural work.

Coffee

Latin America still produces more than half the coffee consumed in the world. Grown on a million hectares, Colombian coffee provides work for more than 400,000 people. Like grapes, coffee was originally imported, and the first coffee trees, originally from Africa, only arrived in the Americas in the 1720s. They produced little red fruits: Arabica beans. The French naval officer Gabriel Mathieu de Clieu actually planted the first coffee tree with its brilliant green foliage in Martinique in this era. Later, in about 1730, the Jesuits brought the plant to Colombia.

The coffee tree blooms with little white flowers as fragrant as jasmine that appear on its branches three times a year. About two months later, the flowers give way to small green berries that take on a reddish colour as they grow until they are dark red at the end of six or seven months. Then a fairly rare phenomenon occurs: new flowers appear, so that the tree is simultaneously blossoming and covered in fruit.

To obtain the best selection, beans must be picked by hand, one by one, the moment that they turn red. The casing of the berry conceals a layer of white meat that in turn protects two coffee beans.

After picking, the ripe berries are washed and put through a threshing machine that removes their skin and meat. As an additional precaution, they are then soaked so that fermentation dissolves the rest of the meat. The beans that remain are then washed again before being set in industrial dryers for a day. Some producers still prefer the old method of natural drying. They place the beans on concrete platforms exposed to the sun. This procedure is longer, requiring four to eight days.

Once dry, the light-green beans are roasted to make coffee. In general, larger companies roast their coffee just before selling it, but it is also possible to buy coffee beans roasted on the premises of specialized shops. Small Colombian *cafeteros*, or coffee growers, grow and roast their own coffee only. It is easy to roast coffee at home, as well. Simply place a few green coffee beans in a cast-iron pan on low heat. This is a long process: the beans must brown evenly for about 20 minutes, or when deemed ready.

Coffee made from beans that are still hot from roasting is a delight, especially when they have been carefully ground in a wood mortar, which adds even more flavour. This is an experience worth tasting! According to the best recipe, the proportions are one tablespoon of ground beans and one spoonful of sugar for one small cup of coffee. Those who have the opportunity to taste fresh-roasted coffee brewed according to this method will confirm that they have drunk the first real coffee of their lives – and the best, of course!

Colombians drink a lot of coffee, and any pretext is sufficient for savouring a *tinto*, a black coffee. Many Colombians claim that the coffee they drink is bad, the best stuff being reserved for export – an irony if ever there was one. In fact, 95 percent of the best coffee is bought on the New York Stock Exchange in the United States, which does not even produce coffee. The Exchange then resells the coffee to about 50 other countries, so international coffee prices are set in New York. However, good coffee is certainly available in Colombia, in places such as large hotels, restaurants that serve espresso, import shops that may be found in most large cities and at the *fincas*, or coffee farms, in the Departments of Caldas, Risaralda and Quindío, among others (see p 222).

Wine

Colombia is not a great wine producer, either in terms of quantity nor quality. In fact, it produces less wine than any other American country and the reputation of its vintages does not extend beyond its borders. Given that Colombia has a very diverse climate that in some regions would be suitable for the cultivation of this temperamental fruit, the question remains: is it simply a matter of lack of interest on the part of investors? After all, neighbouring Chile has a reputation for producing excellent wines, and connoisseurs agree that they are all undervalued. In Colombia, vines produce grapes several time a year, turning the harvest cycle upside down. Colombian vintners produce Manzanilla, which is a type of Porto, and for several years now have been making a number of table wines. Restaurants generally offer lists of imported wines at reasonable prices, especially in large cities and tourist destinations. Some restaurants allow diners to bring their own wine, for the fee of a "cork tax".

POPULATION

A maelstrom of raw colours from the palette of the craziest Fauvist painter, an amalgam of intoxicating, head-turning fragrances, a madness of thundering, harrowing polyphony, Colombia never ceases to spark the imagination. Its mountain chains, valleys, powerful rivers, varied climates and disconcerting landscapes have branded the unique character of its population. Colombians have had to fight fiercely to master their territory from the time of the first arrivals, through the conquest, and up until today, eternally forced to submit to the country's forbidding geography. Thus, it does not seem too farfetched to suggest that violence is the country's most distinctive feature. But shouldn't the difficult countryside unite the people who inhabit to rally against the aggressiveness ascribed to Colombians? This question is unanswerable for the moment, as long as the feverishness and exuberance of recent times still flush Colombians' skin. It is undeniable that they are passionate, dramatic, imaginative, creative, resourceful and even artful, a combination that is not altogether uncontradictory. Culture and the arts – music, among others – are of greater importance to the singularly epicurean people of Colombia.

The fourth-largest country in South America, Colombia ranks second in population after Brazil. It is also one of the most mixed populations in the world. About half, 50% to 55% of the population is mestizo (combined native and white descent), 20% to 25% are mulatto (black and white descent), 20% are white, 3% black, 1% have mixed black and native parentage and 1% to 2% are indigenous, these last being divided into about 50 subgroups representing a dozen cultures: Tayrona, Sinú, Chibcha, Quimbayá, Tolima, Calima, Tierradentro, Cauca, Guane, San Agustín, Nariño and Tumaco. There are also many people from more recent immigrant cultures, such as Italians, Germans, Jews, Turks, Lebanese, Arabs, Asians, all of whom contribute to the national culture.

"South America is an abstraction," Henry Kissinger, former American Secretary of State, once said. His reflection is particularly applicable to Colombia, supreme land of contradictions. One of the top coffee producers in the world, where by the citizens' own admissions they drink lousy coffee. A country of extreme violence, the majority of whose population are tremendously kind. A hot equatorial country, where 70 percent of the population lives in the high altitudes of the Andes where it is often cold, and where the temperature in the capital Santafé de Bogotá even dips down to 4 °C in *invierno*, the rainy season. Winter clothing – scarves and gloves – are not considered emblems of elegance or charm, but necessities. A veritable Babylon of races and colours, but Colombians are not racist. In fact, Colombians claim, and not without irony, that although there are many personality clashes, there is no racism. On the other hand, social segregation is omnipresent – and colour-blind. Slavery was introduced during the early years of colonization, and Cartagena de Indias was a slave trading centre where as many indigenous people were sold as were blacks. More than 100 million black people bore the brunt of this monstrous business in the Americas, fewer than one third of whom survived the passage from Africa. Most were procured in raids in Angola, Sudan, Guinea and Congo. Following

revolts (the first tentative steps toward liberation in South America were made by blacks slaves backed by natives) slavery was finally abolished in Colombia by President José Hilario López in 1851. Groups of blacks settled on the Caribbean coast, in Magdalena, in Cauca and especially in Chocó, and along the Pacific coast, which is still mainly populated by their descendants.

Spanish-speaking and Catholic, Colombians have lost a fair bit of their religious fervour in recent years, at least in the larger centres. In smaller agglomerations, religion is still very present – superficially more than spiritually, it would seem – almost to the point of fetishism. The important Catholic holidays like Christmas and Easter are still celebrated with a great deal of pomp and ceremony, and the churches fill up even for minor religious ceremonies, like baptisms, marriages and first communions. As well, many other sects have sprouted up recently, in direct competition with the Colombian Catholic Church, the most conservative in all of South America.

The family continues to play a primary role in Colombia, even if it is a double-edged sword. Unconditionally protective of all of its members, it demands in return that each do his or her part to support it. This restricts personal development because this last demand has neither chronological nor financial limits: the needs of the "clan" go before those of individuals. Exile and emigration do not abnegate this responsibility either: Colombians living abroad are expected to furnish housing and food to any family member who visits, and are morally bound to send part of their earnings back home to contribute to the family.

Facts and Figures

According to the Departamento Administrativo Nacional de Estadísticas, some 27 percent of Colombians were living below the poverty line in 1997. The real growth rate in gross domestic product fell recently from 5.7% to 3.3%. Unemployment increased to 14.3 percent in 1998, while inflation brushed the 20 percent level. The annual budget deficit is now 3.8 billion US. Foreign investment is the only improving economic indicator, displaying spectacular growth in recent years and increasing 40 percent to approximately four billion American dollars. The birth rate is 2.92 and life expectancy is in the 70s. About 8.7 percent of

PORTRAIT

Two Contrasting World Views

Able to travel for long periods without tiring by chewing the coca leaf with *mambe*, Colombia's native people are generally peaceful and have always tried to maintain their way of life and thinking amid modern society, especially in South America where some groups remain isolated from the "outside" world.

Native society is very spiritual. For example, although gold was the essence of wealth to the Spanish, the precious metal did not have the same meaning to the natives who see it as a tangible manifestation of divine power, mainly that of the sun-god.

Characteristics considered to be virtues by modern society are often seen as flaws by the natives, and vice-versa. Laziness is a necessity for natives who must preserve energy to live in harmony with the nature, geography and climate of their region. Poverty puts natives at a disadvantage when it comes to preserving their traditions. When they succeed in meeting their daily needs and those of their families, they stop working, since work does not figure among their essential life activities. This does not, however, mean that they do not plan their harvests ahead of time. They have a profound respect for the earth and maintain a harmonious relationship with the animals that they hunt and the fish they catch. Surplus harvests are shared with the community, and greed and enriching oneself at others' expense are foreign concepts. In fact, the word "greed" does not even exist in the Quechua language.

Capitalism is another form of enslavement. The rich keep getting richer by making their own people work for them. Even when they have everything, it seems rich people feel the need to outdo each other and look like role models. They also sell things rather than give them away – even sharing is self-centred. The rich also tend to be power hungry and flaunt their wealth.

Natives take their time to complete their work. They respect the tool as much as the product they use it to make. To natives, time is life.

Modern society believes people who take their time are wasting time: time is money.

Natives dream and their dreams are essential guides to life.

Modern society regards dreamers as idealists, intellectuals, artists, lunatics, revolutionaries, and burdens to society.

Natives can be taken at their word, while modern society is bound by contracts signed in due form. And even then, they must often ask the courts to resolve the claims of opposing parties.

Natives were naked at the time of the conquest, with no sense of shame, in perfect harmony with nature. At that same time in Europe a woman could not even display a painted toenail without finding herself being burned at the Inquisition's stake for indecency. The conquistadors and their priests soon forced the natives to cover themselves to avoid sin. Now converted to Catholicism, the natives are embarrassed by nudity while topless Europeans overrun Caribbean beaches!

Native elders continue to live in the heart of the nuclear family and receive care, respect and affection from all of its members. As patriarchs, they constitute an inexhaustible source of information for the children towards whom they display unbridled tenderness.

Modern society confines the elderly to retirement homes. Their children and even their own grandchildren refuse to visit them, because they think of them as old, scary-looking, dying strangers. Instead, seniors must search elsewhere for the human touch, somewhere they can interact with other people's children, cherishing the slightest gesture from a friendly kid.

The gods of the natives are accessible and resemble them. They do not judge humans as weak and inferior creatures. They are much closer to the gods of Far Eastern civilizations, from which they probably originated, migrating at the same time as their worshippers.

The Western god is cruel, arrogant, distant, selfish and vengeful. He judges the actions of humans and does not hesitate to condemn them to all of the horrors of hell for the slightest thought or action.

the population is illiterate, while the education rate for children 12 to 17 years of age is 65.7 percent. The percentage of students who graduate university is 17.5.

Native Peoples

Many natives in the Andes still live according to ancestral traditions, and some groups remain completely removed from the rest of the world. Unlike other great civilizations that share or dominate vast territories, the first peoples of Colombia lived in small, fierce tribes that developed in limited areas. Brief descriptions of the most important of these first nations follow (see also History, p 14).

The Tayrona

The Tayrona (see also p 141) are descended from the Arawaks. They are very proud natives who escaped the influence of the conquistadors by fleeing into the highlands. Today Arawaks, Koguis and Wayuús are direct descendants of the Tayrona. The name Tayrona at one time designated only one tribe, but now the term is used for all of the natives of the Sierra Nevada, although some of them prefer the less common appellation Kogui. While modern-day Tayrona are more open to outside influences than their ancestors were, they still live outside of mainstream society. Their main economic activities are livestock raising and farming.

Archaeologists researching this civilization found vestiges of streets and esplanades in highly sophisticated cities linked by a stone road network of almost 500 kilometres. They discovered stairways in stone slabs and massive stone blocks used as foundations for houses and religious and public buildings. The Tayrona had perfected a rather sophisticated technique for levelling mountainsides into superposed terraces. They then built cities with temples and houses and equipped them with complex aqueduct systems.

The Tayrona worked in ceramics, although their main subsistence activities were agriculture, fishing and the extraction of salt from the marshes of coastal cities. They also traded in myriad other crafts including metalwork. The Tayrona were monogamous, and married women enjoyed a higher status than did women in most other tribes. Their civilization was made up of several societies spread over a tiny territory compared to that of other cultures.

Because there is no gold in the Sierra Nevada de Santa Marta, the Tayrona had to import the precious metal. It is thought that they traded with the Quimbayá of the Río Cauca Valley as well as with the tribes of Panamá, their natural neighbours in the time before modern borders. Tayrona means "goldsmith" in Quechua and gold working was widely practised in the Andes. The Tayrona were especially good at it.

Today, in accordance with the nature and spirit of their ancestors, the Tayrona have decided to open themselves up to the world and allow strangers to visit their territory. Tourists are welcomed to Pueblito and Ciudad Perdida, the "lost city" of the Sierra Nevada de Santa Marta, in an area that is so difficult to travel through that it is nicknamed El Infierno, or "hell". This openness is relatively recent because outsiders did not know that Ciudad Perdida (see p 142) existed until 1975; the Tayrona were so hostile to the intrusion of whites into their territory, they cared little whether they were archaeologists.

The Chibcha

The Spanish were so absolutely determined to conquer South America because they were fervently eager to take possession of the riches to be found on the continent. Were they fooled by the mischievousness of the natives – still evident in Colombians today – who took advantage of their ignorance and then laughed at them? Although the conquistadors shamelessly pillaged every South American civilization, they were not satisfied with the treasures they found. The natives gave them hints of riches hundreds of times more fabulous than those they had succeeded in acquiring. To drive these undesirable barbarians and parasites from their villages, they willingly told them their legends, or any story at all, to send the Spanish away in a frenzy of greed.

Organized into small kingdoms, the Chibcha, whom the Spanish called Muisca, were like many other gold-working and gem-cutting peoples. From 200 BC up until the conquest, they occupied the savanna of Bogotá in the centre of Colombia, the entire high plateau of the Cordillera Oriental. Their civilization was protected by immense, almost impenetrable fortresses – the mountains – and by endless plains that enabled them to spot the enemy from great distances. Although they were not advanced enough to build in stone, they did live in palaces, buildings and houses of wood, the splendour of which fascinated the Spanish, who nicknamed the area Valle de los Alcazares, or "the valley of castles". Their houses were true little gems that exhibited a quality of life superior to those of the Spanish who discovered them: they were solid, carefully built and beautifully decorated. Some had carpets and furniture. The Chibcha wore richly coloured cotton clothing and jewellery made of gold and precious stones. They were not literate but they did have currency, they had even established a credit system by which an unpaid debt doubled every full moon. They were exceptional metalworkers and created many objects by casting them in sculpted clay moulds.

Like the Tayrona, the Chibcha were also uncommonly skilled goldsmiths and did not possess their own gold mines, so they had to import the nuggets from their neighbours, the Quimbayá. Like the Quimbayá, they used hammering, wiredrawing, rivetting and inlaying techniques. But they excelled in a lost wax-work technique and filigree, the interlacing of strands of metal held together by a still-mysterious soldering method.

By aerating a grill of charcoal with blowers, they raised the temperature of their ovens enough to mix pure, supple gold with other metals like silver and copper to make resistant alloys. They were so skilled in this that they often fooled the Spanish who thought the alloys were pure gold. They created many jewels, including pendants, earrings, amulets and nose ornaments of all shapes with this alloy.

In addition to working with gold, the Chibcha exploited salt and emerald mines. They were expert farmers and grew potatoes, and small game was diverse and abundant. They also mastered pottery and cotton weaving and dyeing. Despite the fact that their kings, Bogotá and Tunja, were almost always at war when the Spanish arrived, the two were not really warriors and they often combined forces against their natural, cannibalistic enemies, the Panches. It is thought that the modern Páez (see p 269) are direct descendants of the Chibcha.

The propitiatory ritual of the Chibcha "gold man" is still deeply rooted in the popular imagination. Who has not heard of El Dorado (see p 22), the legend of a Chibcha cacique? And are not legends the dreamlike interpretations of reality? The conquistadors only saw in it what they wanted to believe, leading them on a futile, and often deadly, quest for gold.

The San Agustín Civilization

San Agustín (see p 274), in southern Colombia, is incontrovertibly one of the country's most important pre-Colombian archaeological sites; many stone and terracotta works were found there. Underground tombs and temples were uncovered, as well as hundred of sculptures and limbless statues of humans and animals carved into soft rock. Immense monolithic anthropomorphic steles sculpted in volcanic rock have also been discovered. The most interesting constructions, however, are large round barrows more than 4 metres high and 20 to 25 metres in diameter. It is thought that these barrows concealed underground temples hidden from intruders by huge slabs of stone.

The Quimbayá

The Quimbayá civilization is undoubtedly the most fascinating of Colombia's pre-Columbian societies. The Quimbayá lived in the area that

PORTRAIT

now makes up the Department of Antioquia, along Río Cauca in western Colombia. Archaeologists first learned of their existence when they discovered their tombs. The Quimbayá used two different types of crypts: the first kind were found at ground level, the others about 10 metres underground. The deceased were laid out on the ground itself, surrounded by funerary objects including ceramic and stone implements and necklaces and other items made of gold.

Above all else, the Quimbayá excelled in metalwork. All evidence indicates that they had perfected their technique for working gold about 500 years BC. Their skills were consummate in hammering, wiredrawing, rivetting and inlaying. Although there are significant gold deposits in the central and southern parts of the country, the Quimbayá did not dig mines since they did know how to crush stone. Neither did they have smelting furnaces. But they were skilful gold washers with a thorough knowledge of how to filter gold from the alluvial sediment of rivers. They worked with pans, which they used to filter gold-bearing sand to collect nuggets.

The Quimbayá were polygamous, and the number of wives one man had indicated his prosperity and influence in the community.

The Motilones

The Motilones are apparently descendants of the Caribs; at least, their language is related to that culture. They have resisted assimilation for a long time and, like many other indigenous groups, they have had to confront the disquieting arrival of neocolonialism. They have retreated into the mountains and now live in the most isolated heights of the Sierra Nevada de Santa Marta.

Native Power

The National Organization of Indigenous People of Colombia (ONIC) is an organization that fights for the rights of native people, who are increasingly confronted with claims by *terratenientes*, large property owners, and with small farmers taking over their land. Until the agrarian reforms of 1961, aboriginal Colombians were governed by one law that dates from 1890 and laid out a plan to marginalise natives on state-owned reservations. With the reforms of 1961, the reservations disappeared

and were replaced by *resguardos*, territories handed over collectively to the first nations, who have their own administrative authority. Through universal suffrage they elect a council led by a cacique, which cooperates with the state and presides over tribunals (major crimes still fall under Colombian law).

However, the natives' future is still uncertain. All of these reforms, including the creation of a Ministry of Indian Affairs in 1960 and the adoption of the International Labour Organization's convention on the protection of indigenous peoples in 1967, remain gestures of good will on the part of the Colombian government. The funds budgeted for buying land are insufficient and the ministers involved are continually coming up against the *terratenientes*, whose lordly pretensions are throwbacks to the feudal colonial regime and who refuse to sell their land.

For these reasons, the Páez initiated the first regional council of the natives of Cauca in 1971, which caused a good deal of opposition in Latin America. The council created, among other things, bilingual schools where the majority of lessons are taught in indigenous languages, proving their determination to have their culture respected.

CULTURE AND TRADITIONS

Colombia's large centres and tourist areas are not all that culturally different from Europe or North America. Its bustling cities are overrun with cellular telephones, uniformity and internationalism, and are the domains of a privileged new generation hooked up to satellite dishes, computers and the Internet. And who could blame them? This outward gaze is apparent in the behaviour, fashion, hobbies, gastronomy and the arts generally of prospering Colombians, as well as in their manner of meeting and embracing foreigners.

To get a feeling for authentic Colombia, outsiders must look elsewhere and take an interest in the simplest aspects of daily life. They must get used to unfamiliar fragrances that emanate from all over and are especially powerful after a rain shower. They must witness unfurling waves of colour that hypnotize and intoxicate. They must hear the cacophony of popular songs drowning out conversations in a language that at times sound like a litany and at others like a long cry, never monotone, always harmonic, retelling the tumultuous past, the difficult present and the uncertain future in one lyrical breath full of hope.

Violence

Colombia has an unenviable reputation internationally and reports of the violence that afflicts the country are commonly read and seen abroad (see also p 63). "Colombia is a violent country" seems to be the most frequently heard cliche in the tourism industry. Maybe this attitude benefits other vacation destinations that would lose out if this were proven to be false. Without being obsequious, we can admit that the country merits a second look before being branded by global admonition. In fact, a more serious analysis shows without doubt that a minute portion of the population makes a living out of violent crime – like anywhere else – and this small subsection of society is responsible for the "diabolical" reputation that has tarnished all Colombians and stigmatized them nationally and internationally. As well, the problems of which Colombia is accused are hot topics for the media, which the public likes to hear about: sexism, drugs, guerrilla warfare.

In fact, violence is only endemic to certain very specific regions of Colombia. At least six large groups reap the benefits of power and dominate specific areas. These are the two largest political parties, the Liberals and the Conservatives, then the military, the paramilitary, the guerrillas and organized crime.

The majority of guerrilla groups, who have been active as armed revolutionaries over the last 40 years, have been gaining respect recently. Shortly after the attack on the Bogotá courthouse by the FARC (Revolutionary Armed Forces of Colombia) in 1985, President Belisario Betancur helped create the group Contadora with the goal of ending such conflicts in Latin America. Contadora formulated principles to restore social peace between various political factions, especially in Colombia. During the years that followed, most of the guerrilla groups left the mountains to enter the official political arena. They became a true opposition by denouncing the financial instability, social inequality and poverty resulting from the privileges still enjoyed by large landowners.

In 1992, the economic situation deteriorated and the guerillas returned to the underground. In early 1998 there were no fewer than 75 guerrilla groups in Colombia, ranging from the Marxist FARC to the Guevarist ELN (National Liberation Army), and they were not necessarily always cooperating with eachother. Some of these factions still have dubious associations with drug traffickers, whom they protect in exchange for money to buy weapons. As an aside, the financial power of the drug traffickers is so great now that it can influence elections. Former Liberal President Ernesto Samper Pizano was accused of colluding with the Cali cartel during the elections that brought him to power in 1994. The United States even banned him from entering the country after this accusation. It must be mentioned that the influx of foreign currency that the drug trade attracts creates a paradox for nations in crisis, especially when money laundering is directly responsible for a nationwide construction boom. The former boss of the Medellín cartel, Pablo Escobar, actually offered to pay off the national foreign debt in exchange for amnesty. He also covered the construction costs to build an entire neighbourhood of houses for the poor in Medellín.

Far right extremists (paramilitaries) have appeared with the evocative name *vigilantissimo*. In July 1997, these death squads were responsible for the massacre of 25 people in the region of Mapiripán, about 210 kilometres southeast of the capital of Bogotá. In 1998, shortly after the elections, they killed 25 hostages in the area of Barancabermeja, in the Department of Santander. They accused the villagers of supporting the Guevarist ELN (National Liberation Army). Neither did they hesitate to attack on several other occasions, because, they claim, the army refused to do so.

Do government authorities choose to keep Colombia in this state of violence? The answer to this question is not so simple and implies certain subtleties that cannot be ignored. Although Colombia now claims to be a pluralist democracy, the reality is quite the opposite. At the end of the 1950s, the Conservatives and the Liberals signed a pact to share power by alternating turns in office to avoid civil war. The parties submitted themselves to systematic vote-buying, which created many debts. Additionally, this bipartisanship, which prevailed until the renewal of the constitution in 1991, did not predispose politicians to decisions that might diminish approval from the groups that support this power sharing, which is to say the elite families, large landowners, and industrialists, among others. Thus, nepotism paralysed the entire government apparatus for a long period, with jobs being given not according to competence but rather by relation. Many lucrative positions were created as repayment for services rendered, inexorably depleting government funds, including recipients for social programs. As a result, a "domino effect" affected even in large businesses. As well, it is still claimed that Colombia belongs to 24 dynasties, descended from conquistadors who settled on huge estates in the earliest days of colonization, who have governed by turns for more than 100 years. Subsequently, elections often inspire only indifference in a largely disillusioned population.

It is easy to understand that, in these conditions, the motto "every man for himself" – and for his family – has become a necessity for survival for most of the population. The anarchy this precept creates replaces law, with the logical result that violence is an accepted lifestyle. As well, a sense of honour and virility underlies all relations and discussions. Revenge becomes justice for the slightest disagreement. And ironic as it is, life in Colombia is of unparalleled intensity, as the majority of Colombians will attest with a certain pride. However, a wave of change is presently unfurling. During the last elections, in June 1998, the population clearly expressed to the 10 presidential candidates its discontent with criminal violence and impunity. On June 19, a huge demonstration was organized on Plaza Bolívar in the Colombian capital, with simultaneous symbolic protests in other large cities, which paralysed the entire nation for a half hour and left no uncertainty as to the will of the people.

Machismo

Change has been afoot in the area of gender roles over the last few years. Women are gradually entering the labour force and competing with men financially. They hold ministerial and high-level bureaucratic positions in government, and are increasingly involved in the decisions that affect society as a whole and the role of Colombian women in particular. It's a beginning.

Coca

The small, pointy, green coca leaf is easily mistaken for tea. It grows on bushes that reach a height of three metres. Colombian natives make a mixture of the leaf and ash called *mambe* which they store in a *poporó*, an emptied pear-shaped squash (calabash). As needed, they dip long, narrow, wood straws into the *poporó* and lick them to absorb the *mambe*, which gives them alot of energy. They carry the *poporó* in their *guambia*, a sort of shoulder bag, when they leave their villages for several days, on hunting trips, for example, or to cross the mountains to the market of a faraway village where they sell fruit and vegetables and especially crafts. When used in this way, *mambe* constitutes an inexpensive nutritional supplement that diminishes fatigue, hunger and thirst. The natives can spend entire days travelling without eating or sleeping, which shortens their trip and the time their families spend without their protection.

As well, *naomas*, the shamans, use the coca leaf in religious ceremonies. Other substances are also consumed, including hallucinogenic drinks made from the San Pedro cactus, which contains mescaline, and other plants. "It's cultural," they say. If governments around the world ignore the issue of nicotine addiction and avoid prohibiting the use of tobacco – a custom that is only a few decades old – it is understandable that the Colombian government is hardly in a position to legislate against the use of coca leaves by the natives, a custom that goes back several millennia.

Every aboriginal group has its own recipes of medicinal or hallucinogenic plants that they use to increase their concentration or physical stamina or both.

La Cocaína

During the Vietnam War, American G.I.'s made a fortune selling hashish (readily available all over Asia) to Nixon-supporting soldiers, who enjoyed the effects of being "stoned". Hoping to pursue this lucrative career once back in the United States, they found it was easier to import marijuana by air or by sea from Colombia to Florida than it was to grow it in their own country. They landed in the Guajira Peninsula in search of their product's main ingredient

Mambe

The preparation of *mambe* varies very little from one region to another and from one indigenous tradition to another. First round stones from freshwater streams are heated in a fire for about 30 hours. Then the stones are placed into a cauldron over the fire with boiling water and brown sugar until the stone disintegrates. The water is poured off so as to keep only the powder, which is transferred into the *poporó*.

The coca leaf is then dried and powdered, added to the *poporó*, and mixed into the stone powder. Then a few coca leaves are placed in the mouth and a moistened stick straw is used to sip the *poporó* mixture. The whole is chewed for about 15 minutes and then spit out.

Natives do not use lemon or lime very much because their astringent properties dry the mouth and saliva is necessary to enhance the effects of *mambe*.

so they could continue to supply their old combat buddies and their new American customers who, encouraged by "peace and love", were demanding more and more drugs. In fact, once back from Vietnam, US Marines rekindled the ritual of toasting North America by smoking a nice fat joint, a cone, and this custom soon spread to Europe. México, a top exporter of marijuana and mescaline, was being monitored more closely by the US Drug Enforcement Agency, so traffickers had to find a new supplier quickly.

Once in Colombia, this new generation of conquistadors of Alta Guajira soon discovered the benefits of the coca leaf and put themselves to the task of finding it with the same frenetic energy that their predecessors had applied to the hunt for gold. The substance had been in use in the 1900s in their favourite drink, Coca-Cola, so they knew how to chemically refine it to produce a readily consumable product: *cocaína*, cocaine, or coke(!).

The Americans shared this technology with smalltime Colombian gangster bosses from the start, and were content simply to handle American distribution. These common mobsters soon turned into international super-criminals, furnishing the distribution network already in place in the United States and throughout the world. The rest of the story is common knowledge, including the establishment of Colombian-run networks in North America and Europe, President Bush's and his successors' commitment to the "war on drugs", and the violence that has resulted from the whole mess. Everyone has heard of the incarceration of Pablo Escobar, the head of the Medellín cartel, who drew up the plans for his prison himself and paid for its construction out of his own pocket, including the bomb shelters installed to protect him from air attacks by his enemies. His 1992 escape is also well-known, and his violent death one year later in the middle of a street on his own turf in the Medellín neighbourhood of Envigado was picked up by all the international media.

Freud lauded the therapeutic value of cocaine in his book *Ueber Coca*, published in 1884, and as early as 1844, German Wilhelm Lossen mixed coca leaves with ether and essence to produce a hydrochloride of cocaine now known colloquially as coke.

The production of one kilogram of cocaine, so precious to its users, requires 500 kilograms of coca leaves. The first step is to extract the alkaloid from the leaf. To do this, the leaves are soaked in a mixture of potash or sodium carbonate and water. Then they are mashed in a container of kerosene, which dissolves the alkaloid. When the mixture turns into black mud, sulfuric acid is added, which reacts with the alkaloid and transforms it into a cocaine sulfate. The kerosene is extracted and replaced by an alkali that neutralizes the toxic effects of the sulfuric acid. This leaves a grey paste that is immersed in kerosene again. In a short time, layers of 60-percent-pure cocaine alkaloid are formed. This paste is then washed and dried and immersed in sulfuric acid again, to which potassium permanganate is added. Then the whole thing is filtered. A product of ammonium hydroxide is then added and the blend is filtered again producing raw cocaine. The final product is created by dissolving the raw cocaine in ether and adding hydrochloric acid and acetone. With all of the chemical ingredients that enter into its fabrication, it certainly isn't the sort of thing one might find on the shelves of health-food stores!

"But it's cultural," they natives say. Well, it's also illegal for the entire Colombian population and for tourists (who are in no way directly descended from the indigenous peoples of South America) to possess, sell or export cocaine. These crimes are harshly punished by local and international authorities. Nothing is worse than a stay in a foreign prison. (Not that prison is a holiday in one's own country!) Although Colombians are generally very pleasant hosts, they do not build their luxury hotels simply for rich foreigners to snuff their laws – and their cocaine. Also, drug dealers are disreputable people in any country, and associating with them is truly at your own risk and peril.

Because of international, especially American, "demand" for their products, drug lords are so powerful that they have small armies to defend themselves, which makes them masters of entire regions. According to some sources, the drug trade represents close to 14 percent of Colombia's foreign exports and slightly under five percent of its gross domestic product.

The Colombian government has taken a broad series of actions to fight the traffickers since 1989, following the assassination of the Liberal candidate Luis Carlos Galán by the Medellín cartel in the elections of 1990. It remains obvious that part of national power is in the hands of the cocaine cartels who can pull a lot of strings and now also traffic heroin and other hard drugs. Today, Colombia's priorities are dealing with poverty and drugs, but it will not overcome the latter without the support of the other nations affected by this plague.

Food

Gastronomy is very diverse in Colombia (see also p 72). A variety of international cuisines are well-represented, from Chinese to Italian and French nouvelle cuisine. There are also Japanese, Spanish, Swiss, Argentinian and Russian restaurants, to name but a few. Fast food (*la comida rapida*) is omnipresent: all of the big American chains compete Colombian-style in downtown areas.

The shortage of air and land transportation that existed for so long because of the country's rugged terrain isolated many regions. This, in turn, contributed to the development of original regional cooking styles that are the pride of all Colombians. Everything can be found in Colom-

bia, which is self-sufficient in produce, livestock and fish. Depending on the area, people eat beef, pork, lamb and chicken prepared in every way imaginable, with all of the known exotic vegetables. In coastal areas, all sorts of fish and seafood are consumed in their particular season. Some of the cervids (horned big game) provide exquisite meat, and the *hocco*, a large, loud black bird is the best fowl to be had in all Latin America. In some regions, monkey and iguana are eaten, especially by locals who consider them delicacies.

Traditional restaurants that serve regional cuisine, especially at noon, can be found all over the place. *Almuerzo* is the affordable midday meal; *desayuno* is breakfast and *cena*, supper. Of course, tastes vary. Like all regional cuisines, Colombian local cooking is based on affordable cuts of meat or fish, accompanied by beans and rice, which makes it heavy stuff. Traditional Colombian restaurants share another peculiar trait: they all have televisions that are always blaring, either for atmosphere or to entertain the children. It is very unpleasant and impossible to get used to. Another custom that may be hard to adjust to is that you will be served your main course before you've finished your appetizer.

Hot sauces are concocted everywhere, but are served as an accompaniment rather than used as an ingredient in the dishes themselves. So don't worry about burning your mouth by eating something that is too spicy, which often the case with food in México, the Caribbean and even North Africa.

One culinary must is *arepa*, a fried pancake of cornflour dough kneaded with water that is served with every meal. *Arepa* is definitely not the same as good bread, which is rare in Colombia, but it is found on every Latin American table. Meanwhile, plantains are eaten raw, poached, fried, grilled in stews and in soups. They are even used to make chips: coin-shaped slices of plantain are fried and then flattened and dipped in a deep frier, which makes them crunchy like potato chips.

Coconut is also used in many stewed dishes and gives them an interesting colour but also an exceptional flavour. Coconut oil is commonly used for frying, as is peanut oil. However, to experience the coconut flavour at its best, you must try some of the *postres* (desserts), especially ice cream.

More audacious diners will want to taste *las culonas* (literally, "fat bottoms"), large ants without any real flavour except those of grease and salt from cooking – like snails, which taste mostly like garlic butter. *Las culonas* (see p 211) are one of the specialties of Bucaramanga, the capital of the Department of Santander.

Colombia's best restaurants are found in the Zona Rosas of large cities. The Zona Rosa is a neighbourhood – sometimes identified as such and sometimes not – with a large concentration of bars, nightclubs and restaurants. All of the taxi drivers know their city's Zona Rosa and can take you there, or you can ask for directions at the reception desk of your hotel.

Civic and Religious Holidays

January 1: New Year's Day (*Circuncisión*);
January 6: Epiphany (*Los Reyes Magos*);
March 19: the feast of Saint Joseph (*San José*);
March or April: Holy Week (*Semana Santa*);
May 1: May (Labour) Day (*Día del Trabajo*);
May or June: Corpus Christi;
June: feast day of the Sacred Heart of Jesus (*Sagrado Corazón de Jesús*);
June 29: feast day of Saint Peter and Saint Paul (*San Pedro y San Pablo*);
July 20: Colombian national holiday (*Día de la Independencia*);
August 7: commemoration of the Battle of Bocayá (*Batalla de Bocayá*);
August 15: Assumption (*Asunción de Nuestra Señora*);
October 12: Day of the Race, commemoration of Columbus's arrival in the Americas (*Día de la Raza*);
November 1: All Saints' Day (*Todos Santos*);
November 11: commemoration of the liberation of Cartagena (*Independencia de Cartagena*);
December 8: Immaculate Conception (*Inmaculada Concepción*);
December 25: Christmas *(Navidad)*.

Colombians, it's easy to see, love a party. Everything is a pretext for a celebration and a dance. Many big international events take place in Colombia over the year. Here are a few of them:

January: the fair of Manizales; the Carnaval de Blancos y Negros in Pasto; the Carnaval del Diablo in Riosucio (every two years);
February: the Barranquilla carnival;

March-April: the Cartagena International Caribbean Music Festival; Holy Week all over the country, especially popular in Popayán and Mompós;
April: the Festival of the *Vallenata* Legend in Valledupar; the Bogotá International Latin American Theatre Festival (every two years);
June: the Cartagena International Film Festival; the Folk Festival and crowning of the Bambuco queen in Neiva;
August: the Santa Marta Festival of the Sea; the Medellín flower fair;
September: the Manizales Festival of Latin American Theatre;
November: the crowning of Miss Colombia in Cartagena; the national coconut queen pageant in San Andrés; the Llano Tourism and Folk Festival in San Martín; the Feria Internacional del Vino in Cali;
December: the sugarcane fair in Cali.

ARCHITECTURE

Early colonial architecture in Colombia is characterized by the poor quality of the materials used, especially of the wood. Only toward the end of the 17th century did stone cathedrals and monasteries begin to appear with wooden decorative elements. As for design, Colombia long favoured baroque art that was strongly influenced by the style popular in Spain at the end of the Middle Ages. The Renaissance, which was occurring during the same period, did not become popular because most of the country's new inhabitants were uncultivated and too preoccupied with conquest to be affected by it.

In early colonial architecture, the most remarkable feature is the influence of Mudéjar art, characterized by abstract rococo ornamentation and the complete omission of representations of living beings out of fear of idolatry, proscribed by the Koran, and by the heavily illustrated Plateresque style characterized by a profusion of baroque ornamentation. These two styles were predominant in lay and religious buildings, especially on wood roofs and in the decoration of façades. However, the patina of age on a soft material like wood and especially the ravages of fire have left few remnants of these first architectural steps.

Fortunately, Colombia still possesses a few monasteries from the era, notably the Franciscan monastery of Tunja, the capital of Boyacá and gateway to the *llanos*, which was erected in 1550. You can also admire a few buildings typical of Mudéjar art in Bogotá proper. Other interesting buildings abound in this city and many of its churches are remarkable especially for their interior decoration, which was of utmost importance in the 17th century.

The new leaders of Colombian architecture have developed a common, original, modern style with a special interpretive touch of the baroque, seen in pure lines and the use of wood and wrought-iron decorative elements. Condominium apartments, many hotels and government and private buildings constructed by newer architectural firms are eloquent examples of this movement, especially in the larger cities like Santafé de Bogotá, Medellín, Santiago de Cali and Barranquilla.

THE ARTS

Art has always held an important place in Colombia, whether in the field of architecture, the fine arts, literature or music. Many Colombian artists have gained national and international repute. Mirroring the diversity of the country's population, Colombian art reflects its various regions, each of which has its own values. Despite this diversity of influences, Colombia presents a remarkable homogeneity in comparison to other Latin American countries.

Painting and Sculpture

Colombians have demonstrated great creativity when it comes to painting. After the colonial masters, of whom Gregorio Vásquez de Arce y Ceballos and Ricardo Acevedo Bernal were the foremost representatives, and the impressionist period, of which Andrés de Santa María was the precursor, it is above all contemporary painting that attracts attention.

Colombia is no exception to the rule that every country that is the least bit open to the world experienced the same influences at the same time in contemporary art: its sculpture and painting were strongly influenced by the movements and schools fashionable in the United States and Europe and even in Asia. Colombian artists have adapted to international trends. They are sometimes reproached for a lack of originality, while a synchronous stagnation can be observed even in New York, Paris, London, Berlin or Montreal, because we too often forget

that what is officially accepted as art responds to very precise, and from the outset restrictive, "academic" criteria. The yoke of "modern art" actually leaves little room for individual expression, for figurative work for example, which is the characteristic trait of the visual vocabulary of Latin America and Colombia in particular. Gonzalo Ariza for example, with his heavily Asian-influenced canvases (he studied in Japan), brings to light an uncommon sense of the beauty of Colombian nature through Andean landscapes. In another style altogether, Eduardo Celis and his hyper-realist paintings deserve more than an honourable mention. It suffices to name Alejandro Obregón, Edgar Negret, Fernando Botero (see p 197), Luis Caballero and Dario Morales, who are just a few of the artists who have been in the spotlight of the international art world for a long time now. Of course, this list does not mention the little- or unknown artists who are leading a popular art movement of spectacular originality. They decorate *chivas* (buses), creating veritable masterpieces, especially in the department of Antioquia. These are Colombia's true contemporary artists.

Literature

The European influence in the field of literature has been apparent for a long time in the works of Latin American and Colombian writers who often choose to express themselves in Castilian or even French in order to forge reputations for themselves. However, European literature seems to be becoming a much less important influence on the imaginations of Colombian authors. Jorge Isaacs (1837-1895) described the rural values of his era in his famous novel *María*, while José Eustacio Rivera (1888-1928) evoked the difficult conditions of human survival in the tropical forest in realistic detail in his novel *La Voragine* ("The Abyss"). Eduardo Zalamea Borda shares the hard conditions of life in the Guajira Peninsula just as vividly in *Cuatro Años a Bordo de Mi Mismo* ("Four Years by Myself"). Among Cartagena native authors, Luis Carlos López (1881-1950) wrote several famous anthologies and Rafaël Núñez (1825-1894) was a romantic poet who also played an important role in political life (see p 166). More recently, Colombian writers have followed the international trend and engaged with the symbolic regionalism made popular by *One Hundred Years of Solitude* written by Nobel laureate Gabriel García Márquez. The novel reveals the lives of village families in an imaginary rural burg called Macondo. These families, caught up despite themselves in the political upheavals that are gripping their country, see themselves drawn into a spiralling brutality reminiscent of the cruel period of *La Violencia* (see p 31).

Music

In Colombia, the popular *telenovelas* – soap operas – are not aired on Saturdays and Sundays and the weekend is devoted to dancing, especially salsa (see p 246), after loosening up with big shots of *aguardiente*, an anise-flavoured sugarcane liqueur. The pop music industry is very dynamic in Colombia, as it is all over Latin America. Rich and varied, this music mines sources of all genres especially in the various old traditions of South America and the Caribbean. Salsa and *cumbia* are omnipresent, and the latter, brought over by black slaves from West Africa, is practically the country's national dance. Salsa is a saucy blend of elements influenced by *guaguanco, guaracha, chacha* from México and the mambo from Cuba. The most famous *salsero* from Cartagena is Joe Arroyo, who has won the Congo trophy at the Barranquilla carnival 14 times. All of his shows attract huge crowds like the 80,000-strong one that practically demolished a Bogotá park at a concert celebrating his 25th anniversary in show business.

Within a few days of arriving in Colombia, you will notice the lively, rhythmic, accordion-accompanied folk sounds of *vallenato* music (see p 126), especially on the Caribbean coast. This music comes from the northeast of the country, from the region of La Guajira, and dates from the beginning of this century. It was very much in fashion in the 1960s and 1970s. The *vallenato* is still popular today, and very well-known singers, like Diomedes Díaz, are still recording songs in this style.

PRACTICAL INFORMATION

This section is intended to help you plan your trip to Colombia. It also includes general information and practical advice designed to familiarize you with local customs.

ENTRANCE FORMALITIES

To enter Colombia, you must have a valid passport. As a general rule, the expiration date should not fall less than three months after your date of departure. If you have a return ticket, however, your passport need only be valid for the duration of your stay. If not, proof of sufficient travel funds may be required. For most American and Canadian citizens, as well as Western European citizens, a simple passport is enough, and no visa is necessary. Citizens of other countries are advised to contact the nearest consulate to see whether they need a visa to enter the country. Since requirements for entering the country can change quickly, it is wise to double-check them before leaving.

Travellers are advised to keep a photocopy of the most important pages of their passport, and to write down its number and date of issue. If ever this document is lost or stolen, this will facilitate the replacement process. In case of such an event, contact your country's embassy or consulate (see addresses below) in order to be reissued an equivalent document as soon as possible. Never keep your passport, plane tickets, identity cards, cash, credit cards, proof of insurance and other important documents in one place in case they get lost or stolen. Before you arrive, it is also recommended to make a copy of the ID page of your passport, and upon your arrival, the page stamped with the date you entered the country. Some banks ask to see these pages before exchanging traveller's cheques or currency.

Tourist Card

Besides your passport, you must have a tourist card *(tarjeta del turista)*, which is usually issued on the plane or upon your arrival at the airport. The card allows all visitors (Canadians, Americans, British, Australians, New Zealanders) to stay in the country for 60 days. The card must be returned upon departure, so don't lose it.

Departure Tax

Everyone leaving Colombia must pay a departure tax at the airport, when they check in. **Note** that after arriving in Colombia, presenting your documents to the airport and border police and **before** picking up your luggage, you must go through customs to have your passport marked with the *Exención de Impuestos* stamp (only valid for stays of 60 days or less). This reduces the departure tax, so you only pay about US$20 (or 20,000 pesos). Be sure to have this amount in cash, because credit cards are not accepted. For stays of 30 days or longer, the departure tax is 50,000 pesos or US$50.

Customs

Travellers may enter Colombia with up to two litres of alcohol, 200 cigarettes and up to $100 in other items not including those for personal use. Importing drugs and firearms are of course forbidden.

EMBASSIES AND CONSULATES

In Colombia

Embassies and consulates can provide precious information to visitors who find themselves in a difficult situation (for example: they can replace a lost or stolen passport; in the event of an accident or death, they can provide names of doctors, lawyers, etc.). They deal only with urgent cases, however. It should be noted that costs arising from such services are not paid by these consular missions.

In case of theft or violence, do not hesitate to contact your consulate or embassy. Not only are they there to help you, but they also want to know the dangers affecting their citizens. Emergency services are offered round the clock; after business hours, just leave a clear and detailed message as well as a phone number where you can be reached on the answering machine, and a representative will call you back shortly. Sometimes calls are forwarded directly to a representative in your home country.

Australia
Consulate: Calle 70, No. 10-86, Piso 2, Santafé de Bogotá, ☎212-6576, ⌨312-2410.

Belgium
Embassy: Calle 26 No. 4a-45, 7th floor, Santafé de Bogotá, ☎282-8881.

Consulate: Calle 8, No. 23-29, near Carrera 4, Bocagrande, ☎665-2741.

Consulate: Carrera 113 No. 11-49, Ciudad Jardín, Santiago de Cali, ☎/⌨332-0826.

Canada
Embassy: Calle 76 No. 11-52, Santafé de Bogotá, ☎218-0800.

Consulate: Calle Santo Domingo, No. 3308, near Calle de la Inquisición, Centro, Cartagena, ☎664-7393.

Great Britain
Embassy: Edificio Ing Barings, Carrera 9 No. 76, 49 Piso 9, Santafé de Bogota, ☎317.6690, ⌨317.6265.

Consulate: Carrera 44, No. 45-57, Box 706, Barranquilla, ☎326-936.

Consulate: Edificio Garces, Calle 11 No. 1-07, Office 409, Box 1326, Santiago de Cali, ☎832-752, 832-753 or 861-872.

Consulate: Calle 9 No. 43B-93, Medellin, ☎246-3114 or 246-6835, ⌨266-7318.

Italy
Consulate: Calle 93B, No. 9-92, Santafé de Bogotá, ☎218-6604, 610-7095 or 610-7138, ⌨6105886.

Netherlands
Consulate: Manga Calle del Bouquet Carrera 21 No. 25-116, A.A. 118-1851, Cartagena de Indias, ☎660-4476 or 660-4193, ⌨660-4183.

New Zealand
Consulate: Carrera 7, No. 73 - 55, Office 401, Santafé de Bogotá, ☎312-1231, ⌨620-0130.

Panamá
Consulate: Calle No. 694-97, Crespo, Cartagena de Indias, ☎666-2079.

Switzerland
Embassy: Carrera 9a No. 74-08, Office 1101, Santafé de Bogotá, ☎255-3945, ⌨235-9630.

Consulate: Calle 24, No. 23-29, Manga, Cartagena de Indias, ☎666-3880.

Consulate: Calle 14 No. 3-08, Edificio Los Bancos, Office 805, Santa Marta, ☎214-272.

Consulate: Carrera 68 No. 48d-48, Medellín, ☎230-4563, ⌨260-1881.

Consulate: Carrera 100-16 No. 11-90, Office 316, Santiago de Cali, ☎332-0491, ⋯332-0489.

United States
Embassy: Carrera 45 No. 22d-45, Santafé de Bogotá, ☎315-1566.

Consulate: Calle de la Factoría, No. 36-37, Centro, Cartagena de Indias, ☎665-1887.

Colombian Embassies and Consulates Abroad

Australia
101 Northbourne Avenue Turner, 2nd floor, Act 2601 Canberra, ☎(06) 257-2027 or 257-1458, ⋯(06) 257-1448.

Belgium
Rue Van Eyck, 44, 1050 Brussels, ☎(02) 649.07.68, ⋯(02) 646.54.91.

Canada
Embassy: 360 Albert Street, suite 1002, Ottawa, Ontario, K1R 7X7, ☎(613) 230-3760, ⋯230-4416.

Consulate: 1010, Rue Sherbrooke O., Room 420, Montréal, Québec, H3A 2R7, ☎(514) 849-4852 and 849-2929, ⋯849-4324.

Consulate: 1 Dundas Street West, Suite 2108, Toronto, Ontario, M5G 1Z3, ☎(416) 977-0098 and 977-0475, ⋯977-1025.

Finland
Embassy: Fredrikinkatu 61, 00100 Helsinki, ☎(96) 693-1255, 693-1693 or 693-1529, ⋯(96) 693-3072.

Great Britain
3 Hans Crescent, London SW1X OLR, England, ☎(71) 589-9177 or 589-5037, ⋯(71) 581-1829.

Italy
Embassy: Via Guiseppe Pisanelli 4, 00196 Rome, ☎(06) 320-2531 or 361-2202, ⋯(06) 361-2204.

Netherlands
Groot Hertoginelaan 14, 2517 Eg Den Haag, ☎(70) 361-4545 or 361-4650, ⋯(70) 361-4636.

Consulate: Oranje Nassaulaan, 1075 AK Amsterdam, ☎(20) 671-7867.

New Zealand
Wool House Level 11, Wellington, New Zealand, ☎(64) 472-1080 or 472-1472, ⋯(64) 472-1087.

Spain
Embassy: Zurbano 34, 1a Izquierda, 28010 Madrid, ☎310-0441, ⋯310-0239.

Consulate: Paseo de Gracia 2, 4, 6, 08007 Barcelona, ☎90 34 3 412-7828, ⋯90 34 3 412-7540

Consulate: Alameda de Mazarredo No. 47, 20, 30, 48009 Bilbao, ☎94 34 4 423-0539, ⋯423-0267

Consulate: Av. Molini No. 2, 41012 Sevilla, ☎90 34 423-7883, ⋯423-5930.

Sweden
Embassy: Oestermalmsgatan 46, Box 5627, 114 86 Stockholm, ☎(8) 21 84 89, ⋯(8) 21 84 90.

Switzerland
Dufourstrasse, 47, 3005 Berne, ☎(31) 351 54 34, ⋯352 70 72.

United States
Embassy: 2118 Leroy Place, NW, Washington, DC 20008-1847, ☎(202) 387-8338, ⋯(202) 232-8643.

Consulate: 10 East 46th Street, New York, NY 10017, U.S.A., ☎(212) 949-9898, ⋯972-1725.

Consulate: 500 North Michigan Avenue, Suite 2040, Chicago, IL 60611, ☎(312) 923-1196, ⋯(312) 923-1197.

Consulate: 2990 Richmond Av., Suite 544, Houston, TX 77098, ☎(713) 527-9093 or 527-8919, ⋯(713) 529-3395.

Consulate: 3600 Wilshire Blvd., Suite 1712, Los Angeles, CA 90010, ☎(213) 653-4299 or 382-1137

Consulate: 280 Aragon Avenue, Miami, FL 33134, ☎(305) 448-5558.

Consulate: 595 Market St., San Francisco, CA 94110, ☎(415) 495-7195, ⋯(415) 777-3731.

GETTING TO COLOMBIA

By Plane

Many travel agencies offer all-inclusive vacation packages (plane ticket, accommodations and meals) to the main tourist destinations in Columbia: Cartagena de Indias, Santa Marta and San Andrés. Signature Vacations, Caribe Sol, Royal Vacations and Air Transat are just some of the agencies that plan worry-free trips for travellers.

Most of the big airline companies offer direct flights to Colombia. In winter, however, non-stop charter flights are available for less. Travel agency brochures and advertisements in news-papers often have the best deals. Reserving a vacation package a month in advance is also cheaper. Finally, another way to save is by going last minute with a stand-by company like Club D-7 *(3607 Rue St-Denis, Montréal; ☎514-843-6441 or 800-363-6724)*, but your choice of destinations is limited. Club D-7 only flies to Cartagena de Indias, Santa Marta and San Andrés in Colombia. Despite this, all you really need your airplane ticket and you're set, since accommodations in Colombia are easy to find.

From Canada

During the winter season, a number of airline companies such as Royal Airlines, Air Transat and Canada 3000 offer direct charter flights from Montréal and Toronto to Cartagena. Indirect flights are also offered through various American cities.

● **From Montréal**: Air Canada provides daily service to Miami, where travellers can board an Avianca flight to Cartagena the very same day.

● **From Toronto**: Delta Airlines offers daily service to Miami, where visitors can catch a direct flight to Cartagena with Avianca.

AVIANCA
1 St. Clair Avenue West, Suite 202, Toronto, Ontario, M4V 1K6, ☎800-284-2622 and 800-387-8667, ☞972-1112.

From the United States

● **From New York**: Avianca provides direct weekly service *(Sunday)* to Cartagena.

AVIANCA
720 5th Avenue, New York, NY 10019/4907, ☎399-0858.

● **From Miami**: Avianca offers five nonstop flights a week to Cartagena.

AVIANCA
8125 Northwest 53rd Street, Miami, FL 33166, ☎599-7200.

From Europe

● **From France**: There are two options from Paris:

Avianca offers three flights a week *(Wednes-day, Friday and Sunday)* aboard a Boeing767 to Bogotá, from where about ten flights a day leave for Cartagena. The flight time between Bogotá and Cartagena is 1 hour, 20 minutes. The Avianca AIRPASS is the most convenient way of visiting Colombia's various regions (sold only with tickets for transatlantic flights). There are two options: the "5-ticket" Airpass (US$180) entitles you to five flights within the country (US$80 more for the San Andrés and Providencia islands), and the "3-ticket" Airpass, which includes three flights for the modest sum of US$100.

Air France offers three flights a week *(Thurs-day, Saturday and Sunday)* to Bogotá.

Viasa offers flights from Paris to Caracas, with a connection to Cartagena.

For more information: minitel 3615 COLOMBIE.

AVIANCA
31 Avenue de l'Opéra, 75001 Paris, Métro Opéra, ☎01.42.60.35.22, ☞01.40.15.06.03.

● **From Belgium and from Switzerland**: there are no direct flights to Cartagena. Avianca offers two weekly departures from Frankfurt *(Monday and Friday)* to Bogotá then Cartagena, a departure from Paris (see above), as well as two departures a week from London *(Tuesday and Saturday)*.

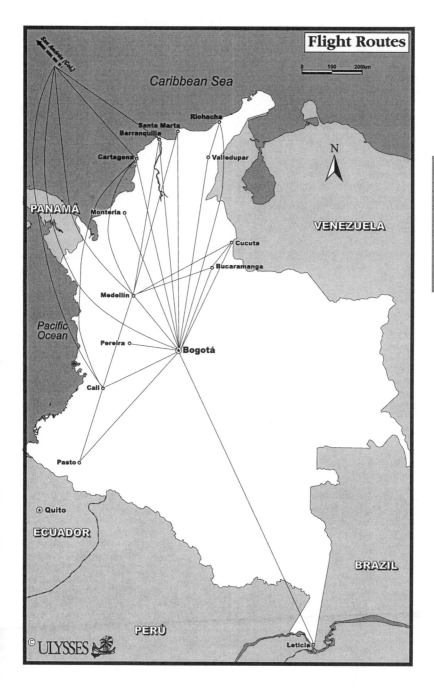

AVIANCA
Avenue Louise 363, 1050 Brussels, ☎(02) 640 85 02 and 640 82 44, ✉(02) 640 12 57.

AVIANCA
Loewenstrasse 51, 8001 Zurich, ☎(1) 212 50 10, ✉(1) 212 50 57.

Other AVIANCA Offices

Denmark
Afgangshallen 1, Sal. Værl. 102, 70 Kastrup, Copehengagen, ☎(45) 32 50 51 44, ✉32 50 51 24.

Finland
Mariankatu 21, 00170 Helsinki, ☎(9) 622 622 77, ✉(9) 622 622 11, avianca@paivi.pp.fi

Germany
Frankenalle 125-127, Frankfurt-am-Main, ☎49 69 7 580 9943, 580 9944 or 580 9945, ✉46 69 7 39 32 00, aviancafra@aol.com

Great Britain
19 Colonnade Walk, Victoria, London, SW1W-9SH, ☎44 99 076 7747, ✉44 99 931 9232, avianca@fltdir.com

Italy
Via Madona Due Ponti 6, Capena, Roma 00060, ☎39 6 930 3835, ✉39 6 930 3834, avianca@uni.net

Netherlands
Evert Vandebeekstraat 11, Amsterdam 1118, ☎31 20 653 2685, ✉31 20 653 4687.

Spain
Gran Via 88, 28013 Madrid, ☎(91) 542 85 53, ✉(91) 542 59 15.

Gran Via Corts Catalanes 617, entlo 1 RA, Barcelona 087000, ☎31 20 653 285, ✉31 20 653 4687, bcnair@nexo.es

Sweden
PO Box 3315, Stockholm 10366, ☎46 8 14 40 55, ✉46 8 24 18 88, www.res.se/avianca

Airports

International airports are found in most of Colombia's big cities like Santafé de Bogotá,

Medellín and Cartagena de Indias. Other destinations within the country can be easily reached with a domestic airline, since all towns have airports for this purpose.

Buses and taxis run from the airport to downtown. Cab drivers may try to tempt you with "special rates," but it is better to stick to the fixed price. If the driver refuses, take another cab.

The major car rental agencies have counters at the airports, so you can rent a car on the spot. They are usually set up one right next to the other, so compare rates. But always remember that you get a better deal by reserving in advance with the company's central reservation network (usually a toll-free number in North America); just take down the reservation number to confirm your rental once there.

INSURANCE

Health Insurance

Health insurance is without question the most useful kind of insurance for travellers, especially since health care costs are always unpredictable and are rising quickly everywhere. Also, though most Western governments cover health care costs for travellers, they will not exceed the fees normally charged in the home country, even if they were more expensive in the country visited. Thus, even a simple *turista* shouldn't take a chance and buy a policy.

Health insurance should be purchased before leaving. The insurance policy should be as comprehensive as possible, because health care costs add up quickly, even in Colombia. When purchasing the policy, make sure it covers medical expenses of all kinds, such as hospitalization, nursing services and doctor's fees (at fairly high rates, as these are expensive). A repatriation clause, in case necessary care cannot be administered on site, is invaluable. In addition, you may have to pay up front at the clinic, so you should check your policy to see what provisions it includes for such instances. During your stay in Colombia, you should always keep proof that you are insured on your person to avoid any confusion in case of an accident.

To make a claim, the following documents must be presented:

- the name and address of the physician
- a detailed description of the treatment
- the date and price for each treatment
- the medical file or report in case of hospitalization
- the surgical chart, in case of operation

N.B.: Charges for a medical file or report are not insured and are therefore not reimbursable.

Cancellation Insurance

This type of insurance is usually offered by your travel agent when you purchase your airplane ticket or tour package. It covers any non-refundable payments to travel suppliers such as airlines, and must be purchased at the same time as initial payment is made for air tickets or tour packages. This insurance allows you to be reimbursed for the ticket or package deal if your trip must be cancelled due to serious illness or death. This type of insurance can be useful, but healthy people should weigh the likelihood of using it against the price. You must confirm your flight with your travel agent or carrier before boarding. Make sure your ticket is stamped with "OK" in the reservation box.

A reservation also does not confirm the price of your ticket, which can change between the date of reservation and the date of final payment, but most carriers charge the price of reservation as final payment.

Airlines also require confirmation of the return flight at least 72 hours before boarding, either by phoning or visiting a travel agent. If you do not do this, you may not be allowed to get on the plane.

Airplane tickets are non-transferrable. Before boarding, a representative from the airline company may ask for a piece of ID. However, another person can pre-pay your ticket in your name, which should appear on the airplane ticket.

You are responsible for your airline ticket, so don't lose it. If this happens, the carrier can replace it for an additional charge, but sometimes it must be paid on the spot, so check this with your travel agent.

Theft Insurance

Most residential insurance policies in North America protect some of your goods from theft, even if the theft occurs in a foreign country. To make a claim, you must fill out a police report. Usually the coverage for a theft abroad is 10% of your total coverage. If you plan on travelling with valuable objects, check your policy or with an insurance agency to see if additional baggage insurance is necessary. European visitors should take out baggage insurance.

Life Insurance

By purchasing your tickets with certain credit cards you will get life insurance. Several airline companies offer a life insurance plan included in the price of the airplane ticket. However, many travellers already have another form of life insurance and do not need extra insurance.

HEALTH

Water

Throughout Colombia, water is sold in bottles or in plastic bags which you drink through a straw. However, drinking water is safe in most of the big cities such as Santafé de Bogotá, Medellín, Pereira, and Santiago de Cali.

Though water is usually safe to drink in most hotels, restaurants and bars in Columbia, it is best not to put ice in your drinks, especially when buying them from street vendors, at campgrounds or places off the beaten tourist track.

Illnesses

Please note that this section is intended to provide general information only.

PRACTICAL INFORMATION

Malaria

Malaria (paludism) is caused by a parasite in the blood called *Plasmodium sp.* This parasite is transmitted by anopheles mosquitoes, which bite from nightfall until dawn, so it is a good idea to protect yourself against mosquito bites (see p 60).

The symptoms of malaria include high fever, chills, extreme fatigue and headaches as well as stomach and muscle aches. There are several forms of malaria, including one serious type caused by *P. falciparum.* The disease can take hold while you are still on holiday or up to 12 weeks following your return; in some cases the symptoms can appear months later.

Hepatitis A

This disease is generally transmitted by ingesting food or water that has been contaminated by faecal matter. The symptoms include fever, yellowing of the skin, loss of appetite and fatigue, and can appear between 15 and 50 days after infection. An effective vaccination by injection is available. Besides the recommended vaccine, good hygiene is important. Always wash your hands before every meal, and ensure that the food and preparation area are clean.

Hepatits B

Hepatitis B, like Hepatitis A, affects the liver, but is transmitted through direct contact of bodily fluids. The symptoms are flu-like, and similar to those of hepatitis A. A vaccination exists but must be administered over an extended period of time, so be sure to check with your doctor well in advance.

Dengue Fever

Dengue is transmitted by mosquitos, and in the mildest cases the symptoms are similar to the flu: headache, fever, sore muscles and nausea. It can be fatal, and though this is rare, protect yourself well against mosquitos (see p 60).

Typhoid

This illness is caused by ingesting food that has come in contact (direct or indirect) with an infected person's stool. Common symptoms include high fever, loss of appetite, headaches, constipation and occasionally diarrhea, as well as the appearance of red spots on the skin. These symptoms will appear one to three weeks after infection. Which vaccination you get (it exists in two forms, oral or by injection) will depend on your trip. Once again, it is always a good idea to visit a travellers' clinic a few weeks before your departure.

Diphtheria and Tetanus

These two illnesses, against which most people are vaccinated during their childhood, can have serious consequences. Thus, before leaving, check that your vaccinations are valid; you may need a booster shot. Diphtheria is a bacterial infection that is transmitted by nose and throat secretions or by skin lesions on an infected person. Symptoms include sore throat, high fever, general aches and pains and occasionally skin infections. Tetanus is caused by a bacteria that enters your body through an open wound that comes in contact with contaminated dust or rusty metal.

Other Health Tips

Cases of illnesses like hepatitis B, **AIDS** and certain venereal diseases have been reported; it is therefore a good idea to be careful. Remember that condoms are the best protection against these illnesses.

Fresh water is often contaminated by an organism that causes **schistosomiasis**. This infection, which is caused by a parasite entering the body and attacking the liver and nervous system, is difficult to treat. It is therefore best to avoid swimming in fresh water.

Remember that consuming too much alcohol, particularly during prolonged exposure to the sun, can cause severe dehydration and lead to health problems.

Many people develop a discolouration of the skin due to the humidity. This is a fungal infection caused by yeast and appears mostly on the chest. The infection is characterized by two distinct symptoms: the skin does not tan and is phosphorescent at night. The best way of preventing this is to take anti-fungal medication one month before leaving.

Airplane Sickness

Airplane travel can cause mild discomfort. Here is some advice for a more pleasant flight:

• The dry air on the plane can irritate your nose and throat, so drink lots of water or juice. Alcohol, coffee and tea are diuretics and therefore dehydrate.
• The dry air can also irritate your eyes, so wear glasses instead of contact lenses.
• Eat light meals that are sugar- and salt-free
and avoid dairy products because they are hard to digest when sit still for so many hours. Make sure to eat vegetables, fruits and bread as part of your meal.
• Some people complain about swollen feet after the plane ride. This is because sitting in one place for a long time reduces blood circulation causing a change in cardiovascular activity, muscular tension and fluid retention. While seated, it is important to stretch your muscles and walk in the aisle every now and then.
• Some people also complain of a blocked nose and ears, especially during takeoff and landing. This is perfectly normal and caused by the change in air pressure in the cabin. To relieve the pressure, just block your nose and close your mouth and breathe out through your ears. This technique is also used on submarines and by scuba divers when water pressure can be felt in the ears at 2 metres underwater. Alternative methods include swallowing hard several times or sucking on a candy.

PRACTICAL INFORMATION

Children can develop impetigo from a bite or a scab. Impetigo is caused by a staphylococci or streptococcal bacteria that infects a sore. Always disinfect any wound with a product recommended by a doctor or pharmacist.

Despite recent medical advances (Dr Pattarayo recently came up with a vaccine against malaria which he offered to the Walter Reed Army Medical Center in Washington, D.C. to be further studied), medical equipment in Colombia may not always be as modern as in your own country. If you need medical care while you are here, don't expect it to be the same as at home. Furthermore, outside of big cities, medical centres might appear somewhat modest to you. Clinics are usually better equipped than hospitals, so visitors are advised to go to the former for any necessary treatment. In tourist areas, there are always doctors who can speak English. If you need a blood transfusion, make sure that the blood has been tested and is safe. Most hotels as well as tourist information offices in larger cities can recommend a good doctor. The International Association for Medical Assistance to Travelers (IAMAT) regularly publishes a list of world-wide medical practitioner that speak English. To obtain this list, call ☎(416) 652-0137.

Insufficiently treated water, which can contain disease-causing bacteria, is the cause of most of the health problems travellers are likely to encounter, such as stomach upset, diarrhea or fever. Throughout the country, it is a good idea to drink bottled water (when buying bottled water, make sure it is properly sealed), or to purify your own with iodine or a water purifier. Most major hotels treat their water, but always ask first. Ice cubes should be avoided, as they may be made of contaminated water. In addition, fresh fruits and vegetables that have been washed but not peeled can also pose a health risk. Make sure that the vegetables you eat are well-cooked and peel your own fruit. Do not eat lettuce, unless it has been hydroponically grown (some vegetarian restaurants serve this type of lettuce; ask). Remember: cook it, peel it or forget it.

If you do get diarrhea, soothe your stomach by avoiding solids; instead, drink carbonated beverages, bottled water, or weak tea (avoid milk) until you recover. As dehydration can be dangerous, drinking sufficient quantities of liquid is crucial. Pharmacies sell various preparations for the treatment of diarrhea, with different effects. Pepto Bismol and Imodium will stop the diarrhea, which slows the loss of fluids, but they should be avoided if you have a fever as they will prevent the necessary elimination of bacteria. Oral rehydration products, such as Gastrolyte, will replace the minerals and electrolytes which your body has lost as a result of the diarrhea. In a pinch, you can make your own rehydration solution by mixing one litre of pure water with one teaspoon of sugar and two or three teaspoons of salt. After, eat easily digested foods like rice to give your stomach time to adjust. If symptoms become more serious (high fever, persistent diarrhea), see a doctor as antibiotics may be necessary.

Nutrition and climate can also cause problems. Pay attention to the food's freshness and the cleanliness of the preparation area. Good hygiene (wash your hands often) will help avoid undesirable situations.

It is best not to walk around bare-foot as parasites and insects can cause a variety of problems, the least of which is athlete's foot.

Insects

Colombia has a unique and varied climate. Thus, there are more insects in certain parts of the country than in others. The Caribbean coast, for example, has few insects because of the dry climate. There are more insects in the cities since they are located in the mountains, notably Medellín, Santafé de Bogotá and Santiago de Cali.

Most insects live in the humid regions such as the Amazon and Chocó on the Pacific Coast. Therefore, cover up well in order to prevent being bitten, especially in the mornings and at sundown when the insects come out in droves.

Mosquitoes are especially plentiful during the rainy season, and certain species can transmit diseases such as hookworm, malaria, encephalitis, lyme disease, the plague, yellow fever and scarlet fever. Protect yourself with a good insect repellent. Repellents with DEET are the most effective. The concentration of DEET varies from one product to the next; the higher the concentration, the longer the protection. In rare cases, the use of repellents with high concentrations (35% or more) of DEET has been associated with convulsions in young children; it is therefore important to apply these products sparingly, on exposed surfaces only, and to wash it off once back inside. A concentration of 35% DEET will protect you for four to six hours, while 95% will last from 10 to 12 hours. New formulas with DEET in lesser concentrations, but which last just as long, are available. If you are allergic to DEET, wear mesh clothing (hats, pants, jackets) sold in outdoor stores. Wear protective clothing that covers the whole body when walking in the woods, including long socks and good shoes.

To further reduce the possibility of getting bitten, do not wear perfume or bright colours.

Sundown is an especially active time for insects. When walking in wooded areas, cover your legs and ankles well. Insect coils can help get a peaceful night's sleep. Before bed, apply insect repellent to your skin and to the headboard and baseboard of your bed. If possible, get an air-conditioned room, or bring a mosquito net.

Since it is impossible to completely avoid contact with mosquitoes, bring along a cream to soothe the bites you will invariably get.

Finally, some people are allergic to insects and can develop a horrible rash after being bitten. Symptoms can be more severe (convulsions) or even fatal. Always carry a first-aid kit with a ventilator (used for asthma patients), which is inhaled to temporarily prevent swelling of the respiratory canals until you reach a hospital or clinic.

There are an estimated 3,000 species of mosquito, and all can be found in the Amazon and Chocó. It is a myth that mosquitoes die after biting: only the female bites, and can do so five or six times before dying. The itching is caused by the mosquito's saliva which is deposited along with 200 eggs. Certain species live longer, and a female can live for five months or more. The have an excellent camouflage that protects them from predators.

The noise produced by the mosquito's wings, which make 250 to 600 movements per second, is annoying enough to disturb the soundest of sleepers. And since the mating season varies from one species to the other, mosquitos are always buzzing about; females can even detect human presence from 10 metres away. Sweat attracts insects, so it is better to take it easy if you want to avoid mosquitos. Remember this proverb: "It is best to put off until *mañana* what you can do today." One good thing is that mosquitos hate wind, and fans are more effective than air conditioners.

Jellyfish

Jellyfish are a type of marine mammal found in many bodies of water. They have a gelatinous umbrella-shaped body with trailing tentacles. Contrary to popular belief, jellyfish do not attack humans, but contact with their tentacles can produce a rash, which can sometimes be fatal, so be careful when going in the water. If you are stung by a jellyfish, do not rub the burn; soak it in salt water instead. Then apply baking soda before removing the tentacles.

The Sun

Colombia is located on the equator, but this does not mean that the sun is always scorching. Rather, Columbia has two rainy seasons; one in October and November and the other one April and May. Since most of the inland cities are in the mountains, the sun is not dangerous and frost is occasional, especially in Bogotá. The sun's rays are stronger on the coast (Atlantic or Pacific) and the Amazon, so remember to wear the proper protection.

It does not rain day and night during the rainy season as imagined, and sometimes not even for months. If it rained non-stop, the vegetation would be so overgrown and drenched that the dry season wouldn't be able to dry it. The rainy season in Colombia is marked by fierce storms that can last several hours and can even cause floods and mudslides. Sometimes it rains for days on end. During the dry season, it is constantly sunny except for a few sporadic showers.

Although the sun is a source of vitamin D, fights acne and gives you a great tan, it can also cause skin cancer. Whether or not you think that this is the fabrication of cosmetic companies to sell their products, wearing protective clothing (hat and sunglasses) is essential to protect yourself against sunburn and other effects of the sun.

UVA rays burn instantly, whereas UVB rays cause more long-term effects. Sunscreen containing dibenzolymethane, mexoril SB and oxybenzone are effective against UVA rays. Creams containing PABA and sulfonic acid protect against UVB rays. Not all sunscreens on the market are effective; ask a pharmacist or read the label.

Apply sunscreen (SPF 30) 20 to 30 minutes before exposure. Too much sun can cause sunstroke (dizziness, vomiting, fever, etc.). Be careful to take sun in small doses, especially during the first few days, as it takes time to get used to it.

First Aid Kit

A small first-aid kit can prove very useful. Bring along sufficient amounts of any medications you take regularly as well as a valid prescription in case you lose your supply; it can be difficult to find certain medications in the small towns. Other medications such as anti-malaria pills and Imodium (or an equivalent), can also be hard to find. Finally, don't forget self-adhesive bandages, disinfectant cream or ointment, analgesics (pain-killers), antihistamines (for allergies), an extra pair of sunglasses or contact lenses, contact lens solution, and medicine for upset stomach. Though these items are all available in Colombia, having them on hand can certainly make life easier.

CLIMATE AND PACKING

Because of its geographic location, Colombia enjoys a wide variety of climates to suit every taste. From the year-round snows of the Sierra Nevada of Santa Marta and the Puracé volcano of the central cordillera to the desert of the Gajira peninsula, the humid tropical climate of the Amazon and the forests of Chocó, and the temperate *sabanas,* many climates exist. Nonetheless, there are only two seasons: the rainy season, called *invierno*, and the dry season, *verano,* from December to March.

Packing

What you bring along depends on what kind of vacation you choose as well as which area of the country you visit. If your trip includes several destinations in Colombia, you will need to bring beach wear, including sunscreen, as well as warmer clothes (woolens and leather) for the mountains and the plateaus of Santafé de Bogotá, where the temperature can drop to 4°C. You should also bring linen clothing if you wish to visit the tropical forests, in the Amazon or the Chocó.

In large cities where proper dress is very important, women are encouraged to wear dresses or skirts, while sports jackets are recommended for men. Jeans should be avoided as much as possible if you plan on making business contacts or wish to visit more upscale places.

For men, a neutral-coloured suit should suffice for evening-wear, while for women a classic black dress and jacket are appropriate for formal outings. Bear in mind that cotton/polyester blends are more wrinkle-resistant than are natural fabrics.

If your trip is only to beach resorts, you should pack casual as well as evening-wear, since Colombians do not look favourably upon beachwear in the city. Going shirtless anywhere other than the beach is also frowned upon. There are as of yet no nude beaches in Colombia, and women should not go topless. In cities and towns, a modicum of modesty is expected when visiting cathedrals, monasteries, churches and other places of worship.

During *invierno,* you should bring the same clothes as above with the addition of rainwear and, of course, an umbrella. For rainy-day pastimes, it is advisable to bring some reading material and a deck of cards or a chess board. Colombians are known for being expert chess players!

It is best to reduce your vacation wardrobe and bring only what is absolutely necessary.

Thieves prefer leather luggage, since its resale price is often higher than anything contained within. Even more tempting is designer luggage, renowned for the high quality of its leather and superior craftsmanship. It is preferable to travel with a solid, sturdy sports bag which will allow you to pack more, and reduces the likelihood of theft.

Carry-On Luggage

All airlines have rules regarding the size, weight and shape of carry-on luggage. It is a simple question of passenger safety. Since most airlines use different types of planes, these rules and restrictions may vary from one flight to another.

Certain airlines also restrict the number of carry-on bags you may bring aboard. Travellers should pay extra attention while packing. Carry-on luggage should not contain anything other than essential items.

Essential items such as prescription medications (e.g. insulin), glasses and contact lens cases should be packed in your carry-on luggage, as should valuable objects, which should never be packed in regular luggage. You must keep your passport, wallet, plane ticket, boarding pass, etc. with you at all times. In order to avoid any possible inconvenience in case your checked luggage is lost or delayed, bring a change of clothing in your carry-on luggage, as well as the basic toiletries and anything else you might need immediately upon arrival.

Every article brought aboard the plane is considered carry-on luggage, and subject to size and storage restrictions. Usually, airlines will charge extra fees for luggage if its weight exceeds the total weight allowed. To find out the fee for excess baggage, contact the airline that issued the ticket.

SAFETY AND SECURITY

When travelling in another country, or even in your own country, you are in a vulnerable position, and this is easily detected by any predator seeking a victim. Criminals looking for easy prey quickly single out people who look innocent or convey a naïve attitude; this, to the criminal, means "come and get me". Thus, it is important to avoid sticking out as a tourist. Sure giveaways are vehicles with rental car license plates. Also, be careful where you stop to ask for directions and who you approach.

When travelling alone (or with a companion) in a country where you don't speak the language, you will often encounter stressful situations. Travelling is always unpredictable, and you can suddenly find yourself without the essentials to which you are accustomed, completely alone, far away from home, family and work, out of your daily routines, or sometimes going from the dead of winter to the heat of summer within a few hours. This can explain the temptation to make new acquaintances with the first person to come along, which is not always advisable, and probably not very safe. It is better to wait several days before taking steps in this direction, and maintain a certain distance until you get a better feel for the region's customs and traditions.

Shady Characters

Tourist attractions are often crowded with many merchants and vendors vying for your attention. These savvy entrepreneurs have mastered the art of selling anything at all, however useless. Some even insist on having you "discover" boutiques where they get a commission for sales made there. If you are not interested, you can simply reply politely but firmly: "*No, gracias.*"

Do not overly respond to someone who is bent on becoming your friend or guide, who will bombard you with the eternal "*¡Hola Amigo!*". With a simple hand gesture, respond to the endless greeting of the would-be friend with a curt *holà*, without conveying aggression or saying anything more, which would surely reveal you to be a foreigner.

Orienting Yourself

Before leaving your room, take note of the exact address of the hotel, including its name, telephone number and the name of the quarter. The hotel reception can provide you with a business card listing all the above information. This way, you can provide the taxi driver with exact information when you return to the hotel, and act as though you know the way. It is always preferable to know where you are going or at least to have a good idea of where you're headed, be it to the beach, the market, or the shopping districts. You should always consult a road map and a more detailed map of the city as well as other information before you leave your hotel room, just as you should verify the address of any friend or acquaintance you may want to visit before going off to explore.

By knowing exactly how to get wherever you are going before you set out, you can avoid appearing lost and vulnerable once you're on the street. When walking, always do so with a normal and confident stride. Do not show surprise if you encounter an unusual situation. Keep your distance and, of course, mind your own business. To verify the name of a street, do so in a discrete fashion, as if you already knew the area well. And if, per chance, you find yourself lost and have no idea in which direction to go, do not panic or become anxious. Stop in a café or an outdoor patio, have a drink, and quietly re-think your plan while going over your notes. You'll no doubt be able to find your way yourself; if not, simply take a taxi.

Addresses

A simple and efficient system of addresses (*dirección*) is used throughout Colombia, in all big cities as well as smaller *pueblos*. First, the number of the *calle* or *carrera*, or the name of the *avenida* is given. This is followed by the number of the *carrera* or the *calle* which intersects the first, followed by the number of the building, these last two numbers being joined by a hyphen. For example: the exact and complete address of the Punta Canoa Hotel in Cartagena de Indias is Calle 7 No. 2-50. Thus, the Punta Canoa is located at number 50, on Calle 7, close to the cross-street Carrera 2. The numbered plaque on the building will show 2-50. By the same token, the address of the Parque Real Hotel, also in Cartagena, is Carrera 3 No. 8-171. This means that the Parque Real is located at number 171 on Carrera 3, close to the cross-street Calle 8. The numbered plaque on the building will show 8-171. This is the only way for taxi drivers to find a location, and many will refuse your fare unless you clearly indicate the *dirección* in this manner. This guide uses this system, and can thus be understood even by Colombians who speak only Spanish when asked to provide this information.

Violence

Violence is a reality in Colombia, especially in large cities. But, of course, no one barricades themselves in their house year-round because of it (see also p 43)! Instead, they take this reality into account during their daily affairs just like residents of New York, Paris, London, or even Rome, by avoiding certain areas and always being careful.

There are three principal types of dangers to beware of: petty crime, guerilla crime, and drugs. In the case of drugs, all you need to do is to stay away from them, since the penalties for drug-related offences are very harsh in Colombia, even for simple consumption. Guerillas are known to kidnap people for ransom; however, they only target important members of Colombian society or foreigners who occupy important roles in international enterprises. They have no interest whatsoever in kidnapping ordinary tourists. However, you should avoid certain risky areas, particularly in the Colombian countryside. As for petty crime, you can safeguard yourself from small-time criminals by planning your outings carefully, keeping safety considerations in mind.

Colombia's major cities can be considered relatively safe, compared to other big cities of the world. Nevertheless, it is better to avoid dangerous quarters not recommended by hotel staff. So as not to find yourself lost or alone in the streets at night, you are better off taking a taxi when returning from a restaurant.

Newspapers

It is always a good idea to get a copy of the morning paper to carry with you under your arm or display on the table beside you, even if you don't speak the language of the country – no one will know! A picture is worth a thousand words, and those found in the large national or local papers announcing a *fútbol* victory of the favourite local team are easy to understand. Thus, no one will be able to affirm with certainty that you don't understand the language. Newspapers are also one of the best ways to learn the language of a country and to familiarize yourself with its traditions and customs. For example, by reading classified ads, you can learn the cost of houses, the price of new cars, and many other useful things. Flipping through the pages of the financial section, you can check the exchange rate and therefore be sure what you exchange at the bank is correct. Suddenly, you will feel less vulnerable. Newspapers create a kind of intellectual rapport which can ward off mishaps.

However, your cover will certainly be blown if you plaster your luggage, handbags and accessories with the flag of your home country. While this is a highly patriotic gesture, it also means you must then avoid those who may have been mistreated by your country. Why attract this kind of problem? In this case, discretion is in much better taste, and will attest to your *savoir-vivre* and a respect for the country you are visiting.

The national newspapers *El Tiempo* and *El Espectador* are published in Bogotá and are available across the country, and each smaller city has one or several local papers.

Jewellery

You are better off wearing as little jewellery as possible, or none at all, as it will only attract attention to you. Unless you spend all your time in casinos, palaces or upscale restaurants, or travel only by limousine and restrict your activities to very safe places, jewellery is nothing but a nuisance. You are better off leaving it at home. Otherwise, you can leave it in the hotel safe. All hotels offer this service; the larger hotels even provide safes in each room. If you are staying in a small hotel and use its safe, make sure that a staff member who knows the combination is available when you wish to retrieve your goods, at a fixed time or date. This having been said, wearing jewellery and fashion accessories is very much in style in Colombia.

Your Camera

Unless you are a professional photographer, it is not necessary to bring along a sophisticated camera which can be easily damaged by water or sand on the beach. All sorts of disposable cameras are available nowadays, and some even come with a flash. There are even disposable underwater cameras, which are protected by a waterproof plastic box. Don't forget that disposable cameras should only be opened in a photo lab. These cameras are sold for 12,000 to 15,000 pesos in Colombia, and can be bought just about anywhere in large centres, including camera stores, souvenir stores, craft shops, and pharmacies. You might be surprised at the quality of the pictures that these little disposables take! On the other hand, if you feel more comfortable with your own camera, it is best to carry it in a discreet case, preferably not readily identified as a camera case, which you can wear over your shoulder.

Not everyone likes being photographed. It is always best to ask permission beforehand instead of coming off as a *paparazzo* who snaps pictures of anyone, anywhere, anytime.

The Police

If you are robbed, make a report to a police officer or at a local police station. Depending on the severity of the incident, the police will investigate accordingly. You might be unsure of their methods, but it is not a good idea to convey this, or appear dubious of their competence. In any case, theft involving tourists are not a priority in Colombia. Even if the police do not seem to act with the urgency that you desire, rest assured that the crime you report will be registered in their system and will be reported. You may not recover your goods, but you will be helping other travellers through your diligence. Nowadays, most countries have a kind of organized tourist police whose aim is to protect the security of tourists, with the obvious goal of getting ahead in the very lucrative but fiercely competitive tourism industry. Certain tourist regions of Colombia have made great strides in this area over the last 10 years or so, while others have been slower to keep up.

While travelling, you are subject to all laws of the country that you are visiting. Your passport does not in any way absolve you from these laws or grant you any sort of diplomatic immunity. If you encounter any problems with the local police, immediately contact your country's nearest consulate or embassy. If this is impossible, ask someone to do so on your behalf.

Police: ☎112
Tourist Police: ☎334 25 01 ext. 33

GETTING AROUND IN COLOMBIA

Distances travelled in Colombia can be very long. Large infrastructure projects have been undertaken in order to improve many of the country's roads and highways, and most notably to finish the *Carretera Panamericana*. Many highways are a full four lanes around Bogotá and most other large cities, which has dramatically reduced the risk of accidents. Still, the majority of roads are still only two lanes, which makes defensive driving a must.

Renting a Car

It is hard to be inconspicuous when the license plate of your rental car clearly indicates that it's rented, and thus obviously driven by a tourist or businessperson who has the means to pay for it. Before renting a car, inquire at the hotel and the rental agency about the possible dangers of driving on your own, and, of course, how to avoid them.

The rules of the road differ from one country to another. European countries are a good example, since most give priority to the driver on the right side of the road, though in some it is to the driver on the left. This is not common practice in North or South America.

Colombians, meanwhile, have a tendency to interpret traffic laws on the spur of the moment. They are not always predisposed to

stopping at a red light, even in big cities. Sometimes they do, sometimes they don't. Once night falls and traffic is less heavy, traffic lights are simply ignored. Therefore, it is preferable to take a taxi or a bus, unless having your own car is absolutely necessary. All things considered, this kind of traffic anarchy makes renting a car highly inadvisable in large cities.

These kinds of traffic problems are less common in the countryside. Bear in mind that there is no police road patrol and no one metes out fines, which opens the door for just about any kind of driving. For example, Colombians do not respect the double line and will pass other cars on curves. This type of driving is accepted and even understood by other drives. Veteran drivers are always prepared for a car coming towards them on a curve or at the top of a hill, and drive accordingly. It might be the only occasion for a driver to pass a large, slow-moving truck which is blocking the road. Other drives understand this dilemma, and respond to it in the same way. They are therefore disposed to yield to the passing driver and even drive on the shoulder of the road if the situation warrants it. If they are annoyed, they will indicate this by honking, but this is equivalent to a shrug of the shoulders rather than a display of anger. Often, the driver of the truck in question will help out by using hand gestures to minimize the risk to all vehicles involved, including his own. Amazingly, accidents are rare, given the frequency of these unorthodox yet effective driving practices on South American roads.

If you rent a car, keep the doors locked and the windows closed while driving. It is recommended that you park in guarded parking lots or in busy areas. Often, parking spots will be indicated on the street, or monitored parking lots will be available. It costs between 200 to 300 pesos for this service. Do not pay until you leave. No matter how long you leave your car or where you have parked it, never leave luggage or clothing inside. To be completely safe, empty out the glove compartment and leave it open.

All major international car rental companies operate in Colombia.

Renting a Motorcycle

In most cities and villages, you can rent a motorcycle for around 12,000 to 15,000 pesos per hour, or 40,000 pesos for the day. You will be required to leave your passport or another form of valid identification. You must verify that the insurance provided covers repair costs in case of an accident, and replacement in case of theft. Even if you have travel insurance that covers automobile accidents, the insurance company may only cover certain vehicles, including cars, sedans, vans and all-terrain vehicles, while excluding trucks, motorcycles and scooters, or cars more than 20 years old, etc. Drive carefully, because even though there are many motorcyclists on the road, car drivers don't always pay proper attention. Be sure to always agree upon the price and all payment conditions before leaving with any rental vehicle.

By Taxi

Taxis are hailed. They are everywhere in large cities as well as larger towns. They are a relatively safe and economical way of travelling, especially if you are sharing the cost. Unless you are travelling with a package that includes hotel and shuttle service, they are the fastest way to get downtown and to large hotels.

Taxis are usually an ochre colour and marked *Servicio Público,* and those in large cities have meters. In other cases, prices are fixed in advance and by sector, regardless of the distance travelled within a given sector. Normally, drivers charge for the number of sectors travelled through, up to 1,000 pesos per sector. Two sectors will therefore cost 2,000 pesos. Prices go up after 5pm. The rates are always clearly indicated on the back right-hand side window. Before your plane lands, ask the flight attendants about the rates to get from the airport to downtown. You'll also get a good idea of what it will cost for other taxi rides.

You can also negotiate with a driver to hire his services for a longer period, a longer distance or even for an entire day. In this case, it is logical to choose a more recent model of car or even a limousine or sedan. It costs the same for a new car as for an old wreck. You are better off waiting a little to choose a car that bests suits your travel needs.

By *Chiva*

If you want to really get a taste of the local scene, you should try the bus or *chiva*. Old, colourful, noisy and bumpy, they will still get you to your destination. *Chivas* in the city cost about 300 pesos for a 20-kilometre trip or more.

Chivas reflect the personality of their drivers. The way they are decorated usually indicates something about his temperament. Often, these will consist of icons and plastic statues of the Virgin Mary that are found everywhere, even stuck on the windows. Or, you might find pictures from the latest *Playboy* or pictures of famous soccer players, boxers, sports teams, etc.

Given that his profits come from the number of passengers he drives, it is in the driver's best interest to offer the best service possible. He will therefore stop just about anywhere to welcome you aboard. You need only flag him down. To get off, say *"Aquí por favor"* (Here, please), or motion to the driver, who will let you off wherever you wish.

By Bus

Public transportation from one city to another, or even to the smallest village, is very efficient service in Colombia. Buses run from the *Terminal de Transportes* (central bus station) of each city (some cities have two), which is always a new and well-organized building serving some 50 bus companies and divided into sections according to the direction of destinations: north, south, east and west. Each company has its own ticket counter in each of these sections. Bus fares are very reasonable in Colombia.

Here, as well, you have a choice, not only between services but also between companies that run to the same destinations and on the same schedule, and whose prices differ by only a couple of dollars. Sometimes, however, they use different routes. Thus, tourists can travel in any class they desire. Depending on your means, you can choose Express First Class with air conditioning, television and hostess

Table of Distances (km)
via the shortest route — ©ULYSSES

													Armenia	Armenia
												Bogotá	286	Bogotá
											Bucaramanga	439	725	Bucaramanga
										Cali	923	484	194	Cali
									Cartagena	1088	917	1178	974	Cartagena
								Florencia	1507	521	986	547	533	Florencia
							Medellín	881	626	462	1543	552	348	Medellín
						Monteria	391	1272	300	933	1217	943	739	Monteria
					Pasto	1253	942	623	1488	400	1323	884	594	Pasto
				Popayán	251	1003	611	372	1237	149	1072	633	343	Popayán
			Quibdo	859	1110	639	248	1129	874	710	1791	800	596	Quibdo
		Riohacha	1189	1552	1803	708	941	1694	406	1403	708	1147	1289	Riohacha
	Santa Marta	191	1091	1454	1705	517	843	1724	217	1305	824	1286	1191	Santa Marta
Yopal	1369	1229	1029	1010	1260	1319	928	923	1783	860	521	376	662	Yopal

Example: The distance between Bogotá and Medellín is 552 km.

service, or to travel for the minimum price with more limited comfort. Since each service has its advantages and disadvantages, here are some points to consider so you can make a more informed choice:

Colectivos are taxis shared between several passengers, and serve all destinations. They are powerful American 8-cylinder 4-door cars, rarely new. Given that the driver must take at least five passengers to make any profit, departures are not at any set time but rather according to demand. The wait can be between 10 and 20 minutes, but rarely any longer than that. The trip is faster, but not necessarily very comfortable, especially for the two passengers in the front, who, along with the driver, often hold the hand-bags. Still, the driver will stop to rest upon request, which makes for a more personalized service. In addition, it is easy to strike up a conversation with the other passengers. *Colectivos* are recommended for short distances of under two hours. This faster and more personal service costs a bit more.

Aerovans are newer minibuses seating 10 to 15 people, which serve the same destinations. Departures are also based on a minimum number of passengers, though the wait is never longer than 10 to 20 minutes. The seats are more comfortable, and the view from the windows is never blocked by window shades. Conversation with other passengers, however, is more difficult, but the driver of an *aerovan* will also stop to rest if the trip becomes long. *Aerovans* are best suited for trips of less than three hours, and the price is somewhere between that of a *colectivo* and an inter-city bus.

First-class inter-city buses (*ejecutivos*) are relatively new and large. A hostess is aboard to assure passenger comfort, and the bus is equipped with toilets. These buses are thus an excellent means of transportation for journeys of over three hours, and can be very pleasant if you come prepared with a few beers to pass the time. The hostess will provide plastic bags for empty cans. If the bus has to stop en route, she will let aboard food vendors of all sorts, especially beer vendors – who will happily replenish your supply.

Nonetheless, the windows on these buses are all shaded, which provides protection from the sun. This necessary accessory diminishes the view of the often grandiose countryside along Colombian roads, still unencumbered by commercial billboards as found in other countries.

The seats are as comfortable as those found on airplanes, offering more leg-room. To keep passengers, entertained, the bus has television sets, whose incessant noise can end up becoming quite a nuisance. As well, the air conditioning, even along coastal regions, is always on at full blast, making some trips unpleasantly cold. To ensure your personal comfort, bring along earplugs and a sweater.

These buses leave the terminal at fixed hours, day and night. There are departures at virtually every hour for short distances. For longer

Identity and Culture Shock

Before going on vacation, we prepare our luggage and get the necessary vaccinations and travel documents, but rarely do we prepare for culture shock. The following text explains what culture shock is and how to deal with it.

In a nutshell, culture shock can be defined as a certain anxiety that may be experienced upon arriving in another country where everything is different, including the culture and language, making communication as you know it very difficult. Combined with jetlag and fatigue, the strain of orienting yourself in a new cultural context can lead to psychological stress that may throw you off track.

Culture shock is a frustrating phenomenon that can easily turn travellers setting out with the best of intentions into intolerant, racist and ethnocentric ones – they may come to believe that their society is better than the new, and seemingly incomprehensible, one. This type of reaction detracts from the whole travel experience.

People in other countries have different customs and lifestyles that are sometimes hard for us to understand or accept. We might even find ourselves wondering how people can live the way they do when their customs run contrary to what we deem to be "normal". In the end, however, it is easier to adapt to them than to criticize or disregard them.

Even though this is the era of globalization and cultural homogenization, we still live in a world of many "worlds", such as the business world, the Western world, etc. Of course, these worlds interact, but each has its own characteristic set of ideas and cultural values. Furthermore, even if they are not in direct contact, each has at least an image of the other, which is usually stereotypical, but in either case is ultimately nothing more than an image. If a picture is worth a thousand words, then our world contains million upon millions of them. Sometimes it is hard to tell what is real and what isn't, but one thing is certain: what you see on television about a place is not the same as when you travel there.

When people interact with each other, they inevitably make sense of each other through their differences. The strength of a group, human or animal, lies in its diversity, whether it be in genetics or ideas. Can you imagine how boring the world would be if everyone were the same?

Travelling can be seen as a way of developing a more holistic, or global, vision of the world; this means accepting that our cultural fabric is complex and woven with many different ethnicities, and that all have something to teach us, be it a philosophy of life, medical knowledge, or a culinary dish, which adds to the richness of our personal experience.

Remember that culture is relative, and that people's social, technological and financial situation shape their way of being and looking at the world. It takes more than curiosity and tolerance to be open minded: it is a matter of learning to see the world anew, through a different cultural perspective.

When travelling abroad, don't spend too much energy looking for the familiar, and don't try to see the place as you would like it to be – go with the flow instead. And though a foreign country might be difficult to understand and even seem unwelcoming at times, remember that there are people who find happiness and satisfaction in life everywhere. When you get involved in their daily lives, you will begin to see things differently – things which at first seemed exotic and mystifying are easily understood after having been explained. It always helps to know the rules before playing a game, and it goes without saying that learning the language will help you better understand what's going on. But be careful about communicating with your hands, since certain gestures might mean the opposite of what you are trying to say!

Prepare yourself for culture shock as early as possible. Libraries and bookstores are good places for information about the cultures you are interested in. Reading about them is like a journey in itself, and will leave you with even more cherished memories of your trip.

Written by Jean-Étienne Poirier

distances, consult the schedules of the bus companies at the terminal.

Certain companies offer better service than others. Inquire at the hotel reception, or even ask a taxi driver, to find out which companies are the best, since they can vary from one region to another.

Finally, the *chivas* are even more basic. With no air conditioning or television and with barely comfortable – or downright uncomfortable – seats, they also provide inter-city transportation, serving more remote destinations. Painted according to the inspiration of an artist paid to decorate them to the local taste, *chivas* frequently stop in unforeseen places on the whim of the driver or passengers. At each stop, they let on board vendors of water, beer, juice, soft drinks, sandwiches, chips, iguana eggs, and so forth. *Chivas* allow you to truly experience the local flavour, with passengers coming from and going to local markets with all sorts of foodstuffs, including live domestic animals, or more often pigs, chickens and roosters (for cockfighting). In Cartagena de Indias, *chivas* are used as tourist attractions and are looked upon as a kind of symbol of Colombia. All across the country, souvenir boutiques sell miniature reproductions of *chivas*, in ceramics or other materials. Think twice, though, before taking a trip on a *chiva*, however, since what may seem like an exotic adventure at first can quickly turn into a nightmare, because of the heat, discomfort and constant commotion.

By Train

There are no passenger trains in Colombia, except in Santafé de Bogotá, where there is a train especially for tourists; the Tren Turístico de la Sabana (see p 88), which links Bogotá with Nemocón.

Hitch-hiking

Given the relatively low bus fares, and obvious risks involved in hitch-hiking, hitch-hike only as a last resort. In this case, be extremely careful. Women travelling alone should never hitch-hike.

MONEY AND BANKING

Currency

The Colombian currency is the peso, which is identifiable by the $ sign. Paper money is available in bills of 20,000, 10,000, 5,000, 2,000 and 1,000 pesos. Coins come in pieces of 100, 50, 20 and 10 pesos. Sometimes, in hotels, prices will be indicated in American dollars. **All prices mentioned in this guide are in pesos, unless indicated otherwise.**

Colombian currency is subject to constant fluctuations, and has suffered several devaluations in the past few years. Newspapers publish exchange rates daily in the economy section, under "Currency". It is wise to consult the exchange rates.

Banks

Banks have different hours depending on what part of the country they are in. Generally, they open at 8am and close at noon, then re-open at 2pm to close again at 4:30pm. In Bogotá, however, they open at 9am and close at 3pm, with the exception of the last Friday of the month, when they close at noon. Banks are closed Saturdays and Sundays, just as in the rest of the world. Therefore, you must make sure to exchange enough money for the weekend. When on vacation, you can quickly lose track of time, and it's not uncommon to forget that Friday is an important day in terms

Exchange Rates

US$1	=	1,626 pesos	1000 pesos	=	US$0.65
CA $1	=	1,113 pesos	1000 pesos	=	CA $0.90
AU $1	=	1,085 pesos	1000 pesos	=	AU $0.92
1 £	=	2,632 pesos	1000 pesos	=	0.38 £
1 Euro	=	1,734 pesos	1000 pesos	=	0.58 Euro
1 DM	=	886 pesos	1000 pesos	=	1.13 DM
1 SF	=	1,081 pesos	1000 pesos	=	0.92 SF
10 BF	=	429 pesos	1000 pesos	=	23.21 BF
10 Lire	=	895 pesos	1000 pesos	=	1,113 Lire
100 PTA	=	1,042 pesos	1000 pesos	=	95.71 PTA

of banking. Luckily, automated teller machines are available throughout the country.

To use an automated teller machine, which allows you to withdraw money in local currency at a competitive rate, you must use an ATM identified with the Visa and Visa Plus symbols, if your bank at home deals with this credit card, or Cirrus if your bank deals with MasterCard. Simply punch in your personal identification number to obtain service in both Spanish and English. There are 368 Visa ATMs and 11 Visa Plus ATMs in Colombia, marked with *V* or *VP*. The Bancafe ATMs are identified with *VP*, those of the Banco de Colombia *V*, those of the Banco Popular *VP* and those of Redeban *V*. Not all ATMs of these banks are identified as above. For those banks affiliated with Cirrus, look for ATMs identified with BIC, Red Multicolor and Davivienda. There are more than 1,500 ATMs affiliated with Cirrus-MasterCard in Colombia. Bear in mind that standard user fees are charged ($2.50 CAN) for each transaction. When withdrawing a sum of money equivalent to $500 US per transaction, these fixed fees represent but a small percentage – less than 0.5% – less than half of the fees charged for the purchase of American Express traveller's cheques. In case of loss or theft of your ATM card or your Visa card, dial ☎980 125 713. For MasterCard holders, the international number is ☎800-307-7309.

American Money

American money should be the currency of choice for travellers to Ecuador. It is easy to exchange and enjoys a better rate than other currencies.

Exchanging Money

It is useless and dangerous to change money in the street. Banks offer a competitive exchange rate, so why risk being robbed or exchanging your money for counterfeit bills?

Cash Advances

The best exchange rate is for credit card cash advances. You save over 10%, which is more than the interest you will have to pay upon your return.

Traveller's Cheques

If you do not use any kind of inter-bank service, traveller's cheques are a safe means of travelling with money. However, you will have trouble exchanging them even if they are in American dollars, except at the Banco Industrial Colombiano (BIC). The BIC will also exchange cheques that are in other currencies. The Banco Unión Colombiano also accepts these transactions, whereas the official representative of American Express in Colombia, TMA (Tierra Mar Aire), will *refuse* to exchange American Express traveller's cheques, even those in American dollars, despite the fact that AMEX commercials portray these as accepted across the world... except in Colombia, one can assume.

Credit Cards

The majority of credit cards, particularly Visa (Blue Card) and MasterCard, are accepted in many businesses such as hotels and restaurants. However, do not count on your credit cards alone, since some smaller businesses refuse them. Again, even if you have traveller's cheques and a credit card, it is best to always carry local currency.

MAIL

Overseas postal service is provided by the national aviation company Avianca. You can buy stamps at the company's offices. Most large hotels also provide this service for their guests. A postcard or letter costs around 800 pesos to the United States, and around 1,000 pesos for Europe.

TELEPHONE

To make long-distance calls within Colombia, dial 09, followed by the area code of the city of the person you wish to reach (the area code for each city or region is indicated at the beginning of each chapter), and then the person's number.

To reduce long-distance fees while travelling abroad, Canadians can use the *Canada Direct* service. This service enables you to call Canada or other countries, or even within the country you are visiting, with the help of an English-speaking operator. All you have to do is dial the *Canada Direct* access number, and an operator will reply immediately. You should ask about the rates before your call is routed. Calls to Canada are billed at the Canadian rate for international calls and may include Canadian time-of-day discounts. The *Teleplus Overseas*, *Intermax* and *Advantage* savings plans also apply for calls made using a *Calling Card* or *Call-Me Card*.

In Colombia, the telephone access number for *Canada Direct* is ☎980-19-0057.

You can also call collect directly, which is the most economical choice. From Colombia, use the following numbers:

For Canada: ☎90-1 + area code + telephone number.

For the United States: ☎90-1 + area code + telephone number, or USA direct at ☎980-11-0010.

For Great Britain: ☎90-44 + area code + telephone number.

For Australia: ☎90-61 + area code + telephone number.

To reach someone in Colombia, use the following numbers:

From Canada and the United States: ☎011-57 + city code + telephone number.

From Great Britain: ☎010-57 + city code + telephone number.

From Australia: ☎0011-57 + city code + telephone number.

Here are some emergency or frequently-called numbers:

Police: ☎112
Tourist Police: ☎334 25 01 ext. 33
Fire: ☎119
Ambulance and 24-hour Pharmacies: ☎115
Local Time: ☎117
Local Information (telephone): ☎113
National Information: ☎00
International Information: ☎08

ACCOMMODATIONS

Many types of accommodations are available throughout Colombia. Depending upon the type of establishments you choose, from the smallest inn to the largest hotel complex, the price for a room will vary greatly, and taxes are not included in the price.

Prices mentioned in this guide are for one room for two people.

$	less than 30,000 pesos
$$	between 30,000 and 50,000 pesos
$$$	between 50,000 and 70,000 pesos
$$$$	between 70,000 and 100,000 pesos
$$$$$	more than 100,000 pesos

Most hotels accept credit cards, except for some smaller ones.

PRACTICAL INFORMATION

Hotels

There are five categories of hotels in Colombia. Close to the downtown cores, you will find budget hotels whose comfort level is often basic. Their rooms usually include a small bathroom and a ceiling fan. The second category, the medium-rated hotels, usually have air-conditioned or heated rooms, and a simple but adequate level comfort level. These are found near city centres and in tourist regions. Hotels of the third category, medium to superior, are usually used by Colombian businesspeople. These hotels are generally bargains for tourists who will find a good level of comfort as well as security, at an advantageous price. Then, there are the high-class hotels, found in tourist destinations as well as in large cities. Finally, there are luxury hotels, for which you can expect to pay a relatively high price compared to prices for similar hotels around the world. Among these luxury hotels are many international chains, notably Inter-Continental, Sofitel, Relais et Châteaux of France and Melía.

With the exception of the most rudimentary of hotels, most establishments are equipped with electric generators, since power outages are frequent outside the large urban centres. Hotels in the medium and superior categories often have guards to ensure the security of guests.

Finally, certain hotels offer "all inclusive" packages, where the price of a room includes two or three meals per day, drinks, taxes and service charges. This is the case with hotels of the Decamerón chain, found only in tourist locations, but who do not accept tourists passing through, with some exceptions. Nothing prevents you from asking the management, however.

Cabañas

Cabalas are motels or chalets which offer rooms with private bathrooms in small, detached cottages. They are generally a little more expensive, and always include a fan or air conditioning, and sometimes a kitchenette.

Bed & Breakfasts

Many *fincas*, particularly in the coffee-production region, have been converted into Bed & Breakfasts. The levels of comfort can vary greatly from one place to another. Rooms in more modest *fincas* do not include a private bathroom, while other establishments may go as far as to have a heated pool! The prices vary according to the amenities available.

Youth Hostels

There are few youth hostels in Colombia, with the exception of Cartagena de Indias (see p 174). If you are looking for a place to stay at a low price, it is better to find a small hotel or inn.

Camping

There are many campgrounds in Colombia, found mostly in tourist regions. You could also try roughing it, but this is discouraged due to the presence of guerillas in many areas, notably in the mountainous regions.

RESTAURANTS AND FINE FOOD

From the smallest cafeterias which serve inexpensive local dishes, to gourmet establishments which cater to more refined tastes, there are a multitude of restaurants across Colombia to suit every traveller's taste, from *comida rapida* (fast food) like pizza, hamburgers and barbecued chicken, all the way to French, Spanish or Italian *haute cuisine*. Large cities offer the most choice, notably Santafé de Bogotá, Medellín, and Santiago de Cali, as well as tourist centres such as Cartagena de Indias and Santa Marta, among others.

Prices mentioned in this guide are for one meal for one person, including taxes, but not including drinks and tip.

$	less than 5,000 pesos
$$	between 5,000 and 10,000 pesos
$$$	between 10,000 and 20,000 pesos
$$$$	between 20,000 and 30,000 pesos
$$$$$	more than 30,000 pesos

Colombian Cuisine

Colombian food is not especially spicy; above all, it is a simple and nourishing cuisine, prepared with local products. Dishes based on fish or seafood, beef, chicken, or pork, served with rice, beans or plantain bananas, are the staples of most menus. By visiting several of these restaurants, you will surely have a chance to taste some of the country's specialties, such as *sancocho,* a soup that is a meal in itself, which varies from one region to another.

BEER, WINE AND LIQUOR

Beer

Certain beers are made locally and are only found in certain regions, such as Poker, found only in Santiago de Cali. Others are distributed across Colombia, including Águila, Club Colombia and Leona (500 pesos at the *mercado* and from 800 to 1,200 pesos in a restaurant or bar). Many hotels, restaurants and bars also serve imported beers.

Wine

Wines have become popular in Colombia over the last several years, even if there is not much local production happening. Wines served in restaurants are usually imported, notably from Chile, France and Italy. They are quite affordable, especially if you order them by the glass (from 4,000 pesos to 4,500 pesos or more).

Liquor

All imported spirits can be found in Colombia. The most popular among them are rum and *aguardiente,* made from sugarcane and anise.

BUSINESS HOURS

Some businesses are open seven days a week, while others have more restricted business hours. In general, business hours are from 8am to noon, and from 2pm to 7pm.

TAXES AND TIPPING

The local tax, *IVA,* is not always included in or indicated along with prices. This must be verified before renting a room or buying any merchandise. The *propina* (tip) is not always included either, therefore 10% to 15% must be added to a bill if no tip is mentioned within. Generally, no tip is required at refreshment stands, convenience stores, or other small stores.

TIME CHANGE

Colombia is one hour behind Eastern Canada and the United States in summer, and on the same time in winter because Colombia does not observe Daylight Savings Time. Thus Colombia is six hours behind Western Europe during winter seven hours during the summer.

TOUR GUIDES

Tour guide services are regulated in Colombia, and individual tour guides and companies such as travel agencies offering excursions must have an official permit from the government to operate. Ask to see the permit, to be on the safe side. These guides are not cheap, however. If you wish to hire such a guide, agree first on services provided and fees charged, and pay only at the end.

WOMEN TRAVELLERS

It is always more dangerous for a woman to travel alone, whether looking for a hotel or even, in some places, finding appropriate washroom facilities. This said, women are relatively safe in Colombia, as long as they avoid more remote areas. While Colombian women may be extraordinarily beautiful, Colombian men are for the most part masters of seduction. They will not shy away from becoming friendly with a pretty foreigner.

PRACTICAL INFORMATION

• Women are often victims of street crime. Be particularly careful when going out alone, and avoid dark areas.
• To avoid problems in this very religious country, it is best to dress conservatively.
• Hotels must be chosen carefully, and be sure that they meet the basic safety standards and that the locks on doors and windows work properly.

MISCELLANEOUS

Supermercados

You can buy just about anything in supermarkets: food, beauty products, alcohol and cigarettes.

Smoking

There are no restrictions on smoking whatsoever. Locally produced cigarettes are more expensive, and it is possible to buy imported cigarettes, especially from the United States. Smoking is permitted in all public places.

Electricity

Electrical appliances run on an alternating current of 110 volts (60 cycles), just as in North America. European travellers will need both a converter and an adapter with two parallel flat pins for any appliances they plan on bringing along.

Weights and Measures

Colombia officially uses the metric system. The following table will make conversions easier:

Weights
1 pound (lb) = 454 grams (g)
1 kilogram (kg) = 2.2 pounds (lbs)

Linear Measure
1 inch = 2.54 centimetres (cm)
1 foot (ft) = 30 centimetres (cm)
1 mile = 1.6 kilometres (km)
1 kilometre (km) = 0.63 miles
1 metre (m) = 39.37 inches

Land Measure
1 acre = 0.4047 hectare
1 hectare = 2.471 acres

Volume Measure
1 U.S. gallon (gal) = 3.79 litres
1 U.S. gallon (gal) = 0.83 imperial gallon

Temperature
To convert °F into °C: subtract 32, divide by 9, multiply by 5
To convert °C into °F: multiply by 9, divide by 5, add 32

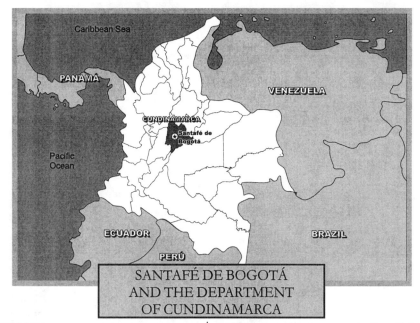

SANTAFÉ DE BOGOTÁ
AND THE DEPARTMENT
OF CUNDINAMARCA

C undinamarca is certainly one of the loveliest regions in Colombia. It has a moderate climate, intriguing biodiversity, beautiful landscapes and friendly people. The word *Cundinamarca* comes from the language of aboriginal people who populated the area before the arrival of the Spanish. Etymologically speaking, it could be a corruption of *cudirrumarca*, *cundalumarca* or *condurcunaca*. According to recent interpretations of the Chibcha language, *cundinamarca* means "heights where the condor dwells."

Eight and a half million people, almost 25 percent of the population of Colombia, live in these 24,210 square kilometres that cover two percent of the country's total area. Clockwise from the north, its neighbouring departments are Boyacá and Meta to the east, Hula and Tolima to the south and, across the Río Magdalena, the departments of Tolima and Caldas to the west. One hundred and fifteen municipalities are found in this mountainous area of the Orientale Cordillero, where the peaks are over 4,000 metres high (El Nevado is 4,560 metres in altitude).The *sabana*, itself a region of high plateaus, averages 2,600 metres above sea level.

When Gonzalo Jiménez de Quesada and his conquistadors first entered this area in 1536, they were astonished to find that the mountains contained vast fertile, irrigated fields. They were in the territory of the rich and peaceful Muisca civilization. Next, the Spanish discovered the city of Bacatá on the Santafé de Bogatá plateau, where the capital city of Bogotá stands today.

Vestiges of indigenous culture still exist in Nemocón and other locations. Cudinamarca was populated by people of the *Chibcha* linguistic family, one of the most advanced civilizations in Colombia. Two caciques (hereditary rulers), El Zipa and El Zaque, ruled the Panche, Muisca, Muzo, Colima, Sutagao, and 51 other Amerindian groups. These people grew many fruits and vegetables, including potatoes, manioc, beans, tomatoes and corn, which was fermented to produce *chicha*, a potent form of beer. Robust, intelligent and hard-working people of average height, they hunted game and certain birds by baiting them with garlic and salt from the mines at Zipaquirá and Nemocón. Commerce with neighbouring peoples involved trading salt, fabric and emeralds, for gold, cotton and shells. The Sun was venerated as Sue, and the Moon as Chía. Religious ceremonies were solemn events, especially the enthroning of a new cacique. The entire population gathered at the shores of a lake where offerings were made to the gods. Chanting and dancing followed the rituals.

The Muiscas were a peaceful people who only waged war in self-defense. They obeyed laws that prescribed harsh penalties for theft and murder. Goldsmiths played an important role in

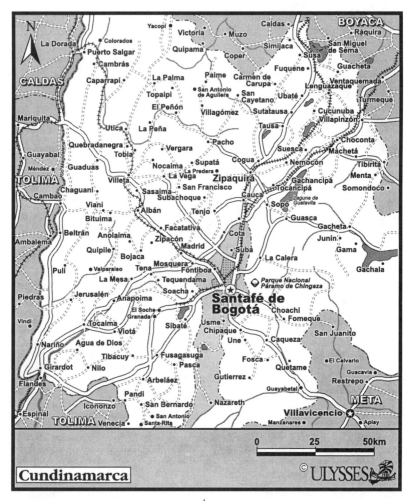

Cundinamarca

© ULYSSES

their society. Artisans lived separately from the community, used tobacco and chewed coca leaves.

The Panches, on the other hand, were ferocious and cruel. They attacked the Muiscas regularly, using bows with poisoned arrows and blowguns. They set traps to capture their enemies alive, then ate them to celebrate.

The Muzos were established on the banks of Río Negro and worked the emerald mines in this region.

When the Spanish entered the Cundinamarca, they rapidly took control of it, first establishing Bogotá as the seat of government. They then built many villages in the region, all with central *plazas* with the church on one side, the town hall on the other, and the homes of important people around the perimeter. They exploited this immense fertile plain with its abundant rainfall for agriculture and raised cattle and horses.

Today, the highways and paved secondary roads that traverse the *sabana* are lined with magnificent trees. Impressive haciendas have replaced the thatched-roofed huts. Some of this land is made up of plantations of cultivated flowers that are famous throughout the world.

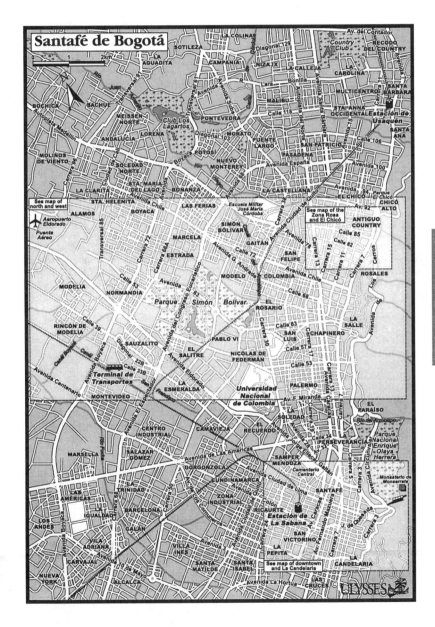

The *sabana* is the garden of Santafé de Bogatá, and perhaps of the country as a whole. In addition to flowers, it produces coffee, corn, plantains, sugar cane, potatoes, barley, wheat, manioc, cotton, beans, tomatoes, string beans, etc. There are also coal, iron, sulfur, emerald, zinc and salt mines. Since the region is self-sufficient, it offers the best prices for just about everything: meals and accommodations, many types of handcrafted objects, clothing and other items.

In terms of cuisine, each village and valley has its own specialties, according to its particular climate, but most have retained a certain Spanish flavour.

Many of the farm workers still wear the traditional Cundinamarca costume. Men wear dark, heavy cotton pants, a cotton shirt, a wool belt, leather sandals and a pale straw hat. Bags slung over the shoulder, bandoleer-style, contain all the necessities for a day spent in the fields: a pocket knife, tobacco and lighter, food and *chicha*, the corn-based beer.

Women wear skirts with colourful, embroidered borders that replicate the motifs of Cundinamarcan mythology and contrast in colour with the hems of the underskirts. The blouses are white cotton with a large collar and are decorated with multicoloured trimmings and fringes at the neck and on the sleeves. The head is usually covered by a black silk or lace scarf that covers a little straw hat. The hair is worn parted in the middle and tied back with a red ribbon to display earrings and an elaborate necklace. White sandals with a black fringe complete the costume.

Santafé de Bogotá

While foreigners generally refer to the capital as Bogotá, the complete name of the city is "Santafé de Bogotá, D.C.," referring to the 1,582-square-kilometre federal district with a population of seven million people. It is in the middle of an immense fertile plateau, the Orientale Cordillera savanna (*sabana*), and lies at an elevation of 2,680 metres. In addition to being the national capital, it is also the capital of the department of Cundinamarca.

North and south of the *sabana*, Santafé de Bogotá is surrounded by high mountains. It is bordered to the east by Monserrate (3,200 m) and Guadalupe (3,320 m), which are home to

a part of its population. The western border is the Funza, a tributary of Río Magdelena. As a city, Bogotá is modern and distinctive whose charm and colour is largely derived from its high altitude and the unusually high mountains around it. Bogotá is the seat of executive, legislative, and judiciary power in Colombia. The city itself has a popularly elected mayor *(Alcade Mayor del Distrito Capial)*, and representatives and administrators (Alcades menores) of the 20 political districts that subdivide the capital.

The Weather

The mean temperature at this high altitude varies between 12°C and 14°C, reaching 22° C to 24°C during the day, and plummeting to 6°C or 4°C at night. This is quite cool, especially given the region's humidity, which averages about 70 percent. Although the room rates are higher, choose hotels with central heating. Some establishments even offer rooms with fireplaces, just to show you how cool the evenings are. There are two summers here, during which rain is scarce, from December to February and from June to September. There are also two winters from October to November and from March to May. Bring rain gear during the winter seasons, and always bring warm clothing for the evenings, as well as lighter clothing for daytime.

A Brief History of the Region

On August 6, 1538, the conquistador Gonzalo Jiménez de Quesada founded Ciudad Nueva de Granada on the site of Bacatá, the former capital of the Chibchas who were among the most highly civilized pre-Columbian people in Colombia. By edict of Phillippe II, King of Spain, the city became "the very loyal city of Santafé" in 1575. Some 200 years later, in 1740, Santafé became the vice-royalty of Nueva Granada under the name, Santafé de Bogotá.

After gaining independence from Spain in 1819, Colombia was part of Greater-Colombia together with Venezuela and part of Ecuador, including Quito. Within this political arrangement, Santafé de Bogotá was the capital of Cundinamarca province. When Greater-Colombia was broken up into separate countries in 1830, the city kept its name and became capital of the republic of Colombia. The constitutional reform instated in June of 1991 amalgamated the city with the municipalities of

Cundinamarca Specialties

Ajaico santafereño is a thick soup made with two kinds of potatoes and flavoured with an herb called *guasca*. Depending on the region, corn, chicken, capers or cream may be added.

Cuchuco is another potato-based soup to which flour, pork and several varieties of beans are added.

Sobrebarriga is prepared from beef entrails. Served Creole style, it is accompanied by tomatoes and onions and flavoured with cumin. Roasted, it is served with steamed rice, potatoes and manioc.

Fritanga is a mixed grill, usually of sausage, blood pudding, pigs' feet, pork tenderloin and entrails. Beef and vegetables are added.

Puchero bogotano is a slow-simmered stew of chicken, pork, beef, cabbage, ears of corn, potatoes, manioc and plantain bananas.

Canelazo is a sweet, hot beverage flavoured with cinnamon, *aguardiente,* rum and cognac.

Viudo pescado is a fish and vegetable soup that is particularly popular in the region of Girardot, on the banks of the Río Magdalena.

Chicha is beer brewed from corn and flavoured with honey.

Chocolate santafereño is prepared according to an old Bogotá tradition that dates from early colonial times. Served from 5 to 6pm, this chocolate drink is diluted with water or milk and is accompanied by cakes, tarts or other sweet treats.

Changua is a milk-based onion soup to which a raw egg is added before serving.

Tama cundinamarqués, a local favourite, is a potpie containing corn, spicy sausages, chicken and pork. It is served with *ratatouille* or other condiments.

SANTAFÉ DE BOGOTÁ

Usme, Bosa, Usaquén, Suab and Engativá to form the capital district which goes by the name of Santafé de Bogotá, in honour of its history.

Bogotá Today

Santafé de Bogotá is an open, international city that, until fairly recently, was called, "the Athens of South America" because of its rich architectural heritage of colonial and republican historical buildings. Unfortunately, these buildings were largely destroyed during the 1948 upheavals known as *La Violencia*, or *El Bogotazo*. The rapid reconstruction that followed in glass and concrete totally altered the face of the city. The only remaining historical architecture is in the old quarter of La Candelaria, and a few narrow streets in the downtown area. Of course, vestiges of the past can be found in the churches, theatres, government buildings and a few houses that were not destroyed. Most of the historic private residences have been converted into restaurants or museums.

If Buenos Aires, Argentina, is the Paris of South America, then Bogotá has become, the New York. The wide, rectilinear arteries and multi-laned boulevards are crammed with cars, buses, trucks and other means of transport. It has a financial district, skyscrapers, commercial centres and poor neighbourhoods that are religiously avoided by the rich elite. The number of the city's inhabitants has swelled more rapidly than the city's ability to absorb them, and most of the population, which currently stands at seven million, fled there from the violence in the more remote areas of the country. Santafé de Bogotá has all the characteristics of a heterogeneous megalopolis without being truly international in character. It also has all the disadvantages of this condition: distrust, insecurity, ghettos formed by people from the same rural regions, endemic poverty in certain areas, ostentatious wealth in others, and so on. In some parts of the city, one or more armed guards protect each street, each building and almost every commercial enterprise. However, the city also benefits from its large population in economic and cultural terms. Bogotá is an important centre of Colombian culture today because almost all the various regions of the country are represented in its population.

Bogotá comes alive in the afternoon...

Bogotanos eat out at lunch time, and only rarely go out for supper. The same pattern is observed on weekends, when customers in search of a family-style brunch head to the restaurants in droves. This is the best time to appreciate the heady atmosphere ofBogotá at its most charming. This is the afternoon siesta : The sun beats down, the Bogotanos are relaxing, the children play. A little girl roller-blades on the sidewalk beside the terrace where her parents are chatting at a table. She falls, lays on the ground for a few moments, then wipes her tears away, gets up and skates on. Bogotá comes alive... in the afternoon.

Internationally known brand names and designer labels from around the world have outlets here that compete for the Mercedes, Corvette and Jaguar set. At the same time, peddlers sell the basic necessities of life to the variegated masses from the backs of donkeys. There is no happy medium here – at least, not yet. The upper class is dominant in every sphere. The middle class practically doesn't exist and since most of the population is from the country-side, they have had problems adjusting to urban life. The most enterprising try to succeed by all means, even at the expenses of the less resourceful. Thus, there are two types of behaviours that distinguish Bogotanos and give them a bad reputation: The first belongs to the tradesmen who try to squeeze the utmost profit from even the smallest transaction. They have no sense of belonging or responsibility to a larger community. Loyalty is reserved for family and *compadres* (pals) from the same region, the same pueblito, or even the same *calle*. At the market, in restaurants and hotels, everything is a pretext for extracting the most money possible from the "stranger", the "adversary", and the "enemy". When a taxi driver charges an overly presumptuous passenger two or three times the normal fare, the passenger will not hesitate to call the driver a thief. However, it is not a question of

theft; in fact, it isn't even a rip-off. It is simply business as usual, and the more gifted of the two individuals will profit from the ignorance of the other. It's shocking and frustrating, but it is the rule of commerce that *Bogotanos* apply indiscriminately. Try to laugh it off, rather than be bitter about it, if it should happen. Don't let it spoil your trip.

Bogotá is a large commercial centre that boasts all sorts of financial institutions. The head offices of the country's 400 largest businesses are here, as well as banks, credit unions and insurance companies that, together, manage about a third of the nations finances.

The city has a large service sector, which is just as economically important to the country as its exports, which are necessary for Columbia's survival on the global market. This sector employs about 30 percent of the city's workforce, which has the highest level of education in Colombia and are highly skilled. In fact, there are over thirty universities and other institutions of higher learning in Bogotá, including the Universidad Nacional de Colombia, the Universidad Autonoma de Colombia, the Universidad Católica de Colombia, the Universidad Cooperativa de Colombia, the Universidad de Los Andes, the Universidad Inca de Colombia, the Universidad Libre and the Escuela Superior de Administración Pública, to name just a few.

Industrial activity also plays an important role in the city's productivity. The most prosperous industries are food, transportation, chemicals, textiles, electrical equipment, beverages, plastics, metallurgy and clothing manufacturing. Bogotá and Cundinamarca represent 25 percent of the total population of the country and produce nearly 23 percent of the gross national product (GNP).

The regional cuisine here is fairly typical and economical, but there is also a host of expensive restaurants that serve every imaginable cuisine, including Chinese, French, Italian, Japanese, Spanish, Russian and others. However, it is fast food, *la comida rapida*, which has become ubiquitous. Almost every second doorway in the downtown area leads into a small Colombian-style fast food restaurant that competes with McDonald's (and other American franchises that feature pizza or barbequed chicken) by delivering to the office buildings around it. As a result, the downtown area is sadly deprived of the terraces, cozy bars and trendy restaurants that are the prerogative of the middle class in all great cities (this sort of scene only exists in the Zona Rosa). It's as if well-to-do *Bogotanos* have decided to ignore the soul of their city and concentrate exclusively on the fat around its bones.

Bogotá has at least three cinema complexes which screen artistic and independent films – Cinematecas del Museo de Arte Moderno, Cinemateca Distrital and Cinemateca del Auditorio –; many theatres, several art galleries, some 50 museums and the national symphony orchestra, which performs here regularly. The place to go for nightlife is Calle 82, for its many chic bars, nightclubs and casinos.

During the day, Avenida Jiménez is an attraction in itself. Situated between Carreras 7 and 8, this is the street where the *esmeraderos*, or emerald merchants, stand in small groups from 8am until five or 6pm to offer prospective buyers, and even passers-by, their merchandise: rough, uncut emeralds in a heavenly shade of green. The unpolished gem lie on unfolded sheets of white paper, attracting scores of people dazzled by their beauty. Some of these pieces can be very valuable and profitable, provided that a quality stone is chosen and expertly cut and polished, and the initial price is not too high. But you have to know how to play the game. Negotiation skills are essential, and it is the golden rule that the first offer must be rejected to maintain credibility. Sometimes the buyer (or the seller) backs away swearing, then returns shortly to accept a second, undoubtedly more advantageous, proposition. All this haggling in the middle of the street is perfectly legal. In fact, since it takes place near the entrance to the building housing the Ministerio de Agricultura (Av. Jiménez No. 7-65), the police are omnipresent so people can buy these rough-hewn, uncut stones without worrying about getting caught. Unless, of course, the "emerald" you lovingly select turns out to be an ordinary chunk of coloured glass. In which case, you won't be the victim of theft, but rather a sore loser in a business – *estilo bogotano* (Bogotá style).

Bogotá is divided into four large districts. The central district, between Carreras 1 and 44 and Calles 5 and 34, contains the old colonial quarter, La Candelaria, which contains many business, political and administrative buildings as well as museums, churches, most of the city's historic monuments and the railroad station. The northern district begins at Calle 72. Modern and commercial, it is the financial centre of the capital, but also includes residen-

tial, commercial and cultural areas. To the south are industrial and working class neighbourhoods with nothing of interest to tourists. The western district includes major industries, many parks, sports facilities, some administrative buildings, the El Dorado airport and the Terminal de Transportes.

The upper-class neighbourhoods in the northern part of the city include Santa Bárbara, Santa Ana, Sotiliza, El Chicó and Rosales. Middle-class neighbourhoods are Soledad, Nicolás de Federman, Palermo, Mandalay, Normandia, Chapinero, Pablo VI, Molinos and Kennedy (founded by John F. Kennedy).

Neighbourhoods to avoid are San Victorino, whose Calle de la Cartucho (sic) is renowned throughout Colombia for its high level of violence, as well as Las Cruces and Perseverancia, g others. Drug dealing and prostitution are a way of life in these areas, and criminal activities like theft and assault are out of control.

It is crazy, if not suicidal, to rent a car here. Only a driver with plenty of experience with the zigzagging, horn-blowing madness that is driving in South America has the lightening-fast reflexes necessary to keep vehicle and passengers intact. It takes time to learn to avoid being hit by the bumpers of trucks and buses, or to slam on the breaks when a bare-footed man pushing a handcart suddenly looms up in the fast lane where the maximun speed limit is 50 to 60 kilometres per hour. The expert driver will enjoy challenging the future cycling champion of Colombia who has decided to do a little training in the middle of a traffic jam. Novices and the claustrophobic should not attempt it.

Noise!

With a chaotic mixture of car, truck and bus horns, shouts of vendors and boosted volumes of sound systems, downtown activity reaches its peak at 4pm when the office buildings empty out and the streets are transformed into market squares.

The cacophony here is overwhelming and constant. It's like a disco or a rave where the melody is completely lost in the staccato beat of the rhythm.

It is also insane to attempt to cross the street anywhere but at an intersection where vehicles actually come to a stop at traffic lights. Even there, motorcyclists are a hazard, since they are not obliged to obey the traffic signals. At night, everyone ignores them; the red and green lights along the streets become merely decorative. However, accidents are surprisingly rare in Bogotá, given the lack of restraint that seems more like anarchy to visitors.

The southern district, where the street numbers decrease, contains poor neighbourhoods and are like pockets of misery. Unless your motive is to work with the poor for humanitarian reasons, nothing is to be gained by going to these extremely poor areas. They contain nothing whatsoever of interest to tourists. Even taxi drivers refuse to go there, not because of the danger, but because people who can not afford to pay for the basic essentials do not take taxis. On the other hand, the northern district is the enclave of the wealthy and the upwardly mobile, where urban development, architecture and zoning are taken into consideration. The streets and avenues are tree-lined and attractive. There are many parks, and the buildings are stylish. Zona Rosa and the neighbourhoods between Calles 70 and 140 are worth a visit for this.

Excursions Around Bogotá

Among many possible destinations for out of town excursions, there are two that shouldn't be missed. The first is the Salt Cathedral in Zipaquirá, which is incontestably the eighth wonder of the world. Also, no trip to Bogotá is complete without seeing the Laguna de Guatavita that inspired the myth of El Dorado and motivated the conquistadors to conquer Colombia.

The most convenient way to travel outside the city is to rent a car with a driver for the day. After hard bargaining, the cost should be between 60,000 and 70,000 pesos. While the highway is the fastest route, it is not yet completely divided into separate lanes therefore it is not in the best of shape, especially on the way out of town. The best way to appreciate Bogotá's unique *sabana* is to take the scenic route, an extension of Carrera 7, via Norte, which becomes Carretera Central del Norte and eventually joins the highway. Along this route there are beautiful *haciendas*, large landed estates with luxurious manor houses that often have in-ground swimming pools. They are bordered by rows of trees, and animals graze in the nearby pastures. Other farms with less imposing residences are called *fincas*. Fields

under cultivation here may be filled with roses, carnations, gladiolas or orchids. There are also golf courses, tennis, horseback riding and swimming clubs, amusement parks, numerous restaurants and frequent gas stations.

Zipaquirá

The little colonial city of Zipaquirá is some 50 kilometres, or about one hour by car, from Bogotá. It has a population of nearly 85,000 and is one of the oldest municipalities in Colombia.

A Brief History

Luis Enríquez founded Zipaquirá on July 18, 1600. The first Spanish to arrive discovered an indigenous village called Chica-Quicha, slightly to the west of the town's current location. The Spanish corrupted the name into "Zipaquirá". In the Chibcha language, *"Chica-Quicha"* means "foot of *chica*," where *chica* probably referred to the salt mountain.

Zipaquirá Today

Zipaquirá is one of the most prosperous small towns in Cundinamarca, because of its salt mine. It is also a renowned centre for handicrafts which can best be appreciated at the Plaza de Merado where all sorts of handmade items are for sale, including woolens as well as religious figurines, ashtrays, vases and candelabras made of ceramic, bronze and other materials, as well as sculptures in marble or blocks of salt from the mine. But it is the visit to the Salt Cathedral that is absolutely not to be missed!

FINDING YOUR WAY AROUND

Like all cities in Colombia, Santafé de Bogotá is criss-crossed by a grid of numbered streets and roads, or *carreras* and *calles*. There are also many *trasversales* and *diagonales* that are named and numbered. *Transversales* go in the same direction as *carreras*; *diagonales* go in the same direction as *calles*.

In Bogotá, *carreras* run north to south, and parallel to the Eastern Cordillera. Carrera 1 starts in the east and the numbers of the carreras reach the double digits as you go west. Buildings on the east side of the carrera are even numbered, and those on the west are odd. *Calles* run from east to west; Calle 1 starts in the southern part of town, and the numbers of the calles hit the double digits as you go north. Buildings on the north side of the *Calle* are even-numbered, and those on the west side are odd. In daily conversation, people speak of *calle siete* (Calle 7) and *carrera séptima* (Carrera 7).

By Plane

The **El Dorado** airport in Santafé de Bogotá (*Av. Eldorado, ☎413 95 00)* has two terminals. The main terminal services international flights, while the **Puente Areo** *(☎413 81 03)* is for flights inside the country. However, Avianca airlines flights to the United States leave from the Puente Areo terminal. While Avianca passengers can use *busetas* (shuttles) to go from one terminal to the other, this service is not systematic. It is best to ascertain the exact departure area of the return flight from the company's information counter upon your arrival. Since these counters are only open during peak hours, it may not be possible to get this information if your flight arrives afterwards. In this case, check with a travel agency or at one of the company's downtown sales counters when confirming your return flight. You can also get from terminal to terminal by cab for 5,000 pesos.

The following is the schedule of Avianca flights to destinations outside Colombia:

Aruba, Mon to Sat 9:29am; Thu, Sun 10:20am; Wed 11:20am; Fri 11:40am.
Buenos Aires, Argentina, Wed 2pm with stop; Thu 4:30pm; Mon, Fri, Sun 9:30pm.
Caracas, Venezuela, Mon to Fri 12:15pm; Sun 3:30; every day 8:35pm.
Frankfurt, Germany, Sun 2:30pm with stop; Thu 3:45.
Lima, Peru, every day 9:45am with stop; Wed, Sun 7pm with stop; Mon, Tue, Fri, Sat 9pm with stop.
London, England, Mon, Fri 6:45pm.
Los Angeles, USA, Mon, Thu, Fri, Sat 10:30 with stop.
Mexico City, Mexico, Mon, Thu, Fri, Sat 10:30am.
Miami, USA, Mon, Fri, Sat, Sun 7am; every day 10am.
New York City, USA, every day 3:45pm.
Panama City, Panama, every day 7:14am.

Paris, France, Tue, Thu, Sat 4:50pm.
Quito, Ecuador, every day 9:45am; Wed, Sun 7pm; Mon, Tue, Fri, Sat 9pm.
Río de Janeiro, Brazil, Wed, Sun 11pm.
San José, Costa Rica, Tue, Wed, Sat 10:10am with stop; every day 2pm.
Santiago, Chili, Wed 2pm; Mon, Fri, Sun 9:30pm with stop.

Avianca has direct flights from Bogotá to the following cities in Colombia:

Armenia, Mon to Thu and Sat 6:02am; Thu 7:50am; every day 11:30am and 6pm; 105,000 pesos.
Baranquilla, every day 7:06am, Mon to Fri and Sun 10:10am; every day 12:20pm, 2:30pm, 4:16pm, 7:15pm; Mon to Fri and Sun 8:42pm; 198,000 pesos.
Bucaramanga every day except Sun 6:04am; every day 6:50am and 10:46am; Tue, Thu and Sun 11:58am; Mon to Fri and Sun 1:05pm; every day 2pm and 3:30pm; Mon to Fri and Sun 4:36pm; every day 6:42pm, 7:36pm and 10:05pm; 141,000 pesos.
Cali, Mon to Sat 6:30am; Mon to Fri 7:54am; Mon to Fri and Sun 9:02am; every day 10:58am, 1:15pm and 2:02pm; Mon to Fri and Sun 3:56pm; every day 5:02pm; Mon to Fri and Sun 6:04pm and 7:08pm; every day 7:40pm, 8:30pm and 10:06pm; 129,000 pesos.
Cartagena, Tue, Thu, Sat and Sun 6:10am; every day 8:40am; Mon, Wed, Fri 10:10am; every day 11:16am, 2:32pm and 4:44pm; Fri 7pm; Mon to Fri and Sun 7:20; 198,000 pesos.
Leticia, Sat 10:10am; Tue 2:30pm; 235,000 pesos.
Manizales, every day 6:30am and 2:10pm; 105,000 pesos.
Medellín, Mon, Wed, Fri 6:20; Mon to Fri 6:38am and 8am; every day 9am; Mon to Sat 11:30, every day 1:noon, 2:15pm and 4:15pm; Mon to Fri and Sun 5:48pm; every day 7:04pm; Mon to Fri and Sun 8:30pm; every day 10pm; 117,000 pesos.
Pereira, every day 6:05am, 8:36am, 10:56am and 1:52pm; Mon to Sat 5pm; Mon to Sun 6pm; Mon, Fri to Sun 8pm Mon to Fri 8:45pm; 105,000 pesos.
Popayán, Mon to Thu and Sat, Sun 2:30pm; 114,000 pesos.
Riohacha, every day 10:28am; 232,000 pesos.
San Andrés, every day 6:10am and 10:10am with stops; Tue, Thu, Sat and Sun 12:50pm; every day 1:22; Fri 2pm; Mon 3:30pm; 237,000 pesos.

Santa Marta, every day 6:22am, Mon to Fri 6:38am; every day 9:32am, Thu and Sun 2:30pm; Mon, Wed, Fri 6:20pm; Thu and Sun 6:35pm; Tue and Sat 6:56pm; 198,000 pesos.

Several airlines fly from El Dorado international airport. Here are their addresses:

Colombian Airlines

Aces, Carrera 10 No. 26-53, ☎281 72 11
AeroRepública, Carrera 10 No. 27-51, office 303, ☎281 51 99 or 281 55 11
Aires, Av. 13 No. 79-56, ☎257 30 00 or 610 96 53
Avianca, Carrera 7 No. 16-36, ☎241 54 97
Intercontinental de Aviación, Carrera 10 No. 28-31, ☎281 51 52 or 283 30 15
SAM, Carrera 10 No.27-91, ☎286 94 02
Satena, Carrera 10 No. 27-51, ☎286 27 10

International Airlines

Aerolinas Argentinas, Calle 85 No. 20-11, ☎616 61 11 or 610 50 66
Aeroperú, Carrera 10 No. 227-51, ☎286-87-11
Aerotaca, Carrera 10 No. 227-51, ☎286 96 82
Air France, Calle 72 No. 10-07, ☎210 14 84 or 210 16 65
Alitalia, Calle 32 No. 7-16, ☎287 13 75 or 287 13 84
American Airlines, Carrra 7 No. 26-20, ☎285 11 11
British Airways, Calle 98 No. 9-07, ☎218 02 00
Copa, Calle 100 No. 8a-49, ☎286 93 70
Continental Airlines, Carrera 7 No. 71-52, ☎312 25 65
Ideria, Calle 85 No. 20-11, ☎616 61 11
KLM, Calle 26 No. 4a-45, tower 6, ☎234 30 01
Ladeco, Calle 100 No. 8a-49, ☎611 15 33
Lufthansa, Calle 100 No. 8a-49, 8th floor, ☎618 04 00
Mexicana de Aviación, Calle 100 No. 8a-49, ☎610 14 77 or 618 16 36
Swissair, Calle 93a No. 14-17, office 605, ☎218 63 00
Varig, Carrera 7 No. 33-24, ☎285 83 00
Viasa, Carrera 20 No. 85-11, ☎610 50 66
Zuliana de Aviación, Carrera 10 No. 27-51, ☎281 56 55.

By Bus

Bus transportation from Santafé de Bogotá to other Colombian cities is highly efficient, as is the case throughout the country. Buses leave from **Terminal de Transportes** *(at the corner of Transv. 66 and Calle 33, or, more precisely, Calle 33b No. 69-59, ☎295 11 00)*, a relatively new and well-designed building that serves some 50 bus companies. It is divided into four sections for departures going north, south, east or west. All the companies have separate ticket counters in each of these sections.

There are also other alternatives. Trips are shorter, although not necessarily more comfortable, if you go by *colectivo*, or shared taxi. Departure times are not set in advance: the taxis leave whenever they are full. *Colectivos* are recommended for trips of less than two hours duration. They are slightly more expensive than buses.

Aerovans, or minibuses, also leave when they have a certain number of passengers. *Aerovans* are recommended for trips of less than three hours duration and charge slightly less than *colectivos*.

First class buses, or *ejecutivos*, are relatively new, large and equipped with washrooms. They are an excellent means of transportation for long distances (trips of more than three hours duration). However, the windows of the buses are tinted to protect passengers from the effects of the sun, so it is more difficult to enjoy Colombia's magnificent scenery.

Buses of lesser quality without air conditioning or television cover the same routes. They charge somewhat less and stop more frequently. Buses leave the Terminal at fixed times. There are hourly departures for nearby destinations. For longer trips, check the bus schedules at the Terminal.

Public Transport

While it is possible to use pubic transportation from the airport to the downtown area during the day (buses stop in front of the main terminal as well as the Puente Aero terminal), there are just too many complications and inherent dangers to attempt it at night. Even *Bogotanos* suggest that it is best to take a taxi into Bogotá after sundown. Just budget the extra expense for the trip. To get to the airport, during the day, public transport leaves from the intersection of Carrera 3 and Calle 19 or from Carrera 10. Take the *ejecutivo (450 pesos)* to Alamos, and then take a *buseta* to the airport

(350 pesos). There are also *ejecutivos* and *busetas* with signs saying "Aeropuerto" on the windshield that go directly to the airport.

Several categories of buses operate in Bogotá with price differences of about one hundred pesos (only a few cents) between them. The route and the final destination are written on a piece of cardboard that appears in the windshield. To make things easier, have the reception clerk at your hotel help map the route for you to a specific destination. Also, people waiting on a street corner for a bus will generally do their best to help you out.

This is my stop!

To signal the bus driver to stop, push the button above the rear exit door. In a *buseta* or an *ejecutivo*, alert the driver by saying, *"Aqui, señor, por favor"* (Here, Sir, please).

Buses accept as many passengers as possible and come to a halt at the red and yellow stops (*paraderos*) to pick up and to let off passengers. However, drivers will also stop the bus, usually at the next corner, at the request or hand signal from a passenger. Fares are indicated on the windshield and vary according to the time of day or night.

Busetas and *ejecutivos* are evidently more comfortable, since they accept only as many passengers as there are seats. Their fares are only slightly higher than ordinary buses and are posted on the windshields.

There is also a *super ejecutivo* type of service, with buses that are air-conditioned and have televisions. They also post the fares on the windshield.

Taxis

There are many taxis waiting at the airport exit. Take a clearly marked, official taxi that has been summoned by the dispatcher in charge of the taxi stand at the far left, as you leave the airport. The ride to downtown will cost 10,000 pesos during the day. At night the driver can charge double fare. It is really a waste of time to try to find a driver who will charge less. Since public transport is unsafe at this hour, double the daytime fare is the norm. Also, you will be tired from the flight and those suitcases will begin to feel heavier by the minute!

Taxis are efficient, clean, inexpensive and plentiful in Bogotá. Passengers can flag them down anywhere on the street. They also have radios and can be summoned by telephone. In general, their work is professional and their service is excellent.

The four-door compact yellow taxicabs have *Servicio Público* written in black lettering on the doors of their cars. Metres determine the fare to be paid, with a minimum fare of 1,000 pesos. If the driver refuses to use the metre, find another cab. If you decide to negotiate the fare, the driver will charge two or three times the agreed upon rate at the end of the ride. This is not being ripped off, it's "doing good business", so use the metre!

If the taxi driver seems pleasant and friendly and you plan to use a taxi several times during the same day, you can make arrangements to hire him for 8,000 pesos per hour. Of course, it costs more during the night. Just take note of his name and personal pager number and his company will willingly make the arrangements with him, providing you with personalized service. This way, there will be someone familiar waiting for you at the door of your hotel the next morning. If you are cleaver, you will have the services of a chauffeur, a guide and an interpreter, all for the same price: and learn to do business Colombian-Style. The game works the other way around, too! An alternative is to use fixed-rate taxis to travel to tourist attractions on the outskirts of Bogotá. The round-trip fare is established according to the destination, usually between 40,000 and 50,000 pesos. One or two hours waiting time during the visit is included in the fare.

As well, all the large hotels offer limousine service that costs some 2,000 pesos more per hour. This service is more discreet, since the vehicles are not identified. Ask for information at the reception desk.

The following is a partial list of taxi companies and their telephone numbers:

Taxi Libres, ☎311 11 11
Taxi Perla, ☎201 04 11
Real Transportada, ☎333 33 33
Telecooper, ☎222 21 11
Proturisme, ☎223 21 11
Texatelite S. A., ☎222 22 22
Astax Dorado, ☎250 36 71

SANTAFÉ DE BOGOTÁ

Tax Q.A.P. S.A., ☎311 66 66
Tax Express, ☎411 11 11
Pronturismo, ☎430 77 77
Teletaxi, ☎226 66 66
Coop. Radio Taxi, ☎288 88 88
Nuevo Taxi Mio, ☎237 47 11

Renting a Car

It is not advisable to rent a car in Bogotá without previous driving experience in South America. However, it might be a good idea to rent a car for visiting the numerous tourist attractions in the areas outside the city. Renting a car let's you set your own schedule and spend as much time as you like enjoying the most interesting places.

Driving in the outskirts of Bogotá is less stressful than fighting city traffic, but there is no highway patrol. Without the threat of a traffic ticket, drivers take all sorts of liberties. While they do not drive excessively fast (amazing, given the circumstances!), Colombians have no respect for the double line and pass on curves and on hills. Nevertheless, very few accidents occur: this unorthodox approach works fairly well in the context of South American driving.

There are several car rental agencies at the airport, but they also have downtown offices. The rates are similar at the different agencies and vary according to the type of rental plan and whatever special rates are available (i.e. weekend packages). An added expense of renting a car is paying the frequent highway tolls (about 1,200 pesos each). Here are some useful addresses:

ABC Rent-a-Car, Carrera 4 No. 65-16, ☎210 01 94
Abordo, Carrera 34 No.160-49, ☎677 13 54
Auto Lima, Calle 98 No. 15-17, ☎621 36 39
Avis Rent-a-Car, Av. 15 No. 101-45, ☎610 44 55 or 620 33 59
Bochica Rent-a-Car, Av. 15 No. 120-59, ☎612 05 95
Budget, Av. 15 No. 107-08, ☎213 63 83, 213 60 20 or 612 50 40
Car Rental, Calle 99 No. 14-27, ☎618 06 42
Colombian Car Rental, Av. 15 No. 118-03, room 9, ☎215 42 02 or 612 64 32
Dollar, Diagonal 109 No. 14-61, ☎620 03 62, 620 00 43 or 612 82 95
Hertz, Av.15 No. 107-24, ☎214 42 28 or 214 97 45; and Carrera 10 No. 26-35, ☎284 14 45

Internacional Travel, Carrra 13 No. 79-09, ☎257 60 71
National Car Rental, Calle 100 No. 14-46, ☎612 56 35 or 620 00 55
Pronto Rent-a-Car, Av. 15 No. 105-22, ☎919 16 84
Rentacar, Calle 71 No. 9-39, ☎235 48 24, 212 15 92 or 212 06 64
Rentamo, Calle 100 No. 11b-95, ☎616 06 57
Rentautos, Carrera 7 No. 46-41, ☎285 96 48, 285 73 39 or 287 96 01
Uno Auto Renta, Diagonal 109 No. 14-61, ☎619 29 77

PRACTICAL INFORMATION

Regional Area Code: 1

Mail

Mail can be sent from the **Avianca Airlines office** *(Mon to Fri 7:30am to 7pm, Sat 8am to 3pm; Carrera 7 No. 16-36).*

Money and Banking

All Colombian banks have their head offices in Bogotá, and they all have the same banking hours, which are not the same in other parts of the country: Monday to Friday from 9am to 3pm, except for the last Friday of the month when they close at noon. Travellers with ATM cards will find ATM counters, *cajas automáticos,* just about everywhere in Colombia, even in the lobbies of some hotels. Trying to cash traveller's cheques is a different story: only a few banks accept them. The most accommodating of these is the Banco Industrial Colombiano (BIC), which will cash most institution's traveller's cheques, even those issued by a few non-American ones. While this is the most efficient place, they still require photocopies of the identification page and the entry stamped page of your passport. Depending on the number of people waiting in line, this process can take up to an hour or more of your precious vacation time. Nevertheless, here are some handy addresses of banks cash traveller's cheques:

Banco Popular, Calle 17 No. 7-43, ☎341 04 88
Banco Unión Colombiano, Carrrera 7 No.71-52,
☎312 04 11
Banco Industrial Colombiana (BIC), Carrera 7
No. 32-33, ☎232 88 61.

Currency exchange offices *(casas de cambio)*
will cash traveller's cheques, but charge excessively high rates compared to the banks. However, they will only cash traveller's cheques
issued by American institutions (AMEX), since
the few travellers cheques issued by institutions in other countries are less popular. Here
are some addresses of currency exchange
offices:

Cambios Country, Carrera 13 No. 84-24,
office 206, ☎256 73 97;
El Dollar, Centro Comercial Unicentro,
room 2-247, ☎619 06 78;
Telecambio, Calle 25 No. 28-58, ☎368 69 41;
New York Money, Av. 15 No 123-30; Centro
Comercial Unicentro, room 2-247,
☎213 22 58, 213 99 47 or 213 07 59;
Carrera 11 No. 82-71, Centro Comercial
Andino, room 348, ☎616 89 55 or 616 89 46;
also at the corner of Carrera 7 and Av. Pepe
Sierra, Centro Comercial Santa Bárbara, room
F-136, ☎214 20 58 or 215 26 83.

Some large hotels also cash traveller's cheques
issued by American institutions to accommodate their clients, but, again, the fees charged
for this are much higher than the banks'. In an
emergency, they may agree to cash traveller's
cheques for someone who is not staying at the
hotel. Try the reception desk at **Teqendama
Inter-Continental** *(Carrera 10a No. 26-21,
☎289 11 11)* or at the **Victoria Regia**
(Carrera 13 No. 85-80, ☎621 16 66). The desk
clerks speak English as well as Spanish.

Tourist Information

The government's tourism development service
was in the process of reorganization when we
were in Bogotá. Here are the addresses of the
main tourist offices that were expected to open
shortly. They should be able to provide maps
and pamphlets for interesting activities and
tourist attractions in Bogotá and the rest of the
country.

Corporación Nacional de Turismo (CNT) *(Mon
to Fri 8:30am to 12:30pm and 2pm to 5pm;
Calle 28 No. 13a-15, ☎283 94 66 or
284 37 61)* is located at street level in the

tallest building in Bogotá, identifiable by the red
and ochre colours of the Bancafé sign on top of
the building.

Instituto Didtrital de Cultura y Turismo *(Calle
10 No.3-61, ☎286 65 55).*

Fundo Mixto de Promoción de Bogotá *(Calle 94
No. 9-84, ☎236 19 70 or 257 07 25).*

Corporación de Turismo de Cundinamarca *(Mon
to Fri 8:30am to 12:30pm and 2pm to 5pm;
Calle 26 No. 47-73, ☎426 00 00).*

Excursions

Several travel agencies offer guided tours of
the city of Santafé de Bogotá that take place
during the day or at night. They provide the
best-organized packages, from day-long walking tours of the city with lunch included, to
excursions that last several days and include
hotel and meals. Here are some possible excursions:

Tour of Bogotá

This four-hour guided tour starts at 8am and
goes to various points of interest in the city
such as the business district and La Candelaria.
The tour also includes a visit to the Museo del
Oro, and, weather permitting, to the mountain,
Monserrate. The price is 30,000 pesos. The
driver picks up passengers at their respective
hotels and brings them back after the tour.

The Salt Cathedral

This four-hour tour goes to the Salt Cathedral
in Zipaquirá, more than an hour's drive from
Bogotá. The cathedral was built some 200
metres underground in a salt mine. Some
consider it the eighth wonder of the world. The
price is 40,000 pesos, and the driver picks up
the passengers at their respective hotels and
brings them back after the tour.

La Laguna de Guatavita

This tour also lasts four hours and heads north
on Carratera del Norte, then follows a perpendicular road more than 3,000 metres up into
the mountains to Laguna de Guatavita, the
mysterious lake of the Muiscas that is the basis

SANTAFÉ DE BOGOTÁ

for the legend of El Dorado. The tour costs 40,000 pesos.

Tren Turístico de la Sabana

Another way to take in the sights in the north is on the **Tren Turístico de la Sabana** *(Sat, Sun and holidays only; departure at 8am from Estación de la Sabana, Calle 13 No. 18-24; and at 8:30am from Estación de Usaquén, Calle 110, between Carreras 9 and 10, ☎257 14 59 or 256 37 51)*. This train is essentially for tourists. It goes from Bogotá to Nemocón, and can take up to three hours for the 100-kilo-metre trip, because it is powered by an old steam engine. Arrival is scheduled for noon, and the return trip from Nemocón is at 3pm, with arrival at Estación de la Sabana at 6pm. There is a dining car on the train, which serves only fast food. Passengers can bring their own food if they wish. The cost of the excursion is 15,000 pesos.

There are approximately twenty other possible excursions in the area around Bogotá, such as a visit to Parque Nacional Chingaza, a tour of a coffee plantation, a trip to the Tequendama waterfalls, a visit to Fusagazugá, a town known for its orchid gardens, or a trip to Boyacá, one of the most beautiful colonial towns in Colombia. Although it might be possi-ble to arrange these outings privately at less expense, the tourist agencies provide security and are flexible in terms of scheduling tours at the convenience of their clients. They offer package deals, not only near Bogotá, but also to the Amazon, to San Andrés, in the *llanos*, or to San Agustín, one of the most important archaeological sites in the Americas. The fol-lowing agencies can provide the appropriate tour. Just ask a few days ahead of time, since some tours require organizing a minimum number of people who are interested and available at the same time.

Tierra Mar Aire (TMA), Carrera 7 No. 35-20, ☎288 20 88 or 288 44 11;
Aviatur, Calle 19 No. 4-62, ☎282 71 11 or 286 55 55;
Bruni Tours, Diagonal 109, No. 19-21, office 203, ☎612 38 12 or 214 42 11;
Aguilatours, Calle 13, No. 7-09, Edificio Murillo Toro, ☎282 82 04 or 324 42 43, ⬛282 55 52;
Anaconda Tours, Carrera 14 No. 77-46, 2nd floor, ☎218 01 23, 218 46 79, 611 32 19 or 256 09 10, ⬛611 23 58. This agency spe-cializes in Amazonian tours.

Amaturs, Calle 85 No. 16-28, office 203, ☎256 11 35, 257 22 00 or 257 03 35, ⬛218 21 13, (amaturs@impsat.net.co). This agency also specializes in Amazon tours.

 EXPLORING

Santafé de Bogotá ★★★

Santafé de Bogotá is tourist oriented. In addi-tion to La Candelaria, which is like an open-air museum, there are some fifty museums to see. Their exhibits reveal the epic of the city's tumultuous past in great detail.

The Downtown Area and La Candelaria

Visitors will see right away that **La Candelaria ★★★** is an important tourist attraction in and of itself. It is an historic neigh-bourhood right in the downtown area that was saved from destruction during *La Violencia*. Today it stands out as the most beautiful neighbourhood in Bogotá. Its colonial buildings have been converted into museums or govern-ment offices. Artists have redesigned the balconies of the houses. There are a few ho-tels, some small restaurants, the Biblioteca Luis-Ángel Arango, a university and other places of interest. A leisurely stroll along the streets, in more or less random fashion, is the best way to get to know the area.

High up in the hills of Monserrate, La Candelaria is an oasis of calm, with its narrow, one-way streets, some for pedestrians only, which discourage heavy traffic. The street names are engraved on plaques on the walls of the buildings. Full of character, they show the wry humour of the colony's early settlers: *Calle de la Fatigue*, *Calle de Agonia*, and *Calle de la Peña*. Their names suggest the strenuous effort that climbing these streets entails (a few of them really are pretty steep). La Candelaria is completely safe during the day, but avoid going there at night, except by taxi or in a group. Some of the streets have no lighting.

Plaza de Bolívar ★★★ *(between Carreras 7 and 8 and Calles 10 and 11)*, at the threshold of La Candelaria, is one of the most famous *plazas* in the whole country, and has an un-usual place in Colombian history. In the early days of the conquest, all important public

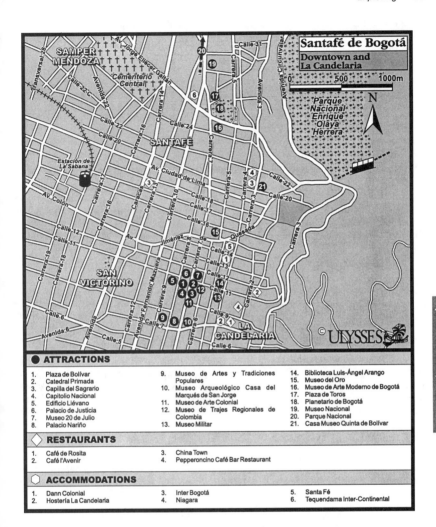

Santafé de Bogotá

Downtown and La Candelaria

0   500   1000m

N

SANTAFÉ DE BOGOTÁ

● **ATTRACTIONS**

1.	Plaza de Bolívar	9.	Museo de Artes y Tradiciones	14.	Biblioteca Luis-Ángel Arango
2.	Catedral Primada		Populares	15.	Museo del Oro
3.	Capilla del Sagrario	10.	Museo Arqueológico Casa del	16.	Museo de Arte Moderno de Bogotá
4.	Capitolio Nacional		Marqués de San Jorge	17.	Plaza de Toros
5.	Edificio Liévano	11.	Museo de Arte Colonial	18.	Planetario de Bogotá
6.	Palacio de Justicia	12.	Museo de Trajes Regionales de	19.	Museo Nacional
7.	Museo 20 de Julio		Colombia	20.	Parque Nacional
8.	Palacio Nariño	13.	Museo Militar	21.	Casa Museo Quinta de Bolívar

◇ **RESTAURANTS**

1.	Café de Rosita	3.	China Town
2.	Café l'Avenir	4.	Pepperoncino Café Bar Restaurant

◯ **ACCOMMODATIONS**

1.	Dann Colonial	3.	Inter Bogotá	5.	Santa Fé
2.	Hostería La Candelaria	4.	Niagara	6.	Tequendama Inter-Continental

events took place here, even mass and other religious ceremonies. Sumptuous celebrations, parades, *corridas*, trials (and their conse-quences: floggings and hangings) – everything happened in the plaza. And it was on this very spot that three conquistadors, all busily discov-ering Colombia, but coming from three differ-ent directions, met for the first time – an event that was marked by a certain amount of aston-ishment and defiance. Gonzalo Jímenez de Quesada started from the Caribbean Coast and founded the city on August 6, 1538. Sebastían de Belalcazár and his troops came from Quito, Ecuador on the Pacific, and Klaus Ferderman came from Venezuela. All three laid claim to the title of governor of the newly conquered regions and to the wealth that came with the position. Nevertheless, they signed a non-aggression pact and formed the first *cabillo* (municipal council) of Bogotá here on the plaza, which was then called Plaza Mayor. Later, in 1821, the plaza was renamed Plaza de la Constitución. Still later, in 1846, the bronze statue of the *Libertador*, commissioned from the Italian sculptor Pietro Tenerani, was installed in the center and the plaza received its definitive name: Plaza de Bolívar."Solemnity" is the word that describes the impression you have when walking onto this hallowed place for the first time.

Catedral Primada ★★★ *(Carrera 7)*, on the northeast side of the Plaza de Bolívar, is its most striking building. Two bell towers rise toward the sky, leading the eye to the monastery of Monserrate that crowns the mountain in the background. Its construction dates back to 1807, and it occupies the same site as the thatched-roof church in the *sabana* of Bogotá where Frey Domingo de las Casas celebrated the first mass in honour of the founding of the city. The sacred vessels and ornaments from this ceremony have been preserved and are kept in the sacristy.

Work on this church was begun by the Capuchin architect Fray Domingo Péres de Petrés, and was finished by Nicolás León in 1823. The first attempt to build a cathedral on this site, in 1556, ended disastrously when the building collapsed. In 1572, a third church was built that was completely destroyed by an earthquake in 1785.

The cathedral that stands today has 17th-century statues from the colonial church displayed in niches in its neoclassical façade. The interior is quite interesting. Fourteen columns support the semi-circular arches of the large vaulted ceiling. To the right are three chapels: the Immaculate Conception, the Sacred Heart and the Dying Christ, which contains a painting by Van Dyck. To the left is a remarkable chapel dedicated to Saint Isabelle of Hungary. On its marble altar are repositories for the ashes of President Antonio Nariño, of the Archbishop of Mosquera and of Gonzalo Jiménez de Quesada, the founder of Bogotá.

Linked to the cathedral by way of the transept, the **Capilla del Sagrario ★★★** was formerly used for congregational meetings. The chapel of the Holy Sacrament (Sagrario) is considered one of the most historically representative and artistically important monuments in Bogotá. The initial phase of its construction took place from 1660 to 1689 through the initiative of Don Gabriel de Sandoval y Arratia. It has endured several catastrophes, including the earthquake of 1743 that partially destroyed the two belltowers. The earthquake in 1827 caused the cupola to collapse over the high altar, which was rebuilt twice after the earthquakes of 1840 and 1917. The entire chapel, including the cupola and the belltowers, was completely renovated in 1950, with support from the government and private funds, mainly from banks.

The façade, whose style is more 16th-century Italian than Baroque, has two steeples and looks out onto the Plaza de Bolívar. The interior, in the shape of a Latin cross, is remarkable for its Moorish vaults and for several paintings by Gregorio Vásquez de Arcey y Ceballos.

The 30-metre-high cupola is decorated with frescos by Ricardo Acevedo Bernal and with the coat of arms of the founder's family and those of the cities of Madrid and of Bogotá. The original high altar was made of carved cedar with inlays of bronze, ivory and mother-of-pearl. The new high altar, installed in 1881, includes several fragments from the original one.

The neoclassical **Capitolio Nacional ★★★** is the most beautiful building on the Plaza de Bolivar. This monumental building covers the entire south side of the *plaza* and houses the Congress. The construction of this legislative building began in 1847, but because of the many political problems and great civil unrest, it was only completed in 1926. It occupies the same site as the former palace of the Viceroy, which burned to the ground in 1786. Too busy with the spanish wars in the mother country, the last representatives of Spain did not have time to order its reconstruction.

Thus it fell to President Tomás Mosquera to initiate the construction of a national building to contain "not just the President but also the Senate, the Supreme Court and the ministerial offices." The project was given to Danish architect Tomas Reed, but the Italian Pietro Cantini took it over in 1871. The edifice was finally completed by two other architects, Mariano Santamaría and Gaston Lelarge, from France.

Another imposing building on the southwest side of the Plaza de Bolivar is the **Edificio Liévano ★★★**, Bogotá's city hall. Though *bogotano* architect Julian Lombada began this building in 1902, the authorities were dissatisfied with his work and gave the contract to Gaston Lelarge in 1905. Lelarge remodeled and completed it. Thus, it can be said to be the product of French craftsmanship.

Due north on the Plaza de Bolívar is the **Palacio de Justicia** ★★★, which houses the Supreme Court. This building has had a tumultuous history. Originally built in 1921, it was destroyed by a fire started by an overexcited mob during the rioting known as *El Bogotazo*. It was replaced by a contemporary-style building. However, in 1985 the second version was also destroyed, this time by the army which attacked it with bazookas and other assault weapons during the hostage taking of the Supreme Court magistrates by the guerrilla group M-19. The building was reduced to rubble. Four years later, it was rebuilt in a style harmonious with that of the Capitolio Nacional, on the opposite side of the *plaza*.

El florero de Llorente

José González Llorente was a Spanish merchant who had his shop in the house on Calle 11 No. 6-94. He refused to loan a certain vase *(florero)* to a *criollo* (Creole, a person of Spanish extraction born in the Americas) who wanted it for the head table at a banquet in honour of José Antonio Villavincencio, a fervent advocate of independence. The confrontation between the two men grew so heated that it started a conflict between the European-born Spanish and the Spanish born in the americas who deposed the governor.

Museo 20 de Julio ★★ *(1,000 pesos; Tue to Sat 9:30am to 5pm, Sun and holidays 10am to 4pm; Calle 11 No.6-94, ☎334 41 50)*. It was in this handsome 17th-century Spanish-Moorish residence that the *El florero de Llorente* incident took place, which sparked the Colombian independence movement on July 20, 1810. This house was designated a national historic monument on July 20, 1960 and now represents an important part of the national heritage.

Adjacent to the Plaza de Bolívar, it is considered one of the best examples of Spanish-Moorish architecture on the American Continent. The first floor contains the famous vase that initiated the independence movement, documents and objects that belonged to the protagonists and a copy of the declaration of independence. There are also the documents, uniforms and period weapons of General Francisco de Paula Santander, donated by *señores* Edwardo Santos and Rafael Martínes Briceño, two eminent *Bogotanos*.

The republican neoclassical-style **Palacio Nariño** ★★★ *(Calle 8, between Carreras 7 and 8)* is now the residence of the President of the Republic. The furniture and interior decoration date from the colonial period. In the square outside the building are two statues: the modern one is by Edgar Negret, while the pre-Colombian one comes from the San Agustin area.

The Palacio Nariño, located behind the Capitolio Nacional, is the birthplace of former President Antonio Nariño who was born on April 9, 1775. The building was acquired by the government in 1888. In 1896 it became part of the university's mathematics faculty. Finally, the government of Rafael Reyes renovated it and made it the official residence of the President of the Republic. It has served this function since 1908.

Museo de Artes Tradiciones Populares ★★ *(700 pesos; Mon to Sat 9am to 5pm, Sun 9am to 1pm; Carrera 8 No. 7-21, ☎284 53 19)*. This building was originally the cloisters of the San Luis Beltrán convent built by the Augustines in the 17th century. During the period of New Grenada, it served as the general quarters of the Presidential Guard. Today it is the headquarters of the Colombian association for the promotion of traditional folk art, created in 1969. Two exhibition halls contain a large collection of handcrafted art from all the regions of Colombia, and another collection of indigenous art made from wood, ceramics and fabrics such as agave fibres, cotton, wool and others. The museum also has a library and an auditorium that hosts temporary folk-art exhibitions.

The Presidential Guard

Don't miss the changing of the Presidential Guard. This ceremony takes place on the square outside the Palacio Nariño every afternoon at 5pm. This formality goes back to the early 19th century, and is quite impressive. Children will especially enjoy it!

Museo Arqueológico Casa del Marqués de San Jorge ★ *(Tue to Sat 9am to 12:30pm and 1:30pm to 5pm, Sun and holidays 10am to 1pm; Carrera 6 No. 7-43, ☎282 09 40)* is located in the former residence of the Marquis de San Jorge, which was built at the end of the 17th century. The Casa del Marqués de San Jorge now belongs to the Banco Popular, which restored it and converted it to a museum. The building itself is a remarkable example of aristocratic colonial construction, with its balconies and wrought iron windows. The museum contains the country's largest collection of pre-Colombian art, displayed in a manner that is informative and easy to follow.

Museo de Arte Colonial ★ *(Tue to Sat 9:30am to 5:30pm, Sun and holidays 10am to 5pm; Carrera 6 No.9-77, ☎284 08 52 or 282 07 40).* The Colonial Art Museum is installed in a former cloister of the San Ignacio church, built by the Jesuit Juan Bautista Coluccini upon the Order's arrival in Colombia. The building later served as the National Library and the Museum of Natural Sciences. It has witnessed many historic events, such as the nomination of President of Antonio Nariño and the drafting of the country's first constitution.

The **Museo de Trajes Regionales de Colombia** ★★ *(700 pesos; Tue to Fri 10am to 5pm, Sat 10am to 1pm; Calle 10 No. 6-36, ☎282 65 31 or 281 19 03),* on the Plazoleta Rufino José Cuervo, was inaugurated in 1972 in a beautiful colonial home. The national costume museum is also the former residence of Manuelita Sáenz, the mistress of Simón Bolívar, who lived here before fleeing to Peru. Today, the house is a national monument. The costumes, furniture, utensils and other everyday objects from different regions of the country are displayed in chronological order, retelling the history of the country.

The **Museo Militar** ★★★ *(600 pesos; Tue to Fri 9am to 12:30pm and 2pm to 3:30pm; Calle 10 No. 4-92, ☎281 30 86 or 281 31 31)* was established in 1982. It deals with the military history of Colombia. The museum displays all sorts of army, navy and air force equipment. It is located in a colonial house that dates from the 19th century and contains all kinds of firearms, from revolvers to cannons, as well as other weapons from the time of the Conquest; replicas and partially preserved antiques from the navy; and costumes, uniforms and flags. The museum's collection is displayed in chronological order and is spread over several floor on two floors. Among the displays are an indigenous warrior with weapons as he would have appeared to the first conquistadors, a soldier from the "Thousand Days" War (1899-1902), a soldier from *La Violencia*, a anti-guerrilla soldier and a soldier from the Colombian-Peru war. In the hall of the FAC (Colombian Air Force) are replicas and models of aircraft used in national aviation and photographs of the

pioneers of Colombian aviation. Outside, the museum exhibits such items as a combat plane, a pilot with parachute and anti-aircraft guns.

In addition to the usual library services such as the reading room, circulation desk, photocopying services and computer assisted research, the **Biblioteca Luis-Ángel Arango** ★★★ *(Mon to Sat 8am to 8pm, Sun 8am to 4pm; Calle 11 No. 4-14, ☎342 06 05 or 286 46 10, ☞286 38 81)* offers guided tours and has both a permanent art collection and special exhibitions by local and international artists. The music section gives audio and visual music appreciation courses, as well as conferences and concerts. Among other events, there are young musicians' nights on Mondays, international music concerts on Wednesdays, family music concerts on Sundays and free Friday concerts at 1pm.

*A gold object from the
Museo del Oro*

The **Museo del Oro** ★★★ *(800 pesos; Tue to Sat 9am to 4:30pm, Sun and holidays 10am to 4:30pm, closed Mon; Calle 16 No. 5-41, next to Parque Santader, between Carreras 5a and 7a, ☎342 11 11, ext. 5424, or 334 87 48)* was originally in the basement of the Banco de la República and was started as an effort to assemble as many gold pre-Colombian art objects as possible. It was only in 1946 that the Museo del Oro de Bogotá was finally built to house this collection. There are over 36,000 of gold objects on display, including jewellery, masks, statuettes, dishes, along with pottery and textiles. Everything is classified and grouped according to its specific indigenous culture.

On the first floor there is a special thematic exhibition hall that focusses on different indigenous cultures and displays archaeological finds from Colombia and other parts of the world.

On the second floor is a five-room gallery for the permanent collection, which comprises objects from the Tumaco, Calima, San Agustín, Tierradentro, Nariño, Tolima, Quimbaya, Sinú, Tayrona and Muisca civilizations. In a windowless room at the entrance, is an impressive sound and light show that transports visitors to the distant past: masks, jewellery and figurines made of gold that appear in the dark to the accompaniment of music played on pre-Columbian instruments.

Other rooms contain models that represent the daily lives of advanced Pre-Columbian civilizations. On display are intricate diadems, chest pieces, medallions, weapons and one of the most extraordinary works by a gold smith in the world, *La Balsa Muisca*, which depicts the legendary El Dorado. The miniature is kept under glass on an emerald green turntable, that represents the Laguna de Guatavita and shows the hereditary ruler Guatavita on his raft *(balsa)* accompanied by his servants. The revolving turntable displays the intricate workmanship from every angle. With a little imagination, you can see the cacique throwing gold and emeralds into the mysterious lagoon.

The third floor explains the significance of gold to the Pre-Columbian people and to the Spanish – not at all the same thing. There is also a library with books about different indigenous civilizations.

You can visit the museum on your own, or take the guided tour in Spanish or English. The Spanish tours are given daily at 11:15am and 2:45pm. The English tours are at 10:15am and at 2:15pm. To arrange a special visit for a private group, call ☎342 11 11 ext. 5424.

Museos del Oro

A word of appreciation: the Banco de la República finances museums of gold and ethnography in all the large cities in Colombia. In adddition to the one in Bogotá, there are museums in Santa Marta, Cartagena de Indias, Manizales, Pereira, Armenia, Cali, Leticia and others. All are exceptionally interesting.

The **Museo de Arte Moderno de Bogotá** ★★★ *(1,000 pesos; Tue to Sat 10am to 6:30pm, Sun and holidays noon to 6pm; Calle 24 No. 6-00, ☎283 31 09 or 286 04 66)* has existed since 1955, but it has only occupied this 5,000-square-metre, four-storey modern building since 1980. The museum sponsors special expositions of the works of modern and contemporary artists from Colombia and around the world throughout the year. The permanent collection includes works by Fernando Boter, David Manzur, Enrique Grau, Edwardo Ramírez Villamizar and Edgar Negret, as well as those of a few women, such as Ana Mercedes Hoyos and María de la Paz Jarmillo. The museum has its own movie theatre and publishes the quarterly magazine *Arte*, which is on sale in the lobby.

The **Plaza de Toros** ★★★ *(open to the public Mon to Fri 9:30am to 12:30 pm and 2pm to 5:30pm, Sat 10am to 2pm; corner of Carrera 7a and Calle 26)* is a circular, Moorish-style red brick building that resembles a Roman arena. Most bullfights take place in January and February, but they are occasionally held at other times of the year, weather permitting. Contrary to the practice in Mexico, the bull here is killed by the toreador. However, if the bull is particularly strong and courageous, or if he makes the toreador appear ridiculous, the spectators insist that his life be spared by waving white flags and cheering loudly.

Planetario de Bogotá ★★★ *(1,000 pesos; shows Tue to Fri 11am, 3:30pm and 5pm; corner of Carrera 7a and Calle 26, at the entrance to Parque de la Independencia, ☎334 45 48, 334 45 71 or 283 63 09, ╍384 78 96)*. The planetarium presents a laser show *(3,000 pesos; Tue to Fri 12:30pm, 2pm and 6pm)*. There is also a small natural sciences museum *(500 pesos; Mon to Fri 9am to 5:30pm, Sat, Sun and holidays 10am to 5pm)*.

The **Museo Nacional** ★★★ *(1,000 pesos; Tue to Sat 10am to 5:30pm, Sun and holidays 10am to 1:30pm; Carrera 7 No. 28-66, ☎334 83 66)* displays an extensive collection of some 10,000 archaeological artifacts from Muisca, Tayrona and other civilizations on the main floor. Most of the rooms on the second floor are devoted to ethnography and anthropology, but there are also displays of weapons, flags and uniforms in the history section. On the third floor are three collections of art works dating from the colonial period through to the beginning of the 20th century.

The modern art gallery includes works by such noted artists as Enrique Grau, Alejandro Obregón and Fernando Botero. This museum is one of the oldest in America, having been opened as a science museum in 1823. In 1945 it moved to the building that formerly housed the largest prison in the country, built in 1874. Designed by Danish architect Tomas Reed along the lines of an existing prison in Philadelphia, it is a so-called "panoptic" structure that allowed guards to observe the 200 prisoners without being seen themselves. The science museum became the Museo Nacional in 1948.

Parque Nacional ★★ *(Carrera 7, between Calles 34 and 40)* is a welcome green space in the heart of downtown Bogotá. It includes sports fields, a theatre and children's playgrounds.

As its name implies, **Casa Museo Quinta de Bolívar ★** *(Tue to Sun 9am to 5pm; Calle 20 No. 3-23 Este, ☎284 68 19)* was formerly a home of Simón Bolívar. Built in 1800, the house belonged to the rich Spanish merchant Don José Antonio Portocarrero who used it to give splendid receptions in honour of the viceroys of the times. In 1820 the government purchased it to present it to the *Libertador* in recognition of his victory over the Spanish at Boyacá. Bolívar stayed here frequently until 1830, and for four years shared its charm and comfort with his mistress Manuelita Sáenz. Classified as a national monument in 1975, the museum reveals the day-to-day life of Bolívar down to the smallest detail. His library, bedroom, dining room and office can be toured among others, and various personal objects, such as weapons and documents, are on display. The interior patio with its garden and fountain is magnificent.

The North

Parque El Chicó ★ *(Carrera 7 No. 94-17)* is in the northern part of Bogotá. It has lots of trees and greenery, playgrounds for children, and the Museo Mercedes Sierra de Pérez El Chicó.

The **Museo Mercedes Sierra de Pérez El Chicó ★** *(1,000 pesos; Mon to Fri 8am to 12:30 and 2pm to 4:30pm, Sat 9am to noon; Carrera 7 No.93-01, ☎623 23 02 or 623 10 66)* opened more than 30 years ago in this house, which belonged to Doña Mercedes de Pérez. Three French-style salons display an admirable collection of furniture and other objects imported from Europe. These rooms and the chapel are rented to the public for private gatherings such as wedding receptions.

The **Museo Francisco de Paula Santander** *(Tue to Fri 8:30am to 12:30pm and 2pm to 5pm,*

Sat 9am to noon; Carrera 7 No. 150-01, ☎258 22 50 or 216 13 33) is a two-storey *hacienda* (large farmhouse) that has an interior patio with walls over a metre wide. Historical interest are General Santander's personal library of over 600 volumes and the collection of Doña Santander's period ball gowns.

The West

Parque el Salitre ★★ *(entrance on Avendida 63)*, adjacent to Parque Simón Bolívar, has bicycle paths, a lake, playgrounds, track and fields, fairground attractions and the Museo de Los Niños.

Museo de Los Niños ★★★ *(adults 3,000 pesos, children 2,500 pesos; Tue to Sun 9am to noon and 2pm to 5pm; Carrera 48, No.63-97, ☎225 52 58 or 225 75 87)* is a non-profit children's museum. All sorts of scientific, technological and cultural knowledge in areas like communications, art, the human body, computers, and so on, are displayed in ways that children enjoy. The explanations are easy for children to understand, and they teach them many valuable things such as how a city works, or about physics, solar energy, television, future technologies, petroleum, health, and even palaeontology. The museum includes a theatre, displays a full-scale airplane donated by Avianca Airlines, and has a real locomotive in working condition. Children from 7 to 12, and grown-ups, will really enjoy this.

Parque Simón Bolívar ★★★ *(between Avenida 63 and Diagonal 53)* is a huge park adjacent to the Museo de Los Niños at the edge of the downtown area. There are bicycle paths, playing fields, a lake, jogging paths and many lovely places to relax. It is both a safe and tranquil area.

The **Museo de Arte Contemporáneo El Minuto de Dios ★★★** *(1,500 pesos; Mon to Fri 8am to 1pm and 2pm to 6pm; Carrera 74 No. 82a-81, ☎252 58 90 or 251 81 00)* has a permanent collection of more than 500 works by the most famous Colombian artists, including Fernando Botero, David Manzur, Enrique Grau, Edwardo Ramírez Villamizar, Edgar Negret, Alejandro Obregón, Omar Rayo, Augusto Rivera, Teresa Cuéllar, Pedro Alcántara, Rafael Penagos, Luis Caballero, Leonardo Nierman, José Luis Cuevas, Oswaldo Vigas and Justo Arosomena. It was Father García Herreros who

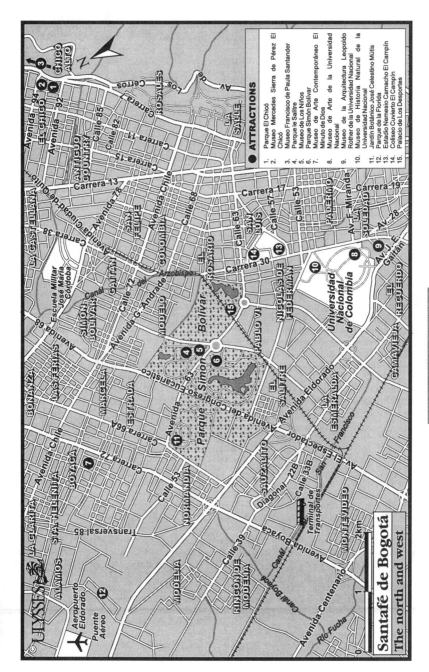

SANTAFÉ DE BOGOTÁ

Santafé de Bogotá
The north and west

ATTRACTIONS

1. Parque El Chicó
2. Museo Mercedes Sierra de Pérez El Chicó
3. Museo Francisco de Paula Santander
4. Parque le Salitre
5. Museo de Los Niños
6. Parque Simón Bolívar
7. Museo de Arte Contemporáneo El Minuto de Dios
8. Museo de Arte de la Universidad Nacional
9. Museo de la Arquitectura Leopoldo Rother de la Universidad Nacional
10. Museo de Historia Natural de la Universidad Nacional
11. Jardín Botánico José Celestino Mutis
12. Parque de la Florida
13. Estadio Nemesio Camacho El Campín
14. Coliseo Cuvierto El Campín
15. Palacio de Los Desportes

started this museum in 1966, well before other contemporary art museums were opened in other parts of the world. Housed in an architecturally innovative building, the Museo de Arte Contemporáneo El Minuto de Dios, is outstanding; an absolute *must* for art lovers!

The **Museo de Arte de la Unversidad Nacional** ★★ *(Mon to Fri 8:30am to noon and 1pm to 5pm; at the corner of Carrera 30 and Calle 45, ☎368 12 75)* presents new artists and new directions in art. Open since the 1970s, it displays paintings, sculptures and engravings.

Devoted exclusively to architecture, the **Museo de la Arquitectura Leopoldo Rother de la Universidad Nacional** ★★ *(Mon to Fri 8am to noon and 1pm to 5pm; at the corner of Calle 26 and Carrera 30, ☎368 14 69)* is the only museum of its kind in South America. Since 1989 it has been a centre for research, conservation information about everything related to Colombian architecture. The museum is named after Leopoldo Rother, a German architect who lived in Colombia in 1936. The four exhibition halls display various architectural projects, among other items. The institution also has an auditorium and a screening room for videos about architecture. Of course, there is also a complete library.

The **Museo de Historia Natural de la Universidad Nacional** ★★ *(Mon to Sat 9am to noon and 2pm to 7pm; corner of Carrera 30 and Calle 53, ☎368 13 80)* dates from 1936 and presents the natural history of Bogotá through a very interesting palaeontology collection of mammals, fish and reptiles. There is also a room devoted to anthropology.

The **Jardín Botánico José Celestino Mútis** ★★★ *(1,000 pesos; Tue to Fri 8am to noon and 1:30 to 4pm, Sat and Sun 10am to 4pm; Carrera 66a No. 56-84, ☎240 04 83 or 240 61 41)* first opened in 1955 and is one of the country's most important centres for research on and conservation of Colombian flora, especially Andean flora. The botanical garden cultivates medicinal plants both in the greenhouse and outdoors in natural settings. Don't miss the Bosquet Andino and El Herbal, two of the most spectacular.

Parque de la Forida *(right next to the El Dorado airport)* contains green spaces, sports fields and an amusement park.

The **Estadio Nemesio Camacho El Campin** ★★★ *(corner of Av. Ciudad Quito and Calle 57)* and the Plaza de Bolívar are probably the two of the most popular places with *Bogotanos*. The local *fútbol* team plays its matches in this stadium, which seat 60,000 fans.

The **Coliseo Cuvierto El Campin** ★★ *(Av. Ciudad Quito, near Calle 57)* can accommodate 40,000 spectators at sports events like boxing matches and basketball games. Big performances like rock concerts are also put on here.

Palacio de Los Deportes ★★ *(corner of Calle 73 and Carrera 50)* is also a sports centre and hosts concerts by internationally known rock stars.

The East

Monasterio de Monserrate ★★★ *(Av. Circunvalar, ☎284 55 77 or 284 57 00)*, at the top of the 3,200-metre-high Mount Monserrate, is reached by a cable-car that has carried thousands and thousands of pilgrims to this enchanting place. The view alone is worth the trip.

Situated high above Bogotá, which lies right on the mountainside, Monserrate is a good vantage point from which to take in the city in all its grandeur. This view is especially striking at nightfall when the city lights up. If you plan on staying for dinner at the La Casa San Isidoro restaurant (see p 105), be sure to bring warm clothing. The temperature can drop below freezing.

The Capilla de Señor Caído de Monserrate was rebuilt after the earthquake of 1917. The original thatched-roof chapel dated from the early days of the colony and was constructed between 1652 and 1657. A small colonial village has been rebuilt around the chapel to house souvenir shops. The overall impression is of stepping into a long-ago era.

The cable-car *(4,600 pesos)* runs on Monday to Saturday from 9am to midnight, and on Sundays and holidays from 6am to 6pm. It is best to go on a weekday to avoid the throngs of tourists that come here on weekends. The total length of the cableway is 820 metres. The lower station is 2,692 metres above sea level, while the upper station is 460 metres higher, creating an 80.5 percent incline. It is possible

The Catedral Primada, with its two bell towers,
at the edge of the Plaza de Bolívar in Santafé de Bogotá.

La Candelaria, with its houses and balconies that are often decorated by artists, is one of the most picturesque neighbourhoods in Santafé de Bogotá.

Catedral de Sal

to make the climb on foot, but this can involve encounters with criminals, especially at night.

While it is an easy walk from downtown to the cable-car station, it involves going through dangerous neighbourhoods. It's much better to take a taxi or one of the buses marked "*Teleféico*".

Zipaquirá

The **Catedral de Sal** ★★★ *(7,000 pesos; every day 10am to 5pm; Via de Sal)* is truly wonderful! Miners contructed the first cathedral in the depths of the mine in 1954, under the leadership of architect José Maria Conzález Concha. It was closed for safety reasons due to the danger of flooding in 1992. The Instituto de Fomento Industrial, the Sociedad Colombiana de Arquitectos and the Corporación Nacional de Turismo joined forces to build another and hired Roswell Garavito Pearl as architect, with Jorge Enrique Castelblanco as technical director. Opened on December 16, 1995, it is a wonderful example of putting technical ingenuity to artistic purposes, using sculpture and the play of light and shadow to create allegory. Irrespective of one's feelings about religion, the majesty of this immense cathedral, built in a mine 200 metres below ground, is sufficient to inspire awe in even the most blasé observer. The 8,500-square-metre cathedral is divided into three sections: the stations of the cross, the cupola and the narthex topped by a jube, and the grand hall. To better convey the scope of this work, groups of 12 visitors are accompanied by student volunteer guides who explain everything in several languages. This service is free, but tipping the guide a minimum of 1,000 pesos per person is appropriate (the tour is worth at least twice that amount).

The Cathedral of Salt

The cathedral can accommodate up to 800 worshippers. Mass is celebrated every Sunday and on holidays. It is even used for weddings and christenings.

The Stations of the Cross, in one of the main galleries, consist of little chapels, each containing a statue carved from a column of salt that represents one of the 14 stations of the cross. They all use the symbol of the cross in allegorical fashion to portray the Passion of Christ. For example, in Christ's burial, the cross is placed inside an excavation shaped like a tomb. Subtle indirect lighting heightens the artistic effect of these works of art. The overall impression evokes the majesty and holiness of the divine mystery. The guide will suggest that you scrape the wall of the gallery with your fingernail and taste it, to prove that the medium is really salt.

The next gallery contains an immense cross, 16 metres high and 10 metres wide that can be seen from below at a distance of 150 metres away. From this perspective, the cross seems to be a gigantic block of pure white that is floating in the heavens. In actuality, the cross is a bas-relief carved out of an area of the wall that appears to be blue thanks to back lighting. The rest of the wall is jade black because of impurities in the unrefined salt. It seems miraculous.

The central gallery consists of the presbytery, the high altar and the grand nave with a marble sculpture of *The Creation of the World* by Carlos Enrique Rodríguez Arango, inspired by the scene from Michelangelo's Sistine Chapel. The *Zipaquireño* sculptor Miguel Sopó executed the statue representing the *Holy Family*, and the Italian Ludivico Consorti created the statue of the *Virgin*.

The nave is flanked by four immense columns, eight metres in diameter, that represent the four evangelists. There are also two enormous blocks of salt with an interstice between them that forms a narrow passageway. Allegorically, it symbolizes the difficulty of going through life, from birth to death.

The **Palacio Municipal** ★★ *(downtown)* is an imposing French-style building with certain Gothic elements. Its baroque-style municipal council chambers have paintings of Simón Bolívar and other historical figures by the local artist Federico Rogrígues Mendoza.

The **Museo Quevedo Zornoza** ★★ is in a 17th-century building that contains souvenirs of several generations of the Quevedos, a family of musicians and artists. There are also costumes and objects dating from the 18th and 19th centuries.

Guatavita

To go to the Laguna de Guatavita, take the scenic route, Carretera Central de Norte, towards Sesquilé. At an intersection a few kilometres from the village, the road leads off towards the mountains and the *laguna*. Since this road is unpaved for more than 15 kilometres, it is best to avoid it if there has been rain, or else rent a four-wheel drive vehicle.

The **Laguna de Guatavita** ★★★ is disturbing. Here, at an altitude of more than 3,200 metres, the legend of Guatavita was born. According to the legend, the cacique of the *Muisca* rode a gold-dust-covered raft into the middle of the lake and tossed emeralds and golden objects into the depths to appease the demon (see p 22). It was mainly the hunt for this fabulous treasure that motivated the conquista-

dors to penetrate the interior of the country despite its inhospitable climate and populations. When they finally arrived at the lagoon, the sight was unbelievable. The Laguna de Guatavita is a small, circular lake less than one kilometre across that appears suddenly, after a long climb. Its still waters are a deep and mysterious green and lie at the bottom of a volcanic crater. Not a single ripple disturbs the surface. It looks like a gigantic emerald among the peaks of the Andes, like a jewel in the setting of a ring.

The Spanish believed it. Seeing this sacred *Muisca* place, they were convinced that the green colour of the surface was reflected from a thick layer of gold and emeralds at the bottom. Over and over, they tried to extract this treasure, even going so far as to drain the lake. This onerous task fell to the Amerindians. Enslaved for the purpose of digging a shaft through the mountainside, many of them died. The rift that was excavated to drain the lake is currently used to make the climb easier for tourists. The government protects the lake now; there will never be another excavation attempt. The place is fascinating by reason of its legend and its history. This is a unique excursion in nature and in time: a pilgrimage into the supernatural mysteries of the Andean Cordillera.

 ACCOMMODATIONS

Santafé de Bogotá

Note: All first-class hotels in Bogotá will provide free taxi service to and from the airport upon request.

Downtown and La Candelaria

From a tourist's point of view, the downtown area and La Candelaria are the most interesting districts of the city. Since they are adjacent, it is easy to explore both on foot and find hotels in every price range.

Hotel **Santa Fé** *($; pb, hw, ℜ; Calle 14 No. 4-48, ☎342 05 60 or 342 05 63, ⊨342 18 79)*, just at the threshold of La Candelaria, is a charming inexpensive older hotel that is sure to please travellers on a small budget. The rooms are simply furnished but spacious, clean and airy, and the hotel provides

Laguna de Guatavita

The Laguna de Guatavita certainly started the conquest of Colombia, and probably that of the South American continent as a whole. The conquistadors heard about El Dorado as soon as they landed, and immediately began a relentless search for the famous lake and its treasure alluded to in the legend. For over a century, hundreds of expeditions covered large areas of South America – the legend of El Dorado is known as far away as Quito, Ecuador, more than 700 kilometres from Bogotá – invading territories infested with jaguars, alligators and serpents, and braving hunger, disease and cannibals. At last, in 1580, a smooth surface of an emerald-coloured lake in the bottom of a crater was identified as the Laguna de Guatavita. Since not a particle of gold was found on the edges of the lake, the Spanish, under the command of Antoniode Sepúlveda, forced the Amerindians to make a breech in the mountain to drain the crater. Even by modern standards, the difficulty of the task was overwhelming. The Spanish would never have embarked on it without the availability of slave labour extracted from the Amerindians at gunpoint.

The sources of the lake had to be rerouted before an opening was dug through the mountain-side to drain the lake. The work was done practically barehanded by Amerindians unused to forced labour, and many died as a result. The opening allowed them to partially drain the lake. The Spanish found gold and even emeralds, but their satisfaction was short-lived. A landslide brought the project to a halt. The opening is still visible, and is used to get to the lake.

Around 1625, miners again got permission from the King of Spain to drain the lake. They dug tunnels and carved out galleries in the shore, and found gold at every step of the way. However, the amounts found were a disappointment to the investors. Later, in 1801, Baron Alexander von Humboldt, a German traveller and naturalist, resumed the excavations and found a series of steps carved out of the rock. His research into the legend of El Dorado led him to believe that the steps were used during the ritual inauguration of the cacique. In 1823, the Colombian José Ignacio París began new excavations, but abandoned the project after his tunnel under the lake collapsed.

The search for gold was refocused on Laguna Seicha, a smaller lake nearby. In 1856 a canal was dug to partially drained it. Gold objects were found, including the figure of a man standing on a raft who was throwing pieces of gold into the water: *La Balsa Muisca*. This work is on display at Museo del Oro de Bogotá (see p 92). In 1870, new excavations were started, but the deaths of two men who were tunneling ended the enterprise.

In 1904, a British firm, Contractors Limited, succeeded in draining the lake completely. All sorts of gold jewellery was discovered, including necklaces and nose ornaments. These articles were auctioned in London to reimburse the sponsors. After many setbacks, including a flood that filled the lake just after it had been completely drained, the company gave up. For the next fifty years, thousands of treasure hunters attempted to excavate gold from the lagoon, until the Colombian government proclaimed it a national monument and put a halt to its desecration in 1965.

a safe environment. Travellers are warmly received and the atmosphere is friendly. However it is necessary to specify shower times to ensure the supply of hot water. Also, there is no central heating and some guests may find the rooms a bit chilly.

The **Dann Colonial** *($$; pb, hw, heating, mb, ☎, tv, ▨, ℛ, P; Calle 14 No. 4-21, ☎341 16 18, ⊶344 99 92)* hotel is situated across from the Santa Fé hotel at the gateway to La Candelaria. This is one of the best bar-gains in Bogotá. The hundred or so spacious rooms in this seven-storey hotel compare very favourably to those of any hotel in this category. They are furnished in unpretentious good taste and have everything a traveller could desire: cleanliness, comfort and tranquillity. For less than 35,000 pesos for single occupancy and 50,000 pesos for double occupancy, Dann Colonial is the perfect choice. The lobby is welcoming and elegantly decorated. The reception is highly professional and worthy of a large hotel chain (the place is part of the Colombian

Dann Hoteles group, which includes hotels in Cali and Baranquilla). The restaurant serves Creole and international cuisine.

L'Hostelería La Candelaria *($$; pb, hw, mb, auxillary heating, ℜ; Calle 9 No. 3-11, ☎342 17 27 or 286 14 79, ⌐282 34 20)* is a colonial-style hotel comprised of two former private residences: one with the rooms around three courtyards planted with trees and flowers, and another housing the reception area and restaurant. The two are separated by a bolted door that must be opened by the personnel. Despite the atmosphere of old world charm, the rooms and suites leave much to be desired in terms of comfort and are in need of renovation. The service at the reception is superficial, inept and above all pretentious. Given these conditions, 49,000 pesos per night might seem like highway robbery. But no, that's just business ...*estilo bogotano*, business Bogotá style!

Adjacent to the Niagara Hotel, the **Inter Bogotá** *($$; pb, hw, heating, ☎, tv, ▣, ℜ, △, ⊘; Carrera 3 No. 20-7, ☎/⌐344 67 12)* is quite decent and caters to guests with limited budgets. The atmosphere is friendly, simple and welcoming. For 50,000 pesos, rooms with sauna are available. Space is slightly more restricted because of the sauna, but on the whole it's a bargain.

The **Niagara** *($$; pb, hw, heating, ☎, tv, ▣, ℜ, Turkish bath; Carrera 3 No. 20-35, ☎294 23 00, ⌐342 76 02)* is just a short distance from the city centre. This is also a great place for those with restricted budgets. For 35,000 pesos, this 30-room establishment provides small but clean and quiet accommodations. For 6,000 pesos more, a Turkish bath is available, and it is offered without charge after a three-day stay. Service is friendly and attentive.

Casa Medina *($$$$$; pb, hw, ⊛, mb, ☎, tv, ▣, heating, ℜ, ⊘, △, ⊛, interior P; Carrera 7 No. 69a-22, ☎217 02 88 or 212 66 57, ⌐312 37 69)* is situated in the new financial and commercial centre of Bogotá and is part of the hotel chain Relais et Chateaux. The Casa Medina is a restored historic monument and has 21 rooms and 37 suites, all of which are comfortable and luxurious. Don Santiago Medina, who constructed this building in 1945, succeeded in blending Spanish and French architectural design to create a new and unique style using ceramic tiles and stone pillars from a Spanish convent in Santo Domingo. Handcrafted wooden doors as well as wrought iron balconies, balustrades and gratings are among

the building's spectacular features. Renovated in April 1988, the building was transformed into an exclusive hotel for the well-to-do, with its antique charm intact. The restaurant is classically furnished and offers prestigious international cuisine in a gracious and subdued atmosphere.

Hotel Tequendama Inter-Continental *($$$$$; pb, hw, =, mb, ☎, tv, ▣, heating, ℜ, ⊘, ⊛, △, interior P; Carrera 10a No. 26-21, ☎286 11 11; toll free from US ☎800 332-4246, ⌐282 28 60, bogha@interconti.com)* is renowned as one of the best hotels in all of South America. Its central location, adjacent to the Centro de Convenciones, affords a panoramic view of the Andes from the downtown area. The rooms are of superior quality, and while the enormous lobby is somewhat impersonal, it provides many conveniences: gift shops, sports shops, a jewellery store, a hairdresser, and even a casino. There are travel agencies, car rentals and a multilingual customer relations service to help with any difficulties a first-time visitor to Bogotá might encounter. The hotel houses a number of bars and restaurants: the Salon Monserrate (known as "Bogotá's balcony" because of its magnificent view of the city), the El Virrey restaurant, the Cafe Vienes, La Cascade (an Italian restaurant), the Chispas (an English pub) and the Lobby Bar, great for business meetings.

La Zona Rosa–El Chicó

The El Chicó district extends from Calle 87 to Calle 100, between Carrera 7 and Avenida Caracas, and is one of Bogotá's most upscale neighbourhoods. Here, luxurious residences border on shady parks. The centre of El chicó, Zona Rosa, a particularly interesting area. It is one of the liveliest spots in Bogotá with all essential and luxury services grouped together along tree-lined boulevards: restaurants, cinemas, art galleries, banks, fashionable boutiques, commercial centres, terraces, bars and nightclubs. All the hotels are first-class (except for the Mediteraneo, see below). However, the Zona Rosa is not recommended for travellers on a small or medium budget.

Hotel Mediteraneo *($$; pb, hw, mb, ☎, tv; Carrera 11 No. 79-43, ☎236 66 30, 218 16 06 or 249 90 55, ⌐218 17 89)* is situated east of the Zona Rosa. It is one of the few inexpensive hotels in this district. The price is probably its best feature, but the atmosphere is friendly enough.

◇ **RESTAURANTS**

1.	Bakara	7.	Lenos	13.	Ricoras Marinas
2.	Bilboquet	8.	Luna	14.	Sandwich Shop
3.	Churrasco's	9.	Na Zdarovia	15.	Tony Roma's
4.	Di Lugga Café Bar Restaurant	10.	Niko Café	16.	Trattoria Bellini
5.	Gran China	11.	Petit Bistro	17.	Victoria Regia
6.	Harry's Cantina	12.	Piazza Luna	18.	Welcome

○ **ACCOMMODATIONS**

1.	Andino Royal	4.	Hamilton Court	7.	Morisson
2.	Charleston	5.	La Bohème l'Européen Royal	8.	Saint Simon
3.	Charlotte	6.	Mediteraneo	9.	Victoria Regia

Hotel **Charlotte** *($$$$; pb, hw, mb, ☎, tv, ▧, ℛ, guarded outside parking; Carrera 15 No. 87-94, ☎218 16 25, 218 16 06, 218 17 84, or 218 17 62, ⤶218 17 89)* is on the outskirts of the Zona Rosa. The Charlotte has about 50 rooms on six floors. Two floors have small balconies facing the park, the Plaza de las Flores, where there is a small flower market and is large enough to do some jogging. One of the staff speaks English well enough to inform and orient visitors. The restaurant menu features continental cuisine.

The **Saint Simon** *($$$$; pb, hw, mb, ☎, tv, ▧, ℛ, guarded outside parking; Carrera 14 No. 81-34, ☎621 81 88, ⤶618 52 79)* has 46 rooms on 7 floors without air-conditioning. The rooms

are clean and some have kitchenettes. The hotel is quiet and offers a good quality to price ratio.

Andino Royal *($$$$$; pb, hw, ≡, mb, ☎, tv, ▧, heating, ℛ, ⊘, ⊛, △, P; Calle 85 No. 12-28, ☎635 11 05 or 635 07 66, ⤶218 64 95, www.colomsat.net.co/hotel/hs.royal)* is an elegant hotel with a spectacular façade featuring French doors and a grandiose stained-glass window above the entrance. Seventy rooms and suites are tastefully furnished. The service is impeccable and the restaurant specializes in Italian cuisine.

La Bohème l'Européen Royale *($$$$$; pb, hw, ≡, mb, ☎, tv, ▧, heating, ℛ, ⊘, △, P; Calle 82*

No. 12-35, ☎617 11 77, toll free ☎800 379 96 36, ⌐618 00 03, hboemer@cdomsat.net.co.) is another small, first-class hotel with a European flavour. It has 66 rooms, a restaurant with terrace that serves continental cuisine and a quiet bar perfect for cocktails. The lobby is charming and the staff is fluent in English.

The **Charleston** *($$$$$; pb, hw, ≈, mb, ☎, tv, ◙, heating, ℛ, ⊘, ⊛, △, interior P; Carrera 13 No. 85-46, ☎257 11 00, ⌐236 79 81)* hotel is located next to the Victoria Regia (see further below). A member of the Relais et Châteaux chain, it offers 65 comfortable and luxurious rooms in a three-towered neoclassical building. This hotel caters to a well-to-do clientele, and the atmosphere is reserved.

Hamilton Court *($$$$$; pb, hw, ≈, mb, ☎, tv, heating, ℛ, ◙; Carrera 14 No. 81-20, ☎621 54 55 or 622 04 04, ⌐218 88 90)*, part of the Forte Travelodge chain, offers 41 expensive classy rooms. Quality accommodations and service are expected from this chain, and travellers will not be disappointed.

The **Morisson** *($$$$$; pb, hw, ≈, mb, ☎, tv, ◙, heating, ℛ, ⊘, ⊛, interior P; Calle 84 No. 13-54, ☎622 31 11, ⌐622 43 88, morisson@impsat.net.co.)* hotel offers 35 rooms and 5 suites, two of which are deluxe with fireplaces. Facing the park León de Greiff, the Morisson has a friendly atmosphere. Half the rooms look out onto the park and have a wonderful view of the charming square. The Centro Comercial Andino is only a few steps away, and quality cinemas and restaurants are nearby.

The **Victoria Regia** *($$$$$; pb, hw, ≈, mb, ☎, tv, ◙, heating, ≈, ℛ, ⊘, △, interior P; Carrera 13 No.85-80, ☎621 26 66, toll-free from the United States ☎800-221-4542 or 914-472-0370, from France ☎01 60 77 27 27, ⌐610 35 16, hvictori@Colomsat.net.co)* is in one of the loveliest neighbourhoods in Bogotá and belongs to the Sofitel chain. This recent construction is an example of sophisticated architecture and mellow English charm. The lobby is remarkable for the varnished wooden staircase that leads to the lounges and sitting rooms. The hotel is near the best shops, art galleries, cinemas, bars and restaurants, and is 20 minutes from the financial district of Bogotá and the World Trade Center. The Victoria Regia is named after Queen Victoria, as is the largest red and white water lily (nymphaea odorata) in the Amazon. There are 94 rooms and 5 suites

offering gracious European service and North American efficiency. All personnel at the front desk are fluent in English and Spanish. The rooms are large, comfortable, tastefully furnished and include desks to accommodate business travellers and tourists who need space to organize their itineraries. There is an excellent restaurant (see p 104), and the Salon Victoria, to the left of the lobby, serves an English-style tea from four to seven, Monday through Friday. The pastries, *petit fours*, and other confections are reputed to be the best in Bogotá. An office complete with desks, computers connected to the Internet, telephones and fax machines is available for business people.

Zipaquirá

Hospederia El Libertador *($$; pb, hw, heating, ☎, tv, ◙, mb, ℛ; via Mina de Sal, ☎852 30 60, 852 68 46, 852 68 48, or 852 68 50, ⌐852 68 51)* is a small neo-colonial hotel nestled in the mountains beside the mine that contains the Cathedral of Salt. With its magnificent view of the city of Zipaquirá and the surrounding countryside and 11 spacious rooms around a courtyard, this hotel is the best-kept secret in Bogotá. The impressive restaurant surrounded by windows, the bar with a cozy fireplace, the warm welcome and reasonable rates *(48,000 pesos per night, double occupancy)* make this a bargain not to pass off.

 RESTAURANTS

Santafé de Bogotá

There are expensive restaurants in all the large hotels in Bogotá, but there is a lack of medium-priced restaurants in the downtown area. There are many fast food outlets such as pizzerias, barbecues, etc. as well as the large fast food chains. However, here are some restaurants that are out of the ordinary, and unique in their own fashion.

Downtown and La Candelaria

Café L'Avenir *($-$$; Mon to Fri 10am to 9pm, Sat noon to 6pm, closed Sun; Calle 11 No. 2-98, ☎284 79 73)* is a small restaurant with only four or five tables, where it is possible to eat well and inexpensively. The atmosphere is bohemian but unpretentious. Artists and students meet here and the thirty-something owner greets and serves the customers. In warm weather the chairs are brought out to the sidewalk to create a terrace. High quality imported products such as virgin olive oil, coffees and homemade marmalade are for sale. With its warm and friendly service, this is an ideal place for cocktails before dinner.

Café de Rosita *($-$$; every day 10am to 8pm; Calle 9 No. 3-11, ☎342 17 27 or 286 14 79)*, the restaurant of the Hosteria La Candelaria (see p 100), has a good but limited menu. The glass-roofed restaurant is located in a courtyard. An exclusive clientele often attends intimate concerts here. Adjoining salons decorated in an old-fashioned style are available for private receptions.

Salma is the Lebanese hostess of the Italian **Pepperoncino Café Bar Restaurant** *($-$$$; Mon to Sat, noon to 4am; Calle 10 No. 3-87, ☎342 27 46)*. To visit this well-known Bogotá establishment, it is preferable to make reservations. An exclusive restaurant, located in a colonial house with a balcony overlooking the courtyard, it reflects the personality of its owner. The atmosphere is unique, and regular customers are sometimes tempted to keep on partying after closing time. "We must keep this secret to ourselves," says Salma. We will!

As the name suggests, **China Town** *($$-$$$; every day, noon to 11pm; Carrera 14 No. 18-58, ☎256 45 95 or 236 62 10, ⬛616 62 45)* is a Chinese restaurant. It provides a welcome change from the usual daily menu.

More than a pizzeria, **El Pozetto** *($$-$$$; every day 11:30am to noon; Carrera 7a No. 61-24 ☎235 84 97, 255 35 84, 255 11 60 or 345 21 17)* boasts a complete Italian menu of pasta, fish, seafood and meat dishes prepared for an exclusive clientele of business people who meet here for lunch. The service is efficient and, if necessary, rapid. The daily menu consists of a variety of dishes including an excellent seafood risotto. The decor is Italian, but simple rather than ornate.

La Zona Rosa–El Chicó

As has already been mentioned, international cuisine is well represented in Colombiá, particularly in Bogotá and most particularly in the Zona Rosa. Choice is limited only by one's budget.

For rapid counter service at any hour of the day or night, the **Sandwich Shop** *($; every day, 24 hours; Calle 82 No. 15-24)* is the place for good sandwiches and coffee. The bread is excellent, a rare thing in Colombia.

Ricoras Marinas *($-$$; every day 10am to 10pm; Carrera 15 No. 83-37, ☎256 50 26 or 530 09 63)* is a small restaurant with a dozen or so wooden tables and benches. From a half-dozen oysters to shrimp served on a bed of rice, seafood casserole or fish soup, everything is good and reasonably priced and can be eaten on the fly. Presentation and service are unpretentious and satisfactory.

In the same category, **Lenos** *($-$$; every day 10am to 11pm; Calle 85 No.13-20, ☎218 02 32 or 218 21 03)* serves roast chicken, but steaks are also on the menu. The wooden furniture is rough-hewn and varnished and the walls are made of brick and stone. The atmosphere is one of simplicity. The terrace on the second floor overlooking the street is very busy from 4pm to 7pm.

Piazza Luna *($-$$$; every day noon to 10pm; Calle 83 No. 12-20, ☎257 20 88)* is the terrace of the Luna Restaurant (see p 104). The menu for both is the same but the terrace is also a sort of country market selling products for Italian cuisine. There are culinary specialties to take out as well as a good variety of fresh pasta, cheese and vegetables. An excellent choice of Italian, Chilean and Spanish wines is also available.

Di Lugga Café Bar Restaurant *($$-$$$; every day 11:30am to 1am; Carrera 13 No. 85-32, ☎611 56 14 or 611 56 65)* is an Italian restaurant serving a much sought-after cuisine. The clientele is exclusive and the atmosphere mellow and subdued. The terrace opens onto the quiet *carrera* and offers more of a *trattoria* menu, with items like pizza.

Bakara *($$-$$$; Tue-Sun noon to 1am; Calle 82 No.12-09, ☎18 80 38 or 239 59 26)* serves Mediterranean and Arab cuisine in the dining room and on the terrace. The European-style service is amiable and customers can relax or read at ease. The dining room and terrace are separated by glass doors and seem to blend together. A small bar in the dining room that seats about ten people creates a bistro atmosphere.

SANTAFÉ DE BOGOTÁ

Harry's Cantina *($$-$$$; every day noon to 1am; Calle 83 No. 12-84,* ☎*616 87 94 or 616 81 74)* has an American-style dining room and terrace where you can have a sandwich or a complete Tex-Mex meal. The furniture and interiors are of polished wood, adorned with lovely tapestries and wall hangings in predominantly green and red hues.

Niko Café *($$-$$$; every day noon to midnight; Carrera 13 No. 83-48,* ☎*610 81 02 or 610 65 53)* offers Mediterranean cuisine in a sophisticated atmosphere. There are two menus: a daily menu served from 7pm for about 10,000 pesos, and the dinner menu at 15,000 pesos or more. The dining room is not very large and the atmosphere is warm and pleasant. The decor is modern and brings to mind certain small, trendy New York eateries. Service is efficient.

Petit Bistro *($$-$$$; every day, noon to 1am; Calle 76 No. 10-28,* ☎*249 40 58)* offers French bistro-style cuisine in a relaxed atmosphere.

Trattoria Bellini *($$-$$$; Mon-Sat noon to midnight; Carrera 13 No. 83-52,* ☎*288 85 60, 288 87 50 or 236 44 01)* is another highly recommended Italian restaurant, serving fine cuisine despite the appellation *trattoria,* which usually describes an ordinary everyday menu. The dining room is tastefully decorated in modern, fashionable style with plexiglas and flowers that suggests creative cuisine. An excellent choice of Italian wines is available.

Welcome *($$-$$$; every day, noon to 3pm and 7pm to 11pm; Carrera 14 No. 80-65, second floor,* ☎*256 47 90)*. This small, intimate restaurant with a Japanese-style decor offers a long sushi bar and excellent service by Spanish-speaking Japanese.

Bilboquet *($$-$$$$; every day midnight to noon; Calle 83 No. 12-19,* ☎*610 52 10)* is a fashionable French restaurant whose reputation has already been established by French residents of Bogotá. Its wine list is especially appreciated.

Churrasco's *($$-$$$$; every day noon to noon; Calle 81 No. 10-50,* ☎*236 522 46)* specializes in meat, fish and seafood prepared on the grill. The decor, presumably Argentinean, features a somewhat somber, heavy style with armchairs and tables in sculpted wood.

Gran China *($$-$$$$; every day 11:30am to midnight; Calle 77-a No.11-70,* ☎*249 59 38 or 211 48 07,* ⌐*312 87 12)*. Open since 1982, this restaurant can pride itself on critical gastronomic success. Situated in the embassy district of Bogotá, the Gran China will not disappoint lovers of oriental cuisine. The menu is extensive and the dining area consists of small rooms, providing an intimate charm.

Luna *($$-$$$$; every day noon to 3pm and 6pm to 11pm; Calle 83 No. 12-26,* ☎*257 20 88)* is an unforgettable Italian restaurant located in an enormous white building with one wall made entirely of glass. The clientele is upscale. The bar at the entrance is an inviting place for cocktails; the two-tiered dining room serves excellent food and the service is attentive. Pasta and pizza are popular, while specialties such as fish fillets with black pepper and seafood linguini are featured on the menu.

Na Zdarovia *($$-$$$$; every day noon to 3pm and 7:30pm to midnight; Carrera 14 No.80-71,* ☎*218 50 72)* is a Russian restaurant that serves different kinds of vodka. On the menu are appetizers of caviar mousse, smoked herring or herring marinated in wine or mustard, and beef Stroganoff, lamb *flambé,* Azerbaidjan duck or shrimp with caviar and champagne sauce as a main course. The staff, however, seemed to pay more attention to the regular clientele and their friends than to tourists, which there were very few of, for that matter.

Tony Roma's *($$-$$$$; every day noon to midnight; Calle 86a No. 13a-10,* ☎*611 31 76 or 256 66 38)* has an interesting lighting system. The dining room here is bathed in light which creates a unique atmosphere. Grilled meat and fish are the specialties, and the service is pleasant.

The restaurant at the hotel **Victoria Regia** *($$$$$; every day 7am to 10pm; Carrera 13 No. 85-80,* ☎*621 26 66)* (see p 102) offers top-notch four-course meals artfully prepared and presented by French chef, Dominique Asselin. Once a month, the chef invites customers to enjoy *The Wine-Maker Dinner,* a gastronomic menu accompanied by the monthly selection of fine wines. For this occasion, a professional wine taster visits each table to explain the subtle ways the wines complement each course.

Other Restaurants

Here are a few more restaurants, which are off the beaten track and interesting for their specialized cuisine.

As the name suggests, the menu at the **Chalet Suizo** *($$-$$$$; Mon to Fri noon to 11pm, Sat and Sun 1pm to 10pm; Av. 22 No. 30a-48, ☎245 61 15)* highlights Swiss specialties, including fondues. Everything is prepared and served under the owner's attentive supervision.

The **Samurai-ya** *($$-$$$$; Mon to Sat noon to 3pm and 6pm to 10pm; Carrera 8a No. 124-22, ☎213 54 40)* serves traditional Japanese food: tempura, sushi, sashimi, sukiyaki and more.

Kyoto Oriental *($$-$$$$; every day 11am to 10pm; Carrera 11 No. 97-32, ☎257 27 28)* is another Japanese restaurant featuring sushi, sashimi and teppanyaki.

Casa San Isidoro *($$$$$; every day 11:30am to midnight; atop mount Monserrate)* is a superb French restaurant spectacularly located at an altitude of 3,200 metres. Food and service are also of a"high" quality. Choose a table near the bay windows for a unique view of the city of Bogotá. At night, a pianist enhances the French atmosphere with some Charles Aznavour tunes.

Zipaquirá

With its population of 85,000, the small city of Zipaquirá is a busy place, which explains why there are so many interesting restaurants here.

Begoña *($-$$; every day 7am to 8pm; Calle 1a, No. 7-50, ☎852 39 32)* is a good-sized establishment serving a variety of local dishes in a warm, relaxed atmosphere. Tables are tastefully decorated with flowers and prices are reasonable, considering quality and service.

Funzipa *($$-$$$$; every day 7am to midnight; Calle 1 between Carreras 9 and 10, ☎852 22 63)* is a large restaurant that serves typical Colombian cuisine in a gracious setting. Local musicians perform here on weekends. Fresh trout is as popular as the specialties described in the section on regional cuisine (see p 79).

ENTERTAINMENT

Santafé de Bogotá

Santafé de Bogotá is well-known for its nightlife, and the nightclubs buzz with activity starting at 11pm. Many bars and hotels have a *feliz hora*, or happy hour, when drinks are sold two for the price of one. Ask around. No one will raise an eyebrow; in fact you will be considered to be a smart traveller: someone in tune with the local customs.

Downtown and La Candelaria

In the downtown area, customers must prove they are not planning to make trouble and go through a metal detector before entering a nightclub. However, you will not be permitted to leave before showing a receipt for your bar bill. Since the downtown district is not safe to venture into at night except by taxi, it is better to head to the Zona Rosa for a night on the town.

Zona Rosa–El Chico

In the Zona Rosa, Calle 82, between Carrera 13 and 11, is lined with the terraces of bars and cafés that share the same lively, young customers. The following bars have similar atmospheres: customers roam from one to the next, listening to loud rock, *vallenato* and even (Yippee!) country music. Drinks are expensive and local beer can cost as much as 2,800 pesos. Many imported beers are available from Europe and elsewhere, including Corona from Mexico, served with a zest of lime.

Admiral Rosa Club, No.12-76
Bar Restaurant Almirante, No. 12-21
Charlies' Roast Beef, No.12-22
Tienda Aguapanela's, No. 12-32, has typical Colombian music from the Caldas region.
Restaurant Bar Burbon Street, No. 12-36
Bar Kaoba, No. 12-44

The terrace of the **Bakara** *(Tue to Sun noon to 1am; Calle 82 No. 12-09, ☎18 80 38 or 239 59 26)* restaurant caters to the thirty-something crowd. The atmosphere is quieter.

Ideal for an aperitif. Beer prices start at 2,500 pesos.

Harry's Cantina *(every day from 10pm; Calle 83 No. 12-84, ☎616 87 94 or 616 81 74)* is a restaurant during the day that turns into a disco every night from 10pm until the wee hours of the morning. Lots of atmosphere!

The **Viejoteca** *(Fri and Sat 10pm to 5am; Carrera 15 No.80-63, ☎218 40 33)* restaurant is a dance club on weekend nights, with a nostalgic ambiance. Local music from the sixties, seventies and (occasionally) the eighties is played. Songs by Los Graduados, Los Hispanos, La Sonara, Fruko and La Billo's are on the DJ list. Prices are reasonable.

Cultural Events

Social and cultural events in Cundinamarca are too numerous for a complete listing, but here are a few that take place in Bogotá itself:

Temporada Tourina: bullfights in January;

Festival Latino-americano de teatro: a drama festival in March;

Feria de Libro: a book fair in May;

Feria Internacional de Bogotá: a fair, every two years, in July;

Salón de Agosto: computer and electronics show in August.

Casinos

Colombians are inveterate gamblers, and casinos and pool halls are found everywhere. Here are a few of the many casinos in Bogotá.

Casino Versailles *(Mon to Sat 2pm to 3am, Sun 7pm to midnight; Carrera 10a No. 26-21, in theTequendama Inter-Continental hotel)*;
Casino Excelsior *(Mon to Sat 9:30am to 1am; Carrera 7 No. 13-73, ☎243 05 91)*;
Casino Caribe *(every day 10:30am to 1am; Carrera 7 No. 21-70, ☎342 99 88)*.

SHOPPING

Santafé de Bogotá

A cosmopolitan city with a worldly flair, Bogotá is an ideal place for shopping. There are a great variety of locally crafted quality products, especially gold, silver and emerald jewellery. Art objects and handicrafts, leather goods, textiles, made-to-order clothing, antiques, musical and manufactured items, as well as a full range of imported goods are readily available. However, bear in mind that prices here are similar to those North America. Don't buy impulsively and perhaps pay a higher price for an item than it would cost in its country of origin. On the other hand, locally made clothing and handcrafted goods are bargains. It would be a shame to pass them up.

For an unforgettable gift, this is the place to purchase articles made of solid silver. They are an excellent value for the money.

It is not a good idea to buy emeralds on the street, unless you know enough to discuss cleavage (splitting along definite planes), fissure (splitting along indefinite planes) or preferential planes (foreseeable splits). Also, you must be able to conduct density tests (potential for being scored by another object) and tests for solubility in hydrochloric acid diluted to 10 percent – not exactly easy to perform on the street! It is obvious that these street dealers are out to rip off tourists. It is better to buy from reputable jewellers who can guarantee the value of your purchase, even though it may not be a real bargain. Remember that the cost of living is high in Colombia.

Bogotanos do not walk about much, probably for safety reasons. Shopping centres provide everything a shopper needs in a concentrated area.

Downtown and La Candelaria

Handcrafted Items

The downtown area is filled with boutiques, and in the evenings many streets are transformed into marketplaces. The many handicraft displays are hard to resist. However, for a greater selection, visit the museum store at the

Museo de Artes y Tradiciones Populares *(Mon to Sat 9am to 5pm, Sun 9am to 1pm; Carrera 8 No. 7-21, ☎284 53 19)*, the headquarters of the Colombian association for the promotion of handicrafts. It has an array of pieces made from wood and ceramics, and textiles made of agave fibres, cotton or wool yarns from all regions of the country.

Artesanías de Colombia *(Mon to Fri 9am to 6pm, Sat 9am to 2pm; Carrera 3 No.118-60, ☎284 32 00)* sells a beautiful collection of arts and crafts inside a cloister, surroundings that really suit them.

Recoleta San Diego *(Mon to Sat 10am to 7pm; Carrera 10a No.26-50, ☎242 32 00)* is another arts and crafts shop with many exquisite pieces. Here, part of the proceeds from sales is reinvested in programs that aid crafts workers, which is a good reason to shop here.

Jewellery

Platería Hector Pena *(Carrera 11a No. 94-45, ☎218 30 03 or 610 41 37)*.

Orfebrería Florentina *(Carrera 15 No. 88-26, ☎256 53 30 or 257 32 24)*.

Photo Developers

Revelado une Demi Hora *(Carrera 7a No.14-12, ☎241 47 42)*.

Shopping Centres

Alhambra, Calle 114a, No. 33-54
Calle Real, Carrera 7, No. 11-72
Terraza Pasteur, Carrera 7, No.23-56

La Zona Rosa–El Chicó

La Zona Rosa is a shopper's paradise with countless stores offering imported goods. But before revamping your entire wardrobe, remember that window-shopping is fun, too, and can save a lot of money! A good place to start strolling is the area of Calles 82 to 85, between Carreras 11 and 15, which contains just about everything the district has to offer. There are jewellers, fashion boutiques, antique shops, record stores, shops selling tableware and other items for home decoration, florists and much more.

Jewellery

Akel Joyeros *(Carrera 15 No. 88-83, ☎236 62 18)*.

Aurigema Internacional *(Carrera 15 No. 78-77, room 156, ☎218 56 31)*.

Gold & Emeralds *(Carrera 15 No. 86a-84, room 1203, ☎218 11 15)*

Greenfire *(Carrera 9 No. 74-08, ☎211 46 21 or 212 03 07)*.

Willis F. Bronkie S.A. *(Carrera 9 No. 74-08, Profinanzas Building, door 207, ☎211 46 21 or 211 10 19)*.

Art and Antiques Galleries

Galería El Museo *(Mon to Fri 10am to 1pm and 3pm to 6pm, Sat 11am to 5pm, closed Sun; Calle 84 No. 13-17, ☎256 69 27 or 256 68 69, ≈256 67 67)* is a private gallery on five floors with 2,000 square metres that can house three or four large exibits simutaneously. Set up in 1971 to present the private collection of Señor Byron López, the gallery has, from its inception, supported young talent such as Fernando Botero, Alejandro Obregón, David Mansur and others of the time. Today, the gallery continues in the same vein by exhibiting the works of promising young artists, as well as those who are now internationally acclaimed, like Botero. The gallery has a permanent collection and presents new exhibits every month. During the time of our visit, the fifth floor displayed a hundred or so women's shoes, arranged with special lighting, and signed Juan Carlos Degado!

At the gallery's entrance there is a shop that sells authentic pre-Columbian art objects and local handicrafts.

Alonso Arte *(Mon to Fri 8:30am to 1pm and 2:30pm to 5:30pm, Sat 10am to 1pm and 2:30pm to 5:30pm, closed Sun; Calle 85, No. 11-53, room 2, ☎618 00 72 or 618 03 86, ≈236 35 19)* is another private gallery owned by Señor Alonso Restrepo, an expert in pre-Columbian art who is a consultant at the Museo Casa del Marqueés de San Jorge. The gallery presents the works of famous Colombian and international painters, and has regular expositions on three floors. When we were there, the gallery was getting ready for a show by the Canadian painter John Fraser. The

SANTAFÉ DE BOGOTÁ

gallery shop sells authentic pre-Columbian art objects.

Bookstores

Oma Libros *(Sun to Wed 12 pm to 8pm, Thu to Sat 11am to 9pm; Calle 15 No. 82-58, ☎256 56 21 or 256 00 59)* bookstore has a great variety of books, and local and international newpapers and journals. It also sells compact disks and laser videos. This bookstore is special in that it has a cafe with a terrace next to it where you can have a coffee and read the paper, or eat a meal while chatting with friends. The **Oma Libros** chain has an another outlet at Avenida 19, No. 118-78 *(☎213 70 83 or 612 91 86)*.

As its name suggests, **Librairie Française** *(Mon to Sat 8am to 12:30pm and 2pm to 6pm; Calle 86a No. 13a-44)* sells books in languages other than Spanish, mainly in French and English.

The Golden Book *(every day 9am to 6pm; Calle 85 No. 12-04, ☎257 91 92 or 257 55 10, ⌐218 35 53; also Av. 19 No.136-04, ☎/⌐258 08 38)* sells international books, periodicals, newspapers and compact disks. Photocopying and lamination are available.

Groceries

Vina del Country *(every day 8am to 11pm; Carrera 15 No. 83-26 and 28, ☎236 71 49 or 256 97 74)* is simple little store selling beer, wine, liquor and cigarettes.

Le Cercle du Vin *(every day 8am to 6pm; Carrera 14 No. 85-75, ☎610 34 01)*. As its name implies, this store sells imported French wine.

Azafran *(every day 8am to 8pm; Calle 13 No. 85-53, ☎618 57 19; and Calle 79a No. 7-72, ☎271 38 24)* are little shops that sell imported foods as well as fresh produce.

Supermercado **Carrulla Country** *(Mon to Sat 7am to 11pm, Sun 8am to 8pm; Calle 85 No. 15-29, ☎218 03 18)*. This is a supermarket with everything needed on a daily basis, from meat (including leg of lamb) to vegetables, and also beer, wine, liquor and cigarettes.

Supermercado **POMODA** *(Mon to Sat 8am to 11pm, Sun 9am to 9pm; Carrera 11 No. 76-19)* is a top-of-the-line Italian supermarket that sells imported products such as wine, high quality oil and cold cuts.

Rigoletto *(Mon to Sat 8am to 7pm; Carrera 13 No. 86a-37, ☎256 69 75)* is a little Italian shop where fresh pasta is always available, along with imported Italian and Argentinean products.

Photo Developers

Revelado une Demi Hora
Carrera 11 No. 81-07, ☎616 39 92;
Calle 72 (Av. Chile) No. 9-29, ☎211 16 57 or 211 28 35

Commercial Centres

Andino, corner of Carrera 11 and Calle 82
Centro 93 corner of Carrera 15 and Calle 93
Centro Suba, Av. Suba or Calle 140, No. 91-19
El Lago, corner of Carrera 15 and Calles 77 to 79
Hacienda Santa Bárbara, corner of Carrera 7 and Calle 116
Iserra 100, corner of Calle 100 and Av. Suba
Unicentro, corner of Carrera 15 and Calle 127
Unilago, Carrera 15, No. 78-33

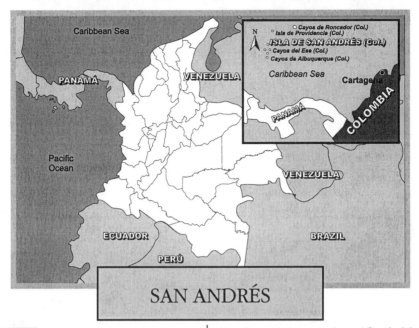

SAN ANDRÉS

The San Andrés y Providencia Archipelago is 700 kilometres northwest of mainland Colombia. The islands look like they are straight off a picture postcard: lush green scenery with white sandy beaches shaded by magnificent palm trees, and a coral sea of transluscent water the colour of emeralds. Comprising a total of 44 square kilometres of land, the islands are spread out over 350,000 square kilometres of sea. The archipelago is primarily made up of the islands of San Andrés and Providencia, which are surrounded by the smaller islands of Santa Catalina, Bolívar, Albuquerque and Cotton Haynes and the reefs Grunt, Johnny Rose, Easycay, Roncador, Serrana, Serranilla, Quitasueño, Brothers, Rocky, Crab and Santander as well as the Alicia and Bajo Nuevo sand banks.

Discovered in 1510 by the Spanish, the San Andrés y Providencia Archipelago abandoned shortly afterward when it was taken over by English Puritans and Jamaican woodcutters according to most historians. This explains why most of the Spanish-speaking inhabitants also speak English. The territory was later recovered by the Spanish during the latter half of the 17th century. For a time, however, the archipelago's flag and coat of arms changed constantly as the English, Dutch, French and Spanish all took possession of it following successive military attacks. These wars ended in 1793 when the Treaty of Versailles was signed recognizing Spanish sovereignty. The pirate Henry Morgan secretly used San Andrés as his base of operations for many years. Legend has it that this is where he buried his fabulous treasures stolen from the Spanish, which have never been found to this day.

San Andrés

In the shape of a seahorse and covered with palm trees, the island of San Andrés has small hills running from north to south that are only about 55 m high. With a surface area of 36 square metres — 12 kilometres long and 3 kilometres wide — the island has about 60,000 inhabitants who are the most highly educated in Colombia. There are more than 40 private schools and special educational centres and about 15,000 students – a quarter of the population!

When the country adopted a new constitution in 1991, the status of the island's administration changed to that of a county, with a governor elected for a three-year mandate. The island's economy is based on tourism — the heavenly temperature is 29°C year-round. The sea is the main attraction, and the beaches are the reason people come here to visit. The beaches are tended with the greatest care, and are groomed almost as meticulously as a golf course: they are cleaned and raked at 5am every day for the tourists who begin to arrive 6am and do not leave before 6pm. The archipelago is part of the second-largest coral reef in the world after the one in Australia. This barrier reef stretches along the coast of Central America, passing close to Belize, Honduras and Nicaragua. It is visited by a great many amateur and professional deep-sea divers. About 500,000 tourists visit the island each year, 20 percent of whom come from outside the country. All parts of the island are completely safe, and you rarely hear about disturbances of any kind. Fishing is also an important source of livelihood here, as is farming since the soil is exceptionally fertile.

FINDING YOUR WAY AROUND

The city of San Andrés is known simply as *El Centro*. Situated in the northern part of the island, this is the capital of the Archipelago but its size is more like that of a village. Other small villages are spread out around the island and on the mountain: for example, Loma is in the centre of the island, San Luis on the east coast and Cove Bay on the west coast.

The Carretera Circunvalar is a paved road of about 30 kilometres that circles the island and can be travelled by car in less than one hour. El Centro, meanwhile, is crisscrossed by *avenidas* that go in every direction and are named. The few *calles* are numbered and run from east to west; their numbers increase from north to south. The rare *carreras* go from north to south, and their numbers increase from east to west. It should be noted that l'Avenida de la Playa—which runs along the beach—is also called Avenida Colombia. It then becomes Avenida Newball, and outside El Centro it is called Carretera Circunvalar or Carretera for San Luis.

By Plane

The only way to reach San Andrés is by plane. No ferries run to the archipelago from the mainland, although cruise ships stop in San Andrés.

Aeropuerto Gustavo Rojas Pinilla *(Avenida Aeropuerto, Sector Swamp Ground, ☎25397)* is less than two kilometres north of the centre of town and spans the width of the island from east to west. the To prevent the island from being overrun by non-residents, visitors arriving here must have a return ticket and a visa which costs 12,000 pesos. There is no bus service to or from the airport, and taxis cost 1,000 pesos. Several airline companies have flights to San Andrés.

Avianca flight schedule to destinations outside of Colombia:

Ciudad Guatemala, Guatemala, Tue, Wed, Sat 1:05pm with stopover.
Ciudad de Panamá, Panamá, Mon, Wed, Fri 3:45pm.
San José, Costa Rica, Tue, Wed, Sat 1:05pm.

Avianca schedule for direct flights to Colombia:

Baranquilla, Mon, Wed, Fri 11:25am; Tue, Thu, Sat, Sun 3:45pm; 178,000 pesos.
Bogotá, Mon, Thu, Sat, Sun 10:05; Mon, Wed, Fri 2:35pm with stopover; every day 4:07pm; Fri 4:50pm; Mon 6:20pm; Tue, Thu, Sat, Sun 7:45pm with stopover; Tue, Wed, Sat 9:05pm; 237,000 pesos.
Cali, every day 11am; 228,000 pesos.
Cartagena, Mon, Wed, Fri 2:35pm; Tue, Thu, Sat, Sun 7:45pm; 178,000 pesos.
Medellín, Mon, Wed, Fri 3:45pm; 202,000 pesos.
Pereira, Sat, Sun 10:05am with stopover; Fri 4:50pm with stopover; 239,000 pesos.
Providencia, every day 7:45am, 9:20am, 10:45am, 10:55am, 1:10pm, 2:40pm, 4:15pm and 4:35pm; 45,000 pesos.

Addresses and telephone numbers of airline companies in San Andrés:

Avianca, Hotel Tiuna, 1st floor, ☎23211, 23212, 23213, or 27018; Avenida Duarte Blum, Edificio Santa Catalina, ☎23307, 26008, 25432 or 26681.
Aces, Avenida Colombia, Centro Comercial New Point, ☎21427.
AeroRepública, Avenida Colón No. 3-60, ☎27325, 27334 or 27619.
Intercontinental de Aviación, Avenida Colombia No, 2-179, ☎25276 or 26115.
Sam, Hotel Tiuna, 1st floor, Av. Colombia, ☎23211, 23212, 23213 or 27018; Avenida Duarte Blum, Edificio Santa Catalina, ☎23307, 26008, 25432 or 26681.

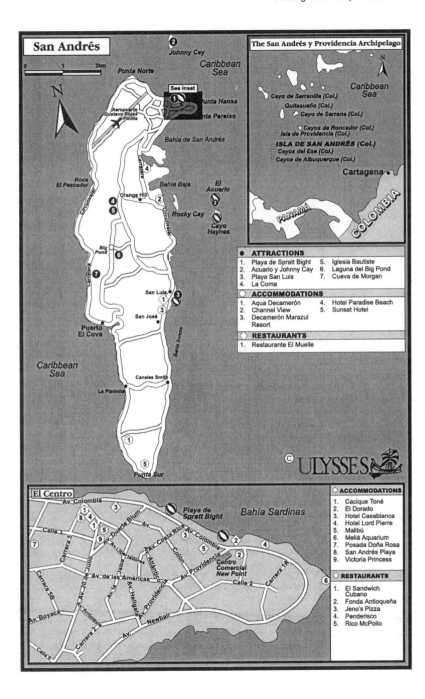

San Andrés

0   1   2km

N

Johnny Cay

Punta Norte

Caribbean Sea

See inset

Punta Hansa

Aeropuerto Gustavo Rojas Pinilla

Punta Paraíso

Bahía de San Andrés

Roca El Pescador

Bahía Baja

El Acuario

Orange Hill

Rocky Cay

Cayo Haynes

Big Pond

San Luis

San José

Puerto El Cove

Caribbean Sea

Canales Smith

La Piscinita

Punta Sur

The San Andrés y Providencia Archipelago

N

Cayo de Serranilla (Col.)

Quitasueño (Col.)

Cayo de Serrana (Col.)

Caribbean Sea

Cayos de Roncador (Col.)

Isla de Providencia (Col.)

ISLA DE SAN ANDRÉS (Col.)

Cayos del Ese (Col.)

Cayos de Albuquerque (Col.)

Cartagena

PANAMA

COLOMBIA

ATTRACTIONS

1. Playa de Spratt Bight
2. Acuario y Johnny Cay
3. Playa San Luis
4. La Coma
5. Iglesia Bautiste
6. Laguna del Big Pond
7. Cueva de Morgan

ACCOMMODATIONS

1. Aqua Decamerón
2. Channel View
3. Decamerón Marazul Resort
4. Hotel Paradise Beach
5. Sunset Hotel

RESTAURANTS

1. Restaurante El Muelle

© ULYSSES

SAN ANDRÉS

El Centro

Av. Colombia

Playa de Spratt Bight

Bahía Sardinas

Calle 3

Av. Duarte Blum

Av. Costa Rica

Av. Colombia

Av. Libertadores

Av. 20 de Julio

Av. Atlántico

Av. Providencia

Colón

Av. de las Américas

Av. Antioquia

Av. Hellgate

Av. Providencia

Centro Comercial New Point

Calle 2

Carrera 1A

Av. Boyacá

Carrera 2

Av. Newball

Carrera 5B

Carrera 5

Carrera 6

Calle 5

Bahía Sonora

Circunvalar

Carrera

ACCOMMODATIONS

1. Cacique Toné
2. El Dorado
3. Hotel Casablanca
4. Hotel Lord Pierre
5. Malibú
6. Meliá Aquarium
7. Posada Doña Rosa
8. San Andrés Playa
9. Victoria Princess

RESTAURANTS

1. El Sandwich Cubano
2. Fonda Antioqueña
3. Jeno's Pizza
4. Penderisco
5. Rico McPollo

By Bus

Old buses run to all parts of the island. They pass frequently — every 15 minutes — and cost 350 pesos. Their destination is indicated on the windshield.

By Taxi

Taxis do not have metres here. In El Centro they cost 1,000 pesos for each trip — but you can cross town on foot in less than half an hour. The price for destinations outside the city should be negotiated as they can vary from one taxi to the next, depending on the driver's mood. Taxis are also willing to show you the main tourist attractions but again, the price must be negotiated. It should be between 15,000 and 20,000 pesos, which is a good deal if it is divided among five passengers.

Car Rentals

You can easily rent all kinds of vehicles in San Andrés: scooters, "quadrimotos" (basically, golf carts), all-terrain vehicles, cars and luxury cars such as BMW convertibles which can be rented by the hour. A VW Golf costs 20,000 pesos for 1 hour; 35,000 pesos for 2 hours; 70,000 pesos for the day from 9am to 6pm and 120,000 pesos for 24 hours. A "quadrimoto" that can carry 4 or 5 people costs 30,000 pesos for 1 hour; 50,000 pesos for 2 hours; 120,000 pesos for the day from 9am to 6pm and 150,000 pesos for 24 hours. As there is hardly any traffic outside El Centro, renting a scooter is an excellent choice since you can go around the island in less than an hour. A driver's licence, the address of your hotel and a 30,000 pesos deposit are required. The rental cost does not vary from one agency to the next and costs around 5,000 pesos for 1 hour, 30,000 pesos for the day from 9am to 6pm and 40,000 pesos for 24 hours. Information can be had from the following agencies:

Bahía Tours Rent a Car (Motos y Carros), Av. Colombia No. 4-189, ☎23323;

Unicar, rents all kinds of vehicles; every day from 8am to 11am; Av. de la Playa, No. 3-137, ☎24791 or 22050;
Portofino Rent A Car, Av. Colombia No. 3-35, ☎25695 or 26935.

By Boat

Contrary to what you might expect, the island of San Andrés is not surrounded by beaches, which are one of the main tourist attractions in the archipelago. The windswept west coast of the island is rocky and not safe for swimming. El Centro's Playa de Spratt Bight in the Bahía Sardinas is a hit with most people thanks to its warm crystal-clear emerald-coloured water and fine white sand.

Other beaches that are just as spectacular await visitors, including Johnny Cay, El Acuario and Cayo Haynes. You can get there by taking a *lancha* (a small boat with a motor) from the Cooperativa de Lancheros de San Andrés. Tickets are sold at the far eastern edge of Spratt Bight beach. The price shown on the door is for a return trip to any one of these islands. It costs 6,300 pesos to visit all three islands.

 # PRACTICAL INFORMATION

Area code: 8.

Mail

Mail service is provided by **Avianca** at the Hotel Tiuna, Av. Colombia.

Business Hours

Generally, the stores and shops are open from 9am to 12:30pm, and from 3pm to 7:30pm. Because the island caters to tourists, the hours may vary from one place to the next, from season to season, and even from day to day, depending on how busy it is.

Banks

Banks are open Monday through Thursday from 8am to 11:30am and 2pm to 4pm, and from 8am to 11:30am and 2pm to 4:30pm on Friday. Money can be changed at the **Banco de la República** *(Av. Colombia No. 2-86,* ☎*23682)* and at the **Banco Popular** *(Av. Las Américas No. 3-161,* ☎*23621).* Money and traveller's cheques can be changed at the BIC, the **Banco Industrial Colombiano** *(Av. Costa Rica No. 2-57,* ☎*24195).* There are also a good many 24-hour bank machines. Most hotels as well as some shops accept American money.

Tourist Information

Secretaría de Turismo, Av. 20 de Julio No. 4-169, ☎25085 or 24346, ⊷24346.

Kiosko de Información Turística, Av. Colombia, ☎24230.

Excursions

Specialised travel agencies in El Centro organise a great many excursions. Here are a few of them:

Tour Vuelta a la Isla, a train that runs on the road, tours the island for three hours; departures every day at 9:30am; 6,000 pesos;

Tour Al Acuario y Johnny Cay, a trip in a small motor boat, leaves from Playa de Spratt Bight every day at 9:30am. It costs 8,600 pesos or 15,000 pesos including an *almuerzo* (lunch) composed of fried fish, rice, a salad and a soft drink;

Tour en semi-submarino Manatí is a 45-minute submarine excursion; departures every day at 10am, 11am, 2pm and 3pm; 12,000 pesos;

Yate con Fondo de Vidrio is a two-hour excursion on board a glass bottom boat; departures Mon, Tue and Thu; 10,500 pesos;

Velero Capitán Morgan is an excursion on board the sailing ship Capitán Morgan that lasts for two hours and includes an open bar with music; departures at 4pm; 15,000 pesos;

Crucero del Atardecer is a two-hour cruise that leaves at sunset and includes cocktails and music; departures every day at 5pm; 10,500 pesos;

Crucero de lujo is a deluxe cruise; departures Wed, Fri, Sat and Sun from 10am to 4pm including an open bar, *almuerzo* (lunch) and even a trip in a motorboat; 30,000 pesos.

These agencies will help you decide on a tour:

Islatur, Av. Colombia No. 1-09, Edificio Hotel Cacique Toné, ☎24127 or 23185;

Viajes Portofino, Av. La Playa, No. 1-120, ☎27773, 22210, 22230, 22211 or 22212;

Fantasia Tropical, Av. Colón, Hotel Caribe, office 9, ☎25158, 25100 or 27001;

Barboat, Carretera to San Luis, ☎29515;

Gema Tours San Andrés, Av. Providencia, Centro Comercial New Point, office 108, ☎28666;

Finan-Tours, Av. Duarte Blum No. 1-34, ☎25810 or 25416;

Receptour del Caribe, Av. Colón, pasaje Comercial Sol Caribe, office 5, ☎22420, 22421, 25857 or 23975; also Carrera 9a No. 10-156, Swamp Ground, ☎28853, 28854 or 28855.

 EXPLORING

San Andrés ★★★

Situated in El Centro beside numerous restaurant and hotel, terraces and restaurants overlooking the Bahía Sardinas, **Playa de Spratt Bight ★★★** is the main beach in San Andrés. With its white sand and crystalline waters, this beach is nestled in a bay protected by a coral reef that is in itself worth the trip to San Andrés. This is where all the tourists flock every day from early in the morning until late in the evening. Sun worshippers will not be disappointed. All the water activities that you could wish for are available, including motorboat *(50,000 pesos/hour)* and windsurfer *(10,000 pesos/hour)* rentals. Volleyball, beach *fútbol* and Frisbee are played while exotic cocktails and cold beer are served on the terrace less than five metres from the beach, on the other side of Avenida de la Playa or Avenida Colombia. Local women gather here every day to *canga* braid visitors' hair.

Just as spectacular as Playa de Spratt Bight is the excursion to **Acuario y Johnny Cay ★★★** *(6,300 pesos)*, with departures at 9:30am from the Cooperativa de Lancheros at the far eastern edge of Spratt Bight beach. Situated 20 minutes from San Andrés by *lancha* (small motor boat), Acuario is a tiny island covered with fine white sand and surrounded by reefs that form a veritable aquarium in the sea hardly 15 metres from the shore. You can go snorkelling to view the area's marine life even if you don't know how to swim, since the water is only one metre deep. The multicoloured fish that swim by seem surprised to see such strange masked water animals: they always approach with the same uneasy curiosity. This excursion lasts one hour, and you can rent the snorkelling equipment (mask and breathing tube) for 1,000 pesos. The organizers will also watch your belongings (bag, camera and other personal effects) for an additional 1,000 pesos.

You then get back in the *lanche* and set off for Johnny Cay, a pear-shaped island opposite El Centro in the Bahía Sardinas. It takes about an hour to reach this genuine pearl in the middle of the sea. You may decide to stay here for the day and return to San Andrés later by one of the other *lanches* that come and go.

Even if you do not stay the whole day, you can still appreciate the beach, its warm water and the sun. When you have had enough sun, you can sit under the magnificent palm trees where about 50 *tiendas* serve refreshing glasses of beer, *aguardiente* or rum. In the cool shade of the trees, the sea breeze also brings the odours of fried fish. The *tiendas* all have the same menu which consists of different fried fish or *sancocho* (fish and vegetable soup) with rice and a fresh vegetable salad *(about 5,000 pesos, with beer)*. After lunch, the *tiendas* are transformed into discotheques with a dance floor on the sand and waiters livening up the place: on the menu are *reggae, salsa, calypso* and... more *reggae*.

Only the part of Johnny Cay situated opposite San Andrés is suitable for swimming because the other side of the island is swept by waves that are too strong and dangerous for swimmers.

Playa San Luis ★★★ is situated some 10 kilometres from El Centro, on the Carretera Circunvalar. It is on the east coast, midway

between the north and south of the island in the tiny village of San Luis. About thirty people live in this calm, pleasant village where the only attraction is its wooden houses built in typical Caribbean style. The nearly-deserted beach is an oasis of tranquillity; it is the perfect place for privacy, since the other beaches are very busy. There are two or three small outdoor restaurants with a great view of the sea (see p 118).

La Loma ★★ is a small village on the mountain in the centre of the island, about 50 metres above sea level. It is the highest spot on the island and has a magnificent view of the surroundings.

Built at the high point in the centre of La Loma, the **Iglesia Bautiste ★** once served as a guide for sailors. Constructed of wood in 1847, and weathered by the sun and wind, it was completely rebuilt in 1896 with wood imported from the United States.

Laguna del Big Pond ★★★ at La Loma measures only 400 metres by 150 metres but shelters thousands of birds, alligators, boas and fish. It is bordered by fruit trees and palms.

Cueva de Morgan ★ is on the west coast, halfway between the north and south. It is an underwater cave where the coral has been hollowed out over time by the waves and is now divided into channels like a labyrinth. Good swimmers can dive down and discover the deserted beach on the other side where English pirate Henry Morgan is said to have hidden his treasure. Nobody has found it yet, but the legend persists on the island and people joke that a lucky tourist will one day discover it.

 OUTDOOR ACTIVITIES

 Diving

The archipelago is situated on the second-biggest coral reef in the world after that of Australia. In fact, the San Andrés coral reef reaches all the way to Belize, and is thus also a part of Honduras. Not surprisingly, it is a favourite deep-sea diving spot for many tourists, to whom some hotels specifically cater. Such hotels are situated in strategic

Angel fish

spots near the reefs on Carretera Circunvalar away from El Centro, and most of their clientele is interested only in the underwater world which is exceptionally beautiful here. The water is between 3 and 40 metres deep, and visibility fluctuates between 20 and 50 metres. However, wetsuits are recommended for deep dives. The six kinds of sites preferred by divers are the small reefs, the large banks of coral, the cliffs, the caves, the flat areas teeming with marine life and, of course, the shipwrecks. Certain excursions are for divers with certificates for the autonomous level and free water 1 or higher from associations such as NAUI, PADI, YMCA, CMAS, DIWA or their equivalent. However, most agencies offer resort-style introductory courses or even intensive courses certified by NAUI and PADI. All the organisations rent equipment and accessories by Mares, Cressi-sub, US Divers, Sherwood and Beuchat; it should be note that American-style regulators are used. The following agencies specialize in deep-sea diving and can help you organise your excursions:

El Centro

Buzos del Caribe, NAUI and FEDECAS, Av. Colombia No. 1a-212, Centro Comercial Dann, ☎23712;
Centro de Buceo Pablo Montoya, PADI, NAUI and FEDECAS, Centro Comercial New Point Plaza, office 110, Av. Providencia, corner of Av. de la Playa, ☎/⌨23141;
Centro de Buceo Blue Life, Transv. 2a No. 2-121, ☎25318 or 29124;
Aquamarina Dive Resort, Av. Colombia, Centro Comercial Acuarium, office 3, ☎26649.

Carretera Circunvalar

Sharky Dive Shop, PADI, NAUI, Sunset Hotel km 13, ☎30420, 30433 or 25940.

ACCOMMODATIONS

The San Andrés y Providencia archipelago's main activity is tourism, so there are hotels to suit all budgets. All the hotel personnel speak English as well as Spanish.

San Andrés

El Centro has a wide selection of hotels on the west side of the Avenida de la Playa opposite Playa Spratt Bight, and also on the side streets only a few minutes' walk from the beach. There are also hotels right on the beach. Hotels specializing in the deep-sea diving tourism are outside El Centro, on the Carretera Circunvalar. **Aqua Decamerón** *(Carretera Circunvalar, km 14, ☎23831 or 27460)* is one of these, and does not accept tourists just passing through. The **Decamerón Marazul Resort** *($$$$$; pb, hw, mb, ⊗, ≈, ☎, tv, ≈, ℛ; Carretera Circunvalar No. 30-45, ☎23539, 23657 or 22013)* also refuses passing tourists since their guests have all bought prepaid packaged tours. If you negotiate with the manager, he may be able to find you a room. The Marazul has 234 rooms in a complex comprised of five two- and three-storey buildings. The rooms have twin beds or one double bed, and some have a balcony or a terrace. The Marazul is situated near San Luis, opposite a very beautiful beach of soft white sand. All kinds of water sports are available here. Less than 30 feet away on the other side of Carretera Circunvalar and shaded by magnificent palm trees are decks with sun shades made from dried palm leaves. Like all the other Decameróns, the price includes all meals and drinks, and even many activities such as tennis during the day or evening, windsurfing, sailing, sea kayaking and so on.

El Centro

Posada Doña Rosa *($; pb, tv, ⊗; Av. Las Américas No. 6-43, ☎23649)* is a family home whose inner courtyard has been modified to accommodate nine motel-type rooms. Situated on a quiet street about one kilomtre from the beach, this is a hotel for travellers on a small budget. For a few pesos more, the San Andrés Playa, the Victoria Princess and the Malibú are better choices:

The **Malibú** *($; pb, ⊗, =, ☎, ℜ; Av. Colón, at the corner of Av. Colombia, ☎24342 or 25644, ⌐25396)* is a new six-storey hotel with balconies. The rooms are pleasant, but that is all. The Malibú is also situated only a few feet from the beach.

The **San Andrés Playa** *($; pb, tv, ☎, =, ℜ; Carrera 5 No. 1-37, ☎25644)* is a new five-storey hotel 50 metres from the beach behind the Cacique Toné hotel. This hotel lacks atmosphere mainly because of the cold functional furnishings but it is nevertheless the best deal in San Andrés for limited budgets. The new administration charges a regular rate of 30,000 pesos per person per day, or accommodation and two meals for two people at 45,000 pesos per day for stays of 15 days if paid in advance. The rooms are gloomy but comfortable. Some are more expensive because they have a balcony with a partial view of the Bahía Sardinas.

The **Victoria Princess** *($; pb, tv, ☎, =, ⊗, ℜ; Av. 20 de Julio No. 1a-116, ☎23189 or 23796, ⌐26130)* is a small, clean hotel with 29 rooms situated in the heart of El Centro. The rooms are simply furnished and the personnel is friendly. This hotel is ideal for travellers on limited budgets and is only a few feet from the beach.

Hotel Casablanca *($$$$; pb, hw, mb, ⊗, =, ☎, tv, =, ℜ; Av. Colombia No. 3-59, ☎24115, ⌐26127)* is a small hotel with 34 rooms, 8 suites and 14 *cabañas* (motel units) opposite the beach. It also has a swimming pool close to the sidewalk of Avenida Colombia. The *cabañas* around the pool are more intimate and feel like private cottages. They are practically but sombrely furnished.

El Dorado *($$$$; pb, hw, mb, ⊗, =, ☎, tv, =, ℜ; Av. Colombia No. 1a-25, ☎24155, 24056 or 24057, ⌐24056)* is a four-storey hotel with balconies and 63 rooms, half of which have a view of the sea. This ordinary hotel in the centre of El Centro can be noisy during high season. The rooms are big and functionally furnished. This hotel also has a play area for children, a wading pool and a swimming pool where entertainment is organized in high season.

The **Cacique Toné** *($$$$-$$$$$; pb, hw, mb, ⊗, =, ☎, tv, =, ℜ; Av. Colombia, corner of Carrera 5, ☎24251, ⌐24256)* is the best-known hotel in San Andrés because it is the first hotel visitors see when arriving from the airport. An imposing building of about a dozen storeys in a "V" shape, it is everything that you would expect from a touristy hotel. The 144 rooms are small but comfortable, decorated with large pale wooden furniture that is nothing special, but functional. The choice rooms are in the front with a view, but even the ones in the back are pleasant and look out over San Andrés and the sea beyond. The personnel is professional and welcoming, knowing from experience what the guests want: pure relaxation for one or two weeks. Beach towels are provided, and in the evening there is organized entertainment for the whole family around the swimming pool, with an orchestra, games, competitions and so on.

The following hotels in El Centro are on the water:

Hotel Lord Pierre *($$$$-$$$$$; pb, hw, mb, ⊗, =, ☎, tv, =, ℜ; Av. Colombia No. 1b-106, ☎27541, ⌐25666)* is a medium-sized hotel with 49 rooms and 11 suites on 3 floors situated right on the sea. Recently constructed, the hotel has its own dock and an elevator with a view. The rooms are large and furnished in the island style of pale wood. The personnel is welcoming.

The **Meliá Aquarium** *($$$$$; pb, hw, mb, ⊗, =, ☎, tv, =, ℜ; Av. Colombia No. 1-19, ☎26918, 23117, 29010, 29030 or 23120, ⌐26918, 26938 or 26471)* is probably the most expensive hotel in San Andrés. Overlooking the sea, this hotel seems more like condominiums, and some rooms have balconies overlooking the water so that you can fish while sipping an aperitif. The Meliá Aquarium also has the only saltwater swimming pool, which is built right next to the sea and is fed by it. The large rooms are comfortable and the personnel are friendly and welcoming.

Carretera Circunvalar

The following hotels are situated outside El Centro. Some of them specialize in deep-sea diving:

The **Channel View** *($$; pb, hw, mb, ⊗, =, ☎, tv, ℜ; Carretera Circunvalar, between Km 5 and 6, San Luis Bay, ☎27057)* is without a doubt the most appealing hotel in San Andrés. Situated amid a forest of palm trees right on the water, this secluded hotel resembles a motel and has 30 rooms. The bamboo furniture is Caribbean island-style. The reception is in an open area from which passageways lead through the trees to the rooms and to the private beach where volleyball nets are set up. The Channel View organizes its own deep-sea diving excursions from the beach that faces Rocky Cay reef or to sites further out to sea depending on which you prefer. Completely removed from all the bustle of San Andrés and yet less than 15 minutes from El Centro's nightlife, the Channel View is a charming hotel with a unique atmosphere. It is the best place to stay in terms of quality for the price. The personnel at the reception desk are extremely warm and friendly and very professional.

The **Sunset Hotel** *($$$; pb, hw, mb, ⊗, ≡, ☎, tv, ≈, ℜ; Carretera Circunvalar No. 12-257, km 13, ☎30433 or 25940)* is another small hotel, with 20 rooms around a swimming pool. The rooms have pure island-style bamboo furniture and balconies with a view of the sea. There are a swimming pool and wading pool, as well as a bar and restaurant. Situated about half an hour from El Centro and on a stretch of seashore that is not safe for swimming, this hotel specializes in deep-sea diving and has its own organization, Sharky Dive Shop (see p 115) to serve its clientele as well as other visitors. The Sunset also has packages that include daily deep-sea diving excursions.

Hotel Paradise Beach *($$$$; pb, hw, mb, ⊗, ≡, ☎, tv, ≈, ℜ; Carretera Circunvalar No. 12-257, between km 1 and 2, ☎25977, 25574, 26384 or 25570, ⇌25622)* is a small motel-style hotel that is situated less than five minutes from El Centro. The reception area has a magnificent view of the sea, and the swimming pool for adults and wading pool for children are placed in a superb setting. The 55 standard-size rooms are comfortable and decorated with pale bamboo furnishings. The personnel are attentive as they are everywhere in San Andrés. Although this hotel does not specialize in deep-sea diving, it does offer the option to its guests.

✗ RESTAURANTS

San Andrés

All the hotels have their own restaurants for their guests and other visitors. As elsewhere in Colombia, San Andrés has many fast food restaurants that serve inexpensive meals. On Avenida de la Playa in the evening, people sell food prepared in advance or charcoal broiled on the street. Most of the restaurants will deliver food.

El Centro

As its name indicates, **El Sandwich Cubano** *($$; every day from 10am to midnight; Av. 20 de Julio No. 1-09, ☎25635)* serves Cuban sandwiches. There is a choice of hot or cold meats with a selection of vegetables, all served on very tasty bread. Excellent! They also make French fries.

For more refined food, choose from among the following restaurants.

Jeno's Pizza *($$; every day from 10am to midnight; Av. Colombia No. 4-189, ☎24392 or 27848)* is a an outdoor pizzeria that serves seafood and a great variety of pizzas.

Rico McPollo *($$; every day from 7am to midnight; Av. Colombia No. 2-63, ☎26896 or 24631)* is also a fast food (*comida rapida*) restaurant where you can eat chicken, of course, but also hamburgers made with chicken, fish soups, breaded shrimps, fish filets and so on. American-style breakfasts are served as well.

 The **Fonda Antioqueña** *($$-$$$; every day from 11:30am to midnight; Av. Colombia No. 1a-16, ☎24185)* serves Antioquian (Medellín) specialities. However, seafood is also on the menu, and the *pargo frito* (fried mullet) alone is worth the trip! The restaurant is situated in a huge old house on the seashore and is decorated with handicrafts from another era. Meals are served at large rustic wooden tables with chairs all around. The service is relaxed but professional and the restaurant offers a complete selection of wines.

The **Penderisco** *($$-$$$; every day from 7am to 8pm; Av. Colombia at the corner of Carrera 5a, ☎24251)* restaurant is in the Cacique Toné Hotel (see p 116). The Penderisco serves continental food consisting of various fish and braised meats in a huge classic diningroom. There is also a selection of pasta dishes and even a decent list of French, Italian and Chilean wines.

SAN ANDRÉS

Carretera Circunvalar

Restaurante El Muelle *($$-$$$; every day from 11:30 to 8pm; Carretera Circunvalar, Playas de San Luis, between km 7 and 8, ☎30128)* is a small restaurant with a terrace situated on the west side of Carretera Circunvalar. The owners have also installed deck chairs with umbrellas on the small beach on the opposite side of the road where they serve food and drinks from the restaurant. The best place to eat is on the shaded terrace refreshed by cool sea breezes. The chef, Carlos Rodríguez, makes the best garlic crab legs in San Andrés – or even the whole archipelago! They are served as a starter, but you can order a double portion for a complete meal. The conch in tomato sauce is also incredible. The waiter may feel uncomfortable with foreign tourists because he does not speak English very well. Make sure he chills the white wine as soon as you arrive if you do not want to be disappointed. A dry white Follonica from the Casa Vinicola de San Paolo di Jesi imported from Italy is highly recommended.

RIOHACHA AND THE DEPARTMENT OF LA GUAJIRA

Most of the Guajira Peninsula, one of the most extreme regions in Central America in terms of climate, belongs to Colombia, though a small strip on the shores of the Gulf of Venezuela belongs to that country. Having long been dependent on the department of Magdalena before becoming an intendancy in 1954, La Guajira become its own department in 1964, with Riohacha as its capital. Divided into three regions, namely Alta Guajira, Media Guajira and Baja Guajira, La Guajira is a huge 20,180-square-kilometre desert where there is virtually nothing but salt and coal mines. In fact, Correjón, the biggest opencast coal mine in the world, is located here. Bounded by the Caribbean Sea to the north and the department of Cesar to the south, the department of Guajira is also bordered by the Caribbean Sea and Venezuela to the east and the department of Magdalena to the west. Home to some 500,000 inhabitants, the desert expanse will only truly please adventurous tourists, though travel agencies do offer organized excursions providing relative comfort.

Riohacha

Riohacha (pronounced *Rio-a-cha*) is located more than a three hours' drive from Santa Marta. This average-size city is the capital of the department of Guajira, with some 120,000 inhabitants, including the neighbouring suburbs.

Truth be told, Riohacha is an unattractive place. Despite all the claims made by travel brochures, which advertize it as a paradise, it must be acknowledged that "heaven on earth" never comes without its faults. Riohacha is not pretty, but that is the least of its faults. The sewer system often overflows, flooding certain streets with dirty, stagnant water that even the sun does not manage to dry. Nor is its beach attractive, characterized by brown, choppy waters and sand that would gain by being better tended. Indeed, the Río Ranchería, in the easternmost part of the city, pours its waters into a rough sea, giving it a rather uninviting brownish colour. These waters ring close to five kilometres of beach like a sombre half-moon for up to one kilometre into the sea. And yet, the water is said to be unpolluted. Pity it hardly seems so. As for the residents of Riohacha, they take advantage of the beach on weekends but do not venture much into the sea itself, and mainly sit beneath the trees to enjoy a respite from the heat.

A Brief History

The city was founded in 1545 and named Nuestra Señora de los Remedios del Río de la Hacha by Venezuelan colonists led by Klaus Federmann.

Once renowned for its rather extensive pearl production, the whole city was repeatedly attacked by French pirate Jean Laffite and sacked by English buccaneer Sir Francis Drake in 1596. Today, it has been reduced to a rather small port city.

Riohacha Today

It is but 8 o'clock in the morning and Riohacha is already scorching hot. The temperature is 30°C, and the air is dry. Breathing alone is difficult. By noon, the temperature will reach 37°C or higher. The sun beats straight down on Riohacha and no one and nothing moves. Even the mosquitos are sweating. At any rate, they suffer enough from the oppressive heat that they refuse to fly. The only slight consolation is the light sea breeze, though it brings no relief (unless, of course, it is the breeze that is responsible for the torpor of the mosquitos). Moreover, the hotel room is like an oven, with neither air conditioning nor a fan due to a general power outage, an all-too-common occurrence in Riohacha. Quick, to a bank, a shop, a pharmacy, a supermarket – anything equipped with a generator and an air-conditioning system! In the meantime, one must seek refuge beneath the few trees on the beach. Merely touching a wrought-iron fence could burn you. Nothing else to do but drink beer, which is what the *Guajiros* often end up doing.

Nights, however, are lively in Riohacha, particularly on weekends: the locals definitely like to have a good time. It is the only city in the world to have erected a bronze monument to an accordion player, Francisco Rodríguez, a.k.a. El Hombre, the creator of *vallenato* music. Need we say more? Though judging by the popularity of *vallenato* in Colombia and even beyond its borders, one can understand the stature of the Riohacha-born musician. The sculpture stands in the very middle of a roundabout, at the intersection of Carrera 7 and Calle 15 (Avenida El Progresso), also known as Carretera Troncal del Caribe. Another popular institution is the *guajira*, a dance of Cuban origin that vaunts the beauty of the *Guajira*, the peasant woman, popularized around the world by the song *Guajira Guantanamera*.

Street performers line the seafront promenade (*Avenida de la Playa* or *Calle 1*), especially to the delight of children. The bars and terraces between Carreras 6 and 9 are overflowing with people, and the ambiance is altogether convivial. The street is sometimes closed off for a special festival with *vallenato* bands on stage and dancing in the street. Indeed, Riohacha is

transformed into an open-air dance club at the drop of a hat. No need to be on your guard here. The locals mind their own business and pay no attention whatsoever to foreigners. They have better things to do, like dancing.

Apart from the *fiesta*, Riohacha is a quiet city where you can walk anywhere, at any time of day or night, worry-free. The city itself consists of a series of low, white houses and narrow, treeless streets with a few skyscrapers in the town centre. Riohacha is not an attractive city, but it is renowned for its sunrises and sunsets, which are unlike any others in the world. This sight alone is worth the trip, when the sun dawns early in the morning, around 5am, to sink below the horizon on the open sea in a riot of colours around 6pm.

 ## FINDING YOUR WAY AROUND

The streets of Riohacha are divided into *calles* and *carreras*. *Calles* (and sometimes *avenidas*) run east-west, their numbers increasing as you head south from the beach. *Carreras* run north-south, and their numbers increase from east to west. Riohacha's main thoroughfare, Calle 1, is also called Avenida de la Playa and, past the Riito bridge spanning the Río Ranchería, becomes Avenida Circunvalación.

By Plane

The **Aeropuerto Almirante Padilla** in Riohacha is located five kilometres southwest of town. It is a local airport served exclusively by Colombian airlines such as Avianca and Intercontinental. Avianca offers one direct Bogotá-bound flight a day at 12:34pm for 232,000 pesos.

Avianca, at Calle 7 and Carrera 8, ☎27 36 24 or 27 36 27.

Intercontinental de Aviación, at Calle 1a and Carrera 7, ☎27 25 89.

By Bus

The Guajira Peninsula is linked to the outside world by a fully paved road, Carretera Troncal

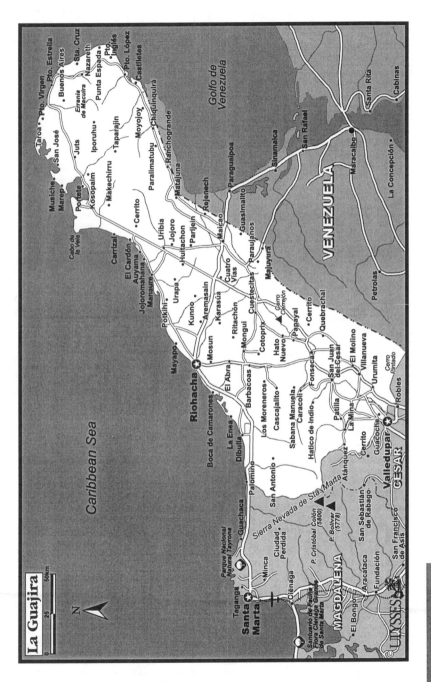

del Caribe, which runs east from Riohacha to Santa Marta, and west to Maicao and Venezuela. Buses leave every hour for destinations such as Santa Marta (3 hours), Barranquilla (5 hours), Maicao (1.5 hours) and Valledupar (4 hours). The bus companies have their ticket offices at the Terminal de Transportes, which is on Calle 15 (or Avenida El Progreso) between Carreras 11 and 12.

Expreso Brasilia, ☎27 22 40
Copertrán, ☎27 25 90
Rápido Ochoa, ☎27 33 02
Cotracosta, ☎27 27 39

Public Transportation

Mini buses roam the streets of Riohacha. Their destinations are indicated by a cardboard sign on their windshields. The beach and the market, however, are easily reached on foot from just about anywhere.

By Taxi

Taxis are not identified as such, but all the big American-made four-door cars, which are at least 10 years old, will take passengers for a flat rate: 1,000 pesos, whatever the distance.

 **PRACTICAL INFORMATION**

Area Code: 54.

Mail

Mail service is provided at the **Avianca** offices, at Calle 7 and Carrera 8.

Banks

Traveller's cheques cannot be changed in Riohacha, which is absurd considering this is a department capital that also promotes itself as an economic and business centre and a tourist destination. Automatic tellers are nevertheless available on Avenida de la Playa and around Parque Almirante Padilla.

Tourist Information

Corporación de Turismo de la Guajira (CORTUGUAJIRA), Calle 1a or Ave. de la Playa, ☎27 24 82.

Excursions

Several excursions are offered by travel agencies that provide relatively comfortable tours in all-terrain vehicles or aboard air-conditioned buses. You can choose between one-day and multi-day excursions, depending on the demand. Excursions are organized for a minimum of four people, and it is best to inquire a few days in advance to allow the agency to plan accordingly. Several destinations are available, such as Boca de Camarones, Uribia, Maicao, Manaure, Musichi, Cabo de la Vela, Parque Nacional Macuira, Parque Nacional Cierro Píntao, and the Cerrejón coal mine. The city of Maicao, which lies at the Colombian-Venezuelan border, is to be avoided, however. This dust-bowl town of 40,000 people has no paved streets, and buses must navigate around the old tires that litter the ground. What is more, because it is near the border, Maicao is a smugglers' den. It is a dangerous place despite the claims made by travel agencies, which describe it as a buyer's paradise. Indeed, everything here is available at half price — at contraband prices, that is. Consult the following travel agencies:

Administradores Costeños Viajes y Turismo, Calle 2 No. 5-02, ☎27 33 93, ⌐27 23 36;
Agencia Guajira Viva, Arimaca hotel, Calle 1a No. 875, ☎27 37 84;
Guajira Tour, Calle 3 No. 6-39, ☎27 33 85;
Awarraíja Tour, Ave. de la Marina No. 3-55, ☎27 58 06.

 EXPLORING

Riohacha ★

Riohacha has few tourist attractions. However, the city is the birthplace of Admiral José Prudencio Padilla, one of the heroes of the war of independence who vanquished the Spanish in a naval battle on Lake Maracaibo on

Riohacha

0   100   200m

N

● ATTRACTIONS
1. Parque Almirante Padilla
2. Catedral de Nuestra Señora de los Remedios del Río de la Hacha

◇ RESTAURANTS
1. Casa del Marisco
2. El Rancho de Rubén
3. El Sabroso
4. Restaurant Antojos

○ ACCOMMODATIONS
1. Arimaca
2. Guimaura
3. Hotel Almirante Padilla
4. Hotel Aremasain
5. Hotel Internacional
6. Hotel Musichi
7. Hotel Tropical
8. Hotel Tunebo

Caribbean Sea

Calle 1 - Av. 14 de Mayo

Calle 2
Calle 3
Calle 4
Calle 5
Calle 6
Calle 7 - Av. Almirante Padilla
Calle 8
Calle 9
Calle 10
Calle 11
Calle 12
Calle 12-A
Calle 13
Calle 14
Calle 14-A
Calle 15 - Av. El Progreso
Calle 16
Calle 17
Calle 17-A

Carrera 2
Carrera 3
Carrera 4
Carrera 5
Carrera 6
Carrera 7
Carrera 8
Carrera 9
Carrera 10
Carrera 11

Río Ranchería

Mercado

Cienaga Salada

Malecón

Aeropuerto José P. Padilla

Aeropuerto Santa Marta

Terminal de Transportes

Valledupar

© ULYSSES

The Wayuú

Wayuú social structure is still organized around matriarchal clans. The Wayuú live in small colonies (*rancherías* or *pichiipalas*) composed of five or six houses inhabited by members of the same family, according to their relation to the female line. Marriage is regarded as a transaction, and polygamy as a token of economic success. With the exception of new brides, all the women live with their children in separate huts where they are regularly visited by their husbands.

The living space is fairly simple and entirely devoid of decoration, while household and luxury articles are kept in bags suspended from the walls. The kitchen is a self-contained building, while the *luma* where social life takes place, is an open structure with a thatched roof supported by columns. The houses themselves are square, though round ones are also found in Alta Guajira. Built since time immemorial with *yotojoros* (the heart of the cactus) or with bamboo, some are now made of stone with sheet-metal roofs, materials imported by coal miners to build their shacks.

The Economy

Economic activity is confined to the breeding of goats and sheep. The more animals a man has, the more women he is entitled to, since wives are acquired in exchange for a certain number of animals. Also, larger flocks and herds enable the owner to meet his moral and material obligations to the community, incurred during previous transactions.

The Authorities

Political organization is non-existent, and the Wayuú recognize no particular authority. When problems arise, they are usually resolved between the parties involved, giving rise to violent grudges and vendettas. The only accepted social institution is that of the *piache*, or healer — usually women — whose powers are magical.

Today, the construction of paved roads, notably for mine development, and the injection of capital from the Colombian and Venezuelan governments on either side of the border are largely responsible for the disappearance of Wayuú customs.

July 24 1823, and you can see his statue in **Parque Almirante Padilla ★★**. The park lies in the city centre, bordered by banks, the most sophisticated shops, and the cathedral.

The **Catedral de Nuestra Señora de los Remedios del Río de la Hacha ★★** *(Parque Almirante Padilla)* stands in the centre of town and is one of the most important places for Riohacha's citizens. The church's style is not particularly interesting, but it is dedicated to the city's patron saint. The ashes of Admiral Padilla are kept in its south wing.

Cabo de la Vela ★★★

Only a sandy trail that changes from day to day depending on which way the wind blows leads to Cabo de la Vela. If you wish to get there without going through an agency, take a Maicao-bound *buseta* or bus early in the morning from the Terminal de Transportes, or from Calle 15, at the corner of Carrera 5. You have to travel 30 kilometres, to a place known as Cuatro Vias — which is indeed a crossroads — where four or five little *tiendas* sell beer under the blazing sun. You must then try to negotiate your way aboard a four-wheel drive truck, which can cost up to 40,000 pesos (a good deal, according to the driver), and travel 160 kilometres along a badly maintained dirt road to Uribia, following the railway which is used solely for the transport of coal from the Cerrejón mine to Puerto Bolívar.

The driver steers the truck with one hand while drinking beer with the other, the hand on the wheel also being used to engage the clutch.

Pelican

The sun beats down. It's as hot as an oven. The red-dirt road has been covered in oil for quite some time, and baked into a bumpy and glazed surface by the sun. The driver is oblivious to this, travelling at 90 kilometres an hour along the uneven road, which nevertheless eventually improves somewhat. This does not much help as he consequently speeds up, now exceeding 110 kilometres an hour. He stops every 20 kilometres to purchase more beer at one of the native huts dotting a flat landscape in the middle of nowhere where only a few emaciated cacti still have the courage to raise their heads to the sky in search of a little water. To no avail. And we set off again faster than ever, the radio-cassette player blasting *rumba*, which does not stop the driver from trying to renegotiate the fare by explaining that his truck needs some repairs and that his suspension is having difficulties. He's got that right!

He stops abruptly after an hour, having noticed a friend whose truck has broken down. After a short discussion, he decides to tow him. We travel slower now, because of the extra load, and finally stop at a garage in Ciudad Uribia.

In **Uribia**, a small city of some 5,000 inhabitants with low houses and treeless streets, there is nothing much to do. And yet, the place is spruced up with lots of banners for the (12th) festival celebrating Wayuú culture, which takes place here every year in October.

And we're off again. At full speed, now. The driver, who has bought more beer, decides that the price charged is unfair and that I will have to pay 10,000 pesos more to reach Cabo de la Vela. Just you try arguing with a drunk driver travelling over 100 kilometres an hour, in the middle of the desert, and been threatening to leave you there! After a good two hours of this hellish journey, we arrive at a hand-written signpost that reads "Cabo de la Vela." We then turn off and take not a road, which is non-existent, but a trail the driver follows roughly, which runs along a sand dune. He points to Cabo de la Vela in the distance, which appears like an indistinct and shimmering mirage in the hazy noontime heat. But it will take yet another hour to reach this village at the ends of the earth. It's hot: 40°C to 42°C, at least.

Cabo de la Vela is a *pueblito* straight out of a Sergio Leone western. Tucked away on the shores of the Caribbean Sea, it boasts some fifty huts and faded white sun-baked stone houses scattered over less than two kilometres. Not a tree nor a cactus in sight. Just sheer desert. In the centre is a single dirt road with two low houses overlooking the desert, one of which also serves as a bar, and a faded white-washed church.

On the seashore are a house, two adjacent hotels, and another house followed by wooden huts. Static *vallenato* plays softly, crackling from a badly tuned-in radio station. The wind angrily whistles and whips through the landscape, sending clouds of sand into the air, rolling tumbleweed across the desert and making a rusted sign advertizing a brand of beer creak. It tolls the bells in the church belfry, producing a sound like a doleful death knell. No one responds. A dog barks. A donkey brays. A toothless drunk man smiles.

There is no electricity in Cabo de la Vela. The La Langosta hotel-restaurant produces its own, using a noisy generator. Visitors can rent a hammock on the open-air terrace right on the beach, or stay in one of two closed rooms. The rooms have two single beds, but no fan, blankets or pillows, and no private bathroom. The pleasant manager explains that he wisely switches off the generator for the night. A fan is therefore out of the question. In any case, the temperature is tolerable at night thanks to the wind. Moreover, there are no mosquitos for the same reason.

The beach, on the other hand, is wonderful – the water is perfect for swimming and is shallow far out into the sea. It is always very

Folklore

Thought to have originated in the northern part of La Guajira, the *chichamaya* (or *yonna*) and the *cabrito* dances are still are still considered very important by its inhabitants. The *cabrito* is the rain dance, but also a dance of rejoicing to celebrate the god Mareiwa, the creator of La Guajira.

Danced by a couple, the *chichamaya* is more profane and the choreography openly sensual, and is performed during a marriage proposal. The man wears his finest *guayaco* or *taparabo* – a piece of fabric that covers the dancer's genitals and buttocks – while the woman is clad in her best *taquiara*, a soft, long and flowing dress that facilitates movement and covers her from neck to toe. Both also wear jewellery and ornaments that indicate their social rank.

The man dances jumping back to the beat of the drums while the woman moves toward him, attempting to throw him off balance and finally succeeding after numerous feigned attempts. The spectators then show their appreciation in accordance with the quality, boldness and general performance of the two protagonists.

Vallenato (literally "born in the valley") is essentially Colombian-flavoured western music that originated in southern Guajira, where it holds a place of honour. *Vallenato* blends the melodious sounds of the *guacharaca* (a hollow bamboo instrument that emits deep tones when rubbed), the accordion and a tambourine, the whole accompanied by a rhythmic *zapateado* (the musicians stamping their feet). Riohacha is the accordion capital and the birthplace of Francisco Rodríguez, better known as Francisco El Hombre ("Francisco the Man"), the father of *vallenato* music.

There are many famous *vallenato* artists today – both solo musicians and bands – including El Binomio de Oro, Hermanos Zuleta, Vallenatos Express, Omar Geles, Miguel Morales, Los Chiches, Miguel Mateus. Originally from Santa Marta, Carlos Alberto Vives has managed to popularize *vallenato* outside of Colombia, having sold over 1.5 million copies of *Clásico de la Provincia* in Latin America alone.

windy and one starts dreaming of windsurfing or sailing. After all, doesn't Cabo de la Vela mean "Cape of the Sail"? The place is certainly destined to become a paradise for this kind of sport. As soon as electricity is put in, that is. This will come about in six months, we are told (though this is undoubtedly a Colombian estimate), and make life more pleasant and fostering the site's development. There are no tourist attractions in Cabo de la Vela – save for the sea of course, which is a marvel. There is also El Pilón de Azúcar, "the sugar loaf", a fairly imposing white rock that looms up out of the water and, according to a *Wayuú* legend, guides the dead on the way to eternity. It was in Cabo de la Vela that Colombia's "discoverer", Alonso de Ojeda, first disembarked in 1499, having sailed from Venezuela with Francisco Pizarro (see p 25) among his crew. Ojeda believed he had seen a sail on the horizon: hence the cape's name. However, there is nothing here to remind us of this historic moment.

So what is there to do? Basically nothing. Take advantage of the sun and the sea, stretch out in a hammock while sipping an ice-cold beer, and discover the mysterious and austere beauty of the desert. Because the desert is indeed beautiful. It is not the exuberance of lush regions or the abundance of colours of a botanical garden, nor the serenity of a remote, gently flowing river in the mountains, but sheer desolation at its most extraordinary.

Though Guajira sunsets are spectacular, the nights here are second to none. Just imagine this enormous plateau – almost as extensive as the Gaspé in Quebec, Calabria in Italy or Cape Cod in the United States – half of which is without electricity. The stars here appear twice as big and five times as bright as they do anywhere else, especially on moonless nights. The scene is quite simply stunning, and like nothing you've ever seen before. It is also the beauty of the desert.

People live here, too. La Guajira is home to the Wayuú Indians (the "sons of the earth"), the direct descendants of the Tayrona. Some 80,000 Wayuús live on the Colombian side, and more still on the Venezuelan side. Most still live according to ancestral customs, which is almost a superfluous statement, given that electricity has yet to reach most of the towns. The Wayuú thus have no reason to change their way of life, which does not seem old-fashioned to them but essentially adapted to their needs — ones that clearly do not include television. They live in thatched-roofed houses and are easily recognizable by their attire. The remarkably beautiful and proud women, for example, wear long, full and uni-coloured (black, white or green) or multi-coloured dresses, and leather sandals on their feet. They have copper-coloured skin, high cheekbones and long, sleek jet-black hair, sometimes held back with a barrette. They often cover their faces with black vegetable gel to protect themselves from the sun. The men are more assimilated and no longer wear traditional dress.

The La Langosta hotel where we stayed is also a restaurant, whose catch of the day is selected straight from the fishing boat. What could be better than that? All the Wayuú's huts and houses along the beach are also restaurants. You have only to inquire and choose one whose owners seem more affable than the rest. They are all friendly. These "restaurateurs" set up a table right on the beach, where you are treated to an incredible amount of fresh shrimp in tomato sauce by candlelight or oil lamp, and all for only 6,000 pesos. What a bargain!

To return to Riohacha, you need only have a flexible schedule and wait for an all-terrain vehicle to drive through Cabo de la Vela on the way to Cuatro Vias (twice a day on average), or for the owner of one of the two hotels to go run errands. The fare is affordable as it is shared between several passengers. Nevertheless, count on spending some 15,000 pesos.

ACCOMMODATIONS

Riohacha

There are many budget hotels and restaurants around the market, though the cleanliness of the streets leaves something to be desired. For better-quality establishments, go to Calle 1a (also called Avenida 14 de Mayo, Avenida de la Marina or Avenida de la Playa), which runs along the beach. All taxis drivers know it well.

Hotel Almirante Padilla *($; pb, ⊗, tv, ℜ; Carrera 6 No. 3-29, ☎27 23 28, 27 36 12 or 27 36 07)* is named after one of the most important figures in Riohacha, Admiral José Prudencio Padilla, a hero of the war of independence. The hotel has 58 rooms, with televisions and fans, some of which have private bathrooms. There is also a small restaurant for guests that serves breakfast only. The three-storey hotel is a former colonial residence and is frequented by a Colombian clientele. The hotel receptionists are attentive and friendly.

Hotel Aremasain *($; pb, ≡, ⊗; Calle 12 No. 7-60, ☎27 32 68)* is a small hotel with a family ambiance whose restaurant, with the same owner, is located right across the street. It is a former family residence converted into a budget hotel. The rooms, some of which have air conditioning and a telephone, are clean and suitably furnished.

In the very heart of the market, **Hotel Internacional** *($; pb, ⊗; Carrera 7 No. 12a-31, ☎27 34 83 or 37 34 84)* may suit low budget travellers. All rooms are clean and have a bathroom with shower. For 7,000 pesos (less than US$7) a day, the place offers friendly and obliging service. The hotel is also a former residence, with a paved interior courtyard onto which most rooms look out. Though the proximity of the market might spell danger, the city of Riohacha does not have a bad reputation for crime.

The pleasant little **Hotel Musichi** *($; pb, ≡; Calle 2a No. 10-16, ☎27 39 65 or 27 67 83)* is some 200 metres from the beach, in a private house that has been converted into a hotel. The place has nine rooms with fans, including two with air conditioning and five with private bathrooms. It is clearly a budget hotel, but one that is clean and offers guests a more attentive welcome than the major hotels.

Adjacent to the market, the 26-room **Hotel Tropical** *($; pb, ≡, ⊗, ℜ; Calle 15 No. 3-82, ☎27 11 73 or 27 11 74)* is located right on Troncal del Caribe, which runs from Santa Marta to Maicao. This is yet another budget hotel, with a common room for the television. Relaxed ambiance.

Hotel Tunebo *($; pb, ≡, ⊗, ℜ; Carrera 10 No. 12a-02, ☎27 33 26 or 27 31 39)* is a small 16-room establishment housed in a white two-storey building. Also for limited budgets, it nevertheless offers comfort and tranquillity.

The **Arimaca** *($$-$$$$; pb, hw, ≡, ⊗, ☎, tv, mb, ▣, ℜ; Calle 1a No. 8-75, ☎27 34 81 or 27 34 82, ⌐27 22 39)* is unquestionably the best hotel in Riohacha, with 45 rooms and 5 suites in a nine-storey building with balconies and a view of the ocean. Moreover, the hotel is equipped with an independent electrical system that allows the establishment to offer all its services without interruption, which is a definite plus in Riohacha, where power outages are common. The place is clean, but no more, and rather disappointing in terms of ambiance. The main entrance consists of a staircase set between a bar and a restaurant that does not herald a well-kept hotel, providing shelter to a mangy dog who was having a siesta there during our visit. Riohacha is still unaccustomed to foreign travellers, and the desk clerks at the Arimaca hotel are not very attentive. That said, it is still the best there is for the price.

The **Guimaura** *($$-$$$$; pb, ⊗, ≡, ☎, tv, mb, ▣, ℜ; Calle 1a, ☎27 22 34 or 27 45 87, ⌐27 45 46)* is a government-owned hotel complex with 40 rooms, 2 suites and 5 *cabañas*. The hotel also has a huge, tree-filled park that also serves as a campsite. Not a bad hotel in itself, with a family ambiance — but it is badly kept and the management is lax. (In all fairness, however, we must admit that the oppressive heat does not encourage the expense of energy.) The rooms require major renovations to live up to the three-star rating that is advertized. Most light bulbs were burned out, the mini bar was rusty, and the walls and furniture were in need of refurbishment. However, all rooms have a balcony overlooking the sea, though access to mine was barred due to a badly hinged door. Moreover, the hotel does not have its own electrical system, which is a necessity throughout the Guajira Peninsula for a hotel that claims to be a certain class. Here, too, hotel receptionists are unused to foreign clients and are not anxious to be at their service, even though this *is* a three-star hotel's distinguishing feature.

Cabo de la Vela

There are at least two hotels in Cabo de la Vela that offer rooms or hammocks. They stand side by side on the beach — you can't miss them. Addresses are useless and probably non-existent. Visitors can also make arrange-

ments to stay with most residents for the same price.

 The most interesting is inarguably the **Hotel Restaurant La Langosta** *($; cellular ☎93 644 0124)*, which produces its own electricity with a noisy generator. The two rooms available only have single beds and do not come with pillows, private bathroom, fan or air conditioning. The hotel itself is a white-washed stone building of basic comfort, and thus recommended for adventurous souls and backpackers. The place also rents out sites to set up your hammocks, which can be rented for 4,000 pesos if you don't have your own. The hotel could claim Alonso de Ojeda and Francisco Pizarro stayed here close to 500 years ago without exaggerating much.

The other hotel, **El Caracol** *($)*, also offers sites with hammocks for the same price. There is no electricity here, however. As the sun sets between 5:30pm and 6pm, guests will have to eat by candlelight or oil lamp.

RESTAURANTS

Riohacha

Riohacha has restaurants for all budgets. Most of them are inexpensive, although, truth be told, one does not eat particularly well at them. There is better choice on Calle 1 (or Avenida de la Playa).

El Sabroso *($-$$; every day 11am to 11pm; Calle 1a No. 4-37, ☎27 04 68 or 27 47 18)* is a small open-air rotisserie with two to three tables on a sidewalk terrace. The place serves all kinds of char-grilled meats — beef, chicken, sausages, etc. — cooked on a grill right in the middle of the street. Unpretentious, good and inexpensive. The restaurant also delivers.

Restaurant Antojos *($-$$; every day 7am to 8pm; Carrera 6 No. 4-01, ☎27 00 18)* serves typical Guajira fare. Owner Gelsomina Gómez de Curiel ensures a relaxed family atmosphere. The place is set up in the two exuberantly decorated front rooms of a private residence, reminiscent of the Caribbean Islands. A great place for an exotic, inexpensive lunch and a real change of scene.

A charming residence in Cartagena de Indias.

Colourful butterflies are among Colombia's fascinating fauna.

A bronze sculpture by Botero in the city of Medellín.

La Casa del Marisco *($-$$$; every day 11am to 11pm; Calle 1a No. 4-43, ☎27 04 68 or 28 34 45)* is another seafood restaurant. Set up by the sea, in a small and narrow room with two rows of tables and a service aisle, the restaurant is pleasant and the service attentive. On the night of our visit, the *cazuela de mariscos* (seafood casserole) with half a lobster was most delicious.

 El Rancho de Ruben *($-$$$; every day 11am to 11pm; Calle 1 No. 1-103, ☎27 35 81)* is probably the best restaurant in Riohacha. Frequented by all of Riohacha, this restaurant specializes in fish and seafood, and is housed in an air-conditioned thatched-roof hut at the east end of Avenida de la Playa, on the other side of the Riito bridge spanning the Río Ranchería. The tables are pleasantly decorated and the ambiance is warm, the place offering a direct view of the sea. The service is friendly and patrons are even invited to discuss the dishes featured on the daily menu with the chef. Ruben, the owner, makes a point of greeting clients himself to make sure that everything is perfect. The *arroz con camarones* (rice with shrimp) was not, however, as one could have sworn the small, overcooked shrimp came straight out of a can. This particular choice, however, fell short of the welcome, but it would be presumptuous to generalize. All things considered, the Rancho de Ruben remains a restaurant worth recommending.

 ENTERTAINMENT

The department of Guajira hosts a few social and cultural events:

La Fiesta Patronale de Nuestra Señora de los Remedios, in Riohacha, is held in honour of the city's patron saint in February;

As its name indicates, the **Festival del Acordeón** is an accordion-music and *vallenato* festival, which takes place in Maicao in July;

The **Festival de las Flores** is a flower fair organized in Urumita in September;

The **Festival y Reinado del Carbón** is held in Barrancas for the crowning of the coal queen, in October;

The **festival of the Wayuú culture** is held in Uribia every October;

The **Festival Cuna de Compositores Monguí** is a *monguí*-music festival that takes place in December in San Juan del Cesar.

 SHOPPING

Riohacha

Riohacha's **public market** *(between Carreras 7 and 8 and Calles 13 and 14)* has it all, even Wayuú handicrafts, including huge two-person hammocks or *chinchorros*, not to mention the famous *manta guajira* or *taquiara*, the loose-fitting dress worn by Wayuú women. Another item to be found here is the *mochila*, a woven bag slung across one's shoulder and made of various fabrics. The market is open every day, from early in the morning to nightfall, at around 6pm.

Riohacha also has a shop specializing in handicrafts, **Casa de la Manta Guajira** *(every day 8am to 12:30pm and 2pm to 6pm; Carrera 6 No. 97-35, ☎27 34 41)*, where you can find all kinds of hand-made goods under one roof.

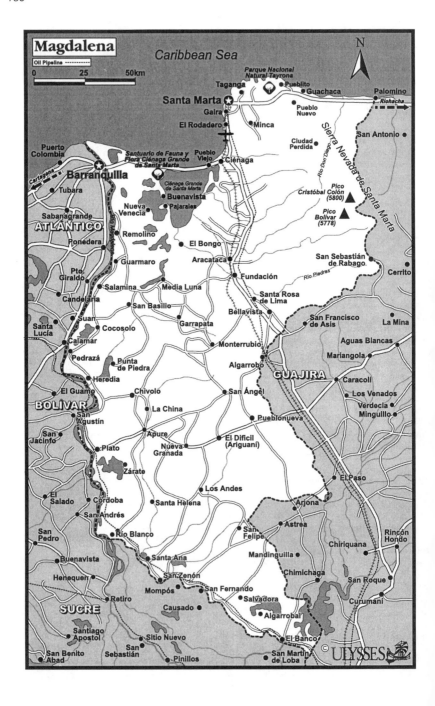

SANTA MARTA AND THE DEPARTMENT OF MAGDALENA

Magdalena is one of the oldest departments in Colombia, after that of La Guajira. Located in the northeastern part of the country, it has a surface area of 22,742 square kilometres and some 1.1 million inhabitants. It is bordered by the Caribbean Sea to the north, the departments of Bolívar and Cesar to the south, Cesar and La Guajira to the east and Atlántico and Bolívar to the west.

Its climate is extremely diverse, varying with the altitude. Indeed, the isolated mountain range known as the Sierra Nevada de Santa Marta creates a variety of climates in this coastal region, ranging from tropical temperatures and lush vegetation at sea level to the perpetual snow of the Bolívar and Cristóbal peaks — the latter being close to 5,800 metres in altitude —, to say nothing of the dry sands of the desert zones. This region has it all!

Santa Marta

One of the oldest cities in Colombia, Santa Marta was founded by Rodrigo de Bastidas on July 29, 1525, becoming the first Spanish outpost on the mainland of the American continent. During its early years, it proved to be one of the most important seaports from which the conquistadors set off to explore the vast interior of the New World.

The city lies in the midst of a singular landscape, fronting a heavenly bay on the Caribbean coast, where the annual average temperature is 28°C, with the constant sea breeze that creates ideal holiday conditions.

With some 350,000 inhabitants, Santa Marta is the capital of the department of Magdalena. It is a congenial little city, in the sense that one can easily tour the city on foot, and its main centres of interest adjoin the beach. Most visitors do not distinguish between Santa Marta and El Rodadero, thinking of them as one and the same destination. And yet, the El Rodadero seaside resort, the most developed tourist attraction in the region, is but one part of Santa Marta — a *barrio* (district) located some five kilometres from town.

A Brief History

Long before the Spanish Conquest, the Santa Marta region was home to indigenous peoples whose origins still elude ethnologists. What is known, however, is that the first inhabitants to permanently settle here lived in small, scattered communities from the outset, most likely because of the region's particular geography. The Tayrona civilization, for example, whose influence spread all along the Atantic coast, settled at the foot of the Sierra Nevada de Santa Marta, on the north side. When the Spanish first arrived, this culture was divided into two main groups, the Carib and Arawak

Indians, the latter being considered the older of the two.

The more warlike Caribs drove the Arawaks into the mountains and settled in their stead, adopting their way of life and their technologies. Thus, they became fishers, hunters and farmers. When the Spanish arrived, these people were expanding and had already conquered vast expanses of the territory that is now Colombia. They grew corn, potatoes, pineapples and other produce, which they traded with neighbouring communities. They also worked in salt mines and were skilled workers of fine metals.

Unlike the Caribs, the Arawaks were peaceful. They were farmers who produced cassava, corn and yams, among other things, and consumed coca leaves in their rituals and other sacred ceremonies.

Like most other Native American people, they wore body ornaments such as bracelets, breastplates, earrings and nose rings. They made handicrafts such as blankets, hammocks, nets and baskets to transport the merchandise that they traded with their neighbours. This is how the emeralds found in the centre of this vast territory made it all the way to the Caribbean coast.

In 1499, Alonso de Ojeda, accompanied by cosmographer Juan de la Cosa, "discovered" Colombia, first setting foot in Cabo de la Vela on the Guajira Peninsula. He had sailed from what is now Venezuela with Francisco Pizarro, the future conqueror of Peru, who had accompanied Ojeda as a simple soldier. Pizarro is the only conqueror to have reached Colombia from both the Atlantic and Pacific oceans (see p 26). Rodrigo de Bastidas arrived a few years later, and explored the entire Colombian coast from Cabo de la Vela to Santa Marta. He set up his headquarters here and chanced upon the estuary of a river he named Grande de la Magdalena. He thought to settle here permanently, but was betrayed by his soldiers who tried to kill him. Seriously injured, he managed to escape and reached Cuba, where he died some time later.

His successor, Rodrigo Alvárez Palomino, engaged in the wholesale destruction and systematic massacre of indigenous peoples on the coast, who subsequently fled to the heights of the Sierra Nevada de Santa Marta. The founding of Santa Marta is thus characterized by the indigenous peoples' battle against the Spanish invaders, and by the succession of governors who fell victim to their troops' voracious appetite for gold. Indeed, they were often forced to flee before they had even been officially appointed by the Spanish authorities.

Several expeditions left Santa Marta for the interior of the country, in search of gold. The biggest of these was inarguably that of Gonzalo Jiménez de Quesada, the man who "discovered" the Sabana de Bogotá (savanna), where he founded the city of Santafé in 1538.

However, with the arrival of Governor Lope de Orozco in Santa Marta in 1596, farming and stock breeding flourished and, more important still, relations with the indigenous peoples improved considerably through a tacit agreement to non-aggression on the part of both communities. Colonists from several countries — particularly England — settled in the region, importing various farming and cattle breeding techniques. A certain prosperity gradually dawned, arousing the envy of other gold-diggers. Santa Marta thus fell prey to pirates who sacked it on several occasions during the 16th and 17th centuries.

With the creation of the viceroyalty of New Granada in 1717, the region became a province called Magdalena, with Santa Marta as its capital, and the country's principal port city. From 1882 to 1911, a railway was built between Santa Marta and Fundación, an enterprise which proved to be the region's main instrument of development. Bananas became the region's most important crop, and were henceforth exported throughout the world from the port of Santa Marta. The North American-based United Fruit Company tended to this very banana production until it pulled out in the 1940s following numerous labour disputes.

As early as the 1950s, however, Santa Marta resolutely turned to tourism, capitalizing not only on its particularly enchanting setting, but also on the interior of the region and especially the Sierra Nevada de Santa Marta, one of the most beautiful landscapes in all Colombia. Several major tourist attractions now draw many Colombian and international visitors. For instance, Santa Marta is where Simón Bolívar, El Libertador, died December 17, 1830. His grave can be visited in the Quinta de San Pedro Alejandrino, a few kilometres from the city.

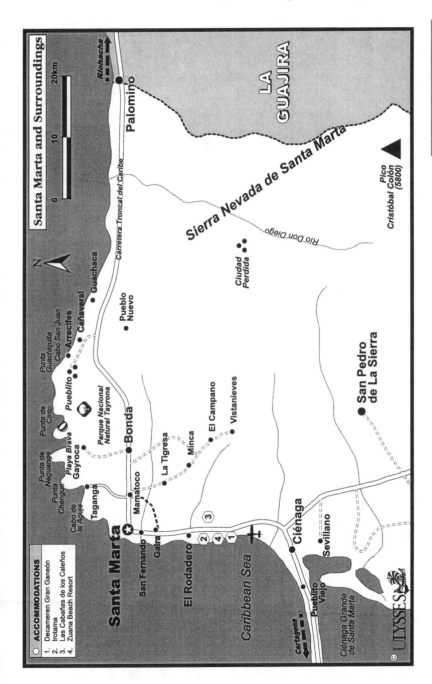

Santa Marta and Surroundings

SANTA MARTA

ACCOMMODATIONS
1. Decameron Gran Ganeón
2. Irotama
3. Las Cabañas de los Caleños
4. Zuana Beach Resort

Santa Marta Today

The first Spaniards settled on the seashore around a central *plaza* (now Plaza Bolívar), with the church on one side and the town hall and other lords' houses on the other. The city then expanded inland, as well as north and south along the coast, all the way to the northwestern extremity of the Sierra Nevada.

Most of the economic activity is centered around the port. Nevertheless, with close to 350,000 inhabitants and a fluctuating population of some 30,000 people, Santa Marta is also a major business centre, with new buildings. Above all, the seaside resort of El Rodadero draws many tourists, and is comparable to those of the Mediterranean.

Sprawled on the sandy shores of the bay of the same name, the city boasts beautiful colonial buildings around Plaza Bolívar, leading to narrow streets lined with scores of shops and many period houses. But it is Avenida Rodrigo de Bastidas (also known as Avenida del Fundador) which impresses tourists the most, with its long and lovely seaside promenade — Paseo de Bastidas — lined with pleasant terraces, affordable hotels and a variety of restaurants for all budgets.

El Rodadero

Some ten kilometres from Santa Marta, El Rodadero, which is in fact a *barrio* (district) of Santa Marta, is the most European seaside resort on the Colombian coast. Here, towering hotels vie with the condominiums (apartments) and the many restaurants, shops and bars to offer a well-to-do clientele everything it could possibly wish for in a "dream" vacation. The white sandy beach draws bathers all year round, but particularly in December and January, when tourists flock here in great numbers. Besides the beach, restaurants and dance clubs, there are few tourist attractions in El Rodadero.

El Rodadero can be reached from Santa Marta by taking the *buseta* marked "El Rodadero-Aeropuerto" on Avenida del Fundador (also known as Carrera 1a), opposite Plaza Bolívar.

In El Rodadero, you can practise every water sport imaginable and make excursions by *lancha* (motor boat) to the neighbouring

beaches. Information is provided right on the beach, at the Corporación de Turismo de Magdalena pavilion on the *paseo de la playa*, Carrera 1a, near Calle 8. This tourist office can give you the details about the excursions to the most interesting and popular beaches (Playa Blanca, among others), and the prices people ask for, as well as the prices that are actually paid.

 FINDING YOUR WAY AROUND

Santa Marta has *carreras* and *calles*, all of which are numbered. There are also *transversales*, *diagonales* and *avenidas* that are named and also numbered. *Avenidas* run parallel to *carreras* and *calles*. *Carreras* run north-south and their numbers increase from east to west, while *calles* run east-west and their numbers increase from south to north.

El Rodadero

Calles in El Rodadero run east-west and their numbers increase from north to south, while *carreras* run north-south and their numbers increase from west to east.

By Plane

Aeropuerto Internacional Simón Bolívar serves the Santa Marta region, receiving local flights from Bogotá, as well as certain international flights, mainly charters. The airport is located about 20 kilometres from Santa Marta, on Carretera Santa Marta-Barranquilla.

Avianca direct domestic flight schedule:

Bogotá, every day 8:28am and 11:23am; Thu and Sun 4:35pm; Mon, Wed and Fri 8:25pm; Thu and Sun 8:35pm; Tue and Sat 8:50pm; 195,000 pesos.
Cali, every day 9:50am with stopover; 232,000 pesos.
Medellín, every day 9:50am; 176,000 pesos.

The following airlines have offices in Santa Marta:

SAM, Calle 14 No. 3-08, Edificio Los Bancos, ☎22 82 11 or 21 07 87

Avianca, Calle 17 No. 2-76, ☎21 02 76 or 21 12 76; El Rodadero, Calle 7 No. 4-27, Edificio Plaza II, ☎22 62 12
AeroRepública, Calle 22 No. 2-14, Room 201, ☎21 01 20 or 21 43 66
American Airlines, Calle 22 No. 2-14, Room 104, ☎21 36 57

By Bus

As elsewhere in Colombia, the bus service between cities is excellent and inexpensive. Several companies offer competitive services and prices to the same destinations, at various prices. All sell tickets at the **Terminal de Transportes** *(Troncal del Caribe, ☎20 90 40)*. You can travel in *colectivos*, *aerovans* or luxury coaches, with departures every hour for nearby destinations like Barranquilla (2 h), Cartagena de Indias (4 h) or Riohacha (3 h), as well as departures at fixed hours for more distant destinations such as Bogotá (20 h), Medellín (15 h) or Bucaramanga (9 h).

Bus Companies

Berlinas del Fonce, ☎23 42 73
Coolibertador, ☎23 85 98
Expresso Brasilia, ☎23 40 88
Copertrán, ☎23 32 22
La Costeña, ☎23 42 73
La Veloz, ☎23 42 73
Rápido Ochoa, ☎20 80 50

Public Transport

A *buseta* (300 pesos) leaves right from the entrance to the airport, and runs through El Rodadero before reaching Plaza Bolívar, in the heart of Santa Marta. A sign on the windshield is clearly marked "El Rodadero-Aeropuerto," with an airplane symbol to indicate the destination. The airport *buseta* also stops in several *barrios* on the way, and crams in as many passengers as the bus will hold, no concern for their comfort. If you have luggage, it is better to take a taxi, which should cost some 5,000 pesos to El Rodadero and 6,000 pesos to Santa Marta.

Public transport is well-organized in Santa Marta, and destinations can be reached either by *busetas* or mini buses. The price is always roughly the same, that is 250 to 350 pesos for all surrounding destinations.

By Taxi

Taxis are yellow ochre and marked *Servicio Público*. They do not have meters, and passengers must negotiate the fare with the driver, which should not exceed 1,000 pesos anywhere within Santa Marta.

Renting a Car or Motorcycle

Renting a car is unnecessary to get around in Santa Marta, since the city can easily be toured on foot. The same holds true for El Rodadero. However, a car can be useful to explore the very lovely countryside toward Riohacha, which can be reached in under three hours.

Though traffic is stressful in Santa Marta itself, the major roads outside the city are much calmer. Bear in mind however, that there is no highway patrol. Colombians do not respect the double line and pass other vehicles on curves or hills.

Some car-rental agencies have offices at the airport as well as in El Rodadero. The rates are more or less the same, depending on the rental option you choose and whether rates, such as weekend specials, are in effect. Here are a few useful agencies for renting a car or motorcycle:

Avis Rent-a-Car, Carrera 4 No. 7-27, Edificio Plaza, Room 105, El Rodadero, ☎28 78 07 or 22 78 09;
Hertz, Carrera 4 No. 7-45, Edificio Plaza, Room 9, El Rodadero, ☎22 71 67 or 22 92 95;
National Car Rental, Carrera 3 No. 7-63, Edificio Centro Internacional, El Rodadero, ☎22 80 78 or 22 87 99;
Las Motos, Carrera 3 No. 9-29, ☎22 97 91. This agency rents out motorcycles by the hour for 12,000 pesos, 30,000 pesos for a half-day and 45,000 pesos for the day. A deposit of 20,000 pesos is required.

 PRACTICAL INFORMATION

Area Code: 5

Mail

Mail goes through **Avianca** *(Mon to Fri 8am to noon and 2pm to 7pm)*, Calle 17 No. 2-76 Santa Marta; El Rodadero, Calle 7 No. 4-27, Edificio Plaza II.

Banks

Santa Marta

Some banks here change currency and traveller's cheques, but it is best to go to the **Banco Industrial Colombiano** (BIC) *(Mon to Thu 8am to 11:30am and 2pm to 4pm, Fri until 4:30pm; Calle 13 No. 4-96, ☎21 23 42, ≈21 17 80).* You can make the most of your day by going in the morning. The bank changes traveller's cheques and currency from just about any country, including Canada, France, Belgium, Switzerland and, of course, the United States.

El Rodadero

No bank in El Rodadero changes traveller's cheques. There are undoubtedly exchange offices, but these charge exhorbitant fees. It is therefore best to do your banking in Santa Marta.

Tourist Information

Santa Marta

Corporación de Turismo de Magdalena, Carrera 2 No. 16-44, Casa de la Cultura, ☎21 24 25.

El Rodadero

Corporación de Turismo de Magdalena also has a branch on the El Rodadero beach *(Mon to Fri 8am to noon and 2pm to 6pm; Carrera 1a, opposite Calle 8)*.

Corporación Nacional de Turismo, Calle 10 No. 3-10, ☎22 94 83.

Santa Marta ★★

The **Catedral de Santa Marta ★★★** *(at Carrera 4a and Calle 17)*, also known as the Basílica Menor, is the oldest church in America. Built in 1529 by Dominican Fray Tomás Ortíz, it was first named the church of Santa Ana. It was promoted to a cathedral in 1533, but it was only much later, in 1766, that the construction of the current whitewashed stone building was undertaken. Built with the blessing of Bishop Fray Agustín Camacho y Rojas and the sponsorship of Governor Andrés Pérez, it is the work of the royal army's architect Don Lucas Gayetano Chacón, and an example of the Romanesque Revival period with a hint of the baroque.

Like all religious structures of the time, the church has a steeple and a raised dome in the centre that dominates the nave, with four main arches made of Italian Carrara marble. The high altar is dedicated to Saint Martha (Santa Marta), sister of Mary Magdalene.

To the right of the main door is the mausoleum where the remains of Don Rodrigo de Bastidas, the founder of the city, are kept. The remains of Simón Bolívar were also kept in this cathedral from 1830 to 1842, at which point they were taken to Caracas, Venezuela, then brought to the Quinta de San Pedro Alejandrino where they now rest. The Santa Marta cathedral holds services at 6pm every day of the week, and Sundays at 7am, 10am, noon and 6pm.

Avenida del Fundador ★★, or **Paseo Bastida**, is the main tourist avenue in Santa Marta. It runs along the length of Santa Marta Bay, and bustles with activity all day long and particularly at night, after 5pm. Having undergone in-depth renovations in 1975 for the festivities surrounding the 450th anniversary of the city's foundation, Avenida del Fundador is now the Santa Marta's "balcony", with its bars, air-conditioned or open-air restaurants, streetfront terraces and gaiety, which cannot help but engage visitors looking for a good time.

The beach is frequented mainly by *Samarios* (residents of Santa Marta), while foreigners

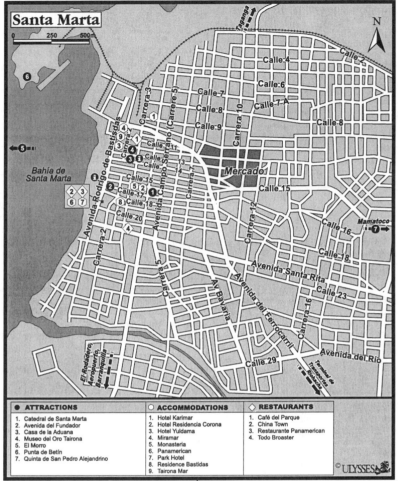

ATTRACTIONS
1. Catedral de Santa Marta
2. Avenida del Fundador
3. Casa de la Aduana
4. Museo del Oro Tairona
5. El Morro
6. Punta de Betín
7. Quinta de San Pedro Alejandrino

ACCOMMODATIONS
1. Hotel Karimar
2. Hotel Residencia Corona
3. Hotel Yuldama
4. Miramar
5. Monasteria
6. Panamerican
7. Park Hotel
8. Residence Bastidas
9. Tairona Mar

RESTAURANTS
1. Café del Parque
2. China Town
3. Restaurante Panamerican
4. Todo Broaster

© ULYSSES

prefer that of El Rodadero, or those of the Parque Nacional Tayrona.

The **Casa de la Aduana** ★★★ *(at Calle 14 and Carrera 2a)* is a beautiful colonial house that is very representative of Santa Marta, since it is infused with the city's past. Built by Governor García de Lerma in 1531, it was the first stone-and-brick house to be constructed on Colombian soil. As such, it was declared a national monument on March 17, 1970. Here began Simón Bolívar's death pangs before he requested to be taken to the Quinta de San Pedro Alejandrino in the dead of night, where he died a few hours later. The construction of the second storey in 1730 is attributed to brothers Nicolás and Domingo Jimeno. Upon Nicolás' death in 1799, the house was repur-

chased by Doña Ramona Oligós, then confiscated by the government in 1855.

After several changes of vocation (it was, among other things, the head office of the United Fruit Company in 1891, and had housed the Cooperativa Bananera del Magdalena in 1933), the Casa de la Aduana now houses the Museo Arqueológico Tayrona of the Banco de la República, better known as the Museo del Oro Tayrona.

The **Museo del Oro Tayrona** ★★★ *(Mon to Fri 8am to noon and 2pm to 6pm; at Calle 14 and Carrera 2a)* is set up in the Casa de la Aduana (see above), an old colonial house restored by the Banco de la República and located north of Plaza Bolívar. All of the numerous museums devoted to gold in Colombia are worth visiting, not only for the pieces featured, but also for their historical and ethnological significance. Though Santa Marta's gold museum is not the most important, it is interesting in that it is devoted to the Tayrona civilization. Featured among the exhibits are pottery and many examples of goldwork produced by highly accomplished Tayrona goldsmiths, including bracelets, rings and pectoral ornaments. The Tayrona people inhabited the Sierra Nevada de Santa Marta, and their main city was named Tayronaca. The name "Tayrona" was later attributed to all peoples who were influenced by this civilization. The culture dates back to 500 BC and declined upon the arrival of the first conquistadors.

El Morro ★ is a rock in the middle of Santa Marta Bay, visible from the beach. In colonial times, the rock was used to defend the city against pirate attacks. Now a lighthouse stands there, but some ruins on the island testify that it once served as a prison for Creole rebels.

The **Punta de Betín ★★** is a rocky headland situated north of Santa Marta. It was also used to defend the city against pirate attacks, and four functional cannons were permanently maintained here during this "glorious" era.

These days, the Punta de Betín is home to the Colombian-German biological and oceanographic research centre. It has a magnificent view that takes in the entire city.

The **Quinta de San Pedro Alejandrino ★★★** *(every day 9:30am to 4:30pm during tourist season, closed Mon and Tue during low season; some 3 km from downtown, follow Avenida Santa Rita, which leads to Avenida del Libertador)* is a villa recognized as a national shrine as it contains the venerated remains of Simón Bolívar. The villa is surrounded by magnificent gardens in which stand 11 smaller buildings, including a distillery and a wine cellar. The museum features a host of objects and curios that once belonged to the great leader. Two statues stand in the entrance of this national treasure: one is of El Libertador, of course, while the other is of his personal physician, Don Alejandro Próspero.

Built to the southwest of what was then the brand-new city of Santa Marta by Don Francisco de Godoy Cortesía in 1608, the Quinta de San Pedro Alejandrino was a farm that specialized in the growing and refinement of sugarcane. Its claim to fame came some 200 years later when the great liberator died here on December 17, 1830.

The main house, the stables, sugar mill, museum and distillery have a very Mediterranean architectural style, while the overall impression is one of calm and serenity, as if Colombia's tumultuous history had decided to rest here.

The Quinta de San Pedro Alejandrino also houses the **Museo Bolivariano de Arte Contemporaneo ★★★** *(Mon to Sun 9:30am to 5pm; ☎20 70 21, ⌐20 65 89)*. Here, visitors can admire contemporary works by artists from countries that were liberated by Simón Bolívar, including Venezuela, Peru, Bolivia, Panamá and, of course, Colombia. Founded on July 24, 1986 by the then-president of the Republic, Belisario Betancur, it fulfils the vision of painter Armando Villegas, in which all the countries liberated by Bolívar would be brought together by the arts even though they were never united as a federation as Bolívar had dreamed. The museum obtained funding from the Colombian government, while artists from the participating nations donated their works to the exhibit. Today, the museum also organizes temporary exhibits by contemporary artists from these nations.

To explore the area surrounding Santa Marta, inquiries can be made at:

Tierra Mar Aire (TMA), Calle 15 No. 2-60, Room 3, ☎21 12 57;
Tayronatur, Calle 16 No. 5-33, ☎21 21 82 or 21 27 83, ⌐21 49 13.

El Rodadero ★★★

The **Iglesia Santa María Estrella del Mar ★★** *(Calle 8, between Carreras 3a and 4)* is a modern, octogonal-shaped, open-air church protected by wrought-iron gates reminiscent of those used in Spanish decoration in colonial times. While not an architectural masterpiece, the church does stand out.

The **Acuario y Museo del Mar Rodadero ★★★** *(5,000 pesos; every day 8am to 6pm; ☎22 72 22)* is a 10-minute boat ride from the El Rodadero beach. The first aquarium in South America, the Rodadero aquarium and sea museum was inaugurated over 30 years ago. Comprising pools of various shapes and sizes, whose waters come straight from the sea, the aquarium allows visitors to appreciate a great

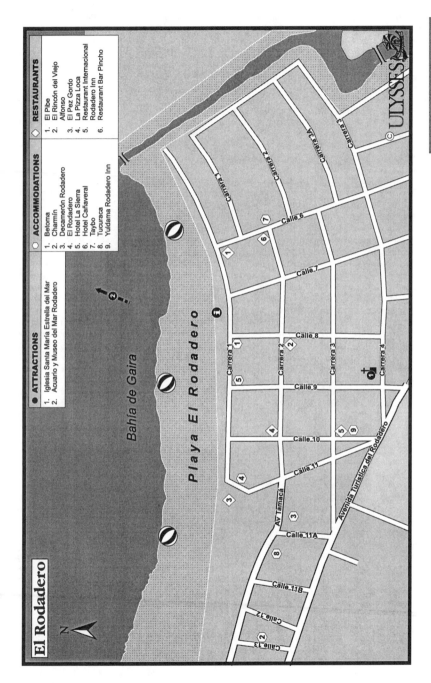

El Rodadero

● ATTRACTIONS

1. Iglesia Santa María Estrella del Mar
2. Acuario y Museo del Mar Rodadero

○ ACCOMMODATIONS

1. Betoma
2. Charmín
3. Decamerón Rodadero
4. El Rodadero
5. Hotel La Sierra
6. Hotel Cañaveral
7. Taybo
8. Tucuraca
9. Yuldama Rodadero Inn

◇ RESTAURANTS

1. El Pibe
2. El Rincón del Viejo Alfonso
3. El Pez Gordo
4. La Pizza Loca
5. Restaurant Internacional Rodadero Inn
6. Restaurant Bar Pincho

Bahía de Gaira

Playa El Rodadero

ⓒ ULYSSES

SANTA MARTA

variety of Caribbean fish and mammals in their natural habitats, including sharks, seals and dolphins. On-site guides provide explanations in Spanish, but it is possible to follow along a little, especially since the pools are identified with names and illustrations.

The seals were trained at the world's best aquariums, and put on a fascinating show, while two species of dolphins stun audiences with their talents.

Smaller aquariums house a wide variety of fish and corallines, including moray eels, tunas, crabs as well as corals, gorgonians, sea urchins, shellfish and sponges — everything, in fact, that makes up the sea bed of the Colombian coast.

The adjoining museum exhibits objects collected from old galleons by the museum's director, Captain Francisco Ospína Návia, an experienced diver as well as a very good storyteller. Visitors can check out the *Darién* craft, in which the captain and his son, Juan Carlos, explored the Colombian coasts, covering 3,000 kilometres from Santa Marta to Esmeralda, in Equador, by sailing the Atrato and San Juan rivers.

The **Agencia de Viajes y Turismo del Valle Tours** specializes in eco-tourism as well as archaeological and sports tourism: Carrera 1a, at Calle 8, El Rodadero, ☎22 45 20, ↝22 87 40.

Parque Nacional Tayrona ★★★

The **Parque Nacional Tayrona** *(every day 8:30am to 5:30pm)* lies at the foot of the Sierra Nevada de Santa Marta and stretches all the way to the Caribbean Sea. It begins east of Santa Marta, extending over 85 kilometres to the Río Piedras. This nature reserve has a long-established reputation in Colombia and throughout the world for the beauty of its white-sand beaches, the crystal-clear waters in its numerous little deserted bays shaded by coconut palms, and its coral formation that follows the mountain, whose fauna and flora are representative of those found throughout Colombia. The park has temperatures ranging from 19°C to 33°C, and landscapes that include deserts where nothing but cacti grow, as well as blooming rain forests where lush vegetation thrives, where the humidity is stifling and where the cries of monkeys, the appearance of

an iguana (hunted for meat) and the song of exotic birds in the enveloping mist transport visitors to a surreal and almost prehistoric world. The boundaries of time seem to melt away in this place, where life has survived for thousands of years.

Parque Nacional Tayrona is dedicated to the research, conservation, propagation and protection of flora and fauna. However, it also boasts the major archaeological site of Pueblito, a Tayrona village, the vestiges of which can be admired in the heart of the forest.

No road leads to Pueblito, and one must walk there accompanied by a guide. Departures leave as early as 6:30am, and return to the hotel around 6pm. The excursion takes four to six hours along a narrow path that is not always as safe as the guide asserts. In fact, the guide must often clear a path through the vegetation with a machete. This famous stone-paved path is itself an archaeological relic. It was built over 1,000 years ago by the Tayrona Indians who populated Pueblito. This path is special because it has many loose stones along it, at more or less regular intervals. Stepping on one of these stones produces a dull sound, an alarm signal as it were, that reverberates through the foliage. The paths were specifically designed this way so that the Tayrona could hear visitors approaching. Friends were then received with all the dignity owed to their rank. Strangers or foes, on the other hand, were killed on the spot, without further ceremony, with a curare-poisoned dart (strychnine poison drawn from nux vomica, a tropical tree) blown from a blowpipe. The system was foolproof. The guide stops to explain and demonstrate this phenomenon. Otherwise, the alarm goes unnoticed by the eyes — and particularly the ears — of visitors who only perceive a fault in the construction!

The path can inflict bumps and sprains on today's enemies, so only the sure-footed should venture here. The path climbs some 400 metres, and the heat and humidity force you to stop every five minutes. Not recommended for children or people not in good physical shape.

The guide assures visitors that the path will stop climbing and will start going downhill exactly three hours after and 400 metres above the point of departure. This is not the case. The trail continues upward for at least 100 metres more. The guide candidly admits estimating the height of the mountain accord-

The Tayrona

When the first conquistadors disembarked on the northeast coast of Colombia in the 16th century, they encountered several groups of indigenous people established in the Sierra Nevada de Santa Marta, on territories that, for want of a better term, they referred to as "provinces". Among these groups were the Tayronas, who inhabited the Río Don Diego valley, and whose main settlement was called Tayronaca. Later, the name "Tayrona" was used to refer to the region's villages as a whole as well as an archaeological zone and a pre-Columbian culture made up of different peoples who lived in a particular region during a certain time.

These native groups began forming a more homogenous society around AD 500, and the civilization reached its height around AD 1000. The majority belonged to the Chibcha linguistic family, which covered a fairly vast territory, from Central America all the way to northern and central Colombia, and part of Venezuela.

The Spanish thus encountered a large hierarchically structured population. The Tayrona population was decimated, and even systematically exterminated soon after it was "discovered". Villages were razed and the few survivors fled to the heights of the Sierra Nevada.

ing to how much his group complains. Such tactics are employed so as not to discourage the less enthusiastic, who are more accustomed to the air-conditioned comfort of hotels. At any rate, we forge ahead! It is wise to bring a few bottles of cold water, insect repellent, a terry-cloth towel (which will prove to be a must!) and good walking shoes. It is another hour and a half of climbing the perilous and narrow paths beneath huge rocks and steep inclines before we reach Pueblito.

It is well worth the effort, though, and the guide's questionable estimates are soon forgiven. Indeed, upon approching the village, one has the impression walking right into a Native American legend. A huge engraved stone stands one-hundred metres before the remnants of Pueblito itself, which lies beneath the rays of the sun that manage to cut through the sombre foliage of trees and the humid and stagnant haze like spotlights. The stone foundations mark the exact location of the native huts that once stood here. That of the cacique was perched on a hill, along with those reserved for religious ceremonies, allowing civil and religious dignitaries a good overview of the community. The other dwellings are tucked away here and there at the edge of the forest, according to the owner's social status. These native peoples practised farming and hunting. Fish also made up a good part of their diet.

The Sierra Nevada de Santa Marta

The Sierra Nevada de Santa Marta — a name that comes from the Spanish — is a mountain range that looms up abruptly on Colombia's Atlantic coast. Stretching over more than 17,000 square kilometres, it spans the departments of Magdalena, La Guajira and Cesar. Its peaks reach elevations of up to 5,700 metres and feed countless rivers and waterways that flow into the narrow valleys. This massif boasts a great diversity of vegetation, ranging from the dry thicket of the desert to a medley of moist groves and the scattered vegetation adapted to the tundra-like regions of perpetual snow. The fauna here is just as diverse, including a variety of birds (seagulls, falcons, buzzards), small mammals (foxes, monkeys, bats) and reptiles (snakes and iguanas). The climate is characterized by heavy precipitation, humidity and cloud cover, but also by drought, as in La Guajira, for instance.

The region is important not only because of its geographical and ecological characteristics, but because it was home to a sizable pre-Hispanic civilization. It is still inhabited by various ethnic groups.

The First Peoples

The region's first inhabitants respected the environment. Their stone terraces, roads and canals were built in such a way as to protect their houses and other buildings on the steep slopes from erosion. Among the best-known Tayrona settlements are Pueblito and Ciudad Perdida.

Way of Life

The native dwelling of the Sierra Nevada was a circular hut made of local materials that were easy to find and to work with, such as wood, bamboo and palm fronds. Similar dwellings are still used today. Tasks were divided according to gender: cooking was the main duty of women, while men took care of pottery making, which was indispensable to daily life. They made vases, mortars to grind seeds into powder or flour, rotating spits and containers of various shapes and colours, that were used for cooking, the distribution of food and the storing of liquids.

While men devoted themselves to weeding and sowing, fishing and hunting, women gathered fruit, fetched water, gathered wool, ground corn and spun cotton.

Social Organization

The Tayrona had a hierarchal social structure. The elite consisted of the *naomas*, or high priests, followed, in order of importance, by warriors, weavers, potters, farmers, sculptors and fine metal workers, and finally the lower classes. Chronicles of the time also mention a political leader who ruled a province that encompassed many villages which were in turn governed by a cacique. These villages were themselves subdivided into districts, which were watched over by a "minor" cacique subject to the cacique of the village.

Music

Tayrona music — probably like all native music — is, above all, a reflection and expression of origins, traditions, the forces of nature, life and death. All religious ceremonies are thus accompanied by flute melodies, and the sounds of resonant plates similar to a gong, and large, hollow shells.

Infrastructure

The hundred or so dwellings that made up the village of Pueblito offer a glimpse of a remarkably advanced civilization. Indeed, all were connected to a system of watertight aqueducts with a stone foundation that were dug in the ground. This network, which dates some 1,000 years before the arrival of the Spanish, supplied the houses with drinking water and drained the waste water from them. It is surprising to note that, at the time of the conquest, Europeans did not enjoy the same quality of life as certain South American native communities living in the heart of the dense forest had known for centuries. Strolling through the peaceful village that is overgrown with huge trees and still inhabited by a native family responsible for greeting visitors, one suddenly finds oneself in direct, spiritual touch with the ancient Tayrona culture. A feeling that is not soon forgotten.

Pueblito ★ ★ ★

Pueblito is located near the sea, and its 3,000-odd inhabitants specialize in fishing and the gathering of seashells. Pueblito was once a trade centre where the fruits of the sea could be traded for products made in the mountains. From an archaeological point of view, Pueblito is characterized by its terraces and its aqueduct, which traverses the village and connects to every dwelling and worship site.

Ciudad Perdida ★ ★ ★

Ciudad Perdida — "Teyuna" in the Chibcha language — was built circa AD 700. It is one of the largest urban centres among the more than 250 settlements discovered in the Sierra Nevada de Santa Marta. Deep in the jungle, Ciudad Perdida is laid out on a sloping stretch of land whose elevation ranges from 950 to 1,300 metres above sea level. Situated on the north side of the Sierra Nevada de Santa Marta, the "Lost City" is spread over the banks of the Río Buritaca and was a major economic and political centre for the Tayrona. In fact, 40 percent of its territory was set aside for public buildings, while the rest was used for private dwellings. Depending on the year and circumstances, its population fluctuated between 1,400 and 3,000 inhabitants. More than 250 terraces were scattered over eight districts or villages, and were surrounded by family dwellings, workshops, temples, and public spaces. Stone-paved roads and stairs provided easy access from one terrace to the other.

Family dwellings were built on circular terraces, the circumference of which depended on the topography. Some terraces were egg-shaped, while others could accommodate several dwellings. Others still were reinforced with a low stone wall. The Tayrona also built sophisticated canals that supplied and collected water. They also had an irrigation system to channel water to the terraced hillside on which they grew crops.

Uncovered in 1975 by archaeologist Julio César Sepúlveda, Ciudad Perdida is one of the most important Tayrona cities, and demonstrates the ability of this culture to adapt to its environment. You can still see 160 terraces in the mountains here today, surrounded by trees standing over 50 metres tall. Tourists now have authorization to visit the place if accompanied by a guide. The three-day trek to Ciudad Perdida is made on a donkey, with sleeping bags or hammocks serving as nighttime accommodations. You can also get there by helicopter during certain periods of the year. The trip by helicopter takes one our each way and costs 500,000 pesos return. Inquire at travel agencies.

Taganga ★★★

The quaint little village of Taganga is definitely worth the trip. Situated in a lovely little bay, it appears suddenly at the foot of the mountain, surrounded by an idyllic landscape right out of a fairytale. But the place is real enough, and less than 20 minutes north of Santa Marta. A mini bus marked "Taganga" will take you there, leaving every 15 minutes from Avenida del Fundador (also known as Carrera 1a), opposite Plaza Bolívar.

Taganga was and remains a fishing village with close to 1,000 inhabitants. Several fishing boats attest to this, and can be seen both on the water and the beach, where necessary repairs are made before they head back out to sea. Some fishers, however, have found it more advantageous to pilot sea excursions, notably to Playa Grande. Inquiries can be made right on the beach. Since they have formed a partnership, these guides all charge the same rates for the same distances and destinations.

Taganga offers few attractions apart from its location and charm. Its many little *tiendas* (stalls) set up right on the beach are definitely part of its charm. Here, you can savour a wide variety of seafood while seated at a table beneath a parasol, refreshed by the salt breeze and a cold beer. Besides the lobster, the *sancocho de pescados*, fish soup (Colombian bouillabaise) with carrots, plantains and corn cobs is a must. Served with rice and a vegetable salad, *sancocho* constitutes a full meal *(3,500 pesos)*. But one could hardly claim to have experienced Taganga without having tasted *pargo frito*, seasoned red snapper, fried and served whole with a vegetable salad with fried plantain slices, the whole liberally sprinkled with lime juice *(5,000 pesos)*. Without a doubt, the best *pargo* in all Colombia.

Ciénaga Grande ★★★

Ciénaga Grande de Santa Marta is the largest swamp lake in Colombia. In fact, *Ciénaga grande* means "large swamp" in Spanish. Located less than a half-hour's drive from Santa Marta, toward Barranquilla, Ciénaga Grande is the largest of nine swamps formed at the mouth of the Río Magdalena. To the southwest is a protected area for flora and fauna that is one of the best places for bird watching, 150 species having been spotted here. Ciénaga was once a huge bay that was altered by the development of a barrier of sand and sediment from the Sierra Nevada. This barrier formed the island of Salamanque, a narrow strip of land on which the Carretera Santa Marta-Barranquilla is built. By permanently cutting off access to the sea, this highway caused a major ecological disaster, modifying the salinity of the water, which led to the destruction of millions of trees. Travellers along this road are met by an apocalyptic vision. The sight of all those dead trees sends cold shivers down your spine. Bleached and mummified by the sun, they look like skeletons that have been left unburied.

On the lake itself, you can visit villages including Nueva Venecia (New Venice), Trojas de Cataca, Pueblo Viejo, Buenavista and Pajarales. These fishing villages are built on islands or on piles, and can only be reached by boat.

ACCOMMODATIONS

Santa Marta

Santa Marta has hotels for all tastes and budgets. Use your intuition to choose a hotel with an *ambiente familiar* (family ambiance), to avoid ending up in a brothel.

Hotel Kalimar *($; pb, ≈, ⊗, ☎, tv, ▣, ℜ; Carrera 4 No. 10-08, ☎21 51 20, ↝23 42 83)* is a small hotel with 20-odd rooms in a renovated building some hundred years old. Very inexpensive for the comfort offered, the establishment is within five minutes' walking distance from the beach, although it also borders on a neighbourhood that is considered unsafe at night. Nevertheless, since the hotel is on a wide and well-lit street, you can reach it safely by taxi. Another plus to consider: its restaurant is open 24 hours a day. Moreover, the owner is fluent in English, having lived some 10 years in the United States.

The **Miramar** *($; ⊗, ℜ; Calle 10c No. 1c-59, ☎21 47 56)* is a Santa Marta institution and is worth a visit for that reason alone. In fact, groups of budget travellers of all ages and from all over the world gather here in an utterly disorderly seventies' ambiance. You can get the latest news about your own country here, as well as tips on just about any destination in Colombia or elsewhere, since one of your roommates is likely to have passed through there. The owner speaks English and organizes the cheapest excursions in Santa Marta, in accordance with guests' budgets. You can sleep in a dormitory for less than 5,000 pesos, or rent a private room. The hotel is a former colonial residence with an interior courtyard that is used for many purposes, including a dining room, a reading or television room and a classroom for foreign languages. The rooms are clean, except for the lingering smell of marijuana, something certain travellers won't mind. Since the place is so crowded, be on your guard to avoid getting robbed, particularly if travelling alone.

The **Monasterio** *($; pb, ⊗, ▣, ℜ; Calle 16 No. 2-08, ☎21 10 60)* is in a historic house undergoing renovation with an interior garden, courtyard and balcony. Several rooms lead onto a large exterior balcony overlooking a narrow street. The reception is friendly, at this budget hotel, and the rooms are clean and very large, with high ceilings and huge varnished-wood doors. The owner assures us that he will keep prices down even after the renovations have been completed. However, one must thus calculate a 20% increase in order to absorb the costs, though this will not change the price category of the hotel.

The **Park Hotel** *($; pb, ⊗, mb, ☎, tv, ▣, ℜ; Carrera 1a, No. 18-67, ☎21 12 15, 21 49 39, ↝21 27 85)* is a rather impressive four-storey building that has 80 rooms, including 25 with a television, telephone and mini bar. Located by the sea, it is a hotel for small and medium budgets. Some rooms have a balcony with a view of the ocean, making them the most worthwhile. It is also advisable to get a room with a mini bar or fridge in order to have cold water at night.

Residence Bastidas *($; pb, ⊗; Carrera 2 No. 18-26, ☎21 16 02)* rents out budget rooms, which is probably its only asset. Nevertheless, it is a good choice for those who only plan on using their room to sleep, since this place is only about 100 metres from the beach.

As its name indicates, the **Hotel Residencia Corona** *($; ⊗, ℜ; Calle 16 No. 3-23, ☎21 30 32)* is more of a budget boarding house than an actual hotel. The hosts show great willingness, but are unaccustomed to receiving foreign guests. Some tourists will enjoy spending some time in an exotic setting, while others will feel ill at ease here due to the lack of communication.

The **Tairona Mar** *($; pb, ≈, ⊗, ℜ; Carrera 1a No. 11-41, ☎21 24 08)* is a very old house made of varnished wood and located a stone's throw from the Yuldama hotel. Set back some 100 feet from the street, with a terrace in front and a very attractive interior courtyard, it is a budget hotel with a great deal of style, and is exclusively frequented by Colombians. The Tairona Mar, however, does not hesitate to double its rates during peak season since, as its name indicates, it is located right by the sea.

The **Panamerican** *($$-$$$; pb, ≈, ⊗, mb, ☎, tv, K, ▣, ℜ; Carrera 1a No. 18-23, ☎21 18 24, 21 39 32, 21 29 61 or 21 12 39, ↝21 47 51)* has 47 rooms, some of which have a balcony and a view of the sea. It is a hotel for medium budgets that offers several rooms with kitchenettes. Moreover, some rooms are air conditioned, while others have but a fan. The latter option is recommended if you only plan on using your room for sleeping. Given the proximity of the beach and the refreshing night breeze, the fan is sufficient, especially since it also chases away the mosquitos. If you choose a room with a kitchenette, opt for air conditioning as well, since the heat can become unbearable around the stove at any time of the day.

The beachfront **Hotel Yuldama** *($$$-$$$$; pb, =, ⊗, mb, ☎, tv, ▨, ℜ; Carrera 1 No. 12 -19, ☎21 00 63, 21 28 89 or 21 46 19, ≈21 49 32)* is an ordinary modern-style hotel. The four-storey establishment has 60 rooms with all the services of a major hotel, but without the cost, and even has a terrace with a view of the sea. Neutral interior decor and decent service, but nothing more.

El Rodadero

Because El Rodadero is the preferred vacation spot in the Santa Marta area, all hotel rates go up by about 20% during the high season, which is from late December to February and during Easter holidays. Moreover, even if the hotels are not located right on the beach, they are not very far away. El Rodadero is easily explored on foot in less than 20 minutes. Everything is thus within reach, be it shopping centres, hotels, restaurants, the beach, or nightclubs. What is more, El Rodadero was built as a tourist resort, so hotel staff are always very open-minded toward vacationers — who are not always compelled to be so themselves.

Budget hotels are easy to find in this area, though none of them have hot water. However, as the temperature only rarely dips below 28°C, the hosts affirm quite plainly that the water here is always as hot as one could wish.

The **Charmin** *($; pb, ⊗, =, ☎, tv, ▨, P; Calle 13 No. 2-41, ☎22 06 16, ≈22 82 53)* is a small, unpretentious 22-room hotel that offers good quality service to budget travellers.

The **Taybo** *($-$$; pb, ⊗, =, K, ☎, tv, ▨, ℜ, P; Calle 6 No. 2-43, ☎22 83 36, 22 74 48 or 22 98 39, ≈22 74 48)* is a four-storey budget hotel in a new building, with 42 plain but quiet rooms and, above all, a staff that is eager to please. The rooms are clean and well furnished, taking the hot climate into account.

The **Tucuraca** *($-$$$; pb, ⊗, ▨, ℜ; Carrera 2 No. 12-53, ☎22 74 93, ≈23 12 76)* is a decent two-storey motel-style hotel less than 100 metres from the beach. The rooms are clean and the welcome gracious.

The **Betoma** *($$-$$$; pb, hw, ⊗, =, ☎, tv, mb, balcony, ▨; Calle 8 No. 1-58, ☎22 73 39, 22 73 40 or 22 71 12, ≈22 80 12)* is a place for travellers with medium budgets. Less than 30 metres from the beach and charging 80,000 pesos per day for two people, the Betoma boasts 65 rooms with balconies and an indirect view of the sea, as well as meeting rooms, a café, a bar, a restaurant, a small swimming pool and shops. The lobby lacks charm, but the reception staff is attentive.

The beachfront **El Rodadero** *($$-$$$; pb, hw, ⊗, =, ☎, tv, ▨, ≈; Carrera 1a No. 1-29, ☎22 72 62, 22 75 23 or 22 84 57, ≈22 73 71)* is a real bargain. The place is clean and offers a family ambiance and a friendly welcome. The 44 rooms and 10 suites are a little sobre, but decently decorated. The hotel is in a low and modern building that looks more like a motel.The entrance blends into the setting of exotic trees. The vast reception area is decorated with rattan furniture. Though this is not a big hotel, even travellers on larger budgets will find it pleasant.

One block from the sea, **Hotel Cañaveral** *($$$-$$$$; pb, hw, ⊗, =, ☎, tv, mb, ▨, ℜ; Carrera 2a No. 11-65, ☎22 70 02, 22 71 46 or 22 71 12, ≈22 80 76)* offers rooms with balcony and a view of the sea or the mountain. It is a modern, six-storey Mediterranean-style building painted in the Greek colours – white and blue. The clean and quiet rooms have ceramic-tiled floors, and a simple but adequate decor. The reception staff is pleasant.

The **Decamerón Rodadero** *($$$-$$$$; pb, hw, ⊗, =, ☎, tv, mb, ▨, ℜ; Carrera 2a No. 11a-98, ☎22 70 28 or 22 70 15)* is an unattractive blue-yellow-and-pink building set right on the beach, in the heart of El Rodadero. Like other Decamerón hotels, this establishment offers all-inclusive packages including accommodation, meals with wine, drinks and even cigarettes. This package enables you to plan a fixed holiday budget for one or two people, or even for the whole family. Not everyone enjoys this type of vacation or not. Although there is little variety, Decamerón hotels are known for their customer satisfaction. The Decamerón Rodadero is a better choice than the Decamerón Gran Galeón (see further below), which is too far off the beaten path. Indeed, the Rodadero is right in the middle of El

Rodadero, so guests can roam the area on foot late into the night.

Hotel La Sierra *($$$-$$$$; pb, hw, ⊗, ≡, ☎, tv, mb, ▤, ℛ, function room; Carrera 1a No. 9-47, ☎22 79 60 or 22 71 97, ⌐22 81 98)* is a modern, Mediterranean-style hotel with 75 rooms and 14 suites, spread over eight floors, whose main entrance leads right onto the beach. The rooms with ceramic-tiled floors are huge and simply furnished: most have a balcony and a view of the sea. Good quality for the price.

The **Yuldama Rodadero Inn** *($$$$-$$$$$; pb, hw, ⊗, ≡, ☎, tv, mb, ▤, ≈, △, nightclub, bar, café, ℛ, ⊘, P; Carrera 3 No. 10-40, ☎22 92 52, 22 92 76 or 22 71 12, ⌐22 92 32)* is a new 90-room hotel that, like the Yuldama hotel in Santa Marta, is a bargain for those with moderate budgets. The hotel has a swimming pool for children and adults, a sauna, a gym, shops, a restaurant (see p 148), a bar, a café and a nightclub – and all less than 500 metres from the sea. Although the decor of the reception area is somewhat cold, this six-storey hotel offers all modern conveniences and a dedicated staff.

Around Santa Marta

Outside El Rodadero, toward Barranquilla via the airport, are a few hotels along some 15 kilometres of beaches with grey but fine sand, only some parts of which are supervised. Signs are clearly marked in French, English and German: "The beach outside this area is no longer under the hotel's supervision." The Sheraton Four Points hotel was under construction here during our visit.

Las Cabañas de los Caleños *($; pb, ⊗, tv; Barrio La Paz, ☎22 40 22)* belong to brothers Dagoberto, Alonso and Arturo Gómez, who come from the region of Cali. Hence the name of the establishment, which consists of motel rooms (five units) located about 100 feet into the La Paz *barrio*, opposite the Irotama hotel, which is 800 metres from the beach. A change of scene is guaranteed, since the hotel lies in an essentially Colombian district that is little frequented by foreigners. The newly-built units are clean, with floors and decent furnishings. You must meet Dagoberto, one of the owners, a Colombian-born naturalized Canadian who lived in Montreal for 20 years and knows everything there is to see off the beaten path in the vicinity of Santa Marta. Dagoberto speaks English and French. Inquiries can be made at the El Pez Gordo restaurant (see p 148), right on El Rodadero beach, at Carrera 1a and Calle 11.

Like the one in El Rodadero, the **Decamerón Gran Galeón** *($$$-$$$$; pb, hw, ⊗, ≡, tv, mb, ▤, ℛ; Km 17, Carretera Santa Marta-Barranquilla, ☎22 80 76 or 22 80 78, ⌐21 80 92)* offers the all-inclusive packages. Here, however, guests are completely isolated and have no other choice but to spend their day at the hotel, unless they take part in an excursion. This formula is ideal for families, but unsuitable for adventurous or curious types. The hotel itself is about ten storeys tall and built in a half-circle by the sea, though it cuts off the view of the mountain. Guests here can enjoy all water sports and facilities in a kind of completely self-contained village.

The **Irotama** *($$$$$; pb, hw, ⊗, ≡, ☎, tv, mb, ▤, ≈, ⊘, Turkish bath, △, ℛ, cafeteria, bars, nightclub, P, function room; Km 14, Carretera Santa Marta-Barranquilla, ☎21 80 21 or 21 81 21, ⌐21 80 77)* is a five-star hotel that is located away from the centre of town and right on the beach, and offers a unique setting with 65 rooms, 14 suites and 25 *cabañas*. These *cabañas* refer to private, stone-built and thatched-roof cabins, each boasting its own terrace beneath the palm trees, with a patio and lawn, and a path leading right to the beach. The *cabañas* are a more worthwhile choice than the rooms because of the intimacy they provide. The hotel offers all the services one might expect from a hotel of this calibre.

Zuana Beach Resort *($$$$$; pb, hw, ≡, ☎, tv, mb, ▤, kitchen and dining room in the suites, ≈, ⊘, Turkish bath, △, ℛ, P, cafeteria, bars, nightclub, shops, supermarket, function room; Carrera 2a No. 6-80, Avenida Tamacá, Bello Horizonte, ☎22 46 52 or 22 46 53, ⌐22 46 71)* is a brand-new five-star hotel that, with its three swimming pools, bars, beach and water sports in a luxurious ambiance, cannot but promote relaxation and blissful idleness. The 167 rooms and 18 suites are huge and all have a balcony with a view of the sea and deluxe furniture. The hotel encloses the pools, which are surrounded by tables with dried palm-frond parasols. There are three bars, including one right in one of the pools. In the vast lobby, decorated with tropical furniture and scores of green plants, are shops that sell souvenirs and beach accessories. The Zu

Market sells everything from beer, wine and 100other alcoholic beverages to kitchen products and frozen food. The hotel staff is affable and speaks English. The hotel recently opened a recreation centre comprising two tennis courts, two squash courts, a park and an arcade. The Zuana Beach Resort is part owner of a nine-hole golf course, which boasts two lakes and about ten sand traps. The clubhouse also has with a swimming pool.

Parque Nacional Tayrona

You can find accommodation right in the Parque Nacional Tayrona, though this will only appeal to nature lovers.

The **Finca El Paraíso y Bukarú** *($; ℜ; Arrecifes, ☎21 47 56)* consists of two campgrounds by the sea, in the Tayrona national park, 40 kilometres from Santa Marta. You can pitch your tent here, rent camping equipment, hang your own hammock outdoors between two trees or rent one if need be. You can also stay in wooden, thatched-roof *cabañas* for 4,000 to 10,000 pesos per person per day. These campgrounds have everything you'll need, including showers. The phone number below is that of the Miramar hotel (see p 144), and departures for the park are every day at 10:30am from the hotel's entrance on Calle 10c No. 1-59.

Taganga

In Taganga, less than 20 minutes from Santa Marta, there are two superb little hotels, one of which is in the very heart of the village, while the other is perched on the mountain. Both are sure to please the most demanding of travellers with the quality of the accommodations, the staffs' friendliness and professionalism, and the beautiful views of the small Taganga Bay.

The **Bahía Taganga** *($$; pb, ⊗, ≈, tv, mb, ℜ; ☎21 76 20)* is perched on a hill at the northernmost tip of the beach. Its superb location ensures that all of its 20 rooms have a view, some with a balcony overlooking the sea, others with no balcony but a view of the mountain. The hotel is comfortable and has family suites. The reception is warm and the whole place is very relaxing.

Facing the Taganga beach, **La Ballena Azul** *($$$-$$$$; pb, ⊗, ≈, ☎, tv, mb, ▣, ℜ;* ☎21 66 68 or 21 50 93, ⊷21 75 80, www.ballena-azul.com)* is a 30-room hotel in the heart of the *pueblo*. This charming hotel is perfect for those seeking tranquillity and a change of scene, while still being able to practise water sports such as snorkelling or diving. Owned by a Franco-Colombian family called Trujillo-Girardot and managed by the son, Sébastien Girardot, the hotel is perfect for a romantic getaway. Renovated less than three years ago, the building was formerly a colonial house with a magnificent interior garden overgrown with flowers, palm trees and cacti, and crowned with a balcony supported by arches onto which the rooms open out. The hotel is painted white, enhanced by touches of blue, a reminder of its name, which means "The Blue Whale". The rooms offer all modern conveniences, and some have a balcony and a view of the sea. For over 15 years now, la Ballena Azul has built its reputation on the quality of its restaurant, which specializes in seafood (see p 149). The staff speaks both English and French. The hotel organizes its own excursions to Ciudad Perdida or the Parque Nacional Tayrona, and also offers a scuba-diving package that includes double-occupation accommodation, a courtesy cocktail, the hotel T-shirt, continental breakfast, dinner on the terrace and two dives a day, for a mimimum of two days, all for 130,000 pesos per person per day.

Visitors can also find a **house for rent** *($$$; ask for Señor Miguel A. Bustamante, at the Casa de Las Ruedas, ☎21 64 62 in Santa Marta and ☎368 44 67 in Barranquilla)* right on the beach for five to eight people at 100, 000 pesos per day. The house comes with a television set, a refrigerator and a kitchenette, a bathroom, fans, and four bedrooms.

 # RESTAURANTS

Santa Marta

Santa Marta has restaurants for all tastes and budgets, many of which have terraces along the Avenida del Fundador. For classier restaurants and a better choice of terraces in a trendy setting, head to El Rodadero. What is more, all upscale hotels have one or two restaurants open to the public.

Café del Parque *($; every day 7:30am until customers leave; Calle 12 No. 3-10,*

☎21 36 29) is a large, open-air European café beneath the trees, facing Plaza Bolívar and adjacent to the Museo del Oro. It is a pleasant place where you can savour all kinds of coffees as well as a variety of pastries and sandwiches. The manager, Gustavo A. Rojas Velásquez, is a good unofficial source of information for tourists, and can get by in English.

As its name indicates, **China Town** *($-$$; every day 11am to 10:30pm; Carrera 1a No. 18-47, ☎21 46 62 or 23 32 17)* is a Chinese restaurant. Boasting a red-painted decor and an air-conditioned, recessed dining room, the beachfront restaurant offers a family ambiance, but cannot lay claim to haute cuisine.

Todo Broaster *($-$$; every day 11am to 11pm; Calle 22 No. 4-21, ☎21 03 29)* is a rotisserie specializing in chicken BBQ. The restaurant delivers, and we're talking fast food here.

Restaurante Panamerican *($$-$$$$; every day 11am to 3pm and 6pm to 11pm; Carrera 1a No. 18-23, ☎21 10 31 or 21 29 01)* has a closed, air-conditioned terrace with a view of the sea. The restaurant is located at the entrance of the Panamerican hotel and specialzes in fish and seafood. Also available here are continental cuisine and Italian-style pasta. The ambiance is pleasant, both in the dining room and on the terrace, with white tablecloths, "captain's" chairs and candles on every table. The service is professional and courteous. The Panamerican restaurant has the best reputation in Santa Marta.

El Rodadero

While El Rodadero can be considered one huge, lively party at night because of the many nightclubs found here, it is also a diner's paradise, offering every type of cuisine a person could wish for.

El Pibe *($; every day 10:30am to 2am; Calle 6 between Carreras 1a and 2a)* is an unpretentious Argentinian rotisserie with a few tables inside but, above all, a terrace with an indirect view of the sea. Featured on the menu are barbecued cutlets and steaks served with fries and salad. The whole washed down with beer. The place generally does not mind if guests bring their own wine, provided they ask politely.

El Pez Gordo *($-$$; right on the beach, in the middle of El Rodadero, left of Carrera 1a, at Calle 11, ☎22 40 22)* is owned by the Gómez brothers, who claim they serve the best *cazuela de mariscos* (seafood casserole) in Santa Marta. The place is more of a *tienda* (stall) than a restaurant, and the terrace is right on the beach, with tables set up on a patio and others right on the sand. All are sheltered from the sun by parasols and giant palm trees. The *cazuela de mariscos* really is out of this world. They also do not mind if you can bring your own wine, as long as you ask them.

El Rincón del Viejo Alfonso *($-$$$; every day 8am to 11pm, later on weekends; Carrera 2a No. 7-63, ☎22 81 13 or 22 77 71)* is a fish and seafood restaurant that also has a table-d'hôte and an à-la-carte menu. The place also serves a variety of sandwiches and burgers. *Viejo* (old) Alfonso greets customers himself, and seems to thoroughly enjoy making them feel at home. His wife waits on customers in this tropical restaurant, whose vast dining room has several fishponds as well as a dance floor. Live music on weekends after 10pm.

As its name indicates, **La Pizza Loca** *($$; every day noon to 3am; Calle 9a No. 1-69, ☎22 00 99, 22 81 15, 22 02 60 or 22 07 07)* is a pizzeria with an air-conditioned dining room and a raised tropical terrace. The place serves every kind of pizza imaginable, as well as a wide variety of Italian dishes on the table d'hôte or à la carte. The decor is modern, with varnished-wood chairs and tables on the terrace.

Restaurant Bar Pincho *($$-$$$$; every day noon to 3:30pm and 6:30pm to midnight; Carrera 2a No. 6-30, ☎/≠22 98 59)* is an upscale restaurant specializing in fish and seafood. Like any self-respecting Colombian restaurant, the daily special here features beef or chicken. The decor is sophisticated, with a bar in the back and tables lined up in the square medium-sized dining room. The place is decorated with suspended fishing nets and supplies, and the subdued lighting creates a pleasant atmosphere. A space is reserved to the left for the band that plays on weekends during tourist season. The service is attentive.

Restaurant Internacional Rodadero Inn *($$-$$$$; every day noon to 3:30pm and 6:30pm to midnight; Carrera 3a No. 10-40, ☎22 92 52 or 22 92 76)* is the Yuldama hotel's (see p 146) French restaurant. In a simple yet sophisticated interior with round tables with white tablecloths, diners will be tempted by porterhouse steak, filet mignon and beef medallion with mushroom sauce. The restaurant's wine list features French, Italian and Chilean vintages.

Taganga

As previously mentioned, Taganga boasts at least 20 little *tiendas* (stands) with terraces on the beach that compete with each other for customers. All have a holiday ambiance and cater to a laid-back, barefoot clientele.

 For more sophisticated dining, head to the restaurant at the hotel **La Ballena Azul** *($$-$$$$; every day 7am to 9pm, right on the Taganga beach; ☎21 66 68 or 21 50 93)*, which has a good reputation (see p 147). Managed by the owner's son, Sébastien Girardot, who studied at the École d'Hôtellerie de Paris, the restaurant maintains high standards, serving refined cuisine in a relaxed but sophisticated ambiance. Its specialities are fish and seafood, served in the dining room or on the terrace. The service is attentive and professional whether you eat inside or outside. The wine list features French, Italian and Chilean wines.

  ENTERTAINMENT

El Rodadero

For cocktail hour, go to El Rodadero, which turns into a veritable open-air dance club at night during peak tourist season. Music blasts from every second door here, and you will have no trouble finding a place to go for a drink simply by walking down the street.

The **Tienda Gaira** *(at Carrera 1a and Calle 8, ☎22 02 04)* is a trendy little open-air bar with a terrace and a view of the sea. The decor consists of an eclectic assortment of objects and photographs relating to navigation. The place serves Colombian beers as well as brands imported from Venezuela, Mexico, Germany and Belgium.

The best-known club in town is unquestionably **La Escollera** *(Calle 5a No. 4-107, El Laguito*

district, *☎22 81 86 or 22 78 59)*, located on a small island in a lagoon, north of El Rodadero.

Events

Social and cultural events are held throughout the department of Magdalena. Here is a selection:

Las Fiestas de Caimán, festivals held in honour of this protected animal, in January in Ciénaga Grande;

Festival de la Cumbia, a dance festival that lasts several days, every June in the small town of El Banco;

Feria Exposición Agropecuaria, in Fundación in July;

Fiesta Nacional del Mar, crowning of a queen of the sea, in Santa Marta in August;

Festival del Hombre Caimán, a festival of folklore and legends, in Plato in December.

SHOPPING

Santa Marta

Early in the morning, artisans set up shop for the day around Plaza Bolívar to sell their wares to the locals and tourists. These goods include sandals, leather belts, silver jewellery, woven garments, hammocks and a host of other items.

Located inside the building that also houses the academy of history, the library and Santa Marta's school of fine arts *(at Carrera 1a and Calle 22)*, the beachfront **Centro Artesanal Siga** has some 20 handicrafts shops. Sold here are leather garments, belts, sandals and jewellery, as well as pottery and ceramic pieces.

El Rodadero

Provisiones Mary *(Carrera 2a No. 8-33, Centro Comercial Los Arcos San Andresito No. 1, Room 3, ☎22 72 95)* is a small shop that offers high-quality imported foodstuffs such as tomato and vegetable juice, Dijon mustard, extra-virgin oils and more.

Supertiendas Olímpica S.A. *(Mon to Sat 8am to 8pm, Sun and holidays 8am to 3pm, until 5pm during high season; at Calle 13 and Carrera 4 No. 13-58, ☎22 75 09)* is a supermarket that sells meat, fruit and vegetables, cold beer and wines imported from Chile and France. At the entrance is a counter of daily ready-cooked meals as well as a sandwich stall where you can eat on the spot or take out. Pharmaceutical products such as sun lotions are also sold here.

CARTAGENA DE INDIAS AND
THE DEPARTMENT OF BOLÍVAR

The Department of Bolívar is probably the best-known in Colombia because of its capital, Cartagena de Indias. The downtown area of this city of some 1.6 million inhabitants has been declared a UNESCO World Heritage Site, and the entire city covers a surface of 26,479 square kilometres. The department is bordered by the Caribbean Sea to the north, the departments of Antioquia and Santander to the south, the departments of Cesar, Magdalena and Atlantico to the east, and the departments of Sucre, Córdova and Antioquia to the west. It is a bustling port city through which bananas, sugar and coffee are shipped. However, it is primarily the tourist industry, which grew up around its beautiful beaches and vacation islands, which truly makes Cartagena de Indias the capital.

Cartagena de Indias

One of the most beautiful cities in Colombia, with almost a million inhabitants living right on the Caribbean Sea, Cartagena de Indias, or, simply, Cartagena, was named after the glorious Spanish city of Cartagena which, in turn, takes its name from Carthage, the great merchant city that once rivalled Rome itself. Carthage, the exalted city of antiquity, was founded by the Phoenicians in the 8th century BC in North Africa, in what is Tunisia today. The conquistadors had a tradition of naming a new colony for one of the cities that had sponsored their expedition, in order to honour their patrons. Thus, the names of the great monarchs of the time appear again and again in the names of places in the New World, since they were the ones to finance most of the voyages. Louisiana, for example, was named after King Louis XIV.

Cartagena was built on several islands located at the end of a bay on the Atlantic coast of Colombia, not far from the majestic Río Magdalena. The marshes that originally surrounded these islands were later filled in order to link the latter to the coast. The city, nestled in the bay, extends onto an L-shaped peninsula called Bocagrande. At the end of this stretch of land are two large islands that appear to be guarding the mouth of the bay: located at the entrance to the bay is Isla Tierrabomba, a natural one, while Isla Barú was created when the Canal Del Dique was dug. This gigantic waterway is 114 kilometres long, and was completed during the colonial era with the aim of linking the Río Magdalena to the sea. The Barú peninsula was thereby cut off from the mainland and transformed into an island. This was one of the largest enterprises of its kind ever to have been carried out in the Spanish colonies, and is used by many boats to this day.

The Del Rosario archipelago lies off the western extremity of Isla Barú. Made up of a multitude of little islands, it has lovely white sand beaches and magnificent coral. Fans of marine life claim that this is one of the most beautiful places on the Colombian coast.

Just south of the downtown area is another island, known as La Manga, which is a residential area for well-off Cartageneros. Several bridges provide access to and from the island, and one of these leads directly to the old city. A number of lagoons separate the suburban areas from the old city, whose centre is surrounded by magnificent ramparts. The only elevated points on the horizon are the Castillo San Felipe de Barajas at the gates of the city, and the Convento de la Popa facing the island of La Manga from its perch atop a 100-metre-high hill.

Thus admirably protected, Cartagena has managed to preserve its military buildings, as well as its lovely upper-class homes and colonial churches. Today, it is one of the finest examples of colonial architecture in South America, and it is not surprising that UNESCO named it a World Heritage Site.

Fauna and Flora

The Del Rosario archipelago is teeming with marine animal life, most of the vegetation consists of mangroves. In the Cartagena region, an amber-coloured stone known locally as *la coralina* is extracted from the soil. Its primary characteristic is its perforation by countless holes, which make it look like a time-worn stone. In the hinterland, the great plains of the Río Magdalena are dominated by typical swampland vegetation, forming a natural habitat for an impressive number of aquatic birds and alligators.

A Brief History

Founded in 1533 by Pedro de Heredia (see p 28), Cartagena de Indias was built on the site of an abandoned Amerindian village, known as Calamarí, located on a small island of the same name. Born into a noble family in Madrid, this illustrious figure left Spain suddenly because of a duel, staying first in Santo Domingo (capital of the present-day Dominican Republic), and later, upon arriving in New Grenada, settling in Santa Marta, where he took up trading with the native inhabitants. After becoming governor, he established himself in the village of Calamarí and founded Cartagena. The little village quickly prospered, with the discovery of numerous treasures in the region, including those in

the tombs of the Sinús, an Amerindian people who customarily buried the dead with all their possessions. In 1552, however, a fire reduced the village (whose buildings were made of wood at the time) to ashes, and Pedro de Heredia ordered that all structures be made of stone from that point onward. In a way, this directive enabled the city to preserve its lovely architectural heritage up until the present day.

As the Spanish continued colonizing South America, they discovered and pillaged the fabulous riches of various Amerindian nations, including the Incas. The port of Cartagena, well protected in a bay, benefited greatly from all of this plundering. Ships loaded with precious cargo arrived from Ecuador and Peru by way of the isthmus of Panamá, and stopped at the city's port to be loaded with other goods from the interior of the country, most of which were brought to the port on the Río Magdalena. Afterward, the ships would continue on their way to Cuba or Puerto Rico, where other merchandise was added to their precious cargo. Finally, fully loaded, they would sail to Spain, the mother country.

Another factor that enabled the city to develop rapidly was the slave trade. In fact, at the beginning of the 17th century, the king of Spain granted the colony a monopoly on this "commerce." It is important to remember that at the time, the Spanish crown had forbidden the enslavement of Amerindians, but granted certain markets and key figures in its new colonies the right to deal in African slaves. Cartagena thus received the dreadful but highly coveted right to be an official slave-trading centre. Veracruz, Mexico was the only other centre of this kind.

All of these activities made it possible for prominent locals to amass enormous fortunes and build superb residences, which still account for some of the town's charm today. Thus, within a few years, Cartagena reached a level of prosperity that aroused the interest not only of other colonial powers, but also of the numerous pirates crisscrossing the seas.

Cartagena's reputation as a flourishing city spread quickly, and the *Jolly Mary* – the black pirate flag with a skull and cross bones – was seen often, hoisted before the Spanish galleons loaded with gold were attacked. In 1543, a Frenchman by the name of Robert Baal launched a successful attack on the city. Surprising the governor in the middle of a banquet, the pirate managed to extort

310 kilos of gold from the city. And that was only the beginning of a long list of attacks by pirates of all different nationalities. They included Englishmen John Hawkins (in 1567) and Francis Drake (in 1586), as well as Frenchmen Jean-Bernard Desjeans and Jean Ducasse (in 1697).

Cartagena managed to fend off at least one attack, mounted by the admiral Edward Vernon sent by King George II of England, along with 15,000 troops, to overthrow the Spanish in 1741. The English, however, were in for a surprise since the small garrison, led by General Basco de Lezo, managed to drive them back to sea. This brave general continued to fight even after losing an arm, a leg and an eye in the battle. No doubt his abilities on the battlefield were somewhat handicapped, but he set quite the example for his troops!

Irritated by the loss of capital to the privateers, the Spanish crown finally decided to fortify the city and its surrounding area. The scale of the project soon made Cartagena the most well-protected colonial city in all of South America. There was one very unfortunate cost though; the shameful exploitation of black slaves.

Among the numerous armed conflicts that have marked the city's history, two major dates should be kept in mind. The first is 1741, the year of the famous Battle of Vernon (see p 168); the second is 1811, when the city was the first to declare its independence from Spain. However, the city came back under the Spanish yoke in 1815 upon being recaptured by General Pablo Morillo. More than a third of the population perished in the fighting – a total of 6,000 people! Later, during the final war of independence led by Simón Bolívar, Cartagena was once again among the first to declare its independence and obtained its liberty once and for all in 1821. Moreover, the *Libertador* nicknamed Cartagena *Ciudad Heroica* (the Heroic City) for its bravery and ability to defend itself.

Cartagena Today

With its forts and handsome colonial buildings, the present-day city peacefully braves an armada of visitors ever year, offering them its sights, services, atmosphere and attractions. The peninsula of Bocagrande and El Laguito is almost entirely devoted to meeting the needs of tourists. From an economic standpoint, the city is dedicated to tourism, while its suburbs and

port (Colombia's second-largest) support a variety of industries.

FINDING YOUR WAY AROUND

Cartagena de Indias

On the entire peninsula, the roads running perpendicular to the waterfront and the bay are known as *calles*, and their numbers increase as you near the downtown area. The roads running parallel to the sea are named *carreras*, and their numbers increase heading away from the coast.

El Centro and San Diego

The heart of Cartagena can be divided into two sections: El Centro and San Diego. As these two areas lie within the fortifications, we will refer to this part of Cartagena as the *intra-muros* city (the Old City and historic centre). In both the *intra-muros* and *extra-muros* parts of the city, the best means of getting around is on foot. Indeed, it is easy to reach any point in these two areas on foot, and, walking at a good pace, it is possible to go from one end of the city to the other in less than half an hour.

Bocagrande and El Laguito

In a car, Bocagrande is easily accessible by way of Avenida Santander, which later becomes Carrera 1 (also known as Avenida del Malecón), and runs alongside the sea for the entire length of the peninsula. At the end, the road branches off to the left on its way into El Laguito, where its name changes to Calle 1A and then Avenida Almirante Brión.

The best way to reach Bocagrande and El Laguito from the intra-muros city is on foot. Indeed, the two places lie only 15 and 25 minutes respectively from the downtown area. Visitors who don't enjoy walking can take one of the many Executivo buses *(300 pesos)* running along Carrera 2 and Carrera 3, or taxis *(700 pesos)* cruising the city. Buses heading downtown from Bocagrande and El Laguito pick up passengers on Carrera 3; those heading from downtown to Bocagrande and El Laguito pick up passengers on Avenida Blaz de Lezo

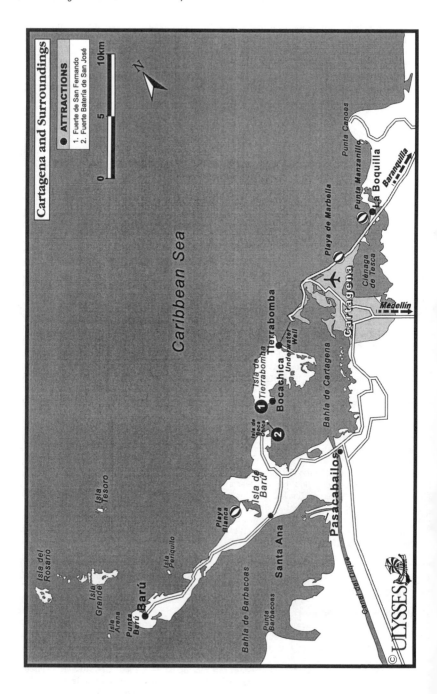

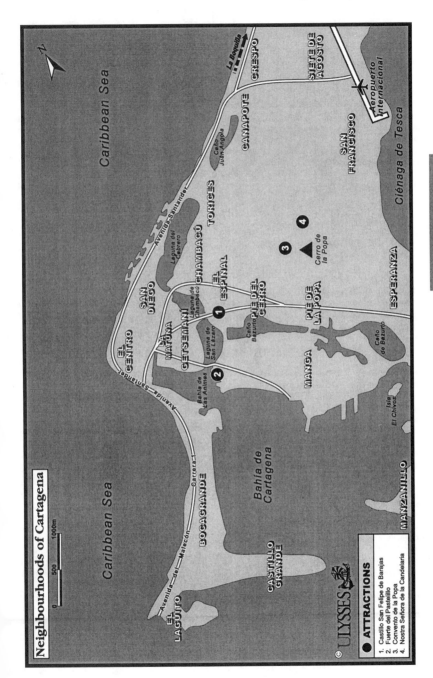

Neighbourhoods of Cartagena

Caribbean Sea

Caribbean Sea

Bahía de Cartagena

CARTAGENA DE INDIAS

Ciénaga de Tesca

ATTRACTIONS
1. Castillo San Felipe de Barajas
2. Fuerte del Pastelillo
3. Convento de la Popa
4. Nostra Señora de la Candelaria

ULYSSES

LAGUITO
BOCAGRANDE
CASTILLO GRANDE
MANZANILLO

Avenida del Malecón
Carrera 1
Avenida Santander

EL CENTRO
SAN DIEGO
LA MATUNA
GETSEMANÍ
Bahía de Las Ánimas
Laguna de San Lázaro
Avenida Santander

CHAMBACÚ
EL ESPINAL
Laguna de Chambacú
PIE DEL CERRO
MANGA
Isla El Chivos
Caño de Bazurto
PIE DE LA POPA
Caño de Bazurto

TORICES
Laguna del Tabero
Caño Juan Angola
CANAPOTE
Avenida Santander

La Boquilla
CRESPO
SIETE DE AGOSTO
Aeropuerto Internacional

SAN FRANCISCO
ESPERANZA

Cerro de la Popa

500   1000m

(near the tourist office of the old port of Los Pegasos). They then run along Carrera 2.

Getsemaní and La Matuna

The Getsemaní area, which we will refer to as the *extra-muros* part of the city, is located near the *intra-muros* part, on the other side of La Matuna. During the day, this is a good place to visit on foot. The entire area is accessible on foot, and, walking at a fair pace, visitors can reach La Matuna from the El Centro area in less than half an hour. After sundown, however, use taxis to get around.

By Plane

Located 1.6 kilometres from downtown Cartagena, the **Rafael Nuñez International Airport** (also known as the Aeropuerto Internacional Crespo) has two sections. The first is used only for arrivals and does not have any dining facilities or other services. There is, however, a small park on the left, which is a pleasant place to pass the time while awaiting your turn to pass through customs. The second section is for departures and offers postal services, duty-free shops (whose products, by the way, are more expensive than those sold downtown) and newspaper stands. There are also a cafeteria and a small coffee counter, but the atmosphere is not very pleasant and the menu is limited. Instead of waiting in the noisy terminal, visitors are advised to opt for a brief outing in the nearby neighbourhood (5 min on foot), to enjoy a drink or a bite to eat without going too far from the airport (see p 183).

Here is the flight schedule for international Avianca flights:

Aruba: Sat 11:20am.
Madrid, Spain: Fri 9:20pm.
Miami, United States: every day 9:20am.
New York, United States: Sat 4:25pm.

Here is the flight schedule for domestic Avianca flights:

Bogotá: Mon-Sat 7am; every day 10:30am, 1:36pm and 4:22pm; Mon, Wed and Fri 4:25pm; every day 6:54pm; Sat 7:40pm; Mon, Thu, Sat and Sun 9:35pm; 198,000 pesos.
Bucaramanga: every day 5pm with stopover; 209,000 pesos.

Cali: every day 3:25pm; Thu and Sun 4:30pm with stopover; 232,000 pesos.
Capurganá: Sun 12:20pm; Mon and Thu 12:40pm; 96,000 pesos.
Cúcuta: every day 5pm; 182,000 pesos.
Medellín: Sat 12:45pm and 3:40pm; Thu and Sun 4:30pm; every day 4:50pm; 167,000 pesos.
San Andrés: Tue, Thu, Sat and Sun 8:10am, Mon, Wed and Fri 1:35pm; 178,000 pesos.

Several airline companies have offices in Cartagena:

AVIANCA: Plaza de la Aduana, ☎665-5504, 665-7740 or 665-8203, ⌐665-0817.
SAM: Plaza de la Aduana, ☎665-5504, 665-7740, 665-8203, ⌐665-0817.
Viasa: Carrera 5a, No. 5-42, Bocagrande, ☎665-4158, ⌐665-1422.
Aces: ☎664-6858, 664-3299, 664-4964 or 664-3131, ⌐664-0117.
AeroRepública: ☎665-8751 or 665-8203, ⌐665-8203.
COPA: ☎664-8289 or 664-4526, ⌐664-5749.
LACSA: ☎664-4352 or 664-7378.

The trip from the airport to downtown Cartagena takes about 20 minutes by car or by bus. Given the bulkiness of most luggage, the risk of theft and the hordes of commuters, it is far more convenient to take a taxi. As the rate is determined by the number of zones crossed, the trip should not cost more than 5,000 pesos. It should be noted, moreover, that most vacation packages offered by travel agencies include transportation to the hotel.

By Bus

A new Terminal de Transportes was opened several years ago, and offers all the services 24 hours a day. You can get there by taking the city bus marked *Terminal*, but this can be difficult if you have a lot of luggage. It is better to take a taxi, which shouldn't cost more than 5,000 pesos.

Several bus companies run the same routes: Expreso Brasilia, Rápido Ochoa, Coolibertador, Unitransco and La Veloz all have regular departures for many destinations. For more detailed schedule information, inquire at the station.

By Taxi

Taxis are available in all holiday resorts as well as in downtown Cartagena. Taking a taxi is probably the safest and most efficient way of getting around. Sharing a taxi can cost less than public transportation. Taxis are usually new yellow four-door compacts, with a sign saying *Servicio Público*. In the city and the suburbs, the fare is determined by how many zones you cross. For example, the ride to the island of La Manga from the *intra-muros* city spans two zones. The current fare for transportation within one zone is 1,000 pesos. Therefore, the trip will cost 2,000 pesos, even if the distance between the two zones is very short. Fares go up to 1,300 pesos per zone in the evening and at night. Wherever you go outside the city, be it to the La Popa monastery or the village of La Boquilla, agree on a fixed price ahead of time, and only pay once you get there. Cab drivers are sometimes willing to wait for you, in return for a previously agreed-upon price, of course. This kind of arrangement is strongly advised if you are heading to remote places. Because the fare is sometimes hard to estimate, we have indicated the approximate fare in the text whenever relevant.

Public Transportation (*Chivas*)

There are many public buses, known as *chivas*, and they go just about everywhere. In general, they are old, slow and uncomfortable. Often jam-packed, they are rather inconvenient for passengers carrying baggage, not to mention that thieves often target tourists on buses. Despite all these drawbacks, *chivas* provide an interesting and inexpensive means of getting around. Painted in bright colours and decorated with assorted objects, these buses are often filled with the loud, brassy music of meringues and salsas, blaring from the driver's radio. Furthermore, you will meet all sorts of interesting characters who often let their curiosity get the better of them and begin questioning you on your life story!

Renting a Car

Because the main attractions in both the city and its surrounding area are located very close to one another, we do not advise those visitors

intending to stay only in Cartagena to rent a car. However, here are some addresses in case you decide to do so:

Avis Rent a Car: Avenue San Martín, No. 6-94, Bocagrande, ☎655-3259.
Auto Costa Rent A Car: ☎665-2427, 665-3259 or 665-3879.
AlquilAuto: Avenue San Martin No. 6-96, Bocagrande, ☎665-5786 or 665-0968.
Budget: Carrera 3 No. 5-183, Bocagrande, ☎665-1764 or 665-6831.
Hertz: Avenue San Martín, No. 6-84, Bocagrande, ☎665-2852 or 665-3359.
International Car Rental: ☎665-5399, 665-1164 or 665-5594, ⊨665-3359.
National Car Rental: Calle 10, No. 2-30, Bocagrande, ☎665-3336 or 665-7145.

Scooter or Moped Rental

On the Bocagrande peninsula, it is possible to rent a scooter for 12,000 pesos an hour. A deposit is also required. It is usually up to motorcyclists, of which there are many, to be careful since motorists do not necessarily watch out for them.

Sasha Motor is open from 9am to 7:30pm, Carrera 1, No. 9-18, ☎665-0844 ext. 230, information available in the clothing store.

 PRACTICAL INFORMATION

Area Code: 5.

Mail

Mail is forwarded through **Avianca** in the company offices, Carrera 3, near Calle 8, No. 129, Bocagrande.

Tourist Information

El Centro and San Diego

Corporación de Turismo
Casa del Marqués de Valdehoyos
from 8am to 12pm and from 2pm to 6pm
Calle de la Factoría, No. 34-56
☎660-0448, ⊨664-6567.

Empresa Promotora de Tourismo
Calle Centanario
near the Paseo de los Pegagos at the landing
stage of the old port, at the beginning of
Avenida Blas de Lezo
☎665-1391 or 665-1843, ⊷665-4877.

Bocagrande and El Laguito

Empresa Promotora de Turismo
Carrera 1, near Calle 4
Beside the tourist police office, in the little park
facing the waterfront.

City Tours

El Centro and San Diego

Many agencies offer tours of the city in a
horse-drawn carriage or a local or air-conditioned bus. Several options are available, some
even including a meal in addition to visiting the
city's major attractions. The prices vary greatly;
a tour of the city in a horse-drawn carriage runs
to about 18,000 pesos an hour, while a
three-hour tour by *chiva* (see p 66, 157) costs
12,000 pesos. Whichever option you choose,
be sure to inquire about the services offered
before setting out. As a general rule, large
hotels have their own tour office, but it is wise
to compare their rates with those of other
establishments before making a choice.

Banks

El Centro and San Diego

Banco Ganadero
Plaza de la Aduana
from 8am to 11:30am and from 2pm to 4pm
Visa; cash advances on the second floor.

Bocagrande and El Laguito

Banco Industrial de Colombia
Carrera 2, near Calle 5
from 8:45am to 11:30pm and 2pm to 3:30pm
MasterCard; cash advances.

Banco de Credito
Carrera 2, near Calle 6
Visa; cash advances.

Good exchange rates also available at the
Cartagena Plaza Hotel, Carrera 1, No. 6-154,
☎665-4000.

Excursions

Many local agencies offer excursions that set
out from Cartagena. Before heading off on an
adventure, be it by sea or by land, it is best to
shop around for the best price and most comprehensive package. Here are some useful
recommendations for making an informed
choice:

● When inquiring about outings by sea, find out
what type of vessel is used, since some companies own small boats which pitch heavily on
the open sea. Occasionally, the captain (especially on tours to the Islas del Rosario) enjoys
turning the trip into a thrill ride by handling the
boat in a somewhat careless manner. Visitors
prone to seasickness are better off choosing a
large boat that can accommodate 100 or so
passengers.

● Always compare the number of stops included in the excursion, since it is possible to
put in at a variety of places on the way to a
single destination, and different agencies don't
always choose the same itinerary.

● **Always** choose a well-established agency and
do not deal with people on the street, who will
often offer you a magnificent excursion that
will never come to pass. Many people have lost
a lot of money on such empty promises.

● Inquire as to the exact length of the trip and
the number of services available (i.e. meal
included or not). Some excursions cannot be
completed in a single day; in such cases, you
will require overnight accommodation along the
way.

● For security reasons, only take along the bare
necessities.

Some Useful Addresses:

Tesoro Tours *(Carrera 2, No. 6-129,
☎665-4713 or 665-3380, ⊷665-6299)*. Eco-
tours and diving excursions (Isla del Rosario,
Playa Blanca etc.). This company has a large
craft.

Puerta del Reloj

Tours Los Pinos *(Corner of Carrera 2 and Calle 9)*. Many excursions at competitive prices.
La Tortuga Dive School *(Avenida del Retorno, El Laguito)*. Diving course and equipment rental.
EcoBuzos *(Av. Almirante Brion, No. 2-50, Room 102, El Laguito, ☎665-2707, ≈665-1129, ecobuzos@axisgate.com)*. Ecological diving.

Sample Rates

The prices listed below are only intended to give visitors a general idea of the cost of an excursion, which can vary greatly from one season to the next.

- Islas del Rosario: 20,000 to 35,000 pesos
- Playa Blanca: 20,000 to 25,000 pesos
- Tierrabomba: 20,000 to 25,000 pesos
- Volcan Totumo: 15,000 to 20,000 pesos

Several agencies also offer excursions within and beyond Cartagena. These include a city tour by bus or on foot, during the day or at night, a visit to a volcano or farm, a day-long or overnight excursion to Barranquilla or Santa Marta, the Islas del Rosario, and more.

Contactos Viajes: Av. San Martin, No. 8-16, Centro Comercial Bocagrande, 2nd Floor, Room 216, ☎665-4959, 665-4561 or 665-2803, ≈665-2327.
Gema Tours Agencia de Viajes y Turismo: Carrera 2a, No. 4-15, Edificio Antillas Bocagrande, ☎665-5206, 665-4832 or 665-5627, ≈665-5628.
Tierra Mar Aire, Agencia de Viajes y Turismo (TMA): Carrera 4, No. 7-196, Bocagrande, ☎665-1062, ≈665-5986.
Viajes El Laguito: Edificio Belmar, Room 102, ☎665-0149, 665-4446 or 665-923, ≈665-3856.

CARTAGENA DE INDIAS

EXPLORING

Cartagena de Indias ★

Before describing the sights of Cartagena, we feel it important to mention that nearly all the streets in the *intra-muros* city are interesting and worth exploring. The countless pastel-coloured private homes with their lovely wooden balconies make a stroll through the streets an adventure of discovery. The play of shadow and light, varying over the course of the day, seems to transform the city's appearance every hour. At night, step several centuries back in time as you slip through the little side streets. After dark, many of the houses are artistically lit up. The *intra-muros* part of the city is relatively safe and, with a few standard precautions, is not a dangerous place to walk around. In recent years, the magical charm exuded by the city of Cartagena has prompted many wealthy Colombians, in search of an idyllic spot and a good investment, to settle here. The consequences of this have been twofold: on the positive side, a large number of beautiful residences have been restored, while on the negative side, the city's original, less affluent residents have left, making way for luxury shops. Hopefully the future holds good things for Cartagena like the growth and preservation of its soul – a soul manifested in the charming population and throughout the streets.

El Centro and San Diego

The neighbourhoods of **El Centro and San Diego** ★★★ are without question the most interesting parts of Cartagena. Well preserved and rich in architecture, they are surrounded by thick walls, forming, like Québec City, one of the few fortified cities in the Americas. Originally, El Centro was mainly inhabited by dignitaries and wealthy merchants, while San Diego was home to soldiers and artisans.

Puerta del Rejol *(Avenida Blas de Lezo)*, known as the "Clock Gate" because of the clock located here, is an integral part of the fortifications (see p 165) surrounding the city, and to this day serves as a symbol of Cartagena. In the past, the gate consisted only of the central archway, which was the main entrance to the city and also linked Cartagena to the village of

Getsemaní by means of a bridge. The two lateral archways, once closed, were used as a munitions depot and a chapel respectively. The present clock tower was added toward the end of the 19th century, replacing the original clock. The central arch is embellished by a Tuscan-style portico.

Just opposite the clock tower, visitors will find a small square adorned with palm trees and a statue of Pedro de Heredia, the founder of the city.

The pleasant square known as **Plaza de los Coches** ★ *(immediately behind the Puerta del Reloj)*, now a hub of commercial activity, was formerly the site of a market, where all sorts of products were sold. Many black slaves who had been brought to the nearby port were sold here. After being branded, they were sent to new colonies. It should be noted that at the time, the Spanish crown had already forbidden the enslavement of Amerindians, but granted certain markets and important figures in its new colonies the right to trade African slaves. Cartagena was thus granted the dreadful but highly coveted privilege of being the official hub of the slave trade for all of Spain's newly discovered colonies (Peru, Venezuela and Ecuador). Veracruz, Mexico was the only other such centre. The name "Coach Square" dates back to the last century, when many coaches set out from here to take Cartageneros across the city. Facing the square, visitors will see a lovely line of archways known as the *"Portal de los Dulces"* (because all sorts of sweets, or *dulces*, are sold there), as well as a picturesque cluster of wooden balconies. Although the styles are somewhat mixed (for example, there is a variety of pediments), the grouping is very pleasing to the eye, and makes this one of the city's loveliest squares.

Plaza de la Aduana ★★★ *(right beside Plaza de los Coches)* is probably the prettiest square and the finest example of civilian architecture from the colonial era still to be found in Cartagena. Once used for military parades, it is the largest square in the *intra-muros* city. All along the walls, visitors will see the perfectly aligned arcades of the **Casa de la Aduana** ★★ (Customs House). This handsome building is thus named because all merchandise entering or leaving the city was taxed here during the colonial era. It now houses a number of administrative services, as well as the mayor's office. Opposite this building, at the left end of the square, stands the **Casa del Premio Real** ★★. This building has an elegant stone pediment,

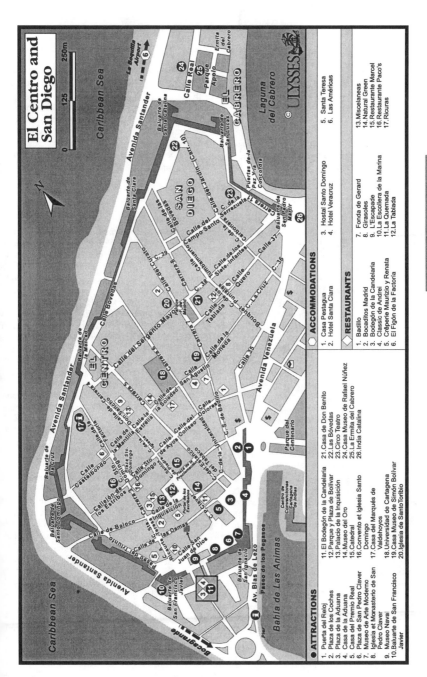

El Centro and San Diego

0   125   250m

Caribbean Sea

CARTAGENA DE INDIAS

● ATTRACTIONS

1. Puerta del Reloj
2. Plaza de los Coches
3. Plaza de la Aduana
4. Casa de la Aduana
5. Casa del Premio Real
6. Plaza de San Pedro Claver
7. Museo de Arte Moderno
8. Iglesia et Monasterio de San Pedro Claver
9. Museo Naval
10. Baluarte de San Francisco Javier

11. El Bodegón de la Candelaria
12. Parque y Plaza de Bolívar
13. Palacio de la Inquisición
14. Museo del Oro
15. Catedral
16. Convento et Iglesia Santo Domingo
17. Casa del Marqués de Valdehoyos
18. Universidad de Cartagena
19. Casa Museo de Simón Bolívar
20. Iglesia de Santo Toribio

21. Casa de Don Benito
22. Las Bóvedas
23. Circo Teatro
24. Casa Museo de Rafael Núñez
25. La Ermita del Cabrero
26. India Catalina

○ ACCOMMODATIONS

1. Casa Pestagua
2. Hotel Santa Clara
3. Hostal Santo Domingo
4. Hotel Veracruz
5. Santa Teresa
6. Las Américas

◇ RESTAURANTS

1. Badillo
2. Bocaditos Madrid
3. Bodegón de la Candelaria
4. Classic de Andrei
5. Crêperie Maurizio y Renata
6. El Figón de la Factoría
7. Fonda de Gerard
8. Girasoles
9. L'Escapade
10. La Escollera de la Marina
11. La Quemada
12. La Tablada
13. Miscelaneas
14. Natural Green
15. Restaurante Marcel
16. Restaurante Paco's
17. Ricuras

A Word About Architecture

Due to its strategic seaside location and year-round warm climate, the city of Cartagena exhibits a number of architectural characteristics found nowhere else in Colombia. In addition to its fortifications, most of its colonial residences are distinguished by having been built with the aim of providing greater protection against invaders arriving from the sea. Very often, these houses are raised, and the windows giving onto the street are protected by wooden bars. The ground floor ceilings are high so as to raise the second floor far above the street. Furthermore, the outer walls are usually smooth, with nowhere to grip on to, so that assailants could not climb the building. The second floor served as living quarters, while the rooms on the main floor were used for storing merchandise. Balconies are another feature related to security and the warm climate. Found everywhere, these are always on the second floor, overhanging the street, which enabled residents to sleep there on hot summer nights and also to defend themselves against attackers.

was the home of the viceroy and was used by the local administration. The wooden balconies, topped with little roofs of terra cotta tiles, are an example of the Andalusian style. Behind them, in the distance, the steeples of the Iglesia de San Pedro Claver seem to remind us that even here, in this wealthy area, it was important not to forget humility. Finally, an elegant statue of none other than Christopher Columbus occupies the place of honour and completes this lovely square. The statue was erected in 1892.

The only discordant, almost aggressive, element in this lovely architectural grouping is the unfortunate Banco de Bogotá building, which seems to want to spoil the serene beauty of this unique square.

Compared to Plaza de la Aduana, **Plaza de San Pedro Claver ★** *(at the end of Plaza de la Aduana)* appears very small, and the church towering over it seems to reinforce this impression. Here, visitors will find the monastery of the same name (right next to the church), as well as the museum of modern art. The square also offers a lovely view of Calle San Pedro Claver, lined with houses with numerous wooden balconies, and the cathedral of Cartagena in the distance.

The **Museo de Arte Moderno** *(500 pesos; on the left side of the square when facing the church)*, which was being restored during our visit, occupies a former colonial home. This museum of modern art comprises three exhibition rooms that feature the works of avant-garde Colombian artists.

The **Iglesia ★** and **Monasterio de San Pedro Claver ★★★** *(1,500 pesos; Mon to Fri 8am to*

6pm, enter through the monastery immediately to the left of the church), attached to one another, were built in the early 17th century. The church underwent a number of modifications up until the 20th century. These include the upper part of the façade, with scrolls surrounding the clock, and the building's cupola which was added in the 1920s. The latter was designed by a French architect named Gaston Lelarge. The façade, like those of most important buildings in the city, was made with the famous local coralline stone and adorned with Tuscan columns. Because they are so low, the two bell towers, set on either side of the entrance, weigh down the elegance of the façade to a certain degree. The relatively unexceptional interior includes a few curious sights, such as the chair made for the Pope's 1986 visit, which is located behind the high altar, and the Black Virgin of Montserrat, at the back of the church. Near the entrance, there is a flying buttress, which supports the chancel, set in the upper part of the church (in some Spanish and Latin American churches, the chancel and the sanctuary are located in different places). When visiting the church, do not bother taking the guided tour, since the information provided is of little use. Instead, ask for regular admission.

Still occupied by five Jesuits, the two-storey monastery is devoted in part to a museum documenting the life of San Pedro Claver, who lived here for 38 years. This monk, born in Catalonia (Spain) in 1580, came to New Granada as a missionary when he was about 30 years old. He dedicated himself to defending the slaves, and it is largely thanks to him that Pedro Zapata de Mendoza, governor of the city at the time, allowed slaves to stop working on Sundays and holidays. The main rooms in which the Spanish monk lived and died are open to the public. The furniture with which they are decorated is quite interesting. A number of religious objects and a few pieces of pre-Columbian pottery are also displayed. San Pedro Claver was the first monk in the New World to be canonized. His remains lie in a glass coffin beneath the main altar of the church. In the pleasant, shady garden of the monastery, visitors can see some beautiful toucans and parrots their brightly coloured feathers.

The **Museo Naval** *(at the end of Calle San Juan de Dios, opposite El Baluarte de San Francisco Javier)*, is in the process of being restored, so only one small room on the main floor is accessible. It features a few model boats, naval charts and other items related to the sea that will mainly interest navigation enthusiasts. Non-authorized people may offer you a "guided tour" of the museum for a few pesos. Unless you are into boat construction, skip this tour, and climb **El Baluarte de San Francisco Javier** ★, in front of the museum, instead. From atop this high wall, there is a lovely view of the dome of the San Pedro Claver church and the cathedral in the distance.

El Bodegón de la Candelaria ★★ *(Calle de las Damas, no. 64)* is a very fine example of a large, colonial upper-class residence. More than three centuries old, the house once belonged to a wealthy merchant named Alonso Alvarez de Armenta. According to legend, the Virgin Mary miraculously appeared in this house and advised Fray Alonso de la Cruz, a priest who was living there at the time, to build a place of worship on the hill where the Convento de la Popa (see p 171) now stands.

Later given to the Church, the residence was used as a monastery and then as a college. Now private property, it houses a restaurant (see p 179), in the centre of which lies a gorgeous patio adorned with greenery. There are lovely wooden screens in the archways above the doors. On the second floor, visitors can walk along a loggia overhanging the inner court, and admire a beautiful series of rooms decorated with period furniture. In one of these, where the apparition supposedly occurred, there is a wooden statue of the Virgin Mary (placed there to recreate the miraculous event) and an assortment of small religious objects. Also on the second floor, is a winding stairway leading to the top of the **El Mirador** ★ (see p 184) tower, which has been converted into a bar. From here, visitors can enjoy a lovely view of the city and the dome of the Iglesia San Pedro Claver.

Parque y Plaza de Bolívar ★ is a small square, with a park lined with large trees, in the heart of Cartagena. It had a series of different names, including Plaza de la Inquisición, before finally being named after the liberator of the country. The city, declared independent for the first time in 1811 and then recaptured by Spanish general Pablo Morillo in November 1815, was liberated once and for all by General Simón Bolívar in 1821. In order to pay homage to its liberator, the city erected a statue of him on horseback in the centre of the park. The sculpture is engraved with one of the general's famous lines, honouring the cities of Cartagena and Mompós: *Si Caracas me dio vida, vosotros me disteis gloria* (If Caracas gave me life, you have given me glory). A number of important buildings, including the Palacio de la Inquisición, the Museo de Oro and the Catedral stand around this pretty square. A vaulted passageway on the south side offers an attractive view of the square and the cathedral.

The **Palacio de la Inquisición** ★ *(1,800 pesos; Mon to Fri 8:30am to 12pm and 2pm to 6pm, Plaza Bolívar)* houses the museum on the Inquisition, whose portal alone is worth the trip. A magnificent example of baroque craftsmanship, it is considered by some historians to be the only "pure" example of this style in all of Colombia. In the centre of the portal, above the door, visitors will see a Spanish coat of arms and, just above that, the inscription "1770", specifying the year in which the building was completed. During the colonial era, this residence served as a tribunal and anyone the Church viewed as a heretic was tried here. This powerful tribunal, which also had jurisdiction over Venezuela, Panamá and several other crown territories, incited terror up until independence. A total of nearly 800 people were sentenced, five of whom were burned at the stake.

CARTAGENA DE INDIAS

The Inquisition

Created by King Philip III in 1610, the Holy Office of the Inquisition enabled the colonial government to brush aside or even physically eliminate anyone considered a nuisance or a "nonconformist." It goes without saying that the authorities had thereby found an easy and "justifiable" means of protecting themselves against any opposition to their power.

Although this is a well-preserved house, the museum inside has outdated, poorly maintained exhibitions. Instruments of torture used during the Inquisition are displayed, along with a number of maps and a somewhat outdated model of old Cartagena. Despite these drawbacks, some of the rooms are worth visiting, especially the one containing the wooden altar (painted red and gold) from the old Iglesia de Santa Clara and the room devoted to pre-Columbian objects. In the latter, the Amerindian masks made of palm fibres and the ceremonial pottery and crowns are very interesting. Unfortunately, the poor lighting and lack of written commentary detract from the exhibit. At the entrance, visitors are offered a guided tour, which is not really necessary, considering the inferior quality of the exhibition. If you do decide to visit the museum, make sure to go to the inner gardens at the back of the building, on the right-hand side. With a little patience and a sharp eye, you will spot, high in the branches of the trees, two sloths who appear to have taken up residence here. Hopefully, an unwanted return of the Inquisition won't ever disturb this rather nonconformist pair!

Upon leaving the museum, visitors will see, to the left of the building, on Calle de la Inquisición, the small, barred window from which the sentences handed down by the tribunal were announced to the public.

At the **Museo de Oro** ★★★ *(1,200 pesos; 8:30am to noon and 2pm to 6pm; on Plaza Bolívar, across from the Inquisition museum)*, visitors will find several very interesting rooms on the region's Amerindian ethnic groups, as well as a "strong room" containing some lovely jewellery, finery and other gold objects from the pre-Columbian era. In this room, located on the main floor, there are numerous pieces of jewellery with water-bird patterns. One reason for this is that birds were venerated as intermediaries between the upper and lower forces (the sky and the water) in native mythology. Also on the main floor, but outside this room, at the back of the building, visitors will find a life-sized reproduction of the living quarters of a Sinú family.

There are two interesting rooms on the second floor as well. In the first, the various phases of expansion of the groups that inhabited the coastal region and its hinterland are explained in Spanish. The exhibition includes a number of lovely pieces of pottery, as well as some curious cylindrical seals used for tattooing. The second room contains a model of a Sinú (also

spelled Zenú) village in its natural setting, namely, the marshes in the Magdalena valley. An assortment of objects relating to their activities, most of which centred around fishing, are exhibited. Visitors will be surprised to learn that the Sinús controlled vast stretches of territory, across which they maintained a complex network of canals.

The **Catedral** ★★ *(at the corner of Plaza de la Proclamación and Calle de los Santos de Piedra)* was begun in 1575, due to the efforts of Pedro Fernández de Busto, who was governor at the time. A contest was held, and the winner, architect Símon González, was put in charge of building the church. In those years, González was one of the city's master builders. The project was supposed to take 10 years, but in 1586, when only the tower remained unfinished, pirate Francis Drake attacked the city and partially destroyed the buildings that had already been completed. It was not until 1598 that work on the cathedral was resumed, this time under the supervision of Benito de Morales. Two years later, however, as a crowning misfortune, the roof collapsed, thus delaying the completion of the building once again. The cathedral was not finished until 1612. It later underwent numerous modifications. In the 19th century, its tower was topped with a Florentin-style dome, and its façade was coated to look like marble. The cathedral's left side and pediment have been restored to their original state, giving the building back its charm.

The interior of the cathedral is somewhat sparse but well-proportioned. The wooden roof and the row of columns separating the three naves help create an impression of harmony. The central nave is well-lit, thanks to the *oculi* (small round windows) and three beautiful wrought iron chandeliers of considerable size. Lastly, a lovely red and gold altar made of wood stands in the chancel.

Though the beautiful façade of the **Iglesia Santo Domingo** ★ *(at the corner of Plaza Santo Domingo and Callejón de los Estribos)* unfortunately appears to be in an advanced state of decay, the building is worth a visit. The neighbouring **Convento Santo Domingo** is unfortunately closed to the public. These two buildings form one of the oldest and most imposing architectural groupings in the city. Commissioned by the Dominicans, the church had to be impressive in size. Begun in 1570, its construction was supposed to take 10 years but, due to a lack of funds and the immoderate scale of the project, ended up taking nearly two centuries. Because of the structure's great size and weight, building the church and its single central nave posed many problems. When the vault was put in place, the central nave had to be reinforced to prevent it from collapsing. For this reason, buttresses were added to the outside of the church (on Callejón de los Estribos). Because of this lack of stability, the cupola that was originally supposed to crown the chancel was never built. The sparse interior of the church is graced with a lovely baroque altar.

The magnificent building known as **Casa del Marqués de Valdehoyos** ★★★ *(Calle de la Factoría)* houses one of Cartagena's three tourist offices, and cultural activities take place there on a regular basis. This large upper-class residence once belonged to the Marquis of Valdehoyos, who made a fortune trading flour and, more importantly, slaves. He was in fact authorized by the Spanish Crown to "import" and sell slaves. No one knows if it was a gesture of thanks for the success of this shameful trade, but it was his wife (the daughter of Marqués Premio Real) who endowed the Convento de la Popa with the beautiful **gold and emerald crown** dedicated to the Virgin Mary. Around 1830, the house was also used temporarily by the illustrious Simón Bolívar as a place of residence. With its wooden balconies and protected windows, this perfectly restored building serves as a fine example of the civilian architecture of the colonial era. Inside, visitors' attention will be drawn mainly to the two lovely connecting rooms on the first floor, which offer a view of the street. They are furnished (somewhat sparsely) with beautiful antiques, and the one used as a sitting room has a remarkable coffered ceiling, as well as an elegant crystal chandelier. It is also worth going out onto the balconies, to see how their height and width enabled the residents of the house to protect themselves against assailants.

Not far from the cathedral, the **Universidad de Cartagena** *(Calle de la Universidad)* occupies a former Augustinian monastery, erected in 1580 and then later completely altered. It has a lovely inner garden, which is a pleasant place to take refuge from the street vendors, whose pushy commercial tactics can become somewhat intrusive. The university's inner court is surrounded by a harmonious row of archways.

Near the bustling Plaza del Estudiante is the **Casa Museo de Simón Bolívar** *(Calle San Agustín)*, the first house the general occupied

during his stay in Cartagena. Converted into a museum, it houses documents on military campaigns led by the *libertador* and his comrades-in-arms. It was also here that Simón Bolívar wrote the Cartagena manifesto in 1812.

Facing onto small Parque Fernández de Madrid, the **Iglesia de Santo-Toribio** *(entrance on Calle del Sargento Mayor)* has a pretty vault made of carved wood, as well as a wooden altar covered with gold ornaments. It was built at the end of the 17th century. Also facing the park, the **Casa de Don Benito** is a fine example of colonial architecture. It was undergoing major repairs during our visit.

Las Bóvedas ★★ *(on the square of the same name, near the Baluarte de Santa Catalina)* means "the dungeons". Located alongside the ramparts, the structure consists of 23 dungeons, which originally served as a military barracks, and then as a munitions depot. Later, after independence, they were mainly used as jails. Built toward the end of the 18th century, these dungeons were the last major structure to be built in the *intra-muros* city during the colonial era. The façade consists of a terrace sheltered by a lovely row of arcades. The dungeons have now been converted into souvenir shops. The ramp located to the right when facing the building was used in the past by automobiles entering and leaving the premises. By climbing up it, visitors will reach the top of the old **ramparts** ★★★, which were built all around the city in order to protect it from pirate attacks. Two series of fortifications were erected: those surrounding the centre of the old city and those protecting the suburb of Getsemaní. The first structures, whose construction was supervised by Italian military engineer Giovanni Bautista Antonelli, were begun in the late 16th century on the site now occupied by the Baluarte de Santo Domingo, a bastion. Later, after extensive damage caused by pirate attacks and, occasionally, by the raging sea, many repairs and modifications were made. A series of different architects worked on the project up until the end of the 18th century. Despite the large number of people involved (Italian, Spanish and even Dutch architects), a Spaniard named Cristóbal de Roda (Giovanni Bautista Antonelli's nephew) may be considered the project's main "author". Today, the best-preserved fortifications are those of the old city, which, except for a small part between Puerta del Reloj and the Baluarte de San Pedro Mártir, have remained intact. Of the 23 bastions *(baluarte)* distributed along the two walls, 16 are still visible and in good condition.

Head toward the Casa Museo de Rafael Núñez, located outside the ramparts, and then take the Puerta de la Paz y la Concordia, in order to see the **Circo Teatro**, also known as **Plaza de Toros** *(Calle de la Serrezuela)*, because bullfights were once held here. Erected fairly recently (in the early 20th century), this round wooden building merits a closer look. Its proportions, in perfect harmony with the city, make it an interesting building well worth preserving. It is unfortunately abandoned at the present time and cannot be visited.

Casa Museo de Rafael Núñez ★ *(Calle Real de El Cabrero, outside of the walls in the El Cabrero area)*. This lovely Caribbean-style colonial residence stands in the El Cabrero neighbourhood, which was once a secondary place of residence for the upper class of Cartagena. It was the home of a renowned Colombian president, Don Rafael Núñez, who, in addition to being a poet and writer, was elected head of the republic four times during his life. This conservative man also wrote Colombia's national anthem and its 1886 constitution, which, despite a few changes, still forms the basis of the country's legislation. He lived in this house, now converted into a museum, for eight years, and many meetings were held here while he was in office. Inside, some of his and his family's personal belongings are exhibited. To reach the second floor, visitors must climb a wooden staircase, which affords a view of the lovely garden. The unusual octagonal dining room is bathed in tropical light filtered through a series of shutters that are part of the finely worked wooden balcony. Also of interest is the Empire-style chandelier. It is not difficult to imagine the opulent lifestyles of the residents of this comfortable suburb. Farther along on the second floor is a series of rooms, including the study equipped with a curious rotating bookcase; the living room, decorated with lovely period furniture, and the bedrooms, with their canopy beds. The entire grouping serves as a fine example of architectural harmony. The balcony leading to the rooms offers a view of the lovely residence next door. Built in the republican style of the early 20th century, it was once the head office of the coffee growers' corporation. Opposite the house, there is an astonishing little church known as **La Ermita del Cabrero**, where the President and his wife are interred.

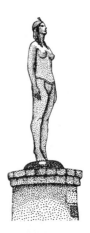

La India Catalina

Heading back to the old city and then on to Puente de Chambacú on the main road, visitors will see a monument in the middle of the traffic circle in front of the bridge. Known as **La India Catalina**, it is dedicated to an Amerindian woman who lived in the area. A courageous warrior according to some, she was used as an interpreter by Pedro de Heredia when the region was being colonized. Nowadays, a miniature copy of the statue is presented as atrophy for the best production at Cartagena's annual film festival (see p 185).

Bocagrande and El Laguito

Within the space of a few years, the peninsula of **Bocagrande ★**, trimmed with a beautiful ribbon of sand, has become the centre of the tourist industry with hotels and all kinds of facilities for visitors. Linked to the downtown area by a seaside road, it is very popular among Cartageneros, who come here on weekends to enjoy the sunny beaches and wonderful warm water. A gigantic underwater construction project was undertaken here, too. From the mid- to late-18th century, the Spanish built an immense underwater stone wall linking Isla Tierrabomba to the tip of the peninsula. Rising up almost to sea level, the wall was intended to prevent ships from entering the bay from the sea.

El Laguito ★, which resembles a small outgrowth at the end of the peninsula, is occupied mainly by luxury hotels, and therefore attracts a more affluent crowd. Shortly before El Laguito, there is another little offshoot of land

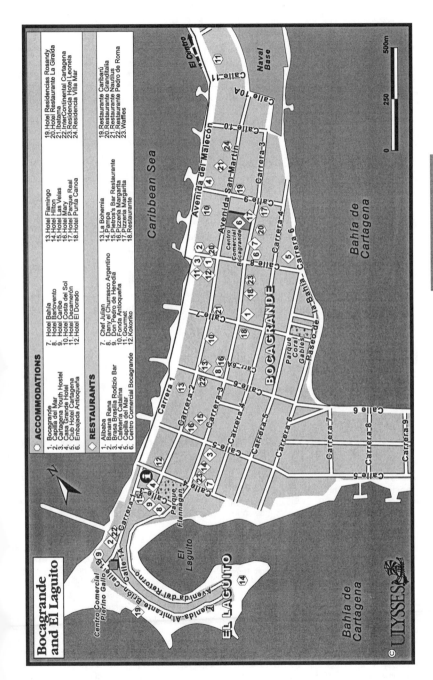

CARTAGENA DE INDIAS

Bocagrande and El Laguito

© ULYSSES

The Battle of Vernon

Of all the battles fought in this city, the most impressive was probably that of 1741, known as the Battle of Vernon. Around 1740, the English, on the pretext that a British ship and a vessel belonging to the Spanish navy had engaged in battle, ordered Admiral Edward Vernon to take possession of Cartagena in order to avenge the affront they had suffered. The king of Spain, who had learned of these plans through his spies, put Don Blas de Lezo in charge of defending the city. Don Blas de Lezo, a Basque of noble birth, was an officer in the royal army, who had taken part in numerous military campaigns. Thanks ironically to the many injuries he had sustained in the course of these battles, including the loss of his right eye, right arm and left leg, he had acquired a reputation for tenacity and courage. In March 1741, the first British warships appeared off the coast of Cartagena. Over the following days, English forces continued to pour into the area, reaching a fleet of 186. Vernon, with 20,000 troops at his disposal, had also been guaranteed the assistance of 4,000 men from the colony of Virginia. (It might interest visitors to learn that the commander of this regiment was none other than Captain Lawrence Washington, the brother of George Washington, who would later become the first president of the United States.) This was the largest force ever assembled to capture the city. Faced with such an opponent, the Spanish forces, numbering some 3,000 men, were almost pathetic. In early April 1741, the battle began, and after 16 days of violent attacks, Vernon succeeded in entering the bay, forcing the Spanish to take refuge in the city's fortifications. The English, thus finding themselves at the gates of the city and, thanks to the American contingent, in control of the Convento de la Popa, were certain they would triumph over the Cartageneros – so certain that Vernon sent messengers to the English colony of Jamaica and to London announcing his victory. Shortly after, the battle resumed, and after a week of sustained firing, the British launched their final assault on the fort. On April 20, 1741, after several hours of intense fighting, and to most people's surprise, the English were defeated. Don Blas de Lezo had stood fast in his impenetrable fortress, forcing his attackers to retreat. Though it does not detract in any way from the bravery of the Cartagenero combatants, it is true that a malaria epidemic had stricken Vernon's men, which helped the courageous inhabitants defend their city. The English thus went home empty-handed, their only consolation the prematurely stamped medal commemorating their "victory" over the city! Don Blas de Lezo, crowned with success, had unfortunately lost his remaining leg during the fighting, and died soon after the battle, in September 1741. A statue was erected in his honour at the foot of the fort.

named Castillogrande, which is a primarily a residential area.

The area's main attraction are its **beaches ★★**. Bordering the coast for nearly half a kilometre, they are clean and well-kept, and very pleasant for swimming. The peninsula also has many shops, restaurants, bars and nightclubs, making this the ideal spot if you're looking for sunshine, water sports, bustling streets and an animated nightlife. Most of Cartagena's large- and medium-sized hotels are also located here.

Getsemaní and La Matuna

Although it is not as rich in architecture as the El Centro and San Diego neighbourhoods, **Getsemaní ★** is also part of the historic section of the city. Originally separated from the two aforementioned areas by a canal spanned by a bridge, it was mainly inhabited by poorer people. It was once entirely surrounded by walls, but only a few pieces of these are still standing today. The relatively modern-looking neighbourhood of **La Matuna** lies nestled between Getsemaní and the old city, where the canal was once located. It is occupied by stores and many services, including the post office and the telephone company.

Once a religious institution, the **Convento de San Francisco ★★** *(Avenido del Mercado, next to the Centro de Convenciones)* consists of a large cloister flanked by two churches, the Iglesia de la Tercera Orden and the Iglesia de San Francisco. The former has remained a house of worship, while the latter has been converted into a movie theatre. The **cloister** *(enter through the long corridor to the right of the movie theatre)* was begun in 1555 and completed in 1628. It is distinguished by the interesting manner in which the arcades have been placed atop the lovely, imposing (albeit slightly heavy-looking) columns. Large trees stand all around the central court, adorning the

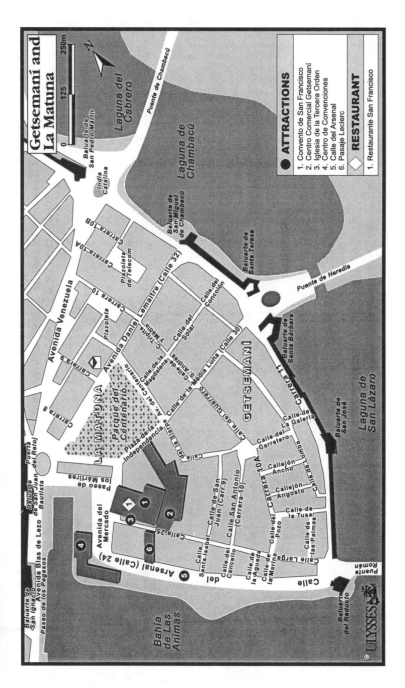

surroundings and shading visitors from the hot sun. A variety of little craft shops have been set up beneath the arcades. At the back of the building, visitors will find the **Centro Comercial Getsemaní**, a veritable labyrinth containing all sorts of shops, which are not particularly interesting. At the front of the monastery, obstructing part of its façade, stands another building whose arcades usually shelter a flower market. The building was being repaired during our visit.

The **Iglesia de la Tercera Orden** ★ *(to the right of the cloister, at the corner of Calle Larga)* is worth visiting for its interesting wooden ceiling, whose central vault has lovely carved crosspieces. Rumour has it that the valiant Don Blas de Lezo (see p 168) is interred here, though no one really knows exactly where.

The **Centro de Convenciones** *(Avenida del Mercado)* is a modern building, erected in 1972, where both commercial and artistic events (exhibitions, trade fairs, conventions, etc.) are held on a regular basis. Criticized by some as being overly modern, the edifice has a certain appeal, thanks to its clean, slender lines and the coralline stone with which it was built. The texture and colour of this material brings to mind the colonial buildings in the *intra-muros* city.

Although there are no real monuments on **Calle del Arsenal**, it is a pleasant place for a stroll. A cobblestone street running alongside the bay, it is lined with pretty houses, which create a romantic atmosphere. In the evening, Calle del Arsenal comes to life, and a motley crowd parades along it. The bars put together makeshift terraces, where live bands play rhythmic tunes. At the beginning of the street, visitors will come across the **Pasaje Leclerc**, a covered passageway sheltering all sorts of shops, selling everything from toys to hardware and household appliances. The market area has a typically Colombian atmosphere.

Around Cartagena

While exploring the area around Cartagena, you will come across a bronze sculpture called *Los Zapatos Viejos*, which stands right before the Puente de Heredia. Its Spanish name translates as "an old pair of shoes". The work was erected in memory of Cartagenero poet Luis Carlos Lopez, whose writings so masterfully glorified his native city.

Near the Gestemaní district, **Castillo San Felipe de Barajas** ★★★ *(1,500 pesos; just past the Puente Heredia, on the way out of Getsemaní)* was the most important military structure built in Latin America during the colonial era. Erected on the hill known as San Lázaro, the fort was originally of only modest size and was essentially limited to the hilltop, which is where visitors will find the oldest parts of the building.

The fort was begun in 1630 and completed in 1657; work on it was greatly accelerated while Pedro Zapata y Mendoza was governor. The design is mainly the work of a Dutch engineer. In 1697, however, French pirates Desjeans and Ducasse destroyed parts of the fort and the city and made off with the impressive sum of 11 million gold pesos. The booty was used in part to replenish the treasury of Louis XIV. Restored by Juan de Herrera y Sotomayor after the attack, the fort underwent significant modifications. The most important, however, were those made by military engineer Antonio de Arévalo, who, after the terrible Battle of Vernon, added a series of imposing lateral batteries to the structure. These were connected by a large number of underground passageways, and completed by large rooms, where weapons could be stored. An underground passageway linking the fort to the old city was also built.

The size of the fort is sure to impress visitors, as are the interesting views of the city from here. Upon arriving, however, get ready to be assailed by a horde of souvenir merchants (you can't stop progress!) prepared to do just about anything to sell their wares. Inside, an impressive series of connected galleries enables visitors to grasp the scale of this project.

Visitors enter the **Fuerte del Pastelillo** *(turn right on Avenida del Pastello immediately after the Puente Román; the entrance to the fort is located at the end of the street)* through a pretty arch-shaped door inscribed with the date of the building's construction, shortly after the Battle of Vernon, on the site of an older fort. The first fort, known as El Boquerón, was erected after a French pirate by the name of Martin Cote besieged and pillaged the city. This series of forts was intended, of course, to protect the port and the Bahía de Las Animas. Well preserved to this day, the Fuerte Del Pastelillo is now a fishing club with an excellent restaurant (see p 183). This place will delight boat lovers most of all, and also offers a panoramic view of Bocagrande.

Fuerte del Pastelillo

The **Convento de la Popa** ★★★ *(1,600 pesos)* was built on the highest hill overlooking the city, at an altitude of 145 metres. Upon the urging of Fray Alonso García de la Cruz, it was begun by the monks of the Augustinian Recollect order in the year 1606. At first, only a small chapel was erected in honour of the Virgin. It was named Nuestra Señora de la Candelaria, in reference to the house (see p 163) in which the Virgin supposedly appeared to Fray Alonso and ordered him to dedicate a sanctuary to her at the top of the La Popa hill. The project continued throughout the 17th century, and after numerous extensions and modifications, the chapel became a real monastery. Shortly after independence, however, it was confiscated by the military and converted into a fort in order to defend the city against a possible Spanish attack. Later, when the country's independence was no longer threatened, the buildings were abandoned for more than a century. In 1961, the same order of monks took over the premises once again. They began major restorations in 1964.

The monastery's entrance opens onto a magnificent cloister surrounded by a double series of arcades supported by massive columns. The coralline stone, the lovely bougainvillaeas, the carved wooden balustrades of the second-floor balconies and the charming little well in the centre of the court create a harmonious setting. In addition to this picture post-card setting, the monastery offers cool shade, which is much appreciated here on this sun-drenched hill. Although it is still inhabited by a few monks, the monastery now serves mainly as a museum, where visitors can see old maps, collections of Gregorian chants and a variety of religious objects. Of particular interest are the astonishing model and the painting depicting the *Adoracíon del Cabro de Oro* (Adoration of the Golden Goat), a pagan religious scene. According to his own account, Fray Alonso surprised a group of slaves and Amerindians worshipping a golden goat at the top of the hill. Deeply offended, he hurled the idol into a crevice now marked by the entrance of the monastery. No one knows if these events really took place, or if the whole story is nothing more than a legend.

A small chapel to the left of the entrance houses the famous wooden statue of **Nuestra Señora de la Candelaria** ★★★, who is also the patron saint of the city of Cartagena. An object of worship (non-pagan this time!), the statue inspires hundreds of believers to make an annual pilgrimage up the hill. Every year, on February 2, there is a procession in honour of the Virgin. A golden crown set with 400 emeralds is also placed on her head once a year (see p 165).

The richly clothed statuette is housed inside a splendid, finely carved wooden altar, which is painted red and covered with gold leaf. The magnificent decor is completed by a beautiful ceiling and several lovely sections of marquetry.

All around the outside of the convent, the panoramic views of the old city, Bocagrande, Isla de la Manga and, in the distance, Isla Tierrabomba will delight photographers.

The **Fuerte de San Fernando**, built on Isla Tierrabomba in 1753, is well preserved. Erected on a small peninsula at the tip of the island, the fort was clearly intended to prevent pirate ships from attacking the city. The construction of another fort, **Fuerte Batería de San José**, which was more modest but well-located on the little island of Boca Chica, immediately opposite, meant the Spanish could easily bombard any hostile ship. Today, as required by the Colombian sovereignty bill, all foreign ships entering the bay must be escorted to the port by navigators from the Colombian military. These two somewhat isolated forts will be of interest mainly to visitors fascinated by military architecture.

Islas del Rosario ★★★

The Islas del Rosario (Rosary Islands), consisting of 26 coral formations in all, are located off the coast of Isla Barú. According to Colombians, these are the most beautiful islands on the country's entire Caribbean coast. Although the archipelago has been classified as a nature reserve, most of the little islands are privately owned and cannot be visited. Many of them belong to political figures, local celebrities or simply wealthy families.

The architecture of some of the buildings reveals a wealth of imagination on the part of the owners, while other properties are in a sorry condition. The abundant marine life, stunning underwater scenery and crystal-clear water make this a heavenly place to explore the sea or simply to go swimming. On Isla San Martín, there is a **water park** where visitors can admire a large variety of fish found in the

Caribbean and watch dolphins perform amazing tricks as well as an impressive shark-feeding session. Finally, there are several aquariums, which are also worth a visit. Right near the park, visitors can swim in a protected area where remarkably beautiful marine life can be observed.

The **Playa Blanca** on Isla Barú is renowned for its lovely white sand and crystal-clear water. It is, however, very remote and facilities are limited; it therefore appeals mostly to those seeking a quiet, secluded setting.

La Boquilla ★★

La Boquilla is a typical little fishing village that lies less than 10 kilometres from Cartagena. Visitors can go swimming here, or simply watch the fishermen go about their business. For the more adventurous, there are boat excursions in the swamp, which offer an opportunity to admire the abundant animal life sheltered by the mangroves. La Boquilla, which attracts large numbers of Cartageneros on weekends, is renowned primarily for its excellent fish dishes.

Volcán Totumo

Visitors fond of spa treatments can opt for a day trip to the Volcán Totumo. Many agencies organize mud-bath excursions. Somewhat peculiar in appearance, the volcano's peak consists of a modest-sized cone with a pool of mud in the middle.

Santiago de Tolú ★★★

Located in the neighbouring department of Sucre, a three-hour-plus drive from Cartagena, Santiago de Tolú makes for a pleasant one-day excursion. You can spend more time here by staying in one of the village's comfortable hotels (see p 178). The Cartagena de Indias countryside east of Santiago de Tolú is magnificent. The green and mountainous landscape is full of charming little fenced-in cattle farms *(fincas)*, and after each sharp curve in the road quaint *pueblos* appear. The spruce houses in these villages are painted white with red round-tiled roofs and patios enclosed by wrought-iron fences. Locals sip coffee or beer at *tiendas* (bars with terraces). You'll think you are somewhere deep in the Mediterranean countryside. But the dream comes to a sudden end here, for some villages tell another story, that of dire poverty that contrast sharply with the rich countryside. A random signpost indicates that a *pueblito* receives aid from international organizations such as Foster Parents. Poverty is rampant — even here, less than one hour from Cartagena, one of Colombia's wealthiest cities.

Santiago de Tolú, more simply known as Tolú, is a fishing village that has become a small tourist resort. Some 15,000 people live here in well-kept houses, some of which have palm-thatched roofs. A few roads are fully paved and all intersect with Avenida 1, or Avenida de La Playa, which runs along the Santiago de Tolú beach for three kilometres. This seafront strip is probably the best thing about Tolú: there are a promenade lined by palm trees, many pleasant little hotels and restaurants, and bars with shaded terraces.

ACCOMMODATIONS

Cartagena de Indias

El Centro and San Diego

The rooms at the **Hostal Santo Domingo** (*$; pb, ⊛; Calle Santo Domingo, No. 33-46, ☎664-2268*), near Iglesia Santo Domingo, are clustered around a small inner court filled with pretty flowers. Although its rooms are not very well insulated, this hotel is very quiet.

Not far from the university, the **Hotel Veracruz** (*$, pb, ⊛; Calle San Agustín, ☎664-1521 and 664-6265*) offers slightly less comfortable rooms, which will nevertheless suit visitors who don't mind a noisy atmosphere; on weekends, there is a discotheque on the main floor. This hotel is popular with travellers on a very limited budget.

 The very lovely **Hotel Santa Clara** (*$$$$$; pb, hw, ≡, ℜ, ≈, tv, △, ⊘; Calle del Torno, Barrio San Diego, ☎664-6070, ≈664-7010*) could easily have been included in the "Exploring" chapter, or even under the "Excursions" heading. Obviously, it is an expensive hotel. Even though high-priced hotels are so old that they creak, this one is aesthetically pleasing in all its simplicity. The Santa Clara is quite

simply exquisite. During renovations, the French hotel chain Sofitel respected the building's charm by preserving the antique character and sober lines of this former Santa Clara de Asis convent, built in the Old City in 1617. The exterior architecture is a perfect blend of Spanish colonial and Republican styles, and the entrance alone is worth the trip. It is accessed through a huge black wrought-iron door and divided into three 10-metre-high rooms: the lobby, the reception area and the room reserved for organizing excursions. Period paintings on wood hang on its red-brick walls and are illuminated by spotlights. A large dark-wood cornice crowns the walls. The effect is stunning, and enhanced by colonial furnishings. The place is a veritable museum, a true work of art that could not have been designed by anyone but a renowned professional. The lobby opens out onto an interior courtyard – a small botanical garden, with each plant and tree identified. The courtyard is surrounded by a colonnade and decorated with antique furniture and objects, and a few wrought-iron chairs and tables where guests can have coffee. In addition to the in-ground swimming pool in a second interior courtyard, the hotel has a fully equipped fitness centre comprising a whirlpool bath, a sauna with Turkish baths and an exercise room with professional equipment. The 162 rooms and 18 spacious suites are in the cloisters. All have balconies, high ceilings and period furniture meticulously selected for maximum comfort. Modern-day amenities include a television set, a telephone, a mini bar and an in-room safe. The staff speak English and French.

 Another beautiful but slightly less expensive hotel, the **Santa Teresa** (*$$$$$; pb, hw, ≡, ≈, ℜ, tv, △, ⊘; Centro Plaza Santa Teresa, Carrera 3a, No. 31-23, ☎664-9494, ≈664-9447 or 664-9448, hsteresa@ns.axisgate.com*) is somewhat more austere but just as spectacular. It is located near the Escolera de la Marina and the Getsemaní conference centre, also in a former convent. The impressive façade is a historical legacy and a successful mix of the Spanish colonial and Republican architectural styles. In the early 17th century, Doña María de Barras y Montalvo, born into a wealthy family, wished to end her days with the Carmelite nuns. She thus had the Convento Santa Teresa built, the first convent erected in the Old City. Later, it served by turns as a military camp, a prison, a school for young girls and finally, a pasta factory, losing more of its original character with each change. The convent was finally bought by the Central Bank of

Colombia and completely restored and converted into a hotel by the Hoteles Pedro Gómez y Cía. S.A. group. The establishment is now part of the French chain *Relais et Châteaux*. This locale can also be considered a museum. The spacious rooms don't have balconies, but are equipped with in-room safes and are decorated with either colonial or Republican furniture. The hotel's biggest draw is its rooftop swimming pool, with a splendid view of Cartagena de Indias and the sea. Other amenities include a fully equipped gym, a sauna, and Turkish baths. The elegantly maintained chapel has a conference room for 220 people and contains several preserved statues.

🏨 The **Casa Pestagua** *($$$$$; pb, hw, ≈, ℜ, ≈, tv; Calle Santo Domingo No. 33-63, ☎664-9514, ≈660-0516)* also belongs to the Hoteles Pedro Gómez y Cía. S.A. group and the French chain *Relais et Châteaux*. This old two-storey colonial house is adorned with the balconies that have made Cartagena famous. The interior courtyard alone is worth the visit, with its marble floors, vaulted colonnades, balcony and eight colossal palm trees that are higher than the roof. The 11 rooms, all of them suites facing the courtyard, are decorated in a way that combines their traditional ambiance with unparalleled elegance. The presidential suite has high beamed ceilings, and a whirlpool bath on the balcony with a view over the Old City. The impeccable service speaks for itself. Sure it's expensive, but you won't find a better place to stay!

Bocagrande and El Laguito

The **Cartagena Youth Hostel** *($; ℗; Carrera 1, No. 8-210, ☎665-0455, ≈665-1074)* offers standard comfort for this type of establishment. It is housed in a large residence with a huge bed of flowers facing the beach, which is less than 20 metres away.

🏨 **Hotel Parque Real** *($; pb, ℗; Carrera 3, No. 8-171, ☎665-5531 and 665-5507)*. The bright, airy rooms are clean and well-maintained. The staff is obliging and efficient.

Visitors on a tight budget should consider the **Hotel Restaurante La Giralda** *($; pb, ℗, ℜ; Carrera 3, No. 8-166, ☎665-4507 and 665-7717, ≈665-7707)*. This villa has old-fashioned charm and a unique style. The rooms are clean but a bit run-down. There is little privacy and the service seems somewhat unprofessional. On the positive side, however,

the hotel is centrally located and offers attractive rates. Rooms equipped with a fan are available for a reasonable price.

Located 100 metres from the beach, the **Hotel Punta Canoa** *($; pb, ≈, ℗; Calle 7, No. 2-50, ☎665-4179 and 665-5672)* is attractive from the outside, but unfortunately the interior does not appear to have been fixed up for a very long time. The only advantages to this place are its proximity to the beach and its low prices. For a little peace and quiet, ask for a room that looks onto the street.

🏨 A clean hotel with a friendly staff, **Ibatama** *($; pb, hw, ≈, ℗; Avenida San Martín No. 7-146, ☎665-4002 or 665-1127, ≈665-8445)* is a worthwhile establishment in this category. Good value for the price.

The **Hotel Mary** *($; pb, hw, ≈, ℗; Carrera 3, No. 6-53, ☎665-2833)* will also appeal to budget travellers. The rooms are clean and simply furnished, and there are a telephone and television set at the reception.

Hotel Residencias Rosandy *($; pb, hw, ≈, ℗; Avenida San Martín No. 9-42, ☎665-5863, 665-5101, 665-4865 or 665-4864, ≈665-3947)* is another budget place in the middle of the tourist district, only 100 metres from the beach. A well-kept hotel that will please those looking for peace and quiet.

The **Embajada Antioqueña Hotel-Restaurant** *($; pb, ≈, ℗, tv, ℜ; Carrera 3a, No. 8-54, ☎665-2718)* is located a stone's throw from the beach and offers clean rooms in a family ambiance. The hotel and its restaurant donate some of their profits to the Fundación Hogar Oscar, a shelter for Cartagena de Indias street children.

The **Residencia Villa Mar** *($; pb, ≈, ℗; Carrera 2 or Avenida San Martín, No. 9-183, ☎665-0425 or 665-6285, ≈665-9145)* is a charming house with an added wing attached to the side. Ask for a room in the house, since those in the wing are poorly insulated and not as comfortable. This place would be more appealing if it were better maintained.

The small **Residencia Hotel Leonela** *($; pb, ≈, ℗; Carrera 3, No. 7-142, ☎665-8595, ≈665-8868)* offers basic rooms in ordinary but clean surroundings.

Another good place for the price, the **Bocagrande** *($$; pb, hw, ≈; Carrera 2,*

No. 7-187, ☎665-4435, 665-4436 or 665-7164, ⇒665-4437) is a decent budget hotel, with about 50 small but clean rooms. Friendly staff.

🏨 The pleasant **Hotel Bahía** *($$$; pb, ≡, ≈, ℜ, tv; Calle 4, near Carrera 4, ☎665-0316, 665-0317 or 665-0318, ⇒665-6170)* has 62 charming, comfortable rooms and two suites on five floors. Some of them face the back of the building, where a large swimming pool and a garden with palm trees adorn the grounds. The hotel is well maintained and tastefully decorated, and the beach is only 300 metres away. Good quality for the price.

🏨 With its interesting interior architecture, the **Hotel Costa del Sol** *($$$; pb, ≡, ≈, ℜ, tv; Carrera 1, No. 9-18, ☎665-0844 and 665-6643, ⇒665-3755)* welcomes its guests in a modern lobby attractively decorated with rattan furniture. The rooms are well-equipped and very tastefully furnished, but there are no balconies. The hotel lies a stone's throw from the beach and has a small roof-top swimming pool. Good quality for the price.

Built on a piece of land stretching from Carrera 2 to Carrera 1, the **Hotel Flamingo** *($$$ bkfst incl.; pb, ≡, ℜ, ℝ, tv; Carrera 1, No. 5-85, ☎665-0301, 665-0302 and 665-3160, ⇒665-6946)* has 32 rooms, which are decorated and equipped in a satisfactory but somewhat unoriginal fashion. While the main floor of the hotel is occupied by a restaurant facing right onto Carrera 2, the part alongside the beach *(Carrera 1)* has a bar and terrace. Located on a fairly busy street, this establishment is most suitable for people who don't mind a noisy atmosphere.

Upon entering El Laguito, you will find the **Hotel Las Velas** *($$$, $$$$ with balcony; pb, ≡, ≈, ℜ, ℝ, tv, Carrera 1, near Calle 1A, No. 1-60, ☎665-0000 and 665-6866, ⇒665-0530)*, which, along with the Hilton, is the only hotel with direct access to the beach. The rooms are tastefully decorated and very bright. Some of them are also equipped with a balcony offering a view of the beach and the sea. A large swimming pool in a lush green setting with a large number of palm trees adds to its already pleasant surroundings. Very good quality for the price.

🏨 The **Casa Grande Hotel Cartagena** *($$$, $$$$ with a view of the sea; pb, ≡, ℜ, tv; Carrera 1, No. 9-128, ☎665-3943 and 665-5893, ⇒665-6806)* has a seaside location

and accommodates guests in a pretty villa, with a pleasant terrace adorned with plants and bushes in front. The decor, embellished with woodwork, gives the interior a cozy appearance. The most attractive rooms are of course those with a view of the sea. Family atmosphere.

Hotel Barlovento *($$$$, $$$$$ with balcony; pb, ≡, ≈, ℜ, tv; Carrera 3, No. 6-23, ☎665-3965, 665-3966, 665-3967, 665-0134 or 665-0616, ⇒665-5726)* is fairly comfortable and reasonably priced. The decor, despite being somewhat haphazard, is acceptable. Rooms with balconies are even brighter, though the view is still relatively uninteresting. Since the hotel is located in a very busy area, these rooms are also noisier. There is a very small swimming pool on the premises.

The **Club Hotel Cartagena Plaza** *($$$$$; pb, ≡, ≈, ℜ, ℝ, tv; Carrera 1A, No. 6-154, ☎665-4000 or 665-4104, ⇒665-6315)* is an imposing, modern structure composed of two huge, beachfront high-rises with rather unoriginal architecture. Each contains about 319 rooms, none of which is equipped with a balcony. The two high-rises (Torre Plaza and Torre Bolívar) are almost identical and sorely lacking in charm. The comfortable rooms are decently decorated, but not remarkable, while the dim corridors, the walls of which are partially covered with dark-coloured ceramic tiles, are not very inviting. Guests have use of a wide range of facilities (roof-top swimming pool, shops, discotheque, restaurant, etc.), as well as deck chairs and beach towels.

The **Capilla del Mar** *($$$$$ with balcony; pb, ≡, ≈, ℜ, ℝ, tv; Carrera 1 and Calle 8; ☎665-1140, 665-1178 or 665-3868, ⇒665-5145)* is a large, modern, oceanfront hotel with 194 rooms, all of which meet the standards of comfort that guests rightfully expect from a hotel in this category (mini-bar, television, etc.). The decor is attractive, though somewhat conventional. Those rooms equipped with balconies have large beds. Many facilities are available on the premises, including a sauna, a gym, a hairdressing salon, a conference room, shops, a travel agency, deck chairs and beach towels. There is a pleasant cafeteria on the main floor and on the roof there is small swimming pool with a lovely view. Unfortunately, the proximity of the fans for the air conditioning system detracts somewhat from the charm of the pool area.

Made up of two separate high-rises, the **Hotel El Dorado** *($$$$$ everything included; pb, ≡, ≈, ℛ, tv; Carrera 2, No. 4-41, ☎665-0211, 665-0914, 665-0272, or 665-0830, ⌐665-0479)* offers packages where everything – all meals, and a wide variety of activities ranging from aerobics classes to evening shows and organized outings – is included. The Torre Los Andes high-rise has an entrance on the beach side, while the entrance of the other building, Torre El Dorado, is located on Carrera 2. Although the corridors are a bit gloomy, the rooms are attractively decorated. However, they do not have balconies. This somewhat lively establishment, most suitable for people fond of both daytime and nighttime activities, also has a medium-sized swimming pool.

The **Hotel Decamerón** *($$$$$ everything included; pb, ≡, ℛ, tv; Carrera 1, No. 10-10, ☎665-7601 or 665-4400, ⌐665-6145)* offers the same sort of package as the El Dorado, and has 280 well-equipped rooms with a modern decor. This hotel's main advantage is that some of its rooms have balconies with a view of the sea. It is also located closer to the old city. Since shows (which are not always in the best of taste) are presented here every night, this place is appropriate mainly for travellers seeking a lively atmosphere.

🏨 The architecture of the **Hotel Caribe** *($$$$$; pb, ≡, ≈, ℛ, ℝ, tv; Carrera No. 2-87, ☎665-0155 or 665-5466, ⌐665-3707 and 665-4970)* is decidedly more interesting than that of many other big hotels in the area. It is probably the oldest hotel on the peninsula. Surrounded by greenery, painted in soft pastel colours with an arched entryway flanked by towers, the building has a pleasant colonial look about it. The rooms are attractively decorated with modern furniture, but none of them has a balcony looking out on the sea. The building is also equipped with a gaming room and slot machines, a chapel and a beautiful small theatre worth visiting for its *trompe-l'œil* decor. There are a number of facilities to satisfy even the most demanding of guests—three restaurants, a bar, a gym *(open every day until 8pm)*, a sauna, a tennis court, shops, a conference room and a large swimming pool with a cafeteria alongside it. A pleasant interior garden complements the overall appearance of the place. The hotel is expensive, but well worth the price.

🏨 The **Inter-Continental Cartagena** *($$$$$; pb, hw, ≡, ℛ, ≈, ℝ, tv, ⊛, ☺; Avenida San* Martín, at Calle 6A, ☎665-8261 or 665-8266, ⌐665-8269)* is an enormous new hotel with three buildings of 21, 15 and 13 floors respectively and about 200 rooms and 50 suites. Of exceptional architecture according to the experts, the hotel has a spacious, impressive lobby that resembles Cartagena de Indias' colonial-era church façades. The rooms are what one would expect of a hotel of this calibre: decently furnished with a high level of comfort. Each room is equipped with an in-room safe. In addition to seven function rooms with a total capacity of 1,000 people, a fully equipped health club, a swimming pool and a casino, the hotel boasts a sophisticated business communications centre with Internet and fax service.

In the luxury category, the **Hotel Hilton** *($$$$$; pb, ≡, ≈, ℛ, ℝ, tv; at the tip of the point on El Laguito, ☎665-0666, ⌐665-2211)* has every facility a person could dream of: a private beach, a gym, tennis courts, a swimming pool, ping-pong tables, a sauna, bars, a discotheque, restaurants, conference rooms, and more. With its tradition of satisfying the most fastidious tastes, it is definitely up to Hilton standards. Regulars of this chain will thus encounter no surprises, other than the live folk music presented every Saturday night (see p 185).

Around Cartagena

Playa de Marbella

The small **Hotel Bellavista** *($; Avenida Santander No. 47-64, ☎664-6411 or 664-0684, ⌐660-0379)* is a ten minutes' walk from the Old City, along the airport road. It is an old colonial-style house with a few comfortable rooms. In addition to its proximity to the beach, the French-owned establishment boasts several patios graced with lovely tropical flora. Because the hotel is slightly off the tourist-beaten path, it is a good place for peace and quiet.

Islas del Rosario

🏨 On the island of Majagua, the **Hotel San Pedro de Majagua** *($$$-$$$$; pb, ⊛, ℛ; ☎664-6070, ⌐664-7010)* offers only a few (11 in total) cottage-style rooms, or *cabañas*, with dried palm-frond roofs in a dream-like setting beneath tropical trees. The place comprises a scuba-diving centre, two magnificent private beaches with a bar, showers, bathrooms, chairs, hammocks, mosquito nets, towels and kayaks, as well as a beachfront restaurant with a splendid view of the sea. The hotel belongs to Sofitel, the chain that owns the Hotel Santa Clara in Cartagena, and the hotels share the same number for reservations. The Sofitel chain preserved the French painter Pierre Daguet's (see box) former studio, and his library — which doubles as a tv room — has also been kept intact. You can read some of the painter's favourite books, including art books and numerous detective novels in both English and French. Splendid marine life and magnificent corals, together with crystal-clear waters, make this "desert island" truly exotic and enchanting. The English- and French-speaking Spanish staff can tell you all about the archipelago, including the best sites for diving. Meals consist of fish and seafood, pasta and grilled meat dishes that cost between 10,000 and 25,000 pesos. And why not wash down that lobster with a wonderful bottle of well-chilled Veuve Cliquot champagne at 130,000 pesos, since staying here is a real bargain at 90,000 pesos per night for one or two people. The return fare to Majagua island is 24,000 pesos. The island has five similar but lower-priced hotels.

Pierre Daguet

Painter Pierre Daguet was born in Clermont-Ferrand, Auvergne, in 1905. He held his first solo exhibition in Paris before taking part in a group show in Santafé de Bogotá, where he settled in 1933. There he worked as an art teacher and founded the first art school with his colleague, Alberto Manrique Convers. He later taught at the Cartagena de Indias art school and opened his "La Majagua" painting studio in 1955, which is now a hotel (see above), on the small island of San Pedro in the Islas del Rosario archipelago. On June 7, 1971, he was awarded the Medal of Honour and Merit by the Secretary of Education and Culture of the Bolívar department for his contribution to Colombian culture. Daguet passed away in Cartagena de Indias on July 20, 1980, at the age of 75.

Crespo

Less than four kilometres from the town centre, Crespo is a small *barrio* with a few hotels.

Its main asset is that it's close to the Rafael Núñez International Airport. These low-budget accommodations will tide you over until there is a vacancy at Las Americas, the best hotel in Cartagena. The beach is just a short walk away, at the end of Calle 70.

The **Hospedaje La Fonda Los Arrieros** *($; pb, ⊗, ℜ; Calle 70, No. 6-142, ☎666-5353)* is a budget hotel and does not pretend to be otherwise. Relaxed ambiance, friendly staff and a small terrace in front.

The **Hotel Aero** *($; pb, ⊗, ℜ; Carrera 70, No. 6-142, ☎666-3249)* has 24-hour reception. Ideal for limited budget travellers who have just gotten off the plane.

Less than two kilometres from the airport, the **Las Americas Beach Resort** *($$$$$; pb, hw, tv, ≡, ≈, ℜ, ◻, ⊘; on the road to La Boquilla, less than one km from Crespo, ☎664-4000 or 664-9650, ≠664-9910, lasamericas@ctgred.net.co)* is a large hotel complex with 250 rooms in seven three-story buildings. Each of the rooms has a balcony and a view of the sea. Its many facilities include bars, restaurants, conference rooms, a discotheque, two small shopping promenades, three swimming pools, two tennis courts, a putting green, a whirlpool bath and different water-sports equipment. The hotel will soon have direct access to the beach. The huge open-air lobby has a bank machine and one of those grand staircases often seen on television shows about the rich and famous. At the top of the imposing staircase are the conference rooms and a café, El mesón de Don Cristóbal, just below a bar. Both the open-air bar and café offer lovely views of the *piscina de niños* (wading pool) and the sea in the distance, which turns scarlet at sundown. A hedge-lined walkway surrounds the swimming pools, where thousands of butterflies (*mariposas*) flutter to the greatest delight of children and lepidopterists. The hotel has also become a refuge for a colony of colourful birds by setting up bird feeders on the grounds. Sometimes these birds eat one of the butterflies for a starter or dessert. Las Americas offers its guests many daytime and nighttime activities. All kinds of children's activities are organized and adults can work out in the hotel's new fully-equipped fitness centre, with a gym, sauna, massage room and more. Free shuttle service is offered at even hours to the town centre and to Bocagrande starting at 8am, with return at odd hours, ending at 11pm. The Cartagena-La Boquilla bus also stops at the hotel: the first bus departs at 6am. The large rooms are comfortably furnished with king-sized beds and large balconies with French doors, where guests can dine or simply lounge in a hammock while listening to the ocean waves break nearby. The dedicated staff speaks both English and French. The hotel's public relations director, Mrs. Patricia Puccetti Carvajal, will be more than happy to help you with any problem.

La Boquilla

A small, quiet family hotel-motel with six rooms, the **Hotel Costa Azul** *($; shower, pb, ⊗; no address or telephone, but right near the Colegio de Bachirato)* stands opposite a dozen small beachfront restaurants. The rooms are clean, but are more suitable for small budgets.

Santiago de Tolú

Most hotels here are located on Avenida de la Playa and do not have official addresses. A few places worth noting:

Brisas del Mar *($; pb, ⊗, ℜ; Avenida de la Playa, ☎88 50 32)* is a small, simple 31-room hotel whose only asset is its proximity to the beach. For limited budgets.

The **Hotel Restaurant El Platana** *($; pb, ℜ; Avenida de la Playa)* is an inexpensive little establishment with 13 rooms; only one has a fan. Also for limited budgets.

The **Hotel Mar Azul** *($; pb, ⊗, ≡; Avenida de la Playa, ☎88 52 15)* is a good choice among the low-priced hotels because it has just been fully renovated. There are twenty rooms, but only one has air conditioning. A good option for budget travellers.

The **Hotel Piedra Verde** *($-$$; pb, ⊗, ≡; Avenida de la Playa, ☎88 52 46)* is housed in a lovely three-storey colonial-style building that has an interior courtyard with ceramic-tiled floor. Friendly staff.

The 16-room **Club Náutico Los Delphines** *($-$$; pb, ⊗, tv, ℝ, K; Avenida de la Playa No. 11-08, ☎88 52 02)* offers accommodation for under 70,000 pesos per night for two people. The hotel seems to be the most dynamic, organizing excursions to the islands. However, it also has a nightclub and as a result may not be the ideal place for light sleepers.

The **Restaurant y Cabañas Macondo** *($$; pb, ⊗, ℜ; Avenida de la Playa, ☎88 51 78)* offers four motel-style rooms with bathrooms and shower, and nothing more. One to four people can stay here for the same price, about 70,000 pesos per night.

 The **Hotel Carib** *($-$$-$$$ bkfst incl.; pb, ⊗, ≡, tv; Avenida de la Playa No. 18-82, ☎88 51 15 or 88 51 33, ☎88 52 47)* is a small hotel with 36 rooms, 17 of them air-conditioned. A large second-floor terrace with chairs and parasols affords a splendid view over the sea, and is a great place for evening cocktails. A room with a fan costs about 70,000 pesos for two people, including breakfast. A room with air conditioning, television and mini bar costs approximately 105,000 pesos for two people, breakfast included. Good value for the price.

The **Montecarlo** *($$-$$$; pb, ⊗, ≡, tv, ℜ; Avenida de la Playa No. 8-30, ☎88 52 30, ☎88 52 31)* is probably the biggest hotel in Santiago de Tolú, and also the most comfortable. It is located at the left end of the beach and boasts some fifty spotless rooms for wealthier vacationers. The warm and friendly welcome make this a highly recommended hotel.

RESTAURANTS

Cartagena de Indias

El Centro and San Diego

At the small restaurant **Galéon de los Mares** *($; Mon to Sat 10am to 7pm, closed Sun; Calle de la Iglesia y Santos de Piedra)*, visitors can enjoy good home-style cooking. The house yucca soup and the *albondiguas* (beef meatballs) are excellent. The service is cheerful and friendly. This is a good spot for an inexpensive, unpretentious meal. The only minor drawback is the noisy television.

The **Maurizio y Renata** *($; Tue to Fri 9am to 9pm, Sat 9am to 5pm, closed Sun; Plaza de Bolívar No. 3-10)* crêperie is a good choice for a quick snack. Sheltered by the arcades of the Plaza Bolívar, this restaurant serves all different varieties of crepes. Try the surprising curried shrimp crepe. Though sitting in the shade beneath the arcades is very pleasant, the place only has a few tables, and would do well to offer faster, friendlier service.

Despite its somewhat misleading name, the **Restaurante Muralla China** *($; Calle del Estanco del Tabaco, No. 35-64)* serves home-style Colombian cuisine. The decor is conventional; the restaurant's main attraction lies in its dishes priced at under 5,500 pesos.

In the same price and food category, **Badillo** *($; Calle Segunda de Badillo, No. 36-47)* serves a *comida corriente* (daily special) in an interior courtyard. The service is relaxed.

A little farther up the same street lies the **Fonda de Gerard** *($; Calle Segunda de Badillo, No. 36-50)*, which offers a wider selection. The decor, however, is not very attractive.

If you have only 2,800 pesos left to buy yourself a meal, don't despair; at **Ricuras** *($; Calle de la Soledad, near the university)*, you can enjoy a home-style dish beneath old-fashioned vaulted ceilings, and television, too!

Yet another inexpensive restaurant, **Miscelaneas** *($; open only during daytime; Calle de Don Sancho, No. 36-44)* is very popular among the local youth, due to its proximity to the university. It offers light daily specials with real home-style flavour: soup, chicken with rice, etc. Very simple cuisine, served in an inner court covered with a thatched roof. Perfect for the easy to please traveller on a tight budget.

In a slightly more pleasant setting, the restaurant **La Tablada** *($; Calle de la Tablada, No. 7-46)* serves daily specials for less than 5,500 pesos in its interior garden.

Girasoles *($; at the corner of Calle Quero and Calle de los Puntales, ☎664-5239)* is a vegetarian restaurant located above the shop of the same name, which sells natural products. The place is poorly decorated, but serves good daily specials, such as coconut rice with beans and gluten. The rather curious interior decor of this restaurant would lead you to believe its owners are devout Christians.

Another option for vegetarians, **Natural Green** *($; Calle de la Soledad, No. 5-41, ☎664-5133)* is a small, slightly stuffy restaurant which serves simple dishes.

Located near Parque Fernández de Madrid, **Bocaditos Madrid** *($; Calle del Curato)* is a most appropriate spot for a light snack or a dessert. It is simple, no frills and inexpensive.

The restaurant/bar **La Escollera de la Marina** *($$$-$$; every day 11am to 3pm and 6pm to 4am; at the corner of Calle San Juan de Dios No. 31-24 and Antonio Ricaurte, near the naval museum, ☎664-2040 or 664-1337)* serves good Spanish cuisine in generous portions. The staff, dressed in colonial-style clothing, serve the tables set up in several different rooms. The one on the second floor, which, unfortunately, is often closed, is worth visiting for its superb colonial decor consisting of old wooden beams, an exposed brick arch and cast iron lamps. The room on the main floor, despite being a bit squeezed up against the bar, is pleasant as well, and has an attractive interior garden. The desserts are somewhat unrefined, but the quality/price ratio is worth the trip.

La Quemada *($$$; every day 11am to 3pm and 6pm to 4am; at Calle de la Amargura No. 32a-33 and Calle de Nuestra Señora del Ladrinal Esquina, ☎664-5312)* looks like a mid-19th-century London pub. In fact, it was built as a set for the film *Burn* (*quemada* means "burn" in Spanish), starring Marlon Brando. The menu features seafood and intercontinental cuisine.

The **Bodegón de la Candelaria** *($$$$; Mon to Fri noon to 3pm and 7pm to 11pm, Sat 7pm to 11pm, closed Sun; Calle de las Damas, No. 64, ☎664-7251)*, located in one of the most beautiful houses in Cartagena (see p 163) welcomes seafood lovers to its charming patio or its air-conditioned dining room. Good food with no surprises. El Mirador (see p 184), the piano bar on the second floor, is worth a visit.

The elegantly decorated **Restaurante Marcel** *($$$$; Mon to Sat noon to 3pm and 7pm to 10pm; Calle de la Inquisición, No. 78, by the Casa Skandia, immediately to the left of the Palacio de la Inquisición, ☎664-7058)*, at the end of a patio at the Casa Skandia, a very handsome colonial building (restored in 1978), will satisfy visitors seeking good, traditional European cuisine. The menu includes Parma ham, jugged duck, pepper steak with cognac sauce, etc. To top off your meal, try the delicious crepes Suzette. The dining room is air-conditioned (perhaps a bit too much so) and the staff friendly. Good quality/price ratio.

The gem of Cartagena's dining scene, **L'Escapade** *($$$$$, menu starting at $$$$; Wed to Sun 7:30pm to 10:30pm; Calle de Don*

Ice Cream and Pastry Shops

El Centro and San Diego

For an inexpensive breakfast, head over to **Calle de la Soledad** *(near the university)*, where the local bakery sells croissants for 19 cents and delicious milk and fruit drinks for less than 60 cents.

Bocagrande and El Laguito

Twenty-four hours a day, the **Panaderia Repostaria** *(Avenida 3, right near Calle 7)* sells bread and all sorts of sweets.

Gran Gelato *(Carrera 2, near Calle 9)* sells excellent Italian ice cream, which is available in an infinite variety of flavours. There is also a wide selection of delicious sorbets. An address to remember!

Getsemaní and La Matuna

Mimo's *(at the corner of Avenida del Pastello, immediately to the right after the Puente Román)* serves good ice cream and sorbet, available in a wide range of flavours.

Sancho, No. 36-15, near Calle La Estrella, ☎660-0858 or 665-5037) can boast unabashedly that it is the best restaurant in the Heroic City. In an attractively renovated house with warm colours, French chef Eric Beldent invites guest to savour exquisite cuisine made with all sorts of delicately prepared fresh vegetables. The rock lobster flan, veal *marengo* and *robalo* (a local fish) *en papillote* are just a few of the surprises awaiting visitors. Excellent desserts, including a delicious *tarte tatin*, which is a kind of apple tart (one of the best we've ever tasted), conclude a flawless menu. The beautiful way in which the dishes are presented blends with the delightful tastes and sounds (Reggiani and Brel are highlighted), making this restaurant a must for connoisseurs of fine food. Excellent value for the money.

In the heart of the old city, **Restaurante Paco's** *($$$$$; Mon to Fri noon to midnight, Sat and Sun 7pm to 1am; Plaza Santo Domingo, ☎664-4294)* serves fish-and-seafood based cuisine and Spanish *tapas*. There is live music on weekends (see p 184). This cozy restaurant is set up inside a lovely colonial-style house with magnificent wooden balconies. With the picturesque Plaza Santo Domingo serving as a backdrop, the setting is extremely beautiful. Expensive, but not to be missed.

For good international cuisine, the exquisitely decorated **Classic de Andrei** *($$$$$; Mon to Fri noon to 3pm and 7pm to 1am, Sat and Sun 6pm to 1am; at the corner of Calle de las Damas and Antonio Ricaurte, ☎660-0968, 664-0284 or 664-2663)* is a must. The main dining room, with its high ceilings, big windows, columns, woodwork and parquet floor, is magnificent. Wrought-iron grates and a little waterfall provide the crowning touches to the decor. The *nouvelle cuisine* is excellent and even includes a few surprises, such as sushi, sesame vegetables and coconut rice. The clientele consists mainly of wealthy Colombians. The service is friendly and efficient.

El Figón de la Factoría *($$$$$; Calle de la Factoria, No. 36, ☎664-1044)* is located in the same building as the Spanish cultural centre. Guests can enjoy authentic Spanish cuisine in a colonial-style residence. Dinner is served either in the lovely inner courtyard, which has Moorish accents, or the very tastefully decorated, air-conditioned dining room. This pleasant restaurant serves good but slightly expensive food.

Bocagrande and El Laguito

La Fonda Antioqueña *($; Mon to Sat 8am to 11:30pm, Sun 11:30am to 11:30pm;*

Avenida San Martín No. 6-164, ☎665-1392 or 665-5805) is a small outdoor restaurant that prepares traditional fare from the Medellín region, such as meat dishes with red beans and fried plantains. Very good value for the money.

Pizzeria Margarita *($; Calle 5 and Carrera 2, ☎653-1454)*, which is part of a chain of restaurants, serves a wide selection of pizzas priced between 8,000 and 15,000 pesos. From its large terrace, located on the corner of bustling Carrera 2, you can watch all sorts of people parade past. This is a very lively spot with a wild mix of music!

Centro Comercial Bocagrande *(Carrera 2, between Calle 8 and Calle 9, ☎635-3939)* is a quieter pizzeria on a terrace below the shopping centre. Another smaller pizzeria belonging to the same chain, but located near the beach on Carrera 1, **Pizza Margarita** *(at the end of the street, just before the beach on the way to El Laguito, ☎665-3931)* serves the same food.

A neighbourhood curiosity, **Kokorico** *($; Carrera 1 and Calle 8)* is like a Colombian McDonald's, which serves light, appealing dishes such as guacamole (avocado puree dip), *mayorca dulce* (corn), chili con carne and of course chicken. Ideal for a quick, inexpensive and simple bite to eat.

Fans of Italian cuisine can treat themselves to a feast at **Pietro's Bar Restaurante** *($$; Carrera 3, No. 5-15, ☎665-1837)*, on a pleasant little terrace slightly set back from the street. In addition to delicious fresh pasta, the restaurant also serves Colombian cuisine. Wine starts at 14,000 pesos a bottle. With efficient service and friendly staff, this is a good place to remember.

Crepes, crepes and more crepes! **Waffles** *($$; Carrera 3, No. 4-76)* serves all different kinds, for dinner or for dessert. On a large, covered terrace with a standard decor, visitors can enjoy crepes with *camarones al curry* (curried shrimp) or, for a change of pace, good *pitas*. The wide selection of desserts attracts large Colombian families, making this a very lively place. The ever-present television (as if there were any need for it!) and the spectacle of the busy street seem to banish the blues. Take note, however, that credit cards are not accepted here.

Graced with a terrace surrounded by plants and facing the beach, the **Restaurante Pedro de Roma** *($$; Carrera 1, on the way to El Laguito,* *at the end of the street)* serves Italian dishes, including good spaghetti for less than 7,000 pesos. Visitors seeking peace and quiet should go early in the evening, since the place gets quite lively later on, due to the proximity of the Banana Rana discotheque (located right next-door).

Banana Rana *($$; Carrera 1, on the way to El Laguito, at the end of the street, in front of the beach)*, located on the same street, serves Japanese cuisine in a Caribbean-style setting. Because of its discotheque (see p 184) the place is very busy late into night.

As indicated by its name, the **Restaurante Granditalia** *($$; Mon to Fri 11:30am to 3pm and 7pm to 11pm, Sat 11:30am to 11pm; Carrera 2, No. 8-19, ☎665-6326)* serves Italian cuisine. Guests can dine either in a pleasant, air-conditioned room or a verdant interior garden. In the latter, however, it is best to choose a table at the end of the terrace in order to avoid the noise coming from both the kitchen and the air-conditioner. The menu features an assortment of high-quality pasta dishes. The vegetarian pasta is excellent. The service is somewhat cool, however, and could be improved.

For good grilled food and to satisfy carnivorous cravings for steak, head over to **Dany el Churrasco Argentino** *($$$; open every day 10am to midnight; Carrera 3A, No. 2-104, ☎665-3059, ⌐665-4523)*. The Argentineans, after all, are experts when it comes to steak. The restaurant's little terrace, which faces the street, is decorated in a simple fashion.

Just across the street, **Pampa** *($$$; open every day 10am to 12pm; Carrera 3A, No. 5-462)* serves the same type of food, namely steaks and grill dishes, in a noisier setting. The terrace, bigger than its competitor's, is neither as intimate nor as charming.

Brazilian cuisine and a wooden decor await visitors at the **Brasa Brasilia Rodizio Bar** *($$$$; Carrera 3, No. 5-104, ☎665-4835)*. The menu consists mainly of grilled meat dishes.

Dressed in sailor suits, the staff of the **Restaurante Nautilus** *($$$$; open every day 11:30am to midnight; Calle 2, No. 9-145, ☎665-3964)* serves guests in a somewhat surprising setting reminiscent of the inside of a boat. The specialty of the house is fish and seafood. There is a second Nautilus restaurant

CARTAGENA DE INDIAS

(☎664-4204) near the Monumento de la India Catalina.

Chef Julian *($$$$; open every day 11am to 11pm; Carrera 3, No. 8-108, ☎665-5220 and 665-2602)* is a good place to go for authentic Spanish cuisine. Guests dine in an elegantly decorated, if overly air-conditioned, room in a lovely house.

🦐 At **La Bohemia** *($$$$; Mon to Thu noon to 3:30pm and 6pm to 1am, Fri and Sat noon to 3:30pm and 6pm to 4am, Sun 6pm to 1am; Carrera 2, No. 6-147, ☎665-3814)*, visitors can enjoy Italian or international cuisine in a cozy atmosphere and refined setting. The menu lists interesting dishes, including a combination of different pastas or meat and fish. There is also a wide selection of wines priced from 20,000 to 40,000 pesos (half-bottle for 15,000 pesos and up). The pianist playing jazz tunes and the friendly, efficient service, create a cozy atmosphere, making this a pleasant place to spend the evening. Good quality/price ratio.

As its name indicates, the **Restaurante Arabe** *($$$$; Wed to Mon noon to 11pm; Carrera 3, No. 8-83, ☎665-4365 and 665-3632)* serves authentic Arabic cuisine in a pleasant air-conditioned dining room and a lovely little interior garden (the plastic furniture detracts somewhat from the charm of the place, however). Cheerful, friendly service.

Farther along on the same street, heading toward the old city, **Alibaba** *($$$$; Tue to Sun noon to 10:30pm; Carrera 3, No. 7-49, ☎665-3573 and 665-3518)* also serves Arabic, as well as Colombian, cuisine in a sophisticated (though somewhat overdone) setting. The interior garden merits a visit.

The **Don Pedro de Heredia** *($$$$; Calle 3, at the end of Carrera 2 on the way to El Laguito, ☎665-0155, 665-0131 and 665-0051)*, located inside the Hotel Caribe, serves international and Colombian cuisine. The menu, though decent, offers no surprises, and the place is somewhat lacking in originality. Immediately opposite, alongside the swimming pool in the same complex, the **Cafeteria Catalina** *($$$)* has a bar and offers a buffet with international dishes. Visitors can eat breakfast here for 11,000 pesos. Very bright and very busy, the place is a little noisy and therefore most suitable for a lively night out. For those fond of meat, grilled food and pizza, the **Jardín Punta de Icacos** *($$)*, located in the hotel garden, is probably the most unique and pleasant place on the premises.

The **Gourmet** *($$$$; Carrera 1 and Calle 8, ☎665-1140)*, found on the third floor of the Hotel Capilla del Mar, will suit visitors seeking a calm, intimate atmosphere. The dining room is air-conditioned and the good but conventional food is served by a friendly, cheerful staff. The cafeteria **Las Ninfas** *($$$)*, located on the main floor of the hotel, offers a buffet featuring home-style cooking (chicken, steak, beans, corn, etc.). The most appealing aspect of this cafeteria, set up on a covered terrace in front of the sea, are its pretty ceramic decorations and wooden shutters, which protect it from the sea breeze.

🦐 The **Capilla del Mar** *($$$$$; open every day 12:30am to 3:30pm and 6:30pm to 11pm; Carrera 5, No. 8-59, ☎665-5001 and 665-4773)*, not to be confused with the hotel of the same name, is a very good choice for quality French food. It occupies a bourgeois residence that once belonged to a French emigrant named Pierre Daguet, a painter by profession, who opened the restaurant in the 1940's. Some of his paintings still grace the walls of the restaurant, adding to its charm. Guests may sit in either a comfortably air-conditioned room or a room equipped with large wrought-iron grates, which let in the sea breeze coming off the bay. Try the appetizer called Capilla del Mar, which offers a taste of various seaside specialties. The *róbalo* (a local fish) au gratin with capers and cheese is a real treat. Each dish is served with a small salad and a good selection of bread (something of a rarity in Cartagena, and elsewhere in Colombia). The portions are very generous, and the service is both cheerful and efficient. Very good quality/price ratio.

Set up inside a modern villa built in the style of Frank Lloyd Wright, the **Restaurante Caribarú** *($$$$$: open every day noon to 10pm; Avenida Almirante Brion, alongside the beach, No. 2-110, ☎665-0783)* serves good international-style cuisine, including a wide selection of fish. Wine can be ordered by the glass. Guests can dine on an attractive terrace facing the sea, where it is pleasant to laze about to the sound of the waves. The service and dishes are meticulous and well worth the price.

Getsemaní and La Matuna

If you're looking for a snack, the **Café de l'Arsenal** *($; Mon to Sat 4pm to 1:30 pm; Calle del Arsenal)* serves all sorts of light dishes at attractive prices.

Set in beautiful rustic surroundings, **Mister Babilla** *($$$; every day noon to 5am; Calle del Arsenal No.8b-137, ☎664-7005 or 664-8777)* is a Mexican restaurant that prepares succulent meats any way you like and classic Mexican cuisine, such as ginger chicken and yucca-based dishes. Simple fare for long Caribbean evenings, but eat early because Mister Babilla turns into a discotheque around 10pm, and revellers dance on the tables by midnight! Because the place is one of the most popular in Cartagena de Indias, the management reserves the right to refuse people at the door. There is also a small interior courtyard.

El Ancora Café *($$$; Mon to Fri noon to 3pm and 5pm to 1am, Sat and Sun 5pm to 1am; Calle del Arsenal, No. 9-47, ☎664-8236)* is a good choice for those seeking cuisine with a touch of the exotic. Quails with grape sauce, shrimp with tamarind and coconut, and cream of celery and blue cheese are just a few of the original dishes on the menu. On the little terrace, which is right on the street, guests can also enjoy delicious home-made juices and cocktails.

La Langosta *($$$; Avenida Daniel Lemaitre, No. 9-50, ☎664-2785)*, whose specialties are fish and seafood, is a friendly place renowned for the freshness of its food. It is not located in the most beautiful neighbourhood, but offers fair value for the money.

The **Restaurante San Francisco** *($$$; open every day noon to 3pm and 7pm to 10pm; in the convent itself, on Avenida del Mercado)* is located in the former convent of the same name. The restaurant serves traditional cuisine in a dining room with a somewhat dark, austere decor. Guests also have the option of eating on the terrace.

Located in the old Fuerte San Sebastián del Pastelillo, the **Club de Pesca** *($$$$; open every day 12pm to 3pm and 7pm to 10:30pm; in the fort itself, immediately to the right after the Puente Román, ☎664-8734 or 664-8736)*

features fish and seafood, as well as Spanish cuisine. The terrace, abounding in flowers and nestled pleasantly beneath the trees, offers a lovely view of the neighbouring ramparts and the marina, where many sailboats are moored. Try one of the tasty paellas (the vegetarian one is excellent; upon request only). The beauty of the surroundings makes up for the service, which is friendly, but a bit slow. A half-bottle of wine starts at 10,000 pesos. Good quality/price ratio.

Around Cartagena

Crespo

Located right across from the airport, at the corner of Carrera 4 and Calle 70, **Piko Rico** boasts a menu of chicken-based dishes for under 7,000 pesos. Bask in the sunshine on its small terrace before flying off to cloudier skies! Right across Carrera 4 is **Rica Carne**, which serves grilled meats. There is also a **Pizzeria Margarita** *(at Calle 70 and Carrera 67, ☎666-5414)* near the airport exit, part of the same chain found on the Bocagrande peninsula. All three establishments are simple and unpretentious.

For those who wish to partake of a more elaborate meal, the **Las Americas Beach Resort** *($$$$$; on the road to La Boquilla, less than one kilometre from Crespo, ☎664-4000 or 664-9650)*, a large seven-building hotel complex (see p 177), features several restaurants and a cafeteria in a setting that harmoniously blends luxury and good taste.

Santiago de Tolú

Most restaurants in the village are located on Avenida de la Playa. Highlights among the many establishments lining the avenue are the restaurant in the hotel **Brisas del Mar** *($; Avenida de la Playa, ☎88 50 32)*, the **Hotel-Restaurant El Platana** *($)*, the **Restaurant Macondo** *($$; every day 7am to 10pm; Avenida de la Playa, ☎88 51 78)* and the restaurant in the hotel **Montecarlo** *($$$; Avenida de la Playa No.8-30, ☎88 52 30)*, the last being the most opulent in Tolú.

ENTERTAINMENT

Bars and Nightclubs

El Centro and San Diego

At **El Mirador** *(7,000 pesos cover charge; from 7pm on; Calle de las Damas, No. 64, ☎664-7251)*, a piano bar located inside the Bodegón de la Candelaria house (see p 163), visitors can enjoy a lovely nighttime view of part of the city while sipping a cocktail to the sounds of the piano. As its name indicates in Spanish, the bar is situated at the top of a tower adjoining the residence, and reaching it requires some acrobatics (the last staircase is fairly steep). The cramped little room, which has a bench covered with comfortable cushioning along the walls, is a perfect place to conclude a romantic evening.

For a mixture of American and Colombian music in a relaxed setting, head over to **El Zorba** *(at the corner of Calle Segunda de Badillo and Calle de la Tablada)*, a little bar which serves drinks at moderate prices. There is an enjoyable view of the Parque Fernández de Madrid from here. This bar caters mainly to local residents.

For upbeat music, try **Bar La Vitrola** *(Mon to Sun 5pm to 3am; Calle de Baloco, No. 33-201, near the city walls)*, which features good live bands Thursday through Saturday from 10pm on. The program includes meringue, *vallenato* and salsa in a lovely pastel decor with lots of atmosphere. Outside, on the sidewalk across the street, small candle-lit tables beckon passers-by to come savour delicious cocktails (which are a bit expensive, however). The place is frequented by Colombians.

A makeshift outdoor terrace on the former city walls and a band playing salsas, *vallenatos* and meringues on weekends – all of this awaits visitors at a bar named **El Baluarte** *(on the Baluarte de San Francisco Javier wall, opposite the naval museum)*. The setting, with the sea in the background, and the big torches casting flickering shadows, combine to make this a magical place that should not be missed. A light menu is available.

Every weekend, **Taberna Paco's** *(Mon to Fri noon to midnight, Sat and Sun 7pm to 1am;*

Plaza Santo Domingo, ☎664-4294) presents live Colombian music played by the band *Los Veteranos* (The Veterans), whose name seems quite appropriate. Indeed, the musicians are all between 60 and 75 years old! There is a lot of atmosphere in this lovely, cozily decorated colonial residence. Food is also served here (see p 180).

Bocagrande and El Laguito

Kaoba *(Avenida Almirante Brion, at the beginning of Calle 1A)* is a trendy bar where a young clientele gets together on a modishly decorated terrace for American music and a light menu. One of the bar's specialties is the evening cocktail. The adventurous can try the *Cabeza de Jabalí*, which will transport you straight into the tropical atmosphere! This is a pleasant spot.

The big bar/discotheque **Banana Rana** *(Carrera 1, on the way to El Laguito, at the end of the road on the left side)* is a good choice for people who like loud, varied music. The place serves Japanese cuisine in a Caribbean-style setting (see p 181), which is a somewhat surprising but pleasant combination. The beach starts right at the foot of the building.

Another spot near the beach, **La Escollera** *(7,000 pesos cover charge; Carrera 1, near Calle 5)*, with an exotic decor, thatched roof and tropical atmosphere, welcomes young disco fans until the wee hours of the morning.

A bit more dressy, the **Portobello Night Club** *(dress code; Calle 1B, on the second floor of the Centro Comercial Pierino Gallo)* is frequented by a particularly affluent crowd.

Whether it be for a drink or dancing in a disco atmosphere, head to the **Nautilus Video Bar Disco** *(Carrera 2, between Calle 9 and Calle 10)*, where people of all ages seem to get together.

Gambling buffs can try the **Casino Caribe** *(Calle 1B, on the second floor of the Centro Comercial Pierino Gallo)*, not to be confused with the casino in the Hotel Caribe. Bets start at 2,500 pesos.

The **Casino Royale** *(inside the Hotel Caribe, Calle 3, at the end of Carrera 2 on the way to El Laguito)* is more expensive than its competitor, but also offers a more elegant setting. Bets starts at 8,000 pesos. In the same hotel, the

Bar Discotec Bolero invites you to enjoy lively evenings to the sounds of its band, which plays on weekends from 9pm to 2am This is a pleasant place, though the drinks are fairly expensive.

Every Saturday at 8pm, the **Hotel Hilton** *(at the tip of the point on El Laguito, ☎665-0666)* presents live folk music in a beautiful setting. Count on spending 30,000 pesos per person, including a Colombian buffet meal.

Getsemaní and La Matuna

The beautiful **Zagera Bar** *(Calle del Arsenal, No. 8-149)*, with its carefully designed decor, will suit visitors seeking a quiet, posh atmosphere in which to finish off the evening in a pleasant fashion.

Tables set up right on the sidewalk and a band playing *vallenatos* and other tropical music await you at the **Terraza de Rafael Ricardo** *(Calle del Arsenal, No. 9-149)*. Furthermore, on some evenings, a group of *mariachis*, who seem to have arrived straight from Mexico, liven up this spot, which is very popular among Colombians. Music and atmosphere are guaranteed every night from 9pm to 4am The cocktails are good, but rather expensive.

Tropical rhythms meld with the latest popular western tunes at the **Tiffany Club** *(2,800 pesos cover charge on weekends; Mon to Sun 7pm to 4am; Calle del Arsenal, No. 24-02)* where the decor is dark and a bit on the kitschy side. It is very popular with Colombians, and there is a small dance floor.

Santiago de Tolú

The **Escotilla Music Bar** *(6pm to 4am)* in the Club Náutico Los Delfines is the most lively nightspot in Tolú. Loud music in a laid-back atmosphere.

Events

Several social and cultural events may be of interest to tourists in the Bolívar district. Among them are:

January: **La Fiesta Brava**, in Cartagena de Indias.

February: the **Festival Patronales de la Candelaria**. The one in Cartagena includes a pilgrimage to the Popa mountain.

March: the **Festival de Música del Caribe**, a music festival in Cartagena, and the **Carnaval de Barranquilla**, one of the most important in Colombia.

April: the **Semana Santa** in Mompóx.

June: the **Festival Internacional de Cine**, which brings together the best South American cinematic productions in Cartagena de las Indias. Some North American films are also shown.

August: the **Festival Bolivarense del Acordeón**, a celebration of *vallenato* held in Arjona.

September: the **Fiesta de San Pedro Claver**, in Cartagena.

November: from November 9th to 10th, festivals are held to **commemorate Cartagena's independence**.

December: the **Reinado Nacional de la Belleza**, the crowning of Miss Colombia, in Cartagena.

SHOPPING

Cartagena de Indias

El Centro and San Diego

Gifts

In terms of selection, the best place to shop is of course **Las Bóvedas** *(Plaza de las Bóvedas)*. Twenty-three shops, one next to the other, have been set up inside an old colonial building (see p 165). Visitors will find a wide variety of handicrafts in every price range. Though it offers a huge choice of products, the place is somewhat lacking in originality.

Located near the cathedral, **La Casa del Joyero** *(Calle Santos de Piedra, No. 34-23)* is a good place to buy all sorts of jewellery or have pieces custom-made. Prices for uncut emeralds start at 14,000 pesos. If you have a little patience, this is a good place to bargain.

Luz Miriam Toro, Arte Precolombino *(Plaza de Santo Domingo, Edificio Cuesta, Room 2,*

☎664-3955) is a charming store that sells pre-Columbian art and is a good place to shop for crafts.

Visitors can buy attractive T-shirts on **Calle de la Soledad** *(No. 5-18, next to the bakery, near the university)*. Though more expensive than those sold by street vendors, they are well-made and decorated with creative patterns.

Antiques

There are many attractive antique shops in the old city. Despite being located on several different streets, they are clustered within a fairly limited area. Try strolling down Calle de las Damas, Calle Santa Teresa and Calle Santo Domingo, where a large number of these shops are located. Generally, the prices are fairly high, but those who know how to poke about can make some worthwhile finds and purchases.

Food

The shop **Girasoles** *(at the corner of Calle Quero and Calle de los Puntalles)* sells natural products, as well as a variety of health foods and vegetarian take-out dishes.

Natural Green *(Calle de la Soledad, No. 5-41)* which sells the same type of products, and has an interesting but smaller selection.

At the **Magali Paris** *(Plaza de los Coches, beneath the arcades of Portal de los Dulces))* supermarket, visitors will find everything they need, from stationery to clothing and food.

Bocagrande and El Laguito

Gifts

The sophisticated **Centro Comercial Pierino Gallo** *(Calle 1B)* shopping centre contains a number of shops selling handicrafts, as well as a jewellery store. The prices, however, correspond to the upscale decor.

At the **Joyería Casa Paris** *(in the Centro commercial Pierino Gallo; also on Carrera 2, No. 6-76)*, visitors will find emeralds in every possible shape and size, as well as a wide selection of gold jewellery. Don't hesitate to bargain, as the shop does offer discounts.

The **Joyería Angel** *(Carrera 2, near Calle 7, No. 127)* makes all sorts of gold jewellery and sells emeralds in every style and price range.

Bookstores and Music Stores

The pleasant **Librería Bitacora** *(Carrera 2, between Calle 8 and Calle 7)* sells Spanish- and English-language literature, and a few books in French. The staff is cheerful and friendly.

The **Disco Store** *(Carrera 1, near Calle 4)* has a good selection of records and compact discs.

Food

Olympica *(open 24 hours a day; Carrera 3, near Calle 6; also on Carrera 2, near Calle 10)* sells liquor at good prices, as well as excellent Colombian coffee.

The **Magali-Paris** *(Carrera 4 and Calle 6)* supermarket, located in a beautiful area, sells merchandise that is a bit more expensive, but also slightly more sophisticated than Olympica's.

España Delicatessen *(Mon to Sat 7am to 11pm, Sun 10am to 11pm; Calle 3a, No. 8-38, Edificio Juviper, ☎665-1890)* is a charming little deli that sells fine meats and imported products such as oils. Here, you can find authentic "Jamón Serrano" from Spain, as well as wines and cheeses. You can sample the products in the store, or try one of their sandwiches.

Getsemaní and La Matuna

Gifts

The **Convento de San Francisco** *(Avenida del Mercado)* contains a large number of shops of all different types. Whether you're looking for a handbag, costume jewellery or a lovely decorative object, you will find everything you need here. Though it would be impossible to list all of the shops in this guide, one of the most noteworthy is the **Artesanías de Colombia** *(Mon to Fri 9am to 1pm and 3pm to 7pm, Sat 9am to 3pm; under the arcades on the patio)*, a co-op with a wide selection of handicrafts. All proceeds go directly to the artisans. The prices, however, are a bit higher than elsewhere.

On the top floor of **Fuerte San Felipe**, visitors will find two adjoining shops, one of which is run by a very friendly Colombian named Bernardo. This store offers a lovely selection of reasonably priced reproductions of pre-Columbian jewellery. In addition to having good taste, the owner takes pleasure in explaining the meaning of various pieces.

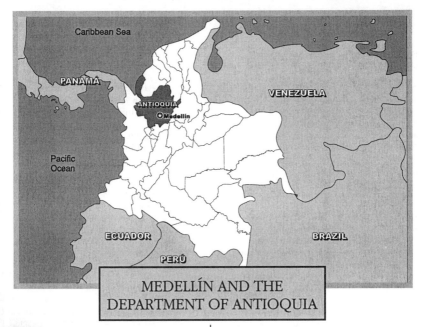

MEDELLÍN AND THE
DEPARTMENT OF ANTIOQUIA

Antioquia is Colombia's seventh largest department. It has a surface area of 64,000 square kilometres, and is bordered by the departments of Bolívar, Sucre, and Córdova, as well as the Caribbean Sea, to the north, by Chocó, Risaralda and Caldas to the south, by Boyacá, Santander and Bolivar to the east, and by Chocó to the west.

Exceptionally rich in natural resources, this department accounts for more than 70 percent of the country's gold production. It is traversed by numerous rivers, including the Río Atrato, Río Cauca, Río León, Río Magdalena, Río San Jorge, Río Sinú, Río Samaná, Río Sur, Río Buey, Río Porce-Nechí and the Río Nus. The climate is temperate and does not fluctuate much.

This region is rugged and mountainous, with peaks in the central as well as the eastern cordillera. These include Mount Frontino (4,080 m), Mount Paramillo (3,960 m), Mont Morro Campana (3,950 m) and Mount Caramanta (3,900 m). Twelve percent of Colombians live in Antioquia; the city's population is seen as dynamic, creative, entrepreneurial and determined. The city also generates approximately 15 percent of the gross national product, since it is the country's primary producer of energy, the main banana and coffee producer and exporter, and the second-largest grower of cut flowers.

A Brief History

The first Spaniards to disembark at San Juan de Urabá in the north of Antioquia during 1500-1501 were the same ones who had discovered Colombia the previous year, when they had landed at Cabo de la Vela under the command of Alonso de Ojeda. This time, however, the expedition was under the command of Rodrigo de Bastidas, who later founded Santa Marta. At the time, the area was inhabited by numerous native groups belonging to the Carib family, including the Yamesís, Niquías, Katíos, Nutabes, Cunas, Tahamíes, Quimbayas and Aburrás.

This initial contact was followed by the arrival of Alonso de Ojeda, who built the fortress of San Sebastián de Urabá. Vasco Núñez de Balboa – who discovered the Pacific in 1513 from the top of a Panamanian peak (see p 166) – then established a command post at Santa María la Antigua de Darién, from which exploration of the country's interior from the Atlantic coast began.

Pedro de Heredia, the founder of Cartagena de Indias, founded San Sebastián de Buena Visa – present-day Necolí – around 1535. On August 24, 1541, Jerónimo Luis Tejelo, a member of marshal Robledo's expedition, discovered the Valle del Aburrá, where Medellín, the capital of Antioquia, is now located.

Robledo himself established a small gold-mining centre in 1541. Gaspar De Rodas moved it to its current location, a little to the west of the Río Cauca, in 1587. Today, it bears the name of Santa Fé de Antioquia.

Around the same time, a small farming community called San Lorenzo de Aburrá (now El Poblado), was established. This name was changed to Nuestra Señora de la Candelaria de Medellín in 1675. The city has been the capital of Antioquia since April 17, 1826. The department's first constitution was signed on March 21, 1812 and on August 11, 1813, the dictator Juan del Corral declared total independence from the Spanish colony.

Antioquia became a department through the Law of the Nation in 1830, after Simón Bolívar had formed Gran Colombia. However, the territory's boundaries were constantly modified and extended, and it was only in 1886 that its current borders were fixed and Antioquia emerged as we know it today, with some 5 million inhabitants.

Medellín

Medellín is the birthplace of world-renowned painter Fernando Botero, and is Colombia's main cultural centre, with art galleries in all the large hotels, in the chamber of commerce and in the town hall. Comprising 24 universities or institutions of higher learning, including the Universidad de Antioquia (22,000 students), Universidad Nacional, Pontificia Bolivariana, Autónoma Latinoamericana and the Universidad de Medellín, it also has a convention centre, 25 shopping centres, numerous theatres, museums, and a subway. Medellín (pronounced *Mey-dey-gin*) is Colombia's second-most important city after Santafé de Bogotá, and is the capital of the department of Antioquia, with a population of approximately 2 million people, which is actually closer to 3 million if you include the neighbouring municipalities of Caldas, La Estrella, Itagüi, Envigado and Sabaneta to the south, Bello, Copacabana, Girardotat and Barbosa to the north. Medellín is located at an altitude of some 1,500 metres in the Aburrá valley, which lies between two branches of the central cordillera, and is bisected by the Río Medellín which runs north-south.

The Spaniards bypassed the city's present-day location in 1541, and it was only in 1616 that

Jewish settlers (*paisas*) fleeing persecution in Europe founded the city. They came not as conquerors, but rather as farmers. They parcelled out the territory into little farms which they cultivated themselves, without using native slave labour. They also lived in isolation, for fear of being persecuted anew, and developed as an independent settlement. Today's inhabitants preserve these olden-day values of self-sufficiency and independence.

Medellín Today

Current-day Medellín is a vibrant, thriving city which *Medellinenses* have transformed into one of Colombia's most important economic centres. From its roots as a gold-mining town early in the century, Medellín has gradually developed into an internationally renowned industrial centre. Metalworking, ceramics, glass, textiles and oil production are its main industries. It is also known for its economical and efficient medical services, particularly organ transplants and plastic surgery.

The town itself is composed of 271 *barrios*, divided into six zones. The southeast includes the well-to-do *barrios* of San Diego, El Poblado (the site of the original settlement), Aguacatala and La Pila Rica. To the southwest are Los Laureles, Guayabal, Belén and La América. Prado, Boston, Buenos Aires, La Milagrosa and downtown are located in the east-central portion, while San Javier, Calazans, Estadio and Carlos E. Restrepo are in the west-central part. The northeast portion includes Manrique, Aranjuez and Campo Valdés, and Castilla, Pedregal and Doce de Octubre lie in the north-west.

From the surrounding hillsides, other *barrios* – including Popular 1, Popular 2, París, Santa Rita, Villa del Socorro, Viejo, Dos de Octubre and Nueva Villa de Aburrá – stretch out as far as the eye can see. These areas served as a refuge for the terrorized rural populations fleeing the *Violencia* (civil war) in the 1950s.

At first, these peasants knew nothing about surviving in an urban environment. They built houses anywhere, anyhow, using whatever scrap material they could get their hands on; this chaotic development provoked even more violence. With the drug traffickers' rise to power in the 1970s and 1980s, and the inception of the Medellín cartel, these desperately poor *barrios* quickly became a virtually inexhaustible source of *sicarios* (hired freelance

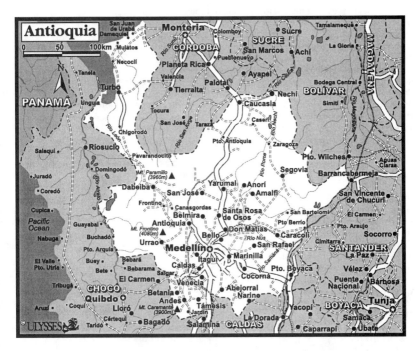

killers), ranging in age from 12 to 20, who were employed by the drug traffickers. As a result, Medellín's reputation for violence spread like wildfire.

The cartel's power was greatly curtailed following an all-out war began in 1983 by the government of Belisario Betancur and the nomination of a new minister of justice, Rodrigo Lara Bonilla. However, this did not happen before the cartel managed to assassinate Bonilla, the editor of Bogotá's *El Espectador*, in March 1984, and Guillermo Cano, in December 1986. Even a prominent presidential candidate, Luis Carlos Galán, was killed in August 1989.

The cartel never recovered from the crackdown; one of its ringleaders, Carlos Lehder, was arrested in February 1987 and extradited to the United States where he is currently serving a life sentence. Gonzalo Rodríguez Gacha ("El Mexicano"), another lieutenant, was shot by police in March 1990.

Finally, in December 1993, the cartel leader himself was brought to justice; police captured Pablo Escobar at his Envigado hideout, in a shootout that also killed six of his lieutenants. The cartel was dismantled and Medellín could

finally breathe a sigh of relief. However, this did not put an end to drug trafficking in Colombia, since the Santiago de Cali cartel, under the more discreet and businesslike brothers Rodríguez Orejuela, took over the drug trade. Today, the Cali cartel continues its lucrative cocaine trade, and has even branched out into opium and heroin, which are currently in high demand in the United States and Europe, their main markets.

Today, Medellín is a relatively quiet town which has blossomed in the past 15 years with its new modern architecture, the renovation of its historic buildings and most of all the construction of a two-line subway with 25 stations and more than 35 kilometres of track, inaugurated on November 30, 1995. In fact, Medellín is the only Colombian city to have a subway, although Santiago de Cali plans to build one in the next few years.

Ninety-nine percent (99%) of the population of the Valle de Aburrá have electricity, and 98 percent have running water and sewage facilities. Empresas Públicas, the organization in charge of providing the region's inhabitants with basic services, is currently installing natural gas pipelines throughout the city, which will allow electricity consumption to be lowered by 30 percent. Medellín is one of South America's most developed cities. With its focus on the trade of manufactured goods and services, the city puts a high premium on quality of life and cleanliness. Ninety-seven percent (97%) of the homes have garbage collection, and 90 percent of its streets are cleaned regularly. Moreover, the Autopista Medellín-Bogotá, which bisects the city from north to south, is closed to vehicles in one direction every Sunday to allow bicycling and roller-blading.

Temperature

Medellín's nickname is "the City of Eternal Spring" because of its temperate climate (average annual temperature of approx. 23°C, at an altitude of 1,538 m), as well as "the City of Flowers" because of the profusion of blossoms that adorn its many parks, gardens, and avenues. However, the city still experiences two "winters", or rainy seasons, as it rains frequently throughout October and November, as well as April and May. Nights can be cool, so it is best to wear a jacket or sweater.

FINDING YOUR WAY AROUND

Carreras run north-south in Medellín, and the numbers of the streets increase from east to west. *Calles* run east-west, and the numbers of the streets increase from south to north, with the exception of the *calles* in El Poblado, whose numbers increase from north to south. Downtown, streets are known by their numbers as well as their names. Calle 50 is also known as Calle Colombia, while Carrera 46 is also called Avenida Jorge Eliécer Gaitán.

By Plane

José María Córdova de Rionegro international airport *(☎287 40 10 or 287 40 11)* is 50 minutes from downtown, and is located at approximately 3,000 metres above sea level. Taxis to Medellín *(7,000 pesos)* follow a steep road which descends along a cliff. On this November night, the illuminated city appears in all its mystical beauty, as if by magic, at the bottom of a valley surrounded by mountains whose peaks are obscured by heavy rainclouds. As car headlights pierce the thick mist, the city briefly appears, like some fantastic supernatural vi-

sion, only to melt away in the next instant. These gorgeous intermittent glimpses of the glittering city continue for a good 10 minutes, bedazzling both the driver and passenger. Incredible!

The **Aeropuerto Regional Olaya Herrera** *(Carrera 65a No. 13-157, ☎285 99 99)*, less than 15 minutes from downtown, also serves Medellín. This regional airport offers daily flights to destinations in Antioquia as well as other Colombian cities.

Here is the schedule for direct Avianca flights to international destinations from José María Córdova international airport:

Aruba, Sun 9:25am with stopover; Sat 9:30am with stopover; Fri 10:05am with stopover; Wed 12:55pm; Thu 4:20pm with stopover
Miami, United States, every day 7:40am with stopover
New York, United States, Sat 2:35pm with stopover
Panamá, Panamá, Mon, Wed, Fri 7:45am

The following schedule is for direct flights to destinations within Colombia, with departures from one of the two airports:

Bahía Solano, Mon, Wed, Fri and Sun 8:30am with stopover (Olaya Herrera), 98,000 pesos.
Baranquilla, Mon-Fri and Sun 9:25am; Mon-Wed, Fri-Sat 2:45pm; Thu 4:20pm (José María Córdova), 167,000 pesos.
Bogotá, Mon-Fri 6:35am; every day 7:06am; Mon-Fri 8:04am; every day 10:24am and 12:20pm; Mon-Sat 12:56pm; Mon-Sat 2pm; every day 2:37pm; Mon-Fri and Sun 4:24pm; Sun 5pm; every day 5:38pm, Mon-Fri and Sun 7:10pm; Mon, Wed, Fri 7:50pm; every day 10pm (José María Córdova), 117,000 pesos.
Bucaramanga, every day 6:55am with stopover; every day 3:35pm (José María Córdova), 151,000 pesos.
Cali, every day 7am, 11:35am and 7:15pm (José María Córdova), 131,000 pesos.
Capurganá, Sun 9:35am; Mon, Thu 9:55am (Olaya Herrera), 120,000 pesos.
Cartagena, every day 7:40am; Sat 9:30am and 2:35pm; Thu, Sun 2:45pm (José María Córdova), 167,000 pesos.
Cúcuta, every day 6:55am; every day 3:35pm with stopover (José María Córdova), 151,000 pesos.
Montería, Mon-Sat 8:05am; every day 3:05pm (Olaya Herrera), 119,000 pesos.
Puerto Berrío, Mon-Sat 6am; Sun 11:45am; Mon-Sat 4pm (Olaya Herrera), 63,000 pesos.

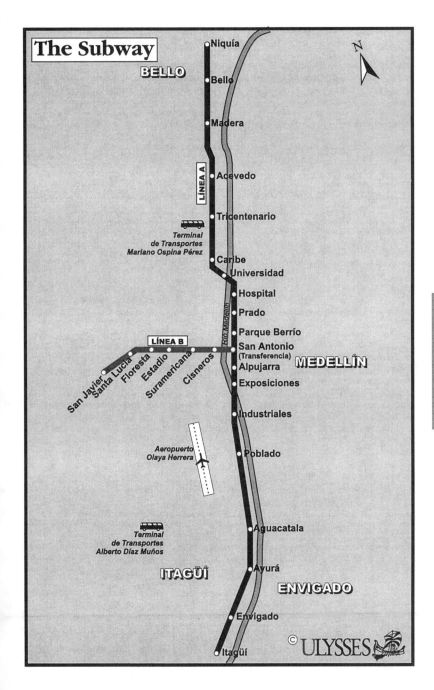

Quibdó, every day 8:30am; Mon-Sat 1:30pm (Olaya Herrera), 68,000 pesos.
San Andrés, every day 7am; Mon, Wed, Fri 7:45am (José María Córdova), 202,000 pesos.
Santa Marta, every day 8am (José María Córdova), 176,000 pesos.

The following airlines serve both airports:

National Airlines:

Aces, Calle 49 No. 50-21, 34th floor, ☎11 22 37
AeroRepública, Carrera 66a No. 34-32, ☎235 09 17
Aires, Carrera 65a No. 13-57, Suite 214, ☎255 95 35
Avianca, Calle 53 No. 45-112, ☎251 55 44
Intercontinental de Aviación, corner Calle 34 and Carrera 43, Centro Comercial San Diego, Suite 243, ☎262 83 17
SAM, Calle 53 No. 45-112, ☎251 55 44

International Airlines:

Aerolinas Argentinas, Carrera 50 No. 56-126, Suite 401, ☎513 11 14
Air Aruba, Carrera 43a No. 19a-87, Suite 22, ☎262 35 17
Air France, Calle 55 No. 46-14, Suite 1102, ☎251 05 44
American Airlines, Calle 16 No. 28-51, Hotel Inter-Continental, Suite 243, ☎268 08 59
Copa, Calle 57 No. 49-44, Suite 215, ☎251 86 52
Iberia, Carrera 50 No. 52-126, Suite 401, ☎511 37 16
Lufthansa, Calle 52 No. 49-28, 4th floor, ☎251 28 30
Tampa, Carrera 76 No. 34a-61, ☎250 29 39
Zuliana de Aviación, Carrera 75 No. 49-29, ☎260 43 99

By Bus

Destinations on the Atlantic coast are easy to reach from Medellín and include Cartagena de Indias (13 h), Barranquilla (15 h) or Santa Marta (17 h). On the Pacific coast, there is Buenaventura (12 h), which is reached via the Troncal Occidental. In fact, you can get to any destination in Colombia by bus from Medellín. For northern destinations, go to the **Terminal de Transportes Mariano Ospina Pérez** *(Carrera 64c No. 78-344, ☎277 77 56)*, while departures for southern destinations in the direction of Santafé de Bogotá (9 h) and Santiago de Cali

(9 h) are from the **Terminal de Transportes Alberto Díaz Muños** *(Calle 8b No. 65-50, ☎361 18 53)*.

The following are the telephone numbers of some of the bus transport companies:

Rápido Ochoa, ☎411 11 00
Expreso Brasilia, ☎230 99 31
Flota Fredonia Ltda., ☎262 12 03
Cootratam, ☎230 59 33
Sotroraba, ☎230 96 96
Coonorte, ☎232 56 42
Coopetransa, ☎230 32 10
Expreso Belmira, ☎230 90 32
Surandina, ☎230 61 52

Public Transportation

Subway

Medellín's subway system has 25 stations, and runs at ground level outside the downtown core and on an elevated rail in the downtown. Line A crosses the city from north to south and covers 22 kilometres of track between the Niquia and Itagüi stations; trains pass every five to ten minutes. Line B is shorter and only covers 8 kilometres of track from the San Antonio station to Barrio San Javier in the west. Tickets can be purchased at station entrances from an attendant or an automatic dispenser for as little as 350 pesos per ticket and 650 pesos for two. Many buses run to specific subway stations, the name of which is displayed on their front windshield.

Bus

More than 25 independent companies provide bus service to all parts of Medellín. As in other large Colombian cities, they offer a first-class, or *ejecutivo*, service which runs to the same destinations as the regular service. Given the city's size, it is necessary to use public transportation when travelling from one neighbourhood to another. However, downtown attractions are within easy walking distance, and the inviting springlike climate is conducive to walking year-round. To reach one of the surrounding metropolitan municipalities such as Itagüi, Envigado, Sabaneta and Copacabana, take one of the minibuses on Carrera 51 in front of the San Antonio subway station.

The Festival Latino-americano de Teatro in Manizales
draws theatre troupes from across the continent each year.

One of the beautifully adorned facades in Manizales.

A brilliant sunset over the Bahía de Buenaventura.

By Taxi

Taxis are a yellow ochre colour and are marked *Servicio Público*. They are everywhere and are inexpensive. For this reason, it may be difficult to find one when it rains. Fares are metered and the minimum is 1,000 pesos per trip, which is usually enough to get halfway across the city, except at night when the fares go up. As in other Colombian cities, most of the cars are recent models of four-door compacts and in good condition. It is easy to hail a taxi, as drivers will stop anywhere on the street to pick up passengers at the slightest wave of the hand. They can also be ordered by telephone, since all cabs have radios. Most drivers are young, highly educated, friendly, curious and valuable sources of inside information on their city, which makes taking a cab that much more pleasurable.

Renting a Car

Although traffic is heavy in Medellín, the city is generally better organized than other large Colombian cities, particularly Santafé de Bogotá. Thus it may be worthwhile to rent a car to visit some of the main *barrios*, since tourist attractions are concentrated in the downtown core. However, you must watch out for motorcyclists, who only rarely obey traffic signals.

Car rental agencies:

Avis Rent-a-Car, Carrera 43a No. 23-40, ☎236 46 70 or 232 38 10
Budget, Carrera 43a No. 23-52, ☎232 82 03
Hertz, Carrera 43a No. 23-50, ☎232 23 07 or 232 48 74
Rentacar, Calle 58 No. 49-50, ☎254 57 66

 PRACTICAL INFORMATION

Area Code: 4

Mail

Mail service is provided by **Avianca**, Calle 53 No. 45-112

Banks

The Banco Industrial Colombiano (BIC) will exchange most currencies and even traveller's cheques in currencies other than US dollars. Although the BIC is more efficient than other banks, they will insist upon obtaining (and keeping) a photocopy of the identification and date of entry pages of your passport before changing any cheques, which is a normal procedure in Colombia.

The **Banco Industrial Colombiano** (BIC) *(Mon-Fri 8am to noon and 2pm to4pm, Fri until 5pm; Av. Columbia No. 51-70)*. There is a photocopying service in front of the bank *(Calle 50 No. 51-81)*.

There is a Visa ATM at the Banco de Columbia's **Llavebanco** *(Carrera 51, corner Calle 50 or Avenida Bolívar)*.

Tourist Information

As was the case everywhere else when we visited the country, the government's tourist information services were in the process of being reorganized. Nevertheless, the following organizations should be able to provide maps and brochures on activities and interesting tourist attractions:

Officina de Turismo y Fomento de Medellín *(Mon-Fri 8:30am to noon and 2pm to 5pm; Calle 57 No. 45-129, ☎254 08 00, ⌐254 52 33, turismo@educam.gov.co)*

Officina de Turismo y Fomento de Medellín *(Mon-Fri 8:30am to noon and 2pm to 5pm; Aeropuerto José María Córdova, ☎260 38 12)*

Officina de Turismo y Fomento de Medellín *(Mon-Fri 8:30am to noon and 2pm to 5pm; Aeropuerto Olaya Herrera, ☎285 10 48)*

Fundo Mixto de Promoción Turistica de Medellín *(Mon-Fri 8:30am to noon and 2pm to*

MEDELLÍN

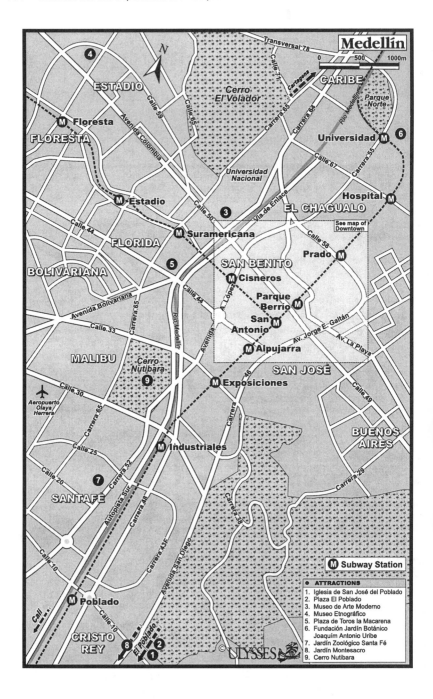

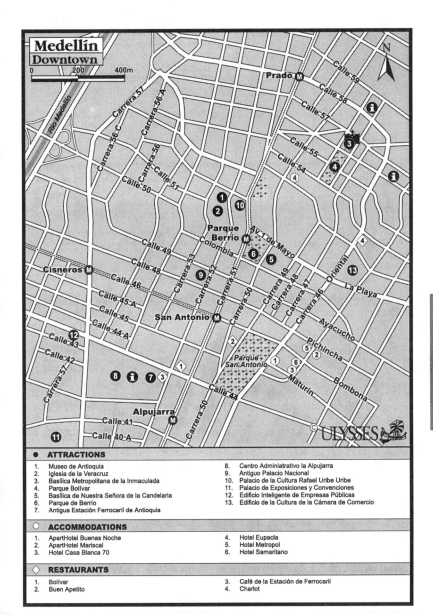

ATTRACTIONS

1. Museo de Antioquia
2. Iglesia de la Veracruz
3. Basílica Metropolitana de la Inmaculada
4. Parque Bolívar
5. Basílica de Nuestra Señora de la Candelaria
6. Parque de Berrío
7. Antigua Estación Ferrocaril de Antioquia

8. Centro Adminiatrativo la Alpujarra
9. Antiguo Palacio Nacional
10. Palacio de la Cultura Rafael Uribe Uribe
11. Palacio de Exposiciones y Convenciones
12. Edificio Inteligente de Empresas Públicas
13. Edificio de la Cultura de la Cámara de Comercio

ACCOMMODATIONS

1. ApartHotel Buenas Noche
2. ApartHotel Mariscal
3. Hotel Casa Blanca 70

4. Hotel Eupacla
5. Hotel Metropol
6. Hotel Samaritano

RESTAURANTS

1. Bolívar
2. Buen Apetito

3. Café de la Estación de Ferrocaril
4. Charlot

*5pm; Aeropuerto Olaya Herrera, Suite 324,
☎285 65 25)*

Turantioquia *(Mon-Fri 8:30am to noon and 2pm
to 5pm; Carrera 48 No. 58-11, ☎291 11 11).*

Excursions

There are many interesting outings in the area
immediately outside Medellín and in the surrounding Antioquia countryside. Its mild spring-
like climate brings to mind the French Alps or
the mountains of Vermont in the United States.

Renting a car and chauffeur by the hour is
probably the most convenient way of getting
around, and only costs 7,000 pesos per hour.
It is also worth inquiring about fixed-priced
tours at the travel agencies. Numerous tours
are available, covering most areas of interest.

In addition to the standard tours of the city,
shopping excursions, "Medellín at Night" and
other tours, the agencies organize visits to the
surrounding metropolitan municipalities including Caldas, La Estrella, Itagüi, Envigado and
Sabaneta, Bello, Copacabana, Girardotat and
Barbosa. There are also eight tours of more
distant destinations.

1- **Región del oriente**, final destination town of
Guatapé;
2- **Región del suroeste**, final destination town
of Jardín;
3- **Región del occidente**, final destination is the
former capital city of the department, Santafé
de Antioquia;
4- **Región del norte**, final destination town of
Santa Rosa;
5- **Región del nordeste**, town of Barbosa is the
main destination;
6- **Región del Río Magdalena medio**, includes
Puerto Triunfo on the Magdalena;
7- **Región del Urabá** or **la Ruta al mar**, includes
Turbo on the Caribbean Sea;
8- **Región del bajo Cauca**, final destination
town of Cáceres.

There are also some ecotourism destinations,
including Parque Natural Los Katios, Parque
Nacional Natural de Las Orquideas and Parque
Natural Paramillo.

For excursions, contact the following travel
agencies in Medellín:

Viajes Turantioquia, Carrera 48 No. 58-11,
☎291 11 11, ⋕291 11 12
Viajes Maya Londoño, Calle 54 No. 45-25,
☎231 46 66, ⋕511 44 08
Agencia de Viajes Naturaleza y Fantasia, Centro
Comercial Villanueva, Suite 990, ☎513 12 84,
⋕251 80 26
Destino Colombia, Carrera 65 No. 49b-21,
Block B, Suite 207, Centro Comercial Los
Sauces, ☎260 68 68, ⋕230 77 50
Seditrans, Calle 9c sur No. 50-161,
☎285 19 78, ⋕285 48 07

 EXPLORING

Medellín ★★★

Medellín lies at the bottom of the Valle del
Aburrá, blessed with a spring-like climate year-
round. This modern city's "tourist" attractions
include its greenery, flowers, and a few historical buildings and churches, most of which are
located downtown. You can visit them on foot,
since *El Centro* is considered safe during the
day. Many streets are pedestrian zones, and
are transformed into public markets with thousands of shops in the streets or running
along them. The boisterous atmosphere is an
integral part of life in Medellín, and as such, is
a tourist attraction in itself.

This guide is not limited to the downtown area
(El Centro), where the main tourist attractions
are found, but also describes El Poblado
(La Zona Rosa), with its many restaurants and
hotels, and indicates other points of interest
that are easily accessible by taxi.

El Centro

The **Museo de Antioquia** ★★★ *(admission
price varies; Tue to Fri 9:30am to 6pm, Sat
9am to 2pm; closed Sun, Mon, and holidays;
Carrera 52a No. 51a-29, ☎251 36 36; ⋕251
08 74)* houses the largest collection of works
by Fernando Botero, with some 32 paintings
and sculptures in two separate exhibition
rooms. The artist depicts characters and situations that are, quite literally, larger than life,
creating an unsettlingly humourous effect. For
example, the pompous self-complacency of a

Fernando Botero

In Spanish, a *bote* is a jar or a bottle, and a *botero* is the person who makes them. Thus, it might come as no surprise that Fernando Botero devotes himself to painting and sculpting puffy, chubby, and sometimes grotesquely paunchy characters and objects, not unlike a big, bubble-shaped blown-glass jar. His well-known 1978 *Mona Lisa* is an enormous lady with an unsettling smile, ridiculous dimples, and plump baby hands. A second *Mona Lisa* was created only a year later, both works in homage to Leonardo da Vinci. Such irony is also at play in the "La Corrida" series, painted between 1984 and 1986, depicting enormous, pretentious bullfighters (*Matador en rojo*, 1986), fighting equally bulls of similar proportions (*Toro muerto*, 1985), all to win over Himalayan dancers (*Mana*, 1984 and *Tablao flamenco*, 1984) with their amusing little beauty marks right under their eye. The evolution and genius of this artist becomes apparent if you look at his earlier works. Paintings like "The Crying Woman" from 1949, and a still life from 1959, are in a style totally different than that of his later works.

Fernando Botero was born on April 19, 1932 in Medellín, the city that would be the source of inspiration for so many of his creations. In 1948, he exhibited two watercolour paintings at the Exposición de Pintores Antioqueños in Santafé de Bogotá. He then moved to this city in 1951, where he took part in two consecutive exhibitions at the Leo Matis gallery. He began to gain recognition during this time when Walter Engel wrote an article on him that was published by Eddy Torres. After winning second prize at the *Frente al mar* Colombian artists' exhibition, Botero began a long journey that would take him to Spain (1952), France (1953, 1969, 1971, 1973), Italy (1953, 1967), Mexico (1956), the United States (1957, 1960, 1972), Brazil (1959), and Germany (1966, 1967). Just as the world was beginning to recognize Botero as one of the great painters of the second half of the century, his son Pedro, then 4, died in a car accident in Spain in 1974, in which Botero himself was also injured. After this date, without having made major changes to his style, critics noticed greater depth in his work, left by the memories of his son. His *Pedrito*, a painting of a child on a wooden horse, is one example, with its bright colours piercing a blue-toned backdrop. This painting is part of a collection of 16 pieces that were donated to the Museo de Antioquia (see p 196) by the artist. The museum now dedicates a permanent gallery, entitled "Pedrito Botero", to the artist. From 1978 to the present, exhibitions of Botero's work are organized in the world's most renowned museums. Botero spends his time between New York, Paris and Tuscany, where he has a workshop in Pietrasanta. In 1984, he made another gift to the Museo de Antioquia – this time a collection of sculptures. The museum created a second permanent exhibition room in his honour to display this collection.

MEDELLÍN

war official is effectively depicted in a 1977 portrait. A plucked chicken, hanging by the neck, provides a shocking interpretation of *nature morte* (still life, literally "dead nature"). The collection also includes the *Mona Lisa Niña*, *Rosita*, *Nuestra Señora de Colombia*, *Dama colombiana*, *Familia colombiana* and *Pedrito*, a portrait of the artist's son. In the sculpture room, *Adán y Eva* is a must-see amongst the dozens of pieces on display. This work is a life-sized bronze of a naked, pot-bellied man and woman, staring aimlessly at the immensity of life. Another Botero bronze depicts a large naked woman, *La Gorda*, and graces the front of the Banco de la Repùblica at the corner of Calle 50 and Calle 51.

Founded in 1881, the Museo de Antioquia, then known as the Museo de Zea, began with a collection of works donated by the president of the time, General Pedro Justo Berrio. The Museo de Antioquia is the oldest in Medellín, and the second-oldest in Colombia. Housed in a newly-renovated colonial building, the Antigua Casa de la Moneda, the museum has two other rooms, in addition to the permanent collection of paintings by Francisco Antonio Cano, which consists of religious works and period paintings. A substantial collection of Columbian paintings can be found on the second floor. The museum also hosts tempo-rary exhibits by artists such as Pablo Picasso, Wilfredo Lam, Alejandro Obregó, Enrique Grau, Marco Tobón, Edgar Negret and Eladio Vélez, has a bookstore and movie theatre, and offers guided tours in English upon request.

You can admire sketches and watercolours and participate in workshops in another building, which is still part of the museum (*Mon to Fri*

8am to noon and 4pm to 6pm, Sat 8am to 2pm; Carrera 45 No. 52-49, ☎251 22 22 or 231 20 13).

The **Iglesia de la Veracruz** ★★★ *(Carrera 52, corner Calle 51, adjacent to the Museo de Antioquia, ☎511 16 24)* is a small church of mixed colonial and Spanish styles, with a stone façade and a belfry with three bells. The church was built between 1791 and 1803, in order to replace the Ermitage de los Forasteros. Designed by José Ortiz and Joaquím Gómez, two Medellín architects, it is the oldest church in the city that is still being used. The bronze holy water font at the entrance was imported from Europe. As its name would suggest, the church is dedicated to the Holy Cross, a popular object of devotion in Antioquia.

The **Basilica Metropolitana de la Inmaculada** ★★★ *(adjacent to Parque de Bolívar, on Carrera 48 No. 56-81, between Calles 54 and 57, ☎513 22 69)* is a Romanesque, Provençal-style cathedral and is one of the oldest structures made from terra cotta brick. Work began in 1875 under the architect Felix Crosti, and was later taken over by the French architect Charles Carré. The church was finally inaugurated in 1931, under the direction of Holieordo Ochoa and Salvador Ortiz. It is the seventh-largest church in Latin America.

Its ornate interior has a high altar decorated with works by various artists, including paintings by Gregorio Vásquez de Arcey y Ceballos (other works by this painter can be seen in the Capilla del Sagrario, at Plaza Bolívar, in Bogotá, see p 88), Van Thuelden, Francisco Antonio Cano, and León Arango. The stained-glass windows and a cross were imported from Italy. Large mahogany Walker organs date from 1933, and have 3,418 metal and wood pipes. Every Sunday, the University of Antioquia symphonic orchestra gives concerts here.

The **Parque de Bolívar** ★★ *(between Carreras 48 and 49 and Calles 54 and 57)* is located in Medellín's downtown and is highly representative of the country's past, with its bronze monument of Libertador Simón Bolívar, the work of sculptor Eugenio Mascagnani (unveiled in 1923) and a bust of Don Fidel Cana, by Francisco Antonio Cano. Also found here is the likeness of Tyrrel Moore, a British immigrant and former owner of the land that is now the park. Moore offered the land to the city as a gift in the 1920s.

The **Basilica de Nuestra Señora de la Candelaria** ★★★ *(adjacent to Parque de*

Berríom Calle 51 No. 49-51, ☎231 33 22) is a whitewashed colonial-style church with two massive belltowers dating back to 1781. Construction began under the architect Don José Barón de Chávez at the end of the 17th century. The church served as Medellín's main cathedral from 1868 to 1931. The Baroque-style high altar is ornamented with Creole gold plating and surmounted with a retable of unknown origin depicting the Virgin of Candelaria, the patron saint of Medellín.

The **Parque de Berrío** ★★ *(between Carreras 50 and 51 and Calles 50 and 51)* is considered to be the heart of Medellín. Sculptures by Fernando Botero and Rodrigo Arenas Betancur adorn the park, and a bronze statue of the former President of the Republic, Pedro Justo Berrío stands in the middle. Unveiled in 1905, it was created by the Italian sculptor Giovanni Auderlini.

The **Antigua Estación Ferrocaril de Antioquia** ★★★ *(corner of Calle 44 or Av. San Juan and Carrera 52)* was officially opened in 1914, and is the work of the architect Enrique Olarte. This old, white, two-storey train station with rib vault windows is now a national monument. Its outdoor court, adjacent to the town hall, was once a loading platform but has been transformed into a restaurant (see p 202).

The **Edificio Inteligente de Empresas Públicas** ★ *(Calle 44, between Carreras 52 and 55)* is a new concept to Medellín. This rectangular, 15-storey building is completely computer-controlled. It stands as a symbol of the efficiency of this governmental branch of public services, responsible for telephone services, electricity, natural gas, water and sewage.

The **Centro Administrativo la Alpujarra** ★★ *(Calle 44, between Carreras 52 and 55)* is made up of a group administrative departmental services buildings. City hall, the municipal council, the government of Antioquia, the Departmental Assembly and the Justice Department are all housed here. In its *plaza* stands a spectacular bronze monument by sculptor Rogrigo Arenas Betancur, dedicated to the people of Antioqueña. You can admire other sculptures by Betancur at Berrío Park between Carreras 50 and 51 and Calles 50 and 51.

The **Antiguo Palacio Nacional** ★★★ *(Mon to Sat 8am to 7:30pm, Carrera 52, No. 48-45)* is one of the most noteworthy and eye-catching buildings in Medellín. In fact, its four storeys and three golden-bronze, sun-deflecting cupolas are visible throughout the city. Long considered the tallest building in Medellín, the Palacio was inaugurated in 1925 and was the work of architect Agustín de Goovaerst. Once used as the main government building, it has since been completely renovated, and is now a shopping mall, with arched balconies and Spanish-style colonnades on every floor. Over a hundred shops look onto this closed courtyard.

The **Palacio de la Cultura Rafael Uribe Uribe** ★★★ (*Carrera 51 No. 52-01*, ☎251 14 44) used to house the government of Antioquia. Its exterior is baroque, if not a bizarre and excessively flamboyant mix of Gothic, English, French, Flemish, Spanish, and Italian – in short, an organized chaos sprung from the imagination of the architect Agustín de Goovaerst in 1925. Considered the city's cultural, historical, and architectural heritage, it now houses the headquarters of the Ministry of Culture for the Department of Antioquia. The building also contains an art gallery, a library, the Antioquia Archives, an auditorium, a movie theatre, and a mural by local artist Ignacio Gómez Jaramillo.

The **Palacio de Exposiciones y Convenciones** (*Calle 41 No. 53-55*, ☎232 45 22) opened in 1971. This modern, cubical building allows for much flexibility in the organization of all sorts of indoor and outdoor exhibitions.

The gallery of the **Edificio de la Cultura de la Cámara de Comercio** ★★ (*Mon to Fri 9am to 7pm; Av. Oriental No. 52-82*, ☎511 61 11, ≈231 86 48) presents graphic arts in three exhibition rooms. In November, the Chamber of Commerce organizes its annual Muestra Grafica Artística, a collective exhibit that brings together a hundred artists specializing in various areas of graphic arts, including silkscreen paintings, lithographs, engravings, etchings, and reliefs.

El Poblado

El Poblado's downtown area is too far away to be reached on foot. You can either take a taxi or take the subway south towards San Antonio station, and get off at El Poblado station.

Iglesia de San José del Poblado ★★ (*Carrera 42 No. 9-11, in front of Parque San José del Poblado*, ☎266 42 46) is built on the original site of the Valle de Aburrá village which was founded in 1616 and later to became Medellín. This original and imposing structure is

the work of architect Horacio M. Rodríguez, and was later adapted by Agustín de Goovaerst, the creator of the Antiguo Palacio Nacional (see p 198) and of the Palacio de la Cultura Rafael Uribe Uribe (see above).

Plaza El Poblado ★ (*Av. El Poblado, at the corner of Calle 10, in front of the San José del Poblado church*) is a little park, known mostly for its life-size bronze depicting a female Indian searching for gold, with a bas-relief of an Indian village and conquistadors in the background. The work is by sculptor Luz María Piedrahita B.

Other Attractions

Other tourist attractions can be found outside El Poblado and El Centro. Here are some that can be easily reached by taxi.

The **Museo de Arte Moderno** ★★★ (*Mon to Fri 10:30am to 7pm, Sat 10am to 5pm; Carrera 64b No. 51-64*, ☎230 26 22, ≈230 27 223) organizes exhibits on visual arts, collage, architecture, and modern design, in four separate rooms on two floors. Guided tours, conferences, and seminars are offered, as well as screenings of films and videos about art.

Founded August 24, 1978, the Museo de Arte Moderno has an educational mandate and organizes travelling exhibits for schools, colleges, and universities, aimed at familiarizing students with modern art. The entire work of Colombian artist Débora Arango is among the collections on display here. During our visit, the museum had organized a retrospective of the works of French painter Olivier, in collaboration with the Jeu de Paume national gallery in Paris.

Museo Etnográfico Miguel Angel Builes ★★ (*Tue to Fri 8am to noon and 2pm to 5pm; Carrera 81 No. 52B-120*, ☎264 22 99 ext. 717) is a small, unpretentious museum dedicated to the preservation of native Colombian culture and artifacts. Amongst the more than 2,000 interesting pieces are a collection of native weapons, a life-size reproduction of a native hut, and the skin of a boa constrictor measuring over six metres long. The building itself was constructed in 1970 by architects Laureano Foreno, Luz Elena de Foreno, Francisco Bayer, and Ocvio Epegui. The price of admission is left to the discretion of the visitor.

The **Plaza de Toros la Macarena** ★ (*Autopista Sur, at the corner of Calle 44*) is a round, red brick building 38.6 metres in diameter that

MEDELLÍN

seats 11,000 spectators. The building is the work of architects Felix Mejía and Gonzalo Restrepo and was inaugurated in 1946. Every January, the Antioqueña bullfight is held here. The Plaza is also used for concerts.

Orchid

The **Fundación Jardín Botánico Joaquím Antonio Uribe** ★★★ (*2,000 pesos; Mon-Sat 8am to 6pm, Sun and holidays, 9am to 6pm; Carrera 52 No. 73-298, ☎233 70 25*) is actually a vast park with over a dozen colonial-style residences, all adorned with more than 250 different species of flowers. The annual orchid exposition is held here every March, and the park is also the site of a permanent collection of various flowers and trees, all of which are labelled. The site includes a lake, an open-air theatre, and an auditorium used for conferences and film and video screenings. It is easily accessible from the Universidad subway station.

The **Jardín Zoológico Santa Fé** ★★★ (*adult 2,000, child 1,000 pesos; 9am to 6pm daily; Carrera 52 No. 20-63, ☎235 09 12*) is home to a wide variety of animals. You can see buffalo, tapirs, bears, lions, jaguars, elephants, zebras, hippopotamuses, rhinoceros, camels, ostriches, crocodiles and monkeys all up close. The zoo is also well-known for its numerous birds, including parrots, toucans, vultures, and pink flamingos, which fly freely around the site. Lama and donkey rides are available for children. A small museum displays a little home with old-fashioned furnishings. The zoo turns into a family park on weekends, and visitors bring their own picnics.

The **Jardín Montesacro** ★ (*Autopista Medellín-Bogotá, Envigado*) also seems like a meeting place for families on weekends, when people

can visit their deceased loved ones and bring flowers to their graves. The tomb of Pablo Escobar, the former leader of the Medellín drug cartel, who died in 1993, is also found here. The site is cared for daily by an employee of the family. The white, hard tombstone reads:

Mientras el Cielo Exista,
Existirán Tus Monumentos
y Tu Nombre Sobrevivirá
como el Firmamento

This translates: "As long as the sky exists above, monuments will bear your name, and it will live on in the heavens".

The **Cerro Nutibara** ★★★ (*between Calles 30a and 33 and between Carrera 55 and Autopista Sur, ☎235 64 96*) is a mountain located right in the middle of Medellín and is considered to be the cultural heart of the city. There is a panoramic view of the entire Valle de Aburrá from a terrace. Here, you will also find an art gallery and a reproduction of an old *antioqueño* village, El Pueblito Paisa, whose main square, fountain, colonial church, town hall, school, artisan shops, and homes with balconies are all true to epoch, and were recreated by architect Julían Sierra Mejía in 1977.

The site also includes an open-air theatre that seats 4,000. It is surrounded by scupltures, including one depicting a heroic chief defending his people from Spanish invaders. The 1955 sculpture is the work of José Horacio Betancur.

Further down, you can visit a sculpture garden, where modern works by Colombian and foreign sculptors are exhibited. John Castles, Carlos Rojas, Edgard Negret, Alberto Uribe and Ronny Vayada (Colombia), Manuel Felguerez (Mexico), Sergio de Camargo (Brazil), Julio Le Parc (Argentina), and Otto Herbert Hajek (Germany) are among the artists whose work is displayed. You can take a bus here from Carrera 46, or a taxi from the Exposiciones subway station.

 ## ACCOMMODATIONS

Medellín

Zona Rosa El Poblado is a new residential neighbourhood in Medellín where you will find not only the best hotels, but also the most expensive. You can, however, find good hotels at a fair price downtown (El Centro) or in the surrounding area.

El Centro

Apart-Hotel Buenas Noche *($; pb, hw, ⊛, mb, ☎, tv, ▣; Carrera 46 or Av. Oriental No. 45-22, ☎251 29 38 or 251 29 36, ⌐251 29 27)* is a budget hotel with 36 rooms on four floors, an elevator, and a central location in the heart of the city. It is good value for the money, but since it is on one of the city's busiest streets, a quieter room at the back of the hotel is recommended.

Hotel Casa Blanca 70 *($; pb, hw, ⊛, ☎, tv, ▣, ℜ; Carrera 45 No. 46 09, ☎251 52 11; ⌐251 47 17)* is another 36-room hotel with a family atmosphere and dedicated staff.

Hotel Samaritano *($; pb, hw, ⊛, mb, ☎, tv, ▣; Carrera 45 No. 45-25, El Palo, ☎251 80 11 or 251 39 42, ⌐252 36 87)* is an inexpensive, clean, decent hotel, with 125 quiet rooms, some with kitchenettes. Good value for small budgets.

Hotel Eupacia *($$; pb, hw, ⊛, ☎, tv, ▣, ℜ; Carrera 50 No. 53-16, ☎231 18 44, 252 6969, or 231 17 65, ⌐511 14 40)* has several inexpensive rooms, but they are in need of some renovation. Since the neighbourhood borders on downtown and is under the surveillance of two police stations, even the hotel reception assures that there is no danger in walking here at night. A definite plus.

Apart-Hotel Mariscal *($$; pb, hw, ⊛, mb, ☎, tv, ▣, ℜ; Carrera 45 No. 46-49, ☎251 54 33, ⌐251 29 27)*, adjacent to the Casa Blanca, offers 28 rooms of superior quality, at a somewhat higher price. Warm reception.

Two blocks from San Antonio subway station is **Hotel Metropol** *($$; pb, hw, ⊛, mb, ⊘, ☎, tv, ▣, △; Calle 47 No. 45-11, ☎513 78 00 or 251 56 98)*, without argument the best hotel for the money in Medellín. With 60 *ejecutivo*-style rooms on five floors, it also has a gym, a sauna and a Turkish bath. This hotel is not an architectural masterpiece, and does not pretend to be one, but offers travellers decent lodgings at a reasonable price. Who could ask for anything more?

El Poblado

The best, but most expensive, hotels in Medellín are found in El Poblado. Expect to pay between US$150 and US$250 or more, unless you get a special rate or weekend deal, which can give you up to 70 percent off. Information about such deals is available at travel agencies or directly at the hotel reception. Some hotels are perched on the mountainside and offer a magnificent view of the area. Others provide peace and quiet in tranquil settings, but are still not far from important business and bank head offices.

Belfort Hotel *($$$$$; pb, hw, ≡, mb, ☎, tv, ≈, ▣, heating, ℜ, ⊘, ⊛, △, outdoor P; Calle 17 No. 40b-300, ☎311 91 71 or 311 00 66, ⌐311 00 76)* is a beautiful new hotel. Its architecture is a blend of audaciousness, conservatism, comfort and style, not to mention charm and warmth – in short, a home away from home. The grounds are surrounded by trees, and the Belfort itself is an eight-storey red brick building that is tastefully designed and decorated, making this one of Medellín's best hotels. The Belfort's 96 rooms are superbly furnished, and 24 of them come with sofas and armchairs. There is no lobby as you enter, but rather a porter who helps you to the elevator which takes you up to the courteous reception on the second floor. The ambiance is posh, and the decor is reminiscent of English style, with lacquered wood. The staff is efficient, and speaks English. Comfortable sofas are tucked away in the alcoves of this little lobby which doubles as a cocktail bar. The dining room leads off from it, followed by an outdoor swimming pool which beckons from beyond the sliding glass doors. The pool alone is worth the trip! Even if you do not stay at the hotel, you should enjoy restaurant (see p 203) or bar, if only to admire the pool with its ceramic blue tiling. The wall at the pool's far end is cleverly camouflaged, so swimmers seem to disappear into the city when they dive in. Impressive! The Belfort art gallery exhibits paintings on the walls of the lobby, the bar, and the dining room.

Hotel Dann Carlton *($$$$$; pb, hw, ≡, mb, ☎, ≈, tv, ▣, heating, ℜ, ⊘, ⊛, △, outdoor P; Carrera 43a No. 7-50 (or Av. Poblado), ☎312 41 41, ⌐268 13 16 or 312 73 23)* belongs to the Carlton Hotel chain and is known as the most expensive hotel in Medellín. The architecture of this 18-storey red brick building is English in style. The main conference room on the top floor offers a spectacular

MEDELLÍN

view of Medellín and the Valle de Aburrá. The white marble lobby is stunning, and the cordial reception staff speaks an impeccable English. The 185 suites are tastefully decorated and elegantly furnished. An art gallery occupies two floors and includes an open bar with a grand piano. Works by the painter Servando Palacios, depicting daily Medellín life, including subway scenes, are on exhibit here. The pool is enormous, and the area is also used as a cocktail bar.

The **Hotel Four Points** *($$$$$; pb, hw, ≡, mb, ☎, tv, ◙, heating, ℜ, ⊘, ⊛, △, outdoor P; Carrera 43c No. 6 Sur-100, ☎311 80 88 or 312 68 06, Sheraton@epm.net.co)* is in keeping with the style of the Sheraton chain: efficient, comfortable, but somewhat cold. The lobby looks up to all ten floors of this grey stone building, which has 123 suites, 3 of them very large, and all tastefully furnished. A lounge on the second floor doubles as an art gallery. The staff speaks flawless English. There is a bank machine in the lobby.

Hotel Inter-Continental *($$$$$; pb, hw, ≡, mb, ☎, tv, heating, ℜ, ⊘, ◙, △, outdoor P; Calle 16 No. 28-51, ☎266 06 80, ↝266 15 48)* was likely the first hotel to be built on the El Poblado mountain. This older nine-storey building has a 1950s decor and some 294 rooms, all comfortable and pleasantly furnished. The large, stark lobby is lacking in charm, but this is compensated for by an attentive staff that speaks English. The art gallery displays naive-style watercolours by Hernan Dario Catano, and includes country- and city-scapes of Medellín. The hotel also offers its guests two tennis courts with night lighting.

The **Park 10 Hotel** *($$$; pb, hw, ≡, mb, ☎, tv, ◙, heating, ℜ, ⊘, ⊛, △, outdoor P; Carrera 36B No. 11-12, ☎381 44 70 or 266 88 11, ↝381 43 55, park10@colomsat.net.co)* definitely caters to an executive clientele. A business centre with desks equipped with computers with Internet access, fax machines, phones, and coffee is set up in a space large enough to fit 10 people. Park 10 also has a library and reference material on various economical and business topics, all for guest use. Located in quiet, shady El Poblado, Park 10 is a new nine-storey building with 55 elegantly furnished split-level suites.

Hotel Poblado Plaza *($$$$$; pb, hw, ≡, mb, ☎, tv, ◙, heating, ℜ, ⊘, ⊛, △, outdoor P; Carrera 43a No. 4 Sur-75, ☎268 53 66 or 288 55 55, ↝268 69 49, 104551@compuserve.com)* is a

stylishly decorated six-storey hotel with a French restaurant whose large windows look out onto a terrace and a flower garden with a lovely pond. Its 85 enormous rooms (the largest in Medellín, according to their ads) are well-furnished, and offer all the comfort expected from a hotel of this calibre.

 # RESTAURANTS

Medellín

Too often, little restaurants in Medellín that might otherwise be stylish tend double as general stores. For example, a potentially charming pizzeria serves local cuisine and rotisserie-style chicken – but also sells chips, pop, jam, chewing gum, milk, bread, fruit juice, cookies, *empanadas*, and so on. As is the case everywhere in Colombia, except Cartagena, the restaurants here are mainly busy at lunchtime.

El Centro has a profusion of restaurants, most of them specializing in fast food. The majority offer an *almuerzo*, a complete luncheon special. Since the area is normally safe for pedestrians during the day, the only drawback to eating here is choosing between so many places!

El Centro

The **Bolívar** *($; every day 6am to 8pm; corner of Carrera 51 No. 44-10 and Av. San Juan, ☎511 68 19 or 511 68 23)* specializes in fast food, but also offers a good, inexpensive breakfast. Just across the street from the Estación de Ferrocaril and the Centro Administrativo La Alpajurra, this is a good place to start the day.

Buen Apetito *($; Mon to Sat 7:30am to 6pm; Torre de Bonbona, room 109, next to Parque San Antonio, between Calles 44 and 46 and Carreras 49 and 46, ☎239 97 77)* is an attractive mid-range restaurant with checkered tablecloths. There are about ten small tables that are slightly too close to each other. Since the restaurant in an office tower, it really fills up at noon. Fish dishes and a daily special are available. Service is fast, attentive and efficient.

The **Café de la Estación de Ferrocaril** *($; every day 8am to 6pm; corner of Calle 44, or*

Av. San Juan, and Carrera 52) is set up in the outdoor courtyard of the station, next to the Centro Administrativo La Alpajurra. Light cafeteria-style meals or sandwiches can be eaten at a table shaded by a parasol. This is the preferred luncheon spot for personnel of the administrative centre and is crowded at lunchtime. The best time for a quiet *tinto* (black coffee) is in the afternoon.

As its name implies, restaurant-bar **Charlot** *($; every day 8am to 6pm; Av. Oriental No. 54-58, ☎231 36 49)* is an unpretentious little restaurant decorated with film posters from Charlie Chaplin movies. Simple dishes are served for the *almuerzo* (lunch special) or for breakfast starting at eight o'clock.

El Poblado

El Poblado offers an excellent choice of restaurants, but expect to pay more than in El Centro.

Empanaditas El Poblado *($; no precise address, but facing the park in El Poblado, to the left of the San José del Poblado church)* is a little outdoor terrace run by two friendly ladies. They greet customers with a smile from as early as six in the morning (a promising way to start the day) until nine at night. Colombian breakfast with *empanadas* seasoned with cumin is on the menu, but American-style breakfasts with eggs prepared however the customer likes and *café au lait* are also available.

El Portal Chino *($$; every day noon to midnight; Av. El Poblado No. 70-58, ☎266 53 46)* is a Chinese-owned Chinese restaurant, but the service is provided by Colombians. The decor of the restaurant is not particularly original; it resembles Chinese restaurants all over the world with its plastic accessories and red walls. The fare, however, is more than satisfactory, and wine is served by the glass or bottle. Since drinking warm *sake* is unusual in Colombia, the owners are not used to having it ordered by customers. They only use *sake* in the kitchen for cooking, and it is not included on the wine list. What a mistake! On the other hand, the shrimp with vegetables dish was excellent, and this restaurant offers good value in terms of price and quality.

🦐 The hotel restaurant at the **Belfort** *($$-$$$$$; every day 7am to 10pm; Calle 17 No. 40b-300, ☎311 00 66)* (see p 201) is sophisticated, but has a relaxed atmosphere, probably because of the friendly staff who speaks English. The chef loves to make a tour of the dining room, and devises a different menu each night according to his imagination and the weather. For example, on some nights he organizes a barbecue on the terrace, but the next night might be Italian, with fresh pasta and sauces that are prepared, and sometimes flambéed, at the table. Everything is done with class and refinement, with no pretense except the chef's insistence on varying the menu and the care taken in the presentation of the food. The memory of the seafood with béchamel sauce will linger for a long time. Also, the bar offers a two-for-one special during *feliz hora* (happy hour). Have a chat with Johnny Salas; the amicable head waiter enjoys speaking English. The wine list includes vintages from France, Italy and Chile.

The **El Claustro de Villa Carlota** *($$$$$; every day noon to 3pm and 6pm to midnight; Calle 16 No. 16-91, on the corner with Carrera 43b, ☎266 85 20)* is a *parrilla* that specializes in cooking over wood coals. Located on a quiet street, this attractive and popular restaurant within the stone walls of a former cloister is considered one of the best in Medellín. The interior decor is in keeping with the architecture. The dining rooms are the former chapels. Expensive, but excellent.

Las Cuatro Estaciones *($$$$$; every day noon to 3pm and 7pm to midnight; Calle 16b No. 43-79, near the Belfort hotel, ☎266 71 00 or 266 71 20)* is an exclusive seafood restaurant that specializes in Spanish cuisine. The meeting place of the business and political classes of Medellín, this restaurant cannot fail to please with its sophisticated cooking, reserved but efficient reception, and highly professional service. Divided into four dining rooms, the Salóns España, Oriental, Europa and Colombia, the decor includes red walls, red ceramic-tile floors and Spanish and colonial-style furniture.

🌿 **La Posada de la Montaña** *($$$$$; every day noon to 3pm and 6pm to midnight; Carrera 43b No. 16-22, ☎266 85 40)* specializes in *antioqueña* cooking. It is located in a former colonial residence, at the top of an embankment that removes it from the noisy traffic on Avenida Poblado below. You enter by way of a flower-filled staircase between magnificent trees. The first outdoor porch with its white linen tablecloths is very tempting; it looks out onto a superb orchard with many flowers and trees, mainly citrus. However,

MEDELLÍN

Medellín: a Leader Among Cultural Cities

It would be difficult to exaggerate the importance that the city of Medellín places on its cultural life; its emphasis on art equals that found in the world's large, cosmopolitan cities. For example, all the stylish hotels in Medellín, and especially those of El Poblado, vie for the privilege of showing the paintings and sculptures of local artists. Not only do they display these works; they also contribute financially to the publication of brochures, the printing of invitations and the expenses of openings. No sooner do we check into the Belfort, than the receptionist volunteers an invitation to that evening's opening by the internationally known local artist, María Victoria Vélez. Even the city hall, Alcadia Major de Medellín, has three rooms devoted to art, displaying the works of a different artist every two weeks. The city bears part of the expenses for openings and invitations, as well as renting the galleries. The permanent collection of more than 50 artworks is hung in municipal offices *(Calle 44, between Carreras 52 and 55)*.

Internationally acclaimed artists and those left waiting in the wings

Without a doubt, Colombia's finest representational artists are found in Medellín. These are uniquely talented painters and sculptors whose techniques would be highly valued were it not for the narrow mindset of critics who refuse to consider anything but abstract art. This constraint leaves little scope for personalized expression, such as figurative painting, which is so important in Latin American art in general, and in Colombian art in particular. The artists exhibiting in the hotel galleries or the city hall may have achieved international recognition, but many of those who are less well-known are equally worthy of attention: painters Lucy Correa, Javier Toro, Fernando E. Muños S., and the sculptor Olga Inés Arango D., to name just a few. To find out more about Colombia's figurative artists, visit the exhibit halls at the Alcacia Major and obtain the program listing current activities in the arts. Also, consult the art book *Galería Gráfica Santandereana*, by Joaquím Romero Díaz, which includes painters Miguel A. Betancur, Alba Helena Pérez Pavony, Léon Molína V, Jorge Cárdenas Hernandez, Jaime Carmona; sculptor Julio Londoño, and many others.

there is more to come. On the other side of the dining room is the terrace of the inner-courtyard, which has a fountain and an ornamental pond and also opens onto a lovely orchard. The full menu is offered, but the *cocina corriente*, daily special, is a must! This lunchtime it was pork chops with a sweet, purple sauce made from cherries and raisins. Marvellous! Has the chef been influenced by *nouvelle cuisine*? The serving was generous enough, but it was a work of art. It was accompanied by a salad perfumed with lemons that might have come from the very tree that was shading our table.

Sakurahana *($$$$$; Mon to Fri noon to 3pm and 7pm to midnight, Sat 7pm to midnight, Sun and holidays noon to 4pm; Carrera 43a No. 3 Sur-98, ☎311 62 51)* is an incredible Japanese restaurant. Also located in a former colonial residence at the end of a private park, Sakurahana is divided into a dozen intimate dining rooms by rice paper partitions that are decorated with dragons. Lighting is provided by rice paper lanterns. The bar has a fireplace and opens onto a classic Japanese garden including

an ornamental pond with a stylized wooden bridge. There is another ornamental pond in the interior courtyard, surrounded by a deck with tables set up on it. Japanese cuisine, including *sushi* and *sashimi* are served here. Customers remove their shoes and are seated at a low table placed on a *tatami*, where they are served a variety of Japanese meat and seafood dishes, cooked in plain view by the Japanese chef. Here the waiters are dressed in Japanese costume; the women as *geishas* with full makeup and fans. The men wear black silk *kimonos* and make the customary gesture of respect of several quick bows of the head with arms beside the body. Despite all this, there are no Japanese staff at Sakurahana. All the employees, including the *geishas* with whitened faces and almond eyes, are Colombians, as are the owners. This is also true of the chef, despite all his skill at the subtle art of *sashimi*. It is as though the attitude, allure and practices were purchased lock, stock and barrel in Japan and imported to Colombia. Good, extremely expensive and very exotic! There is also a small shop that sells Japanese handicrafts, *kimonos* and dishes, among other items.

ENTERTAINMENT

Medellín

For nightlife, nothing compares to the Zona Rosa El Poblado, with its numerous nightclubs and bars. It is hard to choose among so many establishments, most of which are patronized by the young, idle, fashionably-disillusioned offspring of well-to-do families. Nevertheless, try the **Berlín** *(Calle 10 No. 41-65, ☎266 29 05)*. With its odd mix of neon lights and brass musical instruments, the decor is reminiscent of Berlin before the war. There are imported and local beers and the service is laid back. Once a month there is live jazz. The scheduling is so hit or miss that being there on the right night is like winning the lottery, but just like in pre-war Berlin, nobody cares.

There is a second Zona Rosa in Medellín, and all the *Medellinenses* are familiar with Carrera 70, between Calles 40 and 50, affectionately known as *Calle de mariachis*. The bars, restaurants and nightclubs all have terraces on the street that lead right into each other. They get going around 4pm, and don't stop until sometime in the early morning, depending on how busy they are.

At **El Viejo Salón** *(Carrera 70 No. 42-15, ☎412 18 08)* you can have a quiet cocktail, since the music is less loud than elsewhere. Then there is **Estadero Bar Reminiscencias** *(Carrera 70 No. 42-19, ☎250 22 87)*, just a few steps away, which is also quite noisy. Across the street, there are two nightclubs that compete for dancers side by side starting at 6pm, and succeed! In fact, there are already couples getting up for a hot *salsa* number.

For a relaxed, fun evening, **El Chocolo** *(Carrera 70 No. 3-28, ☎260 67 83)*, an elevated terrace known for its beef or chicken *parrilla*, offers entertainment after 9pm. Sure enough, a group of eight *mariachis* straight from Mexico, in costume and sporting *sombreros* strike up a rousing chorus of *Coucouroucoucou Palôôôômaââââ*. There is no cover charge because the show can be seen from the street. However, customers must pass through a metal detector before being seated on the terrace.

Avenidas Las Palmas is also on the mountainside. This is a busy avenue with a multitude of restaurants and nightclubs scattered along its five kilometres. Take a taxi or a car to go from one establishment to another, all of which are very expensive. This is an area of luxury cars and people for whom money is no object.

Events

Medellín is a busy city where many social and cultural events take place during the course of the year. Here are a few of the main attractions:

The **Feria Taurina de la Candelaria** takes place at the Plaza de Toros La Macarena, at the end of January and beginning of February. This annual fair brings together the best toreadors from Spain and Colombia.

The **Exposición Internacional de Orquideas** in March exhibits orchids from many countries.

The **Feria Nacional de Artesanias** assembles all sorts of crafts workers from every corner of the country in July: ceramists, leather workers, wood and stone sculptors and others.

The **Mercado de Sanalejo** takes place on the first Saturday of every month in the Parque de Bolívar. This is an *antioqueño* handicrafts market and flower display.

The **Feria de Las Flores** is the most traditional fair in Medellín. It takes place every year in August and features a sports and cultural program, and the crowning of a flower queen.

The **Sinfonía de Luces** is held from the first week in December to the end of the first week of January. At Christmas, many of the buildings are decorated with multicoloured lights, among them the Empresas Públicas, which is adorned with 200,000.

The **Desfile de mitos y legendas** begins the second week in December in the city centre. This is a parade representing the myths, legends and culture of Antioquia with music and folk dancing.

MEDELLÍN

206

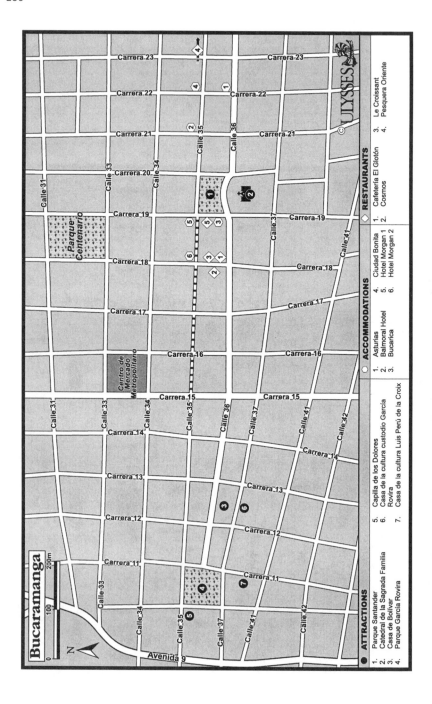

BUCARAMANGA AND THE
DEPARTMENT OF SANTANDER

Santander is named after Bolívar's foremost lieutenant, Francisco de Paula Santander. This area of 30,537 km² was formerly the *santandereana* region, which also included the department of Norte de Santander. Created as a state in 1857, the region officially became a department with the adoption of the constitution in 1886. Santander is located in east-central Colombia, with the eastern cordillera running through it from north to south, making it the most mountainous department of the country. It is, however, blessed with excellent roads. Several canyons cut through this mountainous area, at the bottom of which lie the valleys of the Río Suárez, the Río Fonce, and the Río Chicamocha. The rest of the territory stretches along the eastern bank of the Río Magdalena. Once covered with primary forest, this area is now used for oil production.

The departments of Norte de Santander and Cesar lie to the north of Santander, while Boyacá is to the south. The eastern border is Boyacá, whereas the department's western boundaries touch upon the Río Magdalena, which separates it from the departments of Bolívar and Antioquia. Meanwhile, Santander itself is divided into six provinces: Soto, Mares, Guanentá, García Rovera, Vélez et Comunera. Close to 1.7 million inhabitants live in 87 cities and villages. The temperature varies between 20°C and 28°C.

Bucaramanga was once inhabited by numerous indigenous peoples from various backgrounds: the Yarigüíes and the Agataes on the Río Magdalena, the Guanes in the middle and the mountainside and the Chitareros and the Laches on the elevated plateaus. The Spaniards had colonized Santander as early as the beginning of the 16th century; however, it was a German named Alfinger who first grouped the indigenous people into *pueblos indigenos* in order to control them more effectively and to facilitate their conversion to Christianity.

The indigenous economy mainly practised agriculture, ceramics and weaving, whereas the Spanish focussed on their quest for gold, charcoal mining, the extraction of quinine, growing tobacco, and raising cattle. The villages of Vélez, San Gil, Soccoro and Zapatoca, whose populations were mostly Mestizo, grew rapidly. As of 1778, for example, Soccoro had more than 15,000 inhabitants, but was nevertheless administered by Tunja, the capital of Boyacà, which only numbered 3,000. It is not surprising, therefore, that the first anti-Spanish backlash took place here in 1781, with the uprisings of the *communeros* (see p 29); which began when Manuela Beltrán denounced the public order from the Spanish crown decreeing an increase in market taxes. The Spanish had also implemented some offensive and discriminatory practices, such as forbidding the wearing of traditional Amerindian dress.

Bucaramanga

Bucaramanga is not only the capital of the department of Santander, but also of the northern province of Soto. While it is an important economic and cultural centre of around 500,000 people, Bucaramanga is also known to Colombians as the "City of Parks".

A Brief History

When the Spanish conquered Santander, Bucaramanga was an indigenous *guane* town established on the banks of the Río de Oro, so called because of the large gold deposits found along its shores. It was founded on December 22, 1622, by Andrés Páez de Sotomayor on the cacique of Bucarica's territory, but was declared a *pueblo de indios* by a delegate of the Spanish crown who visited the territory in 1623. It kept this appellation until the founding of a parish and the arrival of permanent Mestizo and Spanish colonists. From then on, Bucaramanga witnessed a phenomenal growth both economically and politically, being elevated to the rank of a city following independence, after which it was declared the capital of the free state of Santander in the mid-19th century. Only when the Constitution was adopted in 1886 did it officially become the capital of Santander. The city welcomed foreigners as of 1825, attracting an influx of immigrants from Britain, who quickly fit in with the Santandereana population, and soon became active citizens of the city. The end of the 19th century saw a second wave of immigrants, this time from Germany, who brought new technologies to Bucaramanga. As a result, Bucaramanga was the first Colombian city to have electricity and natural gas in homes, and also where the first airlines set up business.

Bucaramanga Today

Originally a plateau at an elevation of 950 metres and overlooking the valley of the Río de Oro, Bucaramanga has expanded beyond its boundaries in recent years. By merging with the neighbouring municipalities of Floridablanca, San Juan de Girón and Piedecuesta, it is now a metropolis of over 700,000 *Bumangueses*. Although its balmy

temperature averages 24°C, Bucaramanga has little to offer travellers, except for some sights centred around the Parque García Rovera. Bucaramanga appears after a long drive on the Autopista Girón-Barrancaberjerma, through a striking landscape of towering mounds of soil and deep ravines gauged out of the earth through the constant erosion.

Bucaramanga is a quiet city with pedestrian streets. Calle 35, between Carreras 15 and 19, for example, has been transformed into a market by thousands of vendors, and is complete with air-conditioned shops and outdoor stalls. You can find everything from kitchen utensils to clothing, suitcases and local crafts.

On Sundays, half of Carrera 27, or Avenida Próspero Pinzón, turns into a cycling path, so that the *Bumangueses* can cycle, roller blade, roller board, run, or just walk along it.

Suan Juan de Girón

San Juan de Girón, located nine kilometres west of Bucaramanga, is now part of the latter's metropolitan region, along with Floridablanca. First founded in 1631 by Francisco Mantilla de los Ríos as Villa de los Caballeros de San Juan de Girón, the town, which lies on the Río de Oro, soon became an important economic player of the time, thanks to the gold extracted from the river and its channels. It still remained important even as the gold-bearing channels dried up and the focus of development shifted to deposits in the eastern cordillera that crosses the department.

San Juan de Girón Today

San Juan de Girón's rich colonial architecture, all of which has been preserved, lives up to its National Monument status, which it received in 1963 in order to preserve its characteristic white-washed houses with red-tiled roofs and cobble-stoned streets.

The dozen of arched bridges, also made of stone, which are scattered about the city, are another remnant of its colonial past. Many artists have come here to renovate and establish their homes. In short, Girón is a peaceful and welcoming place.

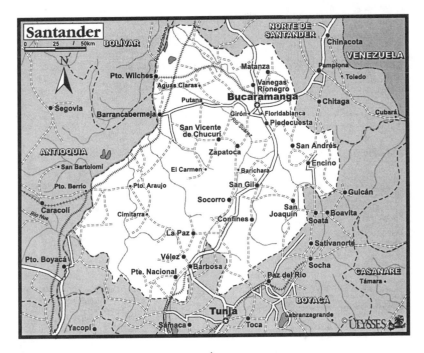

 FINDING YOUR WAY
AROUND

The *calles* of Bucaramanga and San Juan de Girón run east-west, with numbers increasing northward. *Carreras* go from north to south, with numbers increasing eastward.

By Plane

The **Aeropuerto Palo Negro** is located on a high plateau, about one hour north of downtown Bucaramanga. Its elevation makes for a spectacular view at landing. Buses displaying "Aeropuerto" signs head to Palo Negro from downtown, on Carrera 15, and cost 450 pesos. There are also *colectivos* which, for 2,000 pesos, will drop off passengers on Calle 35, between Carreras 19 and 20, in Parque de Santander. Finally, taxis cost 6,000 pesos. While Palo Negro is not an international airport, many Colombian airlines, such as Avianca, offer flights to other cities within the country.

Avianca's schedule:

Baranquilla: every day 7:15am with stopover; Mon, Wed, Fri and Sat 8:15am with stopover; 182,000 pesos.
Bogotá: every day 6:25am; Mon-Sat, 7:29am; Tue, Thu and Sun 9am; every day 12:15pm and 1:59pm; Mon-Fri and Sun 2:35pm; every day 3:25pm and 5:01pm; Mon-Fri and Sun 6:05pm; every day 8:07pm and 10:05pm; 141,000 pesos.
Cartagena: every day 2pm with stopover; 182,000 pesos.
Cúcuta: every day 7:15am, 9:40am, 2pm and 4:50pm; 67,000 pesos.
Medellín: every day 9:40am with stopover; every day 7:05pm; 151,000 pesos.
Valledupar: Mon, Wed, Fri and Sat 8:15am; 139,000 pesos.

Some useful airline information:

National Airlines:

Aces, Carrera 36 No. 26-48, room 104, ☎634 95 95, 632 05 96 or 635 87 91, ⌨634 90 72

AeroRepública, Carrera 33 No. 45-85, ☎643 53 77, 643 79 69 or 643 33 84, ☞643 45 31
Avianca, Calle 37 No. 15-03, ☎642 61 17 or 642 15 19, ☞642 85 26
Helicol, Calle 35 No. 18-65, suite 501, ☎633 47 41
Intercontinental de Aviación, Calle 52, No. 31-71, ☎643 43 52
Satena, Calle 37 No. 17-46, room 202, ☎642 14 77

International Airlines:

Aerotaca, corner of Calle 36 and Carrera 15, 2nd floor, ☎630 51 58
Aerolíneas Argentinas, Carrera 27 No. 36-14, suite 501, ☎634 68 38
Agroaves, Carrera 45 No. 33a-40, ☎634 27 29
Air France, Calle 36 No. 31-39, room 206, ☎634 24 81
American Airlines, Calle 42, No. 34-13, ☎647 45 38
Tas, Calle 42, No. 29-82, ☎645 22 75

By Bus

The **Terminal de Transportes** *(☎644 55 72 ext. 154)* is midway between Bucaramanga and San Juan de Girón, on the Autopista Girón-Barrancaberjerma. The recently built Terminal offers bus service to Colombia's major cities, such as Bogotá, Cartagena de Indias, Barranquilla, Santa Marta and Medellín. The bus companies listed here have a ticket office in the Terminal and/or Bucaramanga:

Autoboy S.A., ☎644 55 96
Berlinas del Fonce, ☎644 52 37
Copetrán, Calle 55 No. 17b-17, ☎644 81 67
Cootransmagdalena, Calle 32 No. 26-06, ☎644 55 88
Cotrasangil, Calle 31 No. 18-55, ☎644 55 62
Expreso Brasilia, ☎644 55 64
Omega, ☎644 55 87
Transportes Reina, ☎644 55 71

Public Transportation

All of Bucaramanga's neighbourhoods have bus service, with their destinations clearly indicated on the bus's windshield. One-way fare costs 350 pesos. For example, you can get to Girón

by hopping on the bus marked "Girón" on Carrera 15 heading south.

Renting a Car

Downtown Bucaramanga is often congested with traffic, though circulation is reasonable during off-peak hours, making it pleasant to rent a car to visit Girón, Floridablanca or Piedecuesta. Try the following car rental companies for more information:

Hertz, Carrera 19 No. 36-40, ☎633 40 06
Alquilauto, Calle 36 No. 31-39, room 315, ☎635 17 56
Bucarautos Rental, Calle 53 No, 36-33, suite 101, ☎643 39 54
Renta Autos Ltda., Carrera 19 No. 36-40, ☎633 07 46

 # PRACTICAL INFORMATION

Area code: 7.

Mail

Mail is forwarded through **Avianca** *(Mon-Fri 8am to noon and 2pm to 6pm; Calle 37 No. 15-03).*

Tourist Information

Fundo Mixto de Promoción Turística, corner of Calle 35 and Carrera 19, Bucarica Hotel, ☎630 75 91 or 630 75 89.

Banks

It's never a problem to exchange currency or traveller's cheques at the **Banco Industrial Colombiano** (BIC) *(Calle 35 No. 18-21, ☎633 12 68).* Automatic bank machines are found around the Parque de Santander, between Calles 35 and 36 and Carreras 19 and 20.

Santander Specialties

Las "hormigas culonas", or "ants with large behinds", or simply "big butts". Since insects are not usually considered edible in northern countries, it may come as a surprise to find that this *Santandereana* specialty, "hormigas culonas" is in fact large ants, fried and salted and served in plastic containers throughout the department, especially at the airport. Most *santandereanos* have tasted these at least once in their lifetime, although eating ants is not part of their daily diet. Enough said; at least, enough to mention their culinary merits. Do not expect to find them accompanying your Big Mac anytime soon.

Fortunately, Santander also has other, non-insect specialties to try:

El cabro o cabrito, a dish of marinated, braised or grilled kid meat;
La pepitoria, kid blood pudding served as an entree;
La carne seca, sun-dried meat cooked on wood charcoal;
La sopa de pichón, pigeon soup made with beef stock, to which milk is added;
El sancocho, meat or fish soup. This dish is served everywhere in Colombia, but has a special local flavour in Santander, where it is made with beef, pork, chicken, cabbage, carrots, celery, onions, plantains, and potatoes;
El ajiaco santandereano, a soup made from corn, pork, and chicken;
El tamal santandereano, a dish of corn, bacon, chicken, beans, onions, garlic and parsley, wrapped in banana leaves;
El masato de arroz, a fermented beverage made from rice.

Excursions

Local travel agencies in the department of Santander can arrange most excursions.

The **Circuito del Cañon** takes you to Santander's main tourist attraction: the le Cañon del Chicamocha *(via the Autopista to Bogotá)*, from where you can see the narrow peaks and steep mountain slopes that give way to the valleys of the *ríos* Suárez and Fonce.

San Gil lies 96 kilometres south of Bucaramanga *(via the Autopista to Piedecuesta)*, and is known as La Perla del Ponce, or "The Pearl of the River Ponce". With century-old willows that dip into the still waters of the river, the Parque Gallineral is one of the main attractions. It is also a lovely place for a walk through the alleys, bridges, and flower gardens.

Barichara, 120 kilometres south of Bucaramanga and 30 kilometres from San Gil *(take the Autopista towards Piedecusta via Barichara, from San Gil)*, is also a National Monument protected by the government of Colombia.

The **Circuito del río** is known as the "safari of Santander", because it leads to the city of Barranca Bermerja *(west of Bucaramanga, via the the Autopista to Girón)*. Many of the *ciénagas*, or marshes, of the Río Magdalena are found here.

The following travel agencies are located in Bucaramanga:

Agencia de Viajes Santur, Calle 36 No. 13-61, ☎630 54 54, ⊶633 33 23;
Galvis Tur Ltda., Calle 36 No. 31-39, room 301, Centro Comercial Chicamocha, ☎645 77 53, 634 33 08, ⊶634 39 09;
Trayectos Tour, Calle 48 No. 24-57, ☎643 58 46 or 643 58 93, ⊶643 58 93.

BUCARAMANGA

Guane Culture

Although researchers know that it was one of the first territories in Colombia to be settled by humans, they still have not been able to pinpoint the exact date when the first inhabitants came to the department of Santander. These people were a nomadic group that bartered with its neighbours and made primitive stone tools designed for multiple uses. They dwelled first in caves on the river banks, but developed an organized social structure based on a stable and sedentary community with the advent of agriculture. The distribution of food and community work were decided upon by one leader, who was supported by secondary members of lesser importance.

For a long time, it was thought that the Guanes were actually the Muiscas, for both groups were neighbours and were in many ways similar. In fact, the Guanes, whose language belongs to the Chibcha family, maintained good relations with the Muiscas, some of whose practices they incorporated into their own culture, as well as that of the Sutagaos, the Laches, the Tunebos, the Chitareros. They even came into contact with peoples as far as the Sierra Nevada de Santa Marta, and groups in Venezuela, which is adjacent to the actual *Santandereano* territory.

The Guanes were farmers, specializing in growing corn, their main food staple. In the colder regions of the Andes, they cultivated potatoes; in warmer climates near the Río Magdalena, they grew beans and fruit, and harvested coca leaves and cotton. The Río de Oro provided them with salt and gold. Expert weavers, the Guanes' beautiful tapestries now constitute the largest collection of archeological textiles in Colombia.

 EXPLORING

Bucaramanga ★★

The **Parque de Santander ★★★** *(between Calles 35 and 36 and Carreras 19 and 20)* is a spectacular park in every sense. During Christmas, for example, Hare Krishnas compete with Santa Claus for charitable donations. Throughout the year, there are shoeshines, newspaper stalls and even a travelling food vendor who sets up cloth-covered tables on Sundays to cater to passing customers. Beyond the parking lot for *colectivos* (collective taxis that run to various destinations, most notably to the airport) are a beautifully lit fountain and a bronze statue of Francisco de Paula Santander.

The **Catedral de la Sagrada Familia ★★★** *(Calle 36, south of Parque de Santander)* is one of the most stunning churches in the region. With white-washed walls and two massive belltowers that are 100 metres high, this colonial-era church speaks volumes of the *Bumangueses'* piety. Inside are 75 magnificent stained-glass windows that provide the only

ambient light in the mornings. A good place of quiet contemplation.

The huge nave is divided into rows which are supported by four rows of nine columns that buttress the vault. The high altar is also surmounted by four columns.

La **Casa de Bolívar ★★** *(Tue-Fri 8am to noon and 2pm to 6pm, Sat 9am to 1pm; Calle 37 No. 12-15, ☎642 25 42)* is where the Libertador once lived, in 1828. Today, it is a museum of history and ethnography where some of Simón Bolívar's belongings still remain on display, accompanied by various artefacts of the Guane culture. The museum houses the chair of the Academia de Historia of the department of Santander. The library is open for public viewing and also serves as research centre for historians.

The **Parque García Rovira ★★★** *(between Calles 35 and 37 and Carreras 10 and 11)* is surrounded by all the remaining colonial buildings found in Bucaramanga. Not only is the beloved Capilla de los Dolores found here, but also the government offices of Santander, as well as Bucaramanga's city council.

The **Capilla de los Dolores ★★** *(Calle 35, corner of Carrera 10)* is the region's oldest

Catedral del Señor de los Milagros

church and the Bucaramanga's architectural treasure dating from the colonial era. Not surprisingly, it is a National Monument. This is where Simón Bolívar came to pray in 1828, as conflicts of interest and power struggles jostled the leaders of the newly liberated nation. The chapel is rarely open to visitors, since services are no longer conducted there.

The **Casa de la Cultura Custodio García Rovera** ★★ *(during exhibits, every day 9am to noon and 2pm to 6pm; Calle 37 No. 12-46, ☎630 20 46)* is another well-preserved colonial edifice that houses Bucaramanga's museum of fine arts which displays works by *santandereanos* and foreign artists. Though paintings outnumber other media, the Casa also has some sculptures and engravings.

The **Casa de la Cultura Luis Perú de La Croix** ★★ *(Calle 37 No. 11-18, ☎633 81 16)* is also an art centre. Simón Bolívar's personality and life story are chronicled in this beautiful colonial house through displays that depict day-to-day life in colonial times. Today, all kinds of artistic activities are organized.

The **Museo Arqueológico Guane** ★★★ *(every day 8am to noon and 2pm to 6pm; Carrera 7 No. 4-35, Floridablanca)* is a cultural centre built around a large sculpted stone bearing a *guane* pictogram in honour of the Sun, known as *la pieda del sol*. Mysterious spirals are also carved into the ground outside, and geometric motifs are carved in bas relief. Once inside the museum, the displays include a collection of *guane* artifacts acquired by Señor Samuel Arenas in 1993, and classified by anthropologist Pablo Fernando Pérez Riaño. The archaeological items include a wide variety of pre-Colombian artifacts, such as jewellery, textiles, ceramic vases and urns, wooden sculptures, clothing and weapons.

The **Jardín Botánico Eloy Valenzuela** ★★★ *(adults 500 pesos, children 300 pesos; every day 8am to 11:30am and 2pm to 5pm; south of the metropolitan region of Bucaramanga, on the Autopista a Piedecuesta, halfway between the districts of Bucarica and Floridablanca)* opened only a few years ago, in 1990. It is located on an 80-metre-long slope with an altitude of 1,800 metres, which shelters over 200 species of plants and trees representing 76 families and 151 genus. Thus, the entire spectrum of the plantlife of the department of Santander, as well as some exotic types from other regions of Colombia, can be found in the 20 gardens growing on different altitudes.

BUCARAMANGA

San Juan de Girón ★★★

As a National Heritage city, San Juan de Girón's sights are best seen on foot, especially in the morning before the temperature reaches its high of 25°C. This city is the meeting place of choice among *Bumangueses*, and local artists flock here in droves, seeking inspiration. The sites listed below are the highlights of San Juan de Girón.

The **Parque Principal** ★★ *(between Carreras 25 and 26 and Calles 30 and 31)* is a beautiful shaded park, surrounded by colonial homes and the cathedral. The park is Girón's main attraction, and all kinds of people come here to relax or just to get some fresh air. Gypsies will read your palm while vendors sell their snacks and beverages.

The **Catedral del Señor de los Milagros** ★★ *(Carrera 26 between Calles 30 and 31)* took 220 years to complete, as construction began in 1656, and only ended in 1876. The Roman-style cathedral is painted white and has two massive square belltowers. Oddly, a star of David hangs over a small cross on the balcony located above the portals. Inside, two rows of six aligned columns support the arches, which in turn hold up the vault of the nave.

The **Mansión del Fraile** ★★ *(every day 7am to 10pm; Calle 30 No. 25-27, ☎646 54 08 or 646 52 22)* is a pretty colonial mansion dating from 1755. Simón Bolívar stayed here on several occasions in 1813, 1822, and again in 1828. This estate is now a museum of its own, with two floors containing numerous rooms that look onto an indoor courtyard, which have been converted into a restaurant. There are guided tours in Spanish and English for 1,000 pesos per person. The place is also a hotel (see p 215) and a restaurant (see p 215) where you can eat and sleep in the same place as the Libertador and his lieutenants did in the 19th century!

 ACCOMMODATIONS

Bucaramanga

Downtown Bucaramanga offers a wide range of hotels for all tastes and budgets. All of them have a good price/quality ratios and are known for being safe.

The **Asturias** *($; pb, mb, ⊛, ≡ ☎, tv, ▨, ℜ; Carrera 22 No. 35-01, ☎635 19 14, 635 29 76 or 645 75 65)* is a very nice hotel with 34 rooms with colonial furniture that match the building. The inviting lobby is lovely, with white walls that contrast beautifully with the dark wooden furniture. A wooden staircase leads to a mezzanine that all the rooms face onto.

The **Balmoral Hotel** *($; pb, hw, ☎, tv, ▨, ℜ; Carrera 21, corner of Calle 35, ☎630 37 23 or 630 46 63)* is a small establishment in a new building. Its 30 rooms are beautifully furnished, and provide better comfort than the Morgan hotels (see below) since they are set back from the noisy street. A budget hotel with a family ambiance.

The **Hotel Morgan 1** *($; pb, mb, ☎, tv, ▨, ℜ; Calle 35 No. 18-33, ☎630 39 49 or 630 37 41)* is a small family hotel with 19 rooms that come with or without mini bars. For the same price, it is better to opt for a mini bar since they also provide cold water bottles. Its central location next to the Parque de Santander is unbeatable for getting to all the downtown sights on foot. However, it can get a bit noisy during local sporting events, when the owners watch *fútbol* on the television.

The **Hotel Morgan 2** *($; pb, mb, ☎, tv, ▨, ℜ; Calle 35 No. 18-83, ☎630 42 26 or 630 46 32)* is a few doors down from its neighbour, the Hotel Morgan 1, and is a better place to stay even though it is slightly pricier. Also only a few minutes away from Parque de Santander, it offers comfort and quality at a good price.

The **Ciudad Bonita** *($$$$; pb, hw, mb, ⊛, ≡, ☎, tv, ▨, ≈, ⊘, △, Turkish bath, ℜ; Calle 35 No. 22-01, ☎635 01 01, ⊷635 61 24)* faces the Asturias. A new and modern building, some of its rooms have balconies with an exceptional view over Bucaramanga. All rooms, however, have the guest's comfort in mind, as they are modern, large and sensibly furnished. Leather sofas rest on the marble floors of the vast entrance hall. The reception is friendly, as it is everywhere else in Bucaramanga.

The hotel **Bucarica** *($$$$-$$$$$; pb, hw, mb, ⊛, ≡, ☎, tv, ▨, ≈, ℜ; Calle 35, corner of Carrera 19, ☎630 15 92, ⊷630 15 94)* may look unimpressive at first sight, even though it is considered a national monument. Once inside, though, the classic building's charm will become perfectly evident. On the left is an indoor courtyard adorned with plants and a fountain within a large pool, around which tables are set up for having a coffee, drinks, or even a full meal, as it is also the terrasse of the restaurant. The swimming pool is in an adjoining courtyard at the back. Warm, friendly staff who speak English await at the reception, where you can catch a glimpse of the large carpeted marble staircase with a dark wooden bannister leading to the three floors of the hotel. Vast corridors with muted lighting run through the hotel, all of them furnished with style, elegance, and functional period pieces. The Bucarica, named for the ancient *guane* chief who once reigned over the *santandereano* territory, is part of the Organización Hotelera Germán Morales E. Hijos, which runs hotels in Bogotá, Santa Marta, and San Andrés.

San Juan de Girón

 Las Nieves *($; pb, tv, ℜ; Calle 30 No. 25-71, ☎646 89 68)* is a small colonial hotel situated on the grounds of the Parque Principal. With no other distinction than being right at the centre of a National Monument, Girón, it is ideal for small budgets.

The **Mansión del Fraile** *($$$; pb, tv, ℜ; Calle 30, No. 25-27, ☎646 54 08 or 646 52 22)*, built in 1755, is a beautiful colonial house with an indoor courtyard with an overhanging balcony onto which the rooms look out. This "hotel-restaurant-museum" (see p 214) offers its guests the same furnishings and decor that were chosen by Simón Bolívar and his lieutenants when they stayed here. Perhaps a bit pricey for its category, this hotel is also located in the Parque Principal in the heart of Girón.

✕ RESTAURANTS

Bucaramanga

Bucaramanga offers ethnic cuisine from all over the world and all types of restaurants, notably around the Zona Rosa, on Calle 33, or Avenida Las Américas, between Calles 35 and 56, where nightclubs and trendy bars and patios are located.

For a quick breakfast downtown, check out **Le Croissant** *($; every day 7am to 8pm; Carrera 17 No. 35-40)* or cross the street to **Cosmos** *($; every day 7am to 10pm; Carrera 17 No. 35-53)*, or even the **Cafetería El Glotón** *($; every day 7am to midnight; Carrera 17 No. 35-23)*. All three offer large, inexpensive breakfasts in an unpretentious atmosphere.

The following are some of Bucaramanga's best restaurants:

The **Restaurante Macaregua** *($$$; every day 7am to 10pm; Calle 35, corner of Carrera 19, ☎630 15 92)* is located on the first floor of the hotel Bucarica in a room with huge windows. Since the regular clientele consists of businesspeople with eclectic tastes, the food is as diverse as it is excellent. The restaurant specializes in continental cuisine, and dishes such as roast beef, Italian pasta, and even fish, are all available. The service is very professional.

Pesquera Oriente *($$$-$$$$; every day 11:30am to 3pm and 6pm to midnight)* specializes in fish and seafood. Seating is available in the dining room or on the patio, but since the latter is next to Bucaramanga's busiest street, it is probably best to eat inside the dining room. Service is fast and courteous; in fact, it is so quick that the waiter will bring out both the appetizer and the main course at the same time unless told to bring one beforehand. The trout *meunière* is exquisite.

San Juan de Girón

The **Mansión del Fraile** *($$; every day 7am to 10pm; Calle 30, No. 25-27, ☎646 54 08 or 646 52 22)* is a famous "hotel-restaurant-museum" (see p 214) in a lovely two-storey colonial home built in 1775. The tables are set up in the courtyard. Here, guests can dine in the exact setting that Simón Bolívar and his lieutenants did while in Girón. The cuisine is typically *Santandereana*, offering local specialties (see p 211) and a variety of fresh-water fish, served with period dining ware.

ENTERTAINMENT

Events

The cultural events listed below all take place in the Department of Santander:

Reinado Departemental, the crowning of the queen of Santader, in Girón in December;
Feria y Reinado de la Piña, the crowning of the pineapple queen, in Lebrija in August;
Feria de Agricultura, in San Gil, in June;
Feria Bonita, Celebraciones Populares, Feria Ganadera, a fair with many organized events, in Bucaramanga in September.

MANIZALES AND THE DEPARTMENT OF CALDAS

According to experts, some of the world's best coffee is produced in Colombia's departments of Caldas, Quindío and Risaralda. This dramatic region of jagged mountains encompasses numerous climates, including the snow-capped peaks of the Andes (the highest is the Nevado del Ruiz, at 5,400 m), the humid tropical forests and the sweltering valleys of the Río Cauca and Río Magdalena.

Caldas was once part of the departments of Quindío and Risaralda, but became its own department in 1905. Today, it covers an area of 7,888 square kilometres and is home to close to one million inhabitants.

Caldas is bordered by the department of Anitoquia to the north, Risaralda and Tolima to the south, Cundinamarca to the east and Risaralda to the west. Maizales is its capital city.

Manizales

Manizales is a tranquil city, but is nevertheless quite dynamic since it is near three of the country's largest economic centres, Santafé de Bogotá, Medellín and Santiago de Cali. Manizales was almost completely destroyed in two separate fires that occurred in 1925 and 1926, but was quickly rebuilt.

A Brief History

Founded by a group of pioneers from Antioquia on October 12, 1849, Manizales began as a small settlement on what is now the eastern fringe of the city, known as La Enea. One year later, on October 1, 1850, the government of Antioquia created the district of Manizales some 250 kilometres from Medellín.

The vitality of these first settlers was passed down through the generations, allowing the small city to grow rapidly. Manizales is now a modern city, which has still managed to preserve aspects of its origins in Antioquia.

Manizales Today

The *ciudad de las puertas abiertas*, or "city of open doors", as it is often called, is an important economic and industrial centre devoted almost entirely to coffee production. Perched at an altitude of 2,500 metres, Manizales has an average temperature of 17°C. This city of less than 500,000 inhabitants nevertheless has six universities: the Universidad Autonoma, Universidad de Caldas, Universidad Católica, Universidad de Manizales, Universidad Nacional de Colombia, and Universidad Antonio Nariño. Manizales was hard hit by the eruption of Nevado del Ruiz in 1985, and the government decreed the devastated area exempt from taxes in order to help the recovery process. This allowed the city to be quickly rebuilt, and new industries to be developed. Today, Manizales has a European flavour and in some ways resembles cities in the interior of Spain with its friendly bars where many *Manizaleños* go to relax after work. A strange tranquillity also pervades the city, which is rare in Colombia! You don't hear music blasting everywhere and at all hours as is often the case in other Colombian cities. Nor do you see many armed guards. Rather, Manizales is refreshing in that you can walk around everywhere without danger.

 ## FINDING YOUR WAY AROUND

Calles run east-west and the numbers increase from north to south. *Carreras* run north-south, and the numbers increase from east to west.

By Plane

The **Aeropuerto La Nubia** is in the far southeastern part of the city *(Km 8, vía Bogotá,* ☎*71 54 39)* and receives only local flights. Here is the schedule for direct Avianca flights: Bogotá, every day 7:55am and 5:25pm, 105,000 pesos.

Here are the addresses for local airlines:

Aces, Calle 24 No. 21-34, Room 1b, ☎83 22 37. Also Carrera 23 No. 62-16, Room 110, ☎85 84 88
Avianca, Calle 23 No. 21-19, ☎84 70 88. Also corner of Carrera 23 and Calle 64, Edicifio Cervantes, ☎86 77 21

By Bus

The **Terminal de Transportes** is in a new building near the downtown *(between Carreras 14a and 17 and Calles 18 and 19,* ☎*83 54 25).* However, it is best to take a taxi to get there. Several bus companies have departures from the bus station, including Expreso Bolivariano, Expreso Palmira, Expreso Trejos and Rápida Tolima, and there are *colectivos* and *aerovans* that run to Medellín (3 h), Bogotá (7 h) and Cali (7 h), as well. There are regular departures, but it is best to find out the schedule in advance if you are travelling long distances.

Public Transportation

Buses run throughout the city on regular schedules, but all the attractions described in this chapter can easily be reached on foot, except, of course, the "Coffee Route", which runs to *fincas* (farms) that grow coffee outside the city.

Renting a Car

Traffic is not too stressful in Manizales, compared to other Colombian cities. Renting a car also allows you to enjoy the beautiful mountainous countryside around Manizales, with its many coffee *fincas*.

Hertz, Carrera 22 No. 20-20, Las Colinas hotel, ☎84 20 09.

 ## PRACTICAL INFORMATION

Area Code: 68.

Mail

Mail service is provided by **Avianca**, Calle 23 No. 21 19.

Banks

Banks are open Monday to Thursday, from 8am to 11:30pm and from 2pm to 4pm, and Fridays until 4:30pm. The **Banco Industrial Colombiano** *(Calle 21, corner of Carrera 22)* cashes traveller's cheques and exchanges currency. The **Banco Anglo Colombiano** *(Carrera 22 No. 17-04)* and **Banco de la República** *(Carrera 23 No. 23-06)* usually cash traveller's cheques, but do not exchange currency.

Tourist Information

Fomento y Turismo, corner of Carrera 22 and Calle 26, Edificio Licorera, 1st Floor, ☎84 62 11.

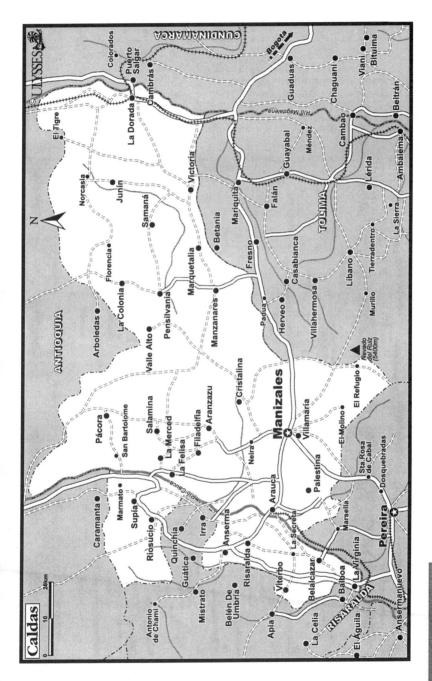

A Notice to Travellers

The city of Manizales and the Department of Caldas were hard hit by the earthquake which struck Colombia in late January, 1999. Because this natural disaster took place shortly before press time, it was not possible to update the information in this chapter. Travellers should thus take note that some of the attractions and establishments listed in this region may have suffered damages, and may be temporarily closed.

Excursions

Local tourist agencies offer various excursions, including winter camping on the Nevado del Ruiz which erupted in 1985, killing more than 20,000 people.

The region is best known for its tours along the Routa de Juan Valdez (the coffee route), which visits coffee *fincas* (farms) along the way. Two such excursions are (see also p 222):

Package 1, **Juan Valdez en la montañas cafeteras**: this excursion explains how coffee, Colombia's main export, is grown. Lasting seven days and six nights, the package includes accommodations at coffee farms, some of which are perched at altitudes of over 4,000 metres, as well as meals, transportation, and even insurance. It costs about 550,000 pesos per person, double occupancy. Bring along beach clothes as well as warmer clothing for the mountains, since the temperatures range from 5°C to 35°C.

Package 2, **Juan Valdez en las murallas, la playa y el cafetal**: this excursion lasts 12 days and 11 nights, and offers the best of both worlds, combining Colombia's beaches and mountains. The first five days are spent in Cartagena de Indias, and include hotel, breakfast, and deep-sea diving, while the last seven days are spent in the mountains and include accommodations, all meals and transportation. It costs about 1,350,000 pesos per person, double occupancy. Bring along beach clothes as well as warmer clothing for the mountains, since the temperatures range from 5°C to 35°C.

You can stay at different *fincas*, whose prices will vary depending on the services they offer. Camping in the snow is available at the Laguna del Otún, the Reserva de Normandia or at Santa Isabel. Other excursions include daytrips to Nevada del Ruiz, the Parque Nacional de Café and various other sites.

Here are the addresses of several travel agencies and tour guides:

Cafetales, Carretera al Magdalena No. 74-71, Edificio Andi, Office 905, ☎/≈87 31 60 or 87 00 36, nrgonzal@col2.telecom.com.co

Condores, corner of Calle 23 and Carrera 21, Room 109, Edificio Tomanaco, ☎80 25 26, ≈80 82 30, condores@eccel.com. Ask for Ximena Dávila Mejía. Ximena has a degree in tourism, speaks English and is a very dynamic and enterprising individual.

Agencia de Viajes Tour Colombia Calle 22 No. 23-23, ☎84 66 99, ≈82 87 56.

Javier Echavarria C. ☎80 83 00 or 74 01 16.

 EXPLORING

Manizales ★

Manizales is a lovely town, but apart from the "Coffee Route" and excursions in the vicinity (see p 222), it does not offer very much in the way of tourist attractions. In fact, due to several cataclysmic natural disasters, including earthquakes in 1875 and 1879, fires in 1925 and 1926, and volcanic eruptions, most notably the devastating explosion of Nevado del Ruiz in November 1985, the city has been almost entirely reconstructed and modernized. Nevertheless, several admirable buildings remain to be explored.

Catedral Basílica ★★★ *(Carrera 22, between Calles 22 and 23, south of Plaza Bolívar)* is a Gothic-style church that marks the exact spot where a little chapel was built when the city's foundations were first laid in 1850. Damaged by severe earthquakes, the chapel was replaced by a more substantial building with three belltowers in 1854. Earthquakes destroyed it in 1886. The strong religious faith of the early colonists led to the prompt erection of another

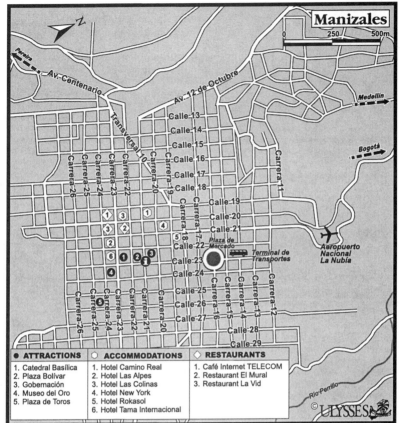

Manizales

0   250   500m

Pereira
Av. Centenario
Transversal-10
Av. 12 de Octubre
Medellín
Bogotá
Calle-13
Calle-14
Calle-15
Calle-16
Calle-17
Calle-18
Calle-19
Calle-20
Calle-21
Plaza de Mercado
Calle-22
Terminal de Transportes
Aeropuerto Nacional La Nubía
Calle-23
Calle-24
Calle-25
Calle-26
Calle-27
Calle-28
Calle-29
Carrera-26
Carrera-25
Carrera-24
Carrera-23
Carrera-22
Carrera-20
Carrera-19
Carrera-18
Carrera-17
Carrera-16
Carrera-15
Carrera-14
Carrera-13
Carrera-12
Carrera-11
Carrera-21
Río Perrillo

● ATTRACTIONS	○ ACCOMMODATIONS	◇ RESTAURANTS
1. Catedral Basílica	1. Hotel Camino Real	1. Café Internet TELECOM
2. Plaza Bolívar	2. Hotel Las Alpes	2. Restaurant El Mural
3. Gobernación	3. Hotel Las Colinas	3. Restaurant La Vid
4. Museo del Oro	4. Hotel New York	
5. Plaza de Toros	5. Hotel Rokasol	
	6. Hotel Tama Internacional	

© ULYSSES

cathedral, built of wood this time. It lasted until March 20, 1926 when it was destroyed by fire.

Architect Julien Polty designed the current cathedral, as the winner of a competition at the École des beaux-arts in Paris, organized by the *Manizaleño* Don Miquel Gutiérrez. The Gothic Revival-style building is made of reinforced concrete. An earthquake in 1979 caused one of its three imposing belltowers to collapse (the highest is 105 metres tall). The cathedral is now restored and is one of the most impressive buildings in Manizales. It stands on the Plaza Bolívar, resplendent with Italian marble, glistening stained glass windows designed by Gerardi and Bonarda, and three bronze doors which depict the history of the city in bas-relief, executed by the Jesuit Eduardo Ospina.

The church's semicircular Romanesque arches were inspired by those of the Hagia Sophia in Istanbul, which was called Byzantium during its domination by the Romans. The pointed arches that contain the stained glass windows are in the Gothic style, whereas the windows themselves come from Greece, Italy and Colombia.

The 12-metre-high canopy over the high altar was designed by the New York firm, Rambush, constructed in Italy by the house of Stuflessu in Ortisei and gilded in Colombia by Don Manuel Vargas.

The style and atmosphere of the **Plaza Bolívar** ★★★ *(between Calles 23 and 23 and Carreras 21 and 22)* in Manizales make it one of the most remarkable in Colombia. Right in the heart of the city, the plaza is constructed of enamelled-brick paving on three levels connected by steps. It is decorated with ceramic murals by *Manizaleño* artist Guillermo Botero, which allude to Colombia's history. Always busy, it is most crowded around 4pm when business offices close. The Cóndor Bolívar is found here, leading to the cathedral and to the building called La Gobernación.

MANIZALES

Cóndor Bolívar

Unveiled on October 12, 1991, the **Cóndor Bolívar** ★★★ *(on the Plaza Bolívar, facing the cathedral)* is an impressive allegorical monument commemorating the Libertador. Perched on a 12-metre-high, tiled-cement pedestal, a six-metre bronze statue of a condor in human form, "a flying centaur", spreads its wings over Manizales (and, by inference, Colombia) to protect it. Attached to the pedestal in front of this figure is a bronze mask of Francisco de Paula Santander, the right-hand man of Bolívar, with an expression that seems to defy time... and today's leaders. Asked about the meaning of the work, the sculptor Rodrigo Arenas Betancur answered sarcastically that they were two demons that had been driven out of the cathedral across the way. This is the same controversial artist who created the bronze dedicated to the Antioqueña people at the Centro Administrativo La Alpujarra in Medellín (see p 221), and three sculptures in Pereira: *El Bolívar Desnudo* on the Plaza Bolívar (see p 238), *El Cristo Sin Cruz* on Avenida 30 de Agosto (see p 238) and *El Monumento à los Fundadores*, Carrera 13 and Calle 13.

La Gobernación ★★ *(north side of the Plaza Bolívar)* is a 19th-century building that was entirely renovated during the years from 1925 to 1927. It is basically in the republican style, with allusions to the Romanesque, baroque, classical and Gothic styles. The building was designed in a rectangular U-shape by architect John Wotard and realized by Italian architect Angello Papio, who was in charge of the construction of several buildings in Manizales. In the inner courtyard is a garden decorated with high relief which lends it a Mudejar character.

The Palacio de Gobierno was declared a national monument in 1984.

Museo del Oro ★★ *(Mon to Fri 9am to 11:30am and 2pm to 5:30pm; Carrera 23 No. 23-06, second floor, ☎84 38 51 ext. 259)* displays a collection of ceramics and gold jewellery from the Quimbaya culture. While it is not the largest gold museum in Colombia, it is a must-see, if only for its description of the ethnographic evolution of the country's first inhabitants. Founded by the Banco de la Repúblic in Santafé de Bogotá in 1939, the Museo del Oro has followed a policy of decentralization. This led to the establishment of the gold museum in Manizales in 1981. This museum specializes in works by the Quimbaya.

Plaza de Toros ★ *(Av. Centenario by way of Av. Pereria)* is an imposing Mudejar structure that was erected some 25 years ago by the engineering firm Borrero y Robledo, and was designed by architect Roberth Vélez. *Corridas* are held here in January to the delight of the *Manizaleños* who are great fans.

La Ruta de Juan Valdez, the "Coffee Route"

The familiar portrait of the *cafetero* Juan Valdez is used in advertising all across Colombia and for Colombian coffee through out the world. Many excursions are based on this image and follow La Ruta de Juan Valdez, leaving from Manizales and lasting from one to several days. They include visits to coffee farms to learn more about the cultivation of coffee. Here is a description of one of the many existing tours on La Ruta de Juan Valdez.

Depart at 9am and return at 12pm. Cost: 30,000 pesos per person. The guide picks up customers at their respective hotels and brings them back at the end of the excursion. His all-terrain vehicle is a truck that has been turned into a sort of bus, with crosswise seats in the back.

Less than 20 minutes from Manizales, the driver turns off onto a small dirt road that climbs up and down the Andes for the rest of the trip. The scenery here is breathtaking: a deep valley where scattered *fincas* appear, some at more than 4,000 metres in altitude, and others down on the floor of the valley.

The guide stops frequently to give explanations. Here, there is a coffee plant, a bush or

El Sombrero Aguadeño

If you like action movies set in Central America, you will, no doubt, be familiar with the Panama, a straw hat named after the country where the ringleaders of the "bad guys" typically reside. These B-flicks are often highly unrealistic, and the Panama is not the least of their inaccuracies. In fact, this *sombrero* originated not in Panamá, but rather in Colombia, in Aguadas to be precise, a small town specializing in handicrafts that is located in the department of Caldas.

The *sombrero aguadeño* – to call it by its proper name – was used by people living in this mountainous region, long before it became popular in Panamá. These people lived on the steep slopes of the Andes, where they cultivated coffee, which became the most renowned in all of Colombia. They used hats woven of dry palm fronds to protect themselves from the intense sun and rain, the two main features of this region's climate.

small tree, beginning to show its small white flowers. There, a plant bears both green and red berries at the same time. Over there is one with flowers as well as berries in both colours, an unusual phenomenon that is characteristic of the coffee plant. The green fruit take seven months to fully ripen. Further on, a *cafetero* (a coffee industry worker) harvests the berries by hand on a slope with a pitch of more than 80 degrees. Is he using a rappelling rope or other climbing equipment? Certainly not! The occupation of *cafetero* is handed down from father to son with many patient demonstrations of traditional technique, although all young *cafeteros* attend one of the department's agricultural schools.

Later, a two-storey white *finca* with a red ceramic-tile roof appears beneath the trees. Of course, the coffee that is served is made from beans (seeds of the coffee berries) grown on the farm. This is a splendid setting with a view of the entire valley from the farm situated right in the middle of it.

Inside, the country kitchen offers every comfort. The walls and floor are covered in ceramic tiles, and the central table and chairs are made from brown wood. Upstairs are a red-painted balcony and bedrooms that are simply furnished but functional. Overnight stays can be arranged by the travel agency. The prices vary according to the quality of the *finca*. Some have heated, in-ground swimming pools and offer amenities worthy of luxury inns.

The other farm buildings are used in the various stages of processing the coffee beans: one is for mechanical drying, another for packing. The guide continues his explanations through questions addressed to a *cafetero*. Another delicious cup of coffee is savoured, and guests are

presented with a gift-wrapped souvenir of the trip. It is a few pounds or kilos of coffee beans in a jute sack encased in a wooden box bearing the name of the *finca* and the image of Juan Valdez.

 ACCOMMODATIONS

Most of the farms in the region of Manizales offer accommodations. Enquire at a travel agency. Otherwise, all of Manizales' recommendable hotels are in the downtown area.

Hotel Las Alpes *($; pb, hw, ☎, ≡, ⊗, tv, ◙, ℜ; Carrera 24 No. 22-52, ☎82 73 39 or 82 14 83)* is small, 12-room hotel with carpets and comfortable furniture. The hotel is set in a recently renovated old colonial house that offers every comfort one could wish for at reasonable rates. The reception is friendly and the owner speaks English.

Hotel New York *($; pb, hw; Calle 20 No. 20-17, ☎82 38 99)* is an old hotel run by an elderly woman. The hotel sets itself apart with its high ceilings and huge rooms. The rooms' wooden double doors are elegant, but the hotel is only suitable for travellers with limited budgets. Single rooms without bathrooms, telephones or televisions are available for 7,000 pesos per person. The common shower has hot running water. Rooms with showers and televisions cost 30,000 for one or two people.

Hotel Rokasol *($; pb, hw, ☎, tv, ◙; Calle 21 No. 19-16, ☎84 20 84 or 84 76 81, ⇝84 77 22)* offers 42 clean rooms and no extras. This is a hotel with neither style nor history, but is adequate for travellers with restricted budgets.

 Hotel Tama Internacional *($; pb, hw, ☎, mb, tv, ▣, ℛ; Calle 23 No. 22-43, ☎84 77 11 or 84 21 24, ⊸84 76 10)* is hard to find because it shares an entrance with a ground-floor restaurant. Nonetheless, it is a very stylish hotel set on the second storey of an old colonial house with high ceilings and an interior balcony that offers a spectacular view of the downstairs restaurant. The 30 rooms are ordinary and simply furnished. Nevertheless, all of the necessary comforts are provided in a warm family atmosphere.

Hotel Camino Real *($$-$$$; pb, hw, ☎, ⊛, ▣, ℛ; Carrera 21 No. 20-45, ☎84 55 88, 84 54 70 or 84 06 32, ⊸84 61 31)* is a two-star hotel with no charm that offers 42 clean, adequate, simply furnished rooms, some of which open onto the street. Since traffic is only busy at the end of the work day, this last detail is not a disadvantage. The staff is likeable and dedicated.

 Hotel Las Colinas *($$$$; pb, hw, ▣, ☎, tv, mb, ℛ, bar; Carrera 22 No. 20-20, ☎84 20 01 or 84 18 16, ⊸84 15 90)* is the best hotel in Manizales. Set in the heart of downtown, next to Plaza Bolívar, this three-star hotel has 63 rooms and 3 adequately furnished suites. Its lobby is dark and haphazardly decorated. The Las Colinas may not be a great hotel, but its staff go out of their way to be pleasant, both at the front desk – where a bit of English is also spoken – and in the restaurant, El Mural (see further below). The same holds true for the bar and the room service. Do not hesitate to call on the public relations agent, Luisa Liliana Velásquez, with any questions about Manizales. Her competence and charm are undeniable.

RESTAURANTS

Downtown Manizales has many restaurants, and you will find a broad selection of fast-food and specialized restaurants simply by walking along the streets. The cuisine is not top-class, but restaurants that serve regional fare are generally good and economical. Here again, restaurants are little frequented at night except in hotels that serve their guests.

Café Internet TELECOM *($; every day 10am to noon and 2pm to 8pm; Carrera 23 and Calle 20, ☎84 20 30, cafealpha@col2.telecom.com.co)* is a small Internet Café. It serves beverages and sandwiches. Clients can use the Internet for 1,200 pesos for 15 minutes, and print documents for 300 pesos per page.

Gran China *($; every day 11:30am to 11pm; Carrera 23 No. 55-30, ☎85 40 25)* offers no-fuss Chinese fare – the beef with vegetables is served with french fries – in a small dining room with a few plain tables. The restaurant mostly delivers.

 Restaurant La Vid *($; Sun to Fri noon to 6pm; Carrera 23 No. 22-26, ☎82 01 77)* is a vegetarian restaurant set in a small, pleasant, second-floor dining room. The hostess is very pleasant. The usual dishes of this type of cuisine are served.

El Mural *($$-$$$; every day 7am to 10pm; Carrera 22 No. 20-20, ☎84 20 09)* is the restaurant of the Las Colinas hotel (see further above). Set in a huge third-floor room, the restaurant is bustling during the week, when the hotel receives convention groups, despite its chilly decor. The international cuisine is excellent and varied. The service is impeccable.

 ENTERTAINMENT

Manizales boasts that it is the first Colombian city to have organized *ferias* (fairs). A few social and cultural events spice up life in the city, its surrounding and the department of Caldas. Here are a few of them:

Feria Anual de Manizales, held every January;

Reinado Internacional del Café, the crowning of the coffee queen, in Manizales, in January;

Carnaval del Diablo, a colourful carnival held in January in Riosucio;

Feria Exposición Equina, the Manizales equestrian exhibition, in March;

Festival del Imagen, a festival of film, video photography and computer graphics, in Manizales, in April;

Festival Latino-Americano de Teatro, a festival that features theatre troupes from all over Latin America, in Manizales, in September.

SHOPPING

Manizales' craft shops are tourist attractions in themselves, displaying the famous *sombrero aguadeño* and the *mulera caldense*. They also sell other handmade clothing and coffee gift packages.

Almacén Artístico, Carrera 23 No. 24-06, ☎84 63 85

Artisanías Dian, Carrera 22 No. 30-64, ☎83 42 85

Artisanías de Aguadas, Carrera 22 No. 28-14, ☎83 44 49

Artisanías de Colombia, Carrera 21 No. 26-10, ☎84 78 74

Coffee Tree

ARMENIA AND THE DEPARTMENT OF QUINDÍO

Q uindío's name is said to have originated with the indigenous tribe of the Quindús. It may also be the misspelling of *quimbaya*, a word that means "eden." Quindío covers an area of 1,960 square kilometres and is bordered by the departments of Risaralda to the north, Valle del Cauca to the southeast, and Tolíma to the southwest. Made into a department only in 1996, Quindío has a population of over 500,000 inhabitants, half of whom live in its capital, Armenia.

Quindío has an unstable climate. Its temperatures range from 10° to 24°C, with an average of 20°C. Summers are usually in December and January, as well as July and August. Winters set in around April and May, and again in October and November. The times of the seasons can vary, as no one can predict them with any certainty.

Coffee is Quindío's main crop. With yields that are the highest per hectare in the world, the department, together with neighbouring Caldas and Risaralda, has one of Colombia's most interesting tourist routes: the "Coffee Road". Other crops include plantain, guava, citrus fruit, sugarcane, cocoa beans, and tomatoes, whose trees reach heights of four to five metres. Asparagus, mushrooms, beans, corn, potatoes, and tobacco are also grown. Beef, sheep and chickens are raised; other agricultural activities include fish farming and beekeeping.

Quindío's industries include construction, the manufacturing of furniture and shoes, and crafts. Situated between 1,200 and 3,000 metres in altitude, Quindío has 12 major municipalities : Buenavista, Filandia, Calarcá, Circasia, La Tabaida, Montenegro, Quimbaya, Córdova, Pijao, Génova, Salento, and the capital, Armenia.

Armenia

On the flanks of the central cordillera, at 1,438 metres altitude, Armenia offers some of Colombia's most pleasant weather, with an average temperature of 20°C. Its inhabitants are friendly and welcoming towards foreigners. Armenia's relative tranquillity resembles that still reigning in the small towns of Spain, Portugal, and Italy.

A Brief History

Quindío was founded on October 14, 1889 by Jesús María Ocampo Toro, accompanied by Jesús María Suáres, Nicolás Macías, Hipólito Nieto and other colonists, on the territory of the Sinús – a tribe related to the Quimbayas. Armenia took its name from a *hacienda* that stood on its territory, which had been named in honour of the peasants killed during that time by Shakir Bajá in the Caucasian country of

Armenia, once a republic that belonged to the former Soviet Union.

A Notice to Travellers

The city of Armenia and the Department of Quindío were hit by several severe earthquakes which struck Colombia in late January, 1999. Because this natural disaster took place shortly before press time, it was not possible to update the information in this chapter. Travellers should thus take note that some of the attractions and establishments listed in this region may have suffered damages, and may be temporarily closed.

 FINDING YOUR WAY AROUND

Armenia's *calles* and *carreras* are all numbered. The calles run east-west, and the numbers increase as you head north. The carreras run north-south, and their numbers increase as you head east.

By Plane

The **Aeropuerto Nacional El Edén** *(vía La Tabaida, ☎47 94 00)* is located to the southwest, about 18 kilometres from downtown, on the road from Santiago to Cali. It is more easily reached by taxi *(6,000 pesos)*, but the bus marked "Aeropuerto" on Carrera 19 will also take you there.

Avianca offers direct flights from Armenia to Bogotá: Mon to Thu and Sat at 7:17am, Fri at 9:05am, every day at 12:51pm and 7:15pm; 105,000 pesos.

The Aeropuerto Nacional El Edén is served by Colombia's two major airlines, as well as American Airlines.

Aces, Carrera 15 No. 21-27, ☎44 40 83.
Avianca, Carrera 15 No. 19-38, ☎44 26 17 or 44 79 30.
American Airlines, Calle 20 No. 14-30, ☎46 35 25.

By Bus

The **Terminal de Transportes** is also located southwest of the city, at the corner of Carrera 19 and Calle 35. Buses running along Carrera 19 from downtown stop here regularly. It costs about 5,000 pesos for a one-way taxi ride from downtown to the Terminal.

The following bus companies service destinations such as Santafé de Bogotá (8 hours) and Santiago de Cali (4 hours).

Expreso Palmira, Calle 35 No. 20-68, ☎44 40 83 or 47 19 31.
Flota Occidental, Calle 35 No. 20-68, ☎47 58 86 or 47 46 16.
Nuevo Rápido Quindío, Calle 35 No. 20-68, ☎47 45 15 or 47 72 49.

Public Transportation

City buses regularly run in all directions across the city *(350 pesos)*, but all the attractions can be reached on foot, except for the *fincas* and the "coffee road".

By Taxi

Taxis are ochre yellow and marked *Servicio Público*. They are equipped with taximetres, and a short trip should not cost more than 1,000 pesos, and never more than 2,000 pesos for longer distances within the city limits, such as to the Museo del Oro. You can also hire a cab by the hour for a rate of 6,000 pesos.

 PRACTICAL INFORMATION

Area code: 6.

Mail

Mail service is provided at the offices of **Avianca**, Carrera 15 No. 19-38.

ARMENIA

Quindío

N

Pereira
RISARALDA
Cartago
Filandia
Villa Rodas
Quimbaya
Salento
Juntas
Circasia
Parque Nacional del Café
Montenegro
Armenia
Calarca
Toche
La Tebaida
QUINDÍO
Ibague
TOLIMA
Bógotá
Buenavista
Córdoba
VALLE DEL CAÚCA
Pijao
La Cima
La Floresta
Guadual
Sevilla
Aures
Genova
Rovira
Ríomanso
Cumbarco
Santa Helena

© ULYSSES

0   12.5   25km

Banks

The **Banco Industrial Colombiano** *(every day 8am to 4pm; Calle 20, between Carreras 15 and 16)* cashes traveller's cheques and exchanges foreign currency.

Tourist Information

Anato is the Colombian association of travel agents, Calle 20 No. 14-30, ☎41 11 11; **Corporación de Fomento y Turismo de Armenia**, Calle 20 No. 15-31, ☎41 04 41, 41 35 86 or 41 35 96;

Secretaría de Cultura, Artesanía y Turismo, Calle 20 No. 13-22, first floor, ☎41 42 80, extension 276;
Fundo Mixto de Promoción Turística del Quindío, Carrera 14, corner of Calle 13, Edificio Cámara de Comercio, second floor, ☎41 28 10.

Excursions

Many organized excursions leave from Armenia, since travel agents offer trips to the numerous *fincas* and cities within Quindío, as well as the must-see Parque Nacional del Café (see p 230). The following travel agencies can plan excursions according to any traveller's needs:

Viajes Palma de Cera, Calle 19 No. 13-45, ☎41 42 43;
Viajes Armenia, Carrera 15 No. 21-61, ☎44 95 44;
Viajes Quindío, Carrera 14 No. 20-12, ☎44 11 94;
Quinditour, Calle 20 No. 14-30, ☎41 11 11.

 EXPLORING

Although it is a quaint town, Armenia offers but few tourist attractions, as most of the interesting sites are in the countryside. Just remember that while the downtown core is considered safe, other areas are to be avoided at night.

The **Catedral de la Inmaculada** ★★ *(Plaza de Bolívar, Carrera 14, between Calles 20 and 21)* is one of Colombia's most modern cathedrals. It is shaped like a Latin cross and its structure forms a capital 'A' that is contained within a larger A-shaped exterior. The cathedral's impressive exterior is flanked by a 40-metre obelisk that is its belltower. Inside, there is a splendid Byzantine-style mural, as well as marble sculptures and stained-glass windows by artist Antonion Valencia.

The **Plaza Bolívar** ★★★ *(between Carreras 13 and 14 and Calles 20 and 21)* is the civic heart of the city. It contains an admirable bronze sculpture dedicated to the vision, effort, and tenacity of the first colonists, the *Monumento al Esfuerzo*, inaugurated on December 17, 1979. The work was created by sculptor Rodrigo Arenas Betancur, whose pieces are also displayed in the Plaza Bolívar: *El Bolívar Desnudo*, the *Monumento a los Fundadores* and the *Cristo sin Cruz Pereira* (see p 238). Elsewhere, Betancur's *Cóndor Bolívar* stands in the Plaza Bolívar de Manizales (see p 221) and another graces the Centro Administrativo La Alpujarra in Medellín. Finally, Plaza Bolívar does indeed display a bronze of Simón Bolívar himself, inaugurated on December 17, 1930, and the work of *quindiano* artist Roberto Henao Buriticá, who poured it in Paris.

The **Museo del Oro** ★★★ *(Tue to Fri 10am to 5pm, Sat to Sun 10am to 5pm; Av. Bolívar, corner of Calle 40n, ☎49 38 20 or 321 33 00, ⊷49 44 26)* is the most modern gold museum in Colombia, and is owned by the Banco de la República. Opened on July 25, 1986, it was designed by architect Rogelio Salmona, who then went on to win Colombia's first prize in

architecture for his work in 1986-1987. The museum is located on the outskirts of Armenia, but is easily reached by taking the bus heading north on Calle 14.

The museum is divided into seven lower rooms built of red brick that lead to two spacious interior courtyards enjoined by red-bricked hallways. There are a reading room, a documentation room, a cafeteria, gardens, and an open-air theatre. Many beautiful gold pieces from the Quimbaya culture are on display here, includes chest plates and bracelets and other items that they commonly used.

The **Parque Nacional del Café** ★★★ is less than a 20-minutes' drive from Armenia, and just a few kilometres outside the small town of Montenegro. Here, visitors can learn more about coffee cultivation and the manufacturing process, from the choice of the beans at the plantation to the care, harvest, drying, roasting, packaging of the coffee, and finally the shipping to the stores and sales.

Located in a vast lush environment, the *Parque Nacional del Café* is home to the Coffee Museum, conference rooms, and a 30-metre watchtower from which there is an exceptional view over the entire region. The two-hour stroll takes visitors along a four-kilometre path through magnificent gardens, including one that highlights South American Indian legends and another filled with orchids, which are the emblem of the department of Quindío.

 ACCOMMODATIONS

Most of the coffee *fincas* (farms) in the department of Quindío offer accommodation; however this kind of lodging also requires the assistance of a special agency since the *fincas* are located outside the cities. As for hotels, most are situated downtown, but beware of the hotels used by prostitutes near the market. Instead, try the following:

The **Hotel Zatama** *($; pb, hw, ⊗, ☎, tv, ℜ; Carrera 15 No. 16-22, ☎45 35 76 or 45 15 24)* has 72 cheap rooms with no special charm, though it should satisfy travellers on a small budget.

The **Hotel Izcay** *($$; pb, hw, ▣, ⊗, ☎, tv, ℜ; Calle 22 No. 14-05, ☎41 02 63, 41 02 64, 41 02 65 or 41 02 66, ⊷44 05 68)* though

ARMENIA

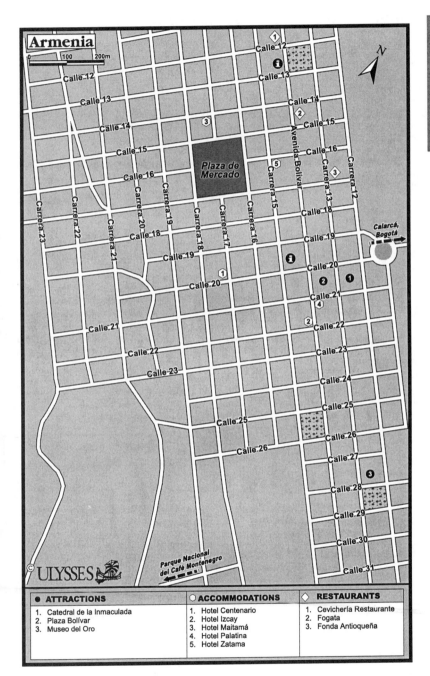

Armenia

0   100   200m

Calle 12
Calle 13
Calle 14
Calle 15
Calle 16

Calle 12
Calle 13
Calle 14
Calle 15
Calle 16

Calle 18
Calle 19

Plaza de Mercado

Avenida Bolívar

Carrera 23
Carrera 22
Carrera 21
Carrera 20
Carrera 19
Carrera 18
Carrera 17
Carrera 16
Carrera 15
Carrera 13
Carrera 12

Calle 18
Calle 19
Calle 20

Calle 19
Calle 20

Calle 21
Calle 22
Calle 23

Calle 20
Calle 21
Calle 22
Calle 23
Calle 24
Calle 25
Calle 26
Calle 27
Calle 28
Calle 29
Calle 30
Calle 31

Calle 25
Calle 26

Calarcá, Bogotá

Parque Nacional del Café Montenegro

© ULYSSES

● ATTRACTIONS	○ ACCOMMODATIONS	◇ RESTAURANTS
1. Catedral de la Inmaculada	1. Hotel Centenario	1. Cevichería Restaurante
2. Plaza Bolívar	2. Hotel Izcay	2. Fogata
3. Museo del Oro	3. Hotel Maitamá	3. Fonda Antioqueña
	4. Hotel Palatina	
	5. Hotel Zatama	

The Indians of Viejo Caldas

Quimbaya is the name of the indigenous peoples who once inhabited present-day El Viejo Caldas, a region comprising the departments of Caldas, Risaralda and Quindío and Valle del Cauca, on the western flank of the central cordillera. There, they farmed and were excellent goldsmiths. Other than the Spanish, who were their main enemy, the Panches and the Pijaos, also dwelled on the western slope.

The Quimbaya were peaceful people, offering little or no resistance to the conquistadores, unlike their warring neighbours, the Armas, the Paucuras, the Pozos, and the Picaras, who cannibalised each other, a war ritual that involved eating the defeated enemy's flesh and keeping the remaining body parts as war trophies. Dismembered and embalmed bodies could be found at the entrance to the tribal chief's dwelling, along with skulls which, when covered with sculpted beeswax, still looked alive, sending a clear and foreboding message to any enemy.

Extinction

The beginning of the Spanish Conquest and the arrival of General Jorge Robledo in the 16th century meant the beginning of the end for the Quimbaya. The numerous confrontations provoked by the Spanish and the loss of their freedom and ancestral autonomy through slavery only contributed to the disappearance of their culture whose remnants still haunt the Viejo Caldas today.

During the 19th century, people became more aware of this culture's past as farmers began unearthing tombs and discovering precious objects belonging to the Quimbaya. More recently, archaeological digs and ethnographic research have led to great advances in the reconstruction of their history along with that of neighbouring groups at the time, which constitute an important part of Colombia's past.

admittedly not an attractive hotel, is good value for the price. It is located near the downtown amenities, inside a five-storey building with 60 average-looking rooms. Friendly staff. A good bet for those looking for simple and quiet accommodation.

The **Hotel Maitamá** *($$; pb, hw, ▣, mb, ⊗, ☎, tv, ℛ; Carrera 17 No. 14-05, ☎41 04 88, ⊷44 93 08)* has 70 rooms and four suites on six floors. The price includes either continental or American breakfast. An average hotel.

The **Hotel Palatina** *($$; pb, hw, ▣, mb, ⊗, ☎, tv, ℛ; Calle 21 No. 14-49, ☎41 27 30, 41 27 40 or 41 27 44)* is another unpretentious hotel. It is mid-sized and clean, with a staff devoted to their clientele. Rooms are well-furnished and comfortable.

The **Hotel Centenario** *($$$; pb, hw, ⊘, ▣, mb, ⊗, ☎, tv, ℛ, bar; Calle 21 No. 18-20, ☎43 31 43, ⊷41 13 21)* is a convenient hotel with 60 clean and decent rooms on four floors of a modern but rather unattractive building. Here as well, personnel is warm and welcom-

ing. It has a workout room, a sauna, a Turkish bath and even some parking.

 RESTAURANTS

As in the rest of Colombia, fast-food chains abound throughout downtown Armenia. However, these following restaurants offer surprising value and good service.

Fonda Antioqueña *($; every day 7am to 10pm; Carrera 13 No. 18-55, ☎44 49 58)* serves regional cuisine, such as *bandeja paisa*, a generous portion of beans and ground meat, plantains and rice. And then there are the famous *arepas*. Or even *sancocho*, a soup made from potatoes, plantains and guava served with either chicken, pork, or beef, used to make the bouillon. Of course, it is also eaten with *arepas*.

The **Cevichería Restaurante** *($$; Mon to Sat 11:30am to 10pm, Sun 11am to 4pm; Carrera 14 No. 11-62, F45 32 05)* serves fish and

Parque Nacional del Café

seafood from the Pacific. It is a small and charming restaurant, but unfortunately it does not seem to be catching on.

 Asadero Sierra Dorada *($$$ every day 11am to 10pm; Av. Bolívar No. 1-160, ☎46 37 50)* is another seafood restaurant with seating either inside or on its patio. Furnished with long wooden tables, the dining room has such a laid-back atmosphere that you feels like you're right on the beach. But don't be fooled. The service here is professional and efficient, and the food is renowned for good reason, as rave reviews often appear in the Quindío media

 Fogata *($$$; every day 11:30am to 11pm; Av. Bolívar No. 14n-39, ☎49 59 80)* is without a doubt Armenia's best restaurant. It is also the preferred meeting place for the city's elite who often come there. It has a patio hidden behind some beautiful trees; however, since Fogata is at the corner of two major avenues, it may be more pleasant to sit in the V-shaped dining room with glass panels on both sides. The menu offers meat and fish entrees which are cooked on wooden charcoals in the kitchen just next to the entrance. French and Chilean wines make up the extensive wine list.

ENTERTAINMENT

Several cultural and social festivals are organized in Quindío throughout the year. Here are a few of interest:

Temporada Taurina, the corridas that take place in January in Armenia;

Reinado Nacional del Café, the crowning of the coffee queen in June in Calarcá;

Concurso del Alumbrado, a competition involving candles and lanterns in December in Quimbaya.

 SHOPPING

Armenia produces many crafts including items made in plaster, wood, and clay, as well as cotton and woolen clothing. Since horses and donkeys still abound in the countryside, leather has remained an important commodity. Armenian artisans are thus expert saddle-makers, and produce other riding accessories. Try the following shops:

Tumbaga, Calle 20a No. 15-30, ☎44 86 20;
Savi, Carrera 16 No. 21-29, ☎44 01 15;
Ema, Calle 19 No. 13-38, room 3, ☎44 31 27.

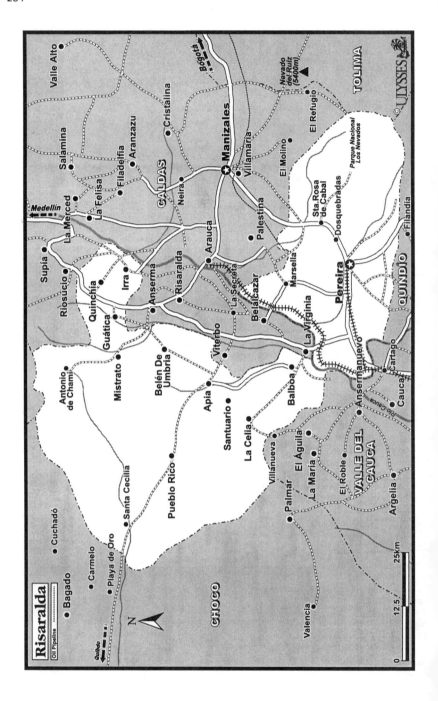

Caribbean Sea

PANAMÁ

VENEZUELA

Pacific
Ocean

RISARALDA
Pereira

Pacific
Ocean

ECUADOR

BRAZIL

PERÚ

PEREIRA AND THE DEPARTMENT OF RISARALDA

R isaralda covers a surface area of 4,014 square kilometres, or barely three percent of the whole country, with a population of close to one million people, most of whom are city-dwellers (88%). The department is bordered by Antioquia and Caldas to the north, Quindío and de Valle del Cauca to the south, Caldas and Tolima to the east and Chocó to the west. The volcanic ash found in the region's soil renders it exceptionally fertile. Numerous rivers and their tributaries flow through the territory, including the Río Risaralda, Río Otún, Río La Vieja, Río Cauca and the Río Barbas. The department's climate varies from the humid warmth of the lower valley to the cold temperatures of the high Andes. The region's annual average temperature is 21°C, with two rainy seasons from April to June and September to November.

Risaralda is composed of 14 municipalities including Apía, Balboa, Belén de Umbría, Dos Quebradas, Guática, La Celia, La Virginia, Marsella, Mistrató, Pueblo Rico, Quinchía, Santa Rosa de Cabral, Sanctuario and the capital, Pereira. The well-developed road network allows for easy travel between cities. Risaralda prides itself on the cooperation that exists between the department's government, industrial and commercial enterprises and schools, which furthers development.

Pereira

Pereira, the capital of the department of Risaralda, is located in a small valley of the central cordillera at some 1,400 metres above sea level, and is bathed by the Río Otún. Covering a surface area of 609 square kilometres, it has a population of some 500,000 inhabitants known for their amiability, entrepreneurial spirit and ingenuity.

A Brief History

The city's history begins in the distant past, at a time when Quimbaya goldsmiths were developing more advanced methods which influenced the work of neighbouring peoples for many generations.

In 1541, several years after the region was first discovered, marshal Jorge Robledo established a small settlement that he named Cartago. Following numerous altercations with the neighbouring native communities, he moved the town to its present-day location on the shores of the Río La Vieja, in 1691.

Some 150 years passed before Francisco Pereira Martínez decided to re-establish a settlement on the original site. However, he died before he could realize his dream, and it was his friend, the priest Remigio Antonio

Cañarte, who ultimately brought it about. Together with a group of men, he made his way to what is now Plaza Bolívar and celebrated a mass there on August 30, 1863.

Pereira Today

Although it is only a medium-sized city, Pereira is the department's capital and one of Columbia's main urban centres, boasting a total of eight universities (Universidad Tecnológica de Pereira, Universidad Católica Popular de Risaralda, Universidad Cooperativa, Universidad Libre, Universidad Antonio Nariño, Universidad del Area Andina, Universidad de Santo Tomás and the Seccional de EAFIT). Its main industries include food processing (chicken, coffee and beverages), textiles (high-quality clothing and leather), lumber (including paper and furniture), metal work and heavy machinery and related equipment. Pereira's dynamic nature can be observed by strolling through the downtown core between 4 and 7pm, when offices close and even the sidewalks are overrun with people. Pereira is a peaceful town, however, and you can walk around taking a minimum of safety precautions.

 FINDING YOUR WAY AROUND

Pereira's *calles* run north-south and the numbers increase from east to west. *Carreras* run east-west and their numbers increase from north to south. If there are avenues, they follow the direction of the *calles* or *carreras* and are similarly numbered.

By Plane

Aeropuerto Internacional Matecaña *(Av. 30 de Agosto, ☎36 00 21)* is located less than 15 minutes south of town. Buses run from the airport to downtown; look for the "El Centro-Matecaña" sign in the front windshield.

There is a flight to Miami with stopovers every day at 6:39am.

Avianca's schedule for direct flights to Bogotá is: 6:39am, 7:25am, 9:59am, 12:21pm, 3:15pm, 6:20pm every day; 7:25pm Mon to Fri; Mon, Fri to Sun 9:20pm; 105,000 pesos.

The following national and international airlines currently serve Pereira:

National Airlines

Aces, Av. Circunvalar, room 111, ☎24 22 37, at the airport ☎36 00 21.
Avianca, Calle 19 No. 6-28, ☎35 85 09, at the airport ☎36 00 29.
Aires, Aeropuerto Internacional Matecaña, ☎26 11 48 or 36 96 03.
Intercontinental de Aviación, Calle 22 No. 7-38, ☎35 04 81, at the airport ☎36 49 91.
SAM, Carrera 8a No. 22-02, ☎35 21 12, at the airport ☎36 00 29.
Air Pereira, Aeropuerto Internacional, Matecaña, ☎26 10 66.
Saturno Ltda, Aeropuerto Internacional Matecaña, ☎26 06 51.

International Airlines

Aerolinas Argentinas, Calle 21 No. 8-48, 3rd floor, ☎34 37 61, 34 08 50 or 35 17 72.
Aeroperú, Calle 21 No. 8-24, ☎34 20 50.
American Airlines, Calle 18 No. 7-59, Suite 501, ☎34 40 82.
British Airways, Calle 21 No. 8-24, ☎34 20 50.
Copa, Calle 100 No. 8a-49, ☎26 93 70.
Iberia, Calle 21 No. 8-48, 3rd floor, ☎34 37 61, 34 08 50 or 35 17 72.
KLM, Av. Circunvalar No. 12-32, Suite 201, ☎35 77 29.
Lan Chile, Calle 21 No. 8-24, ☎34 20 50.
Lufthansa, Carrera 7a, Suite 301, ☎25 89 30.
Mexicana de Aviación, Carrera 7a No. 18-21, Suite 301, ☎25 89 29.
Norwegian Cruise Line, Calle 21 No. 8-24, ☎34 20 50.
Viasa, Calle 21 No. 8-48, 3rd floor, ☎34 37 61, 34 08 50 or 35 17 72.

By Bus

The department considers its road network a priority; as a result, it is easy to reach all municipalities by bus. The region's bus companies are Expreso Bolivariano, Velotax, Flota Magdalena to Bogotá (360 km), Flota Occidental to Medellín (235 km), Expreso Palmira and Expreso Bolivario to Santiago de Cali (230 km) and Buenaventura (372 km). All are located at the **Terminal de Transportes** *(Calle 17*

Pereira

0   200   400m

Carrera 3
Carrera 3
Carrera 4
Carrera 4
Carrera 5
Carrera 5
Carrera 6
Carrera 6
Carrera 7
Carrera 7
Carrera 8
Carrera 9
Carrera 9
Carrera 10
Carrera 10
Carrera 11
Carrera 11
Carrera 12
Carrera 13
Carrera 14

Aeropuerto Internacional Matecaña

Av. 30 de Agosto

Terminal de Transportes

Av. del Ferrocarril

© ULYSSES

● ATTRACTIONS	○ ACCOMMODATIONS	◇ RESTAURANTS
1. Catedral de Nuestra Senora de la Pobreza 2. Iglesia de Nuestro Senora del Carmen 3. Plaza Bolívar 4. Museo del Oro 5. Museo de Arte de Pereira 6. Lago Uribe Uribe 7. Parque de la Libertad	1. Hotel Amarú 2. Hotel Cosmos 3. Hotel Monaco 4. Meliá	1. Dos Castillas 2. El Rincón Costeño 3. Zar Polo La 14

A Notice to Travellers

The city of Pereira and the Department of Risaralda were hit by several severe earthquakes which struck Colombia in late January, 1999. Because this natural disaster took place shortly before press time, it was not possible to update the information in this chapter. Travellers should thus take note that some of the attractions and establishments listed in this region may have suffered damages, and may be temporarily closed.

No. 23-157, ☎35 44 37, 35 44 38 or 35 44 39) south of town.

Public Transportation

Although bus routes service the entire city, it is best to walk during rush hour as traffic is very heavy.

Taxis are new cars clearly marked *Servicio Público*, and are an economical option. It is rare to pay more than 1,000 pesos for a trip. They carry CB radios and can be hired on the street as well as by phone.

Cooperativa de Taxis Consotas, ☎35 51 11, 33 76 66 or 33 77 77.
Cooperativa de Taxis Covichoralda, ☎24 44 44, 24 02 43 or 24 02 44.
Cooperativa de Taxis Luxor, ☎34 73 10, 34 74 00 or 34 75 00.

Monuments, Busts, Sculptures and Murals

Pereira is well-known for its many monuments and busts honouring the country's founders, or other themes depending on the artist's inspiration. Numerous sculptures and murals can also be seen in public squares and in the lobbies of banks or other institutions. These works of art are worth lingering over, as much for their interesting subject matter as for their artistic merit.

Monuments

El Bolívar Desnudo, the "naked Bolívar" *(Plaza Bolívar)*, is a spectacular bronze sculpture by Rodrigo Arena Betancur, the same provocative artist who created the Cóndor Bolívar on the Plaza Bolívar de Manizales (see p 221) and the bronze of the Centro Administrativo La Alpujarra in Medellín (see p 198);

El Monumento a los Fundadores *(Carrera 13, corner Calle 13)*, also by Rodrigo Arena Betancur;

El Cristo Sin Cruz *(Av. 30 de Agosto, between Calles 49 and 50)*, another of Rodrigo Arena Betancur's works, his controversial Christ without a cross;

La Virgen de la Ofrenda *(Calle 21, corner Carrera 7a)*, by Leonidas Méndez.

Busts

Jorge Eliecer Gaítan *(Carrera 4a, between Calles 24 and 25)*, by Alexandra Ariza;

Rafael Uribe Uribe *(Lago Rafael Uribe Uribe)*, by Francisco A. Cano, whose permanent collection is on display at the Museo de Antioquia de Medellín (see p 196) and whose paintings can also be seen at the Basílica Metropolitana de la Inmaculada, also in Medellín (see p 198);

Benito Juárez *(Av. 30 de Agosto)*, a gift from the Mexican government;

Oscar Teherán *(Calle 24, corner Carrera 12)*, a gift from the Rotary Club.

Sculptures

El Argonauta *(Calle 19, between Carreras 6 and 7)*, by Martín Abad Abad;

Hombre y Progreso 1 *(Calle 18, corner Carrera 7a)*, by Jaime Mejía Jaramillo;

Hombre y Progreso 2 *(Calle 19, corner Carrera 7a)*, by Jaime Mejía Jaramillo;

Colombia *(Calle 17, corner Carrera 6a)*, by Carlos Nicholls;

El Obelisco *(Calle 17,corner Carrera 6a)*, by Hernado Hoyos;

El Vigia *(Calle 17, between Carreras 23 and 24)*, by Carlos Nicholls;

La Bohemia *(Av. 14, between Carreras 21 and 22, Edificio La Bohemia)*, also by Carlos Nicholls;

Vendedora de Mango *(Carrera 7, between Calles 21 and 22)*, by Jaime Mejía Jaramillo;

Totem de Rostros *(Carrera 13, corner Calle 22)*, by Ruben Germanchs;

La Familia y el Café *(Av. 30 de Agosto No. 50-54)*, by Salvador Arango.

Murals

Guaca Pobre y Guaca Rica *(Carrera 9a No. 18-23, Banco de la República)*, by Lucy Tejada;

Al Estudiante *(Parque de la Libertad)*, by Lucy Tejada;

Bestiaro Geométrico de la Faunaamericana *(Edicifio Comercio La 16)*, by Jaime Mejía Jaramillo.

Primer Tax, ☎34 80 40.
Tax San Lázaro, ☎33 31 00.

Renting a Car

Driving in Pereira is stressful, especially downtown because of the narrow streets. It is better to rent a car for visiting the surrounding mountainous countryside, which offers stunning scenery. Moreover, the town's tourist attractions are easily accessibly on foot. Otherwise, it is even simpler to take a taxi.

Hertz, Aeropuerto Internacional Matecaña, ☎36 00 36 ext. 264.
Renta Car, Aeropuerto Internacional Matecaña, ☎26 17 38.
Uno Auto Renta Lida, Carrera 10 No. 46-81, ☎26 30 33.

 PRACTICAL INFORMATION

Area code: 6.

Mail

Mail service is provided by **Avianca**, Calle 19 No. 6-28.

Banks

Many banks have branches in Pereira, but for better service for foreign exchange and traveller's cheques, go to the **Banco Industrial Colombiano** or the **Banco Anglo ColombiaNo.** Both are located on Carrera 7, at the corner of Calle 19, northeast of Plaza Bolívar. Automatic tellers (ATMs) are found on Calle 19, between Carreras 6a and 7a and between Carreras 8a and 9a. There are also some on Avenida Circunvalar between Calles 13 and 14.

Tourist Information

Tourist information can be obtained through the following organizations:

Fomento al Turismo, Carrera 7a No. 19-28, 3rd floor, Suite 403, ☎35 71 32 or 35 71 72, ⊷26 76 84. Also at the Aeropuerto Internacional Matecaña, Suite 101, ☎36 00 21, ext. 274.
Fondo de Promoción Turística, Calle 20 No. 8-73, 3rd floor, ☎34 63 95 or 34 68 00.
Compañía Regional de Turismo (Corturis), Club Social Alcides Arévalo, Suite 308-310, ☎35 07 86, ⊷25 25 87.
Corporación de Turismo de Risaralda, Calle 20 No. 8-73, 3rd floor, ☎35 64 27 or 35 64 89.

Excursions

Pereira's travel agencies offer several guided tours of the area surrounding the capital and elsewhere in Risaralda, including: Parque Nacional Natural de Los Nevados, Parque Regional Natural Ucumari, Estación Piscícola El Cedral, La Suiza, Sanctuario de Flora y Fauna and Otúm Quimbaya. Also offered are city tours by *chiva* (a type of bus, see p 66, 157), coffee plantation tours, and tours of Colombia's wine country. Pereira's main travel agencies offering excursions include:

Sin Fronteras, Carrera 13 No. 15-73, Meliá Hotel, ☎35 07 70 ext. 117, ⊷35 06 75;
Operadores Colombiana de Turismo, Calle 18 No. 4-64, Suite 103, ☎35 41 73 or 34 40 17;
Pereira Travel, Carrera 7a No. 19-28, Suite 801, ☎25 86 41 or 25 86 42;
Turismo Café y Montaña, Carrera 6a No. 17-62, Suite 203, ☎25 07 38; **Excursiones Fidel García,** Carrera 8a No. 20-04, ☎35 85 67 or 35 58 08.

PEREIRA

EXPLORING

Pereira ★

Pereira is a relatively new town and forms a metropolitan region together with its neighbours, Dosquebaras and La Virginia. Middle-class and a bit straight-laced, it distinguishes itself more by its monuments, murals, parks, and pedestrian streets *(Calle 28 between Carreras 7 and 8, where artisans do leather and metal work on the spot and make wool garments, jewellery, and bracelet charms; Calle 27 and Calle 18, again between Carreras 7 and 8, among other areas)* than by its rather nondescript modern buildings. Also quaint are the public scribes *(Calle 19 between Carreras 9 and 10)* on the sidewalk with their typewriters who will, for only a few pesos, pen love letters or formal requests, as the case may be.

The **Catedral de Nuestra Señora de la Pobreza ★** *(Calle 20, corner Carrera 7, ☎35 65 45)* has two steeples and faces the Plaza Bolívar. Although it is not a historical building, its interior columns and numerous stained-glass windows give it a majestic appearance.

The Gothic Revival-style **Iglesia de Nuestra Señora del Carmen ★★** *(Calle 15, corner Carrera 13, ☎33 29 18)* is more architecturally interesting. It has numerous stained-glass windows, as the church is a replica of the Catedral del Buen Pastor de San Sebastián in Spain.

The **Plaza Bolívar ★★** *(between Calles 19 and 20 and Carreras 7 and 8)* is one of the busiest and most popular places in Pereira. The department's public events are held here, the plaza having been renovated in August 1993 for this very purpose. Moreover, a powerful earthquake devastated the city in 1995, and certain buildings are still being renovated. It is here that the Bolívar Desnudo bronze (see p 238) honouring the *Libertador* can be found.

The **Museo del Oro ★★** *(Mon to Fri 9am to 11:30am and 2pm to 5:30pm; Carrera 9 No. 18-23)* is also dedicated to the Quimbaya culture. Although it is hardly Columbia's most important gold museum, it does have a significant number of Quimbaya gold pieces and explains how they were created by pre-Colum-

bian goldsmiths. First, the piece was sculpted in wax and covered with several layers of clay and semi-liquid mud. The whole was left to dry before it was covered with a final coat of more solid clay. The object was then placed into the fire to melt the wax and bake the clay. Finally, the mould was filled with liquid gold, left to cool, and then broken open to reveal the finished work in all its glory. The artistic legacy of the *Quimbaya* goldsmiths is still being studied today, as all the steps in the refining process have not yet been understood.

The **Museo de Arte de Pereria ★★** *(Mon to Fri 10am to noon and 2pm to 6pm, Sat and Sun 11am to 4pm; Av. Las Américas Sur No. 19-88, ☎25 55 08 or 25 50 09, ⌐34 43 54)* is a modern museum on two floors. A collection of contemporary art from Risaralda, other parts of Columbia and throughout the world takes up three rooms. The museum organizes regular expositions of Colombian and foreign artists in two separate rooms. Films and videos can be viewed.

Lago Uribe Uribe ★ *(between Calles 24 and 25 and Carreras 7 and 8)* is one of Pereira's most beautiful and most peaceful parks, with an artificial lake and a fountain with water jets and special lighting.

Parque de la Libertad *(between Calles 13 and 14 and Carreras 7a and 8a)* is a small, pleasant park, but nothing more. It is one of the numerous places where the town's shoeshines gather.

ACCOMMODATIONS

All of Pereira's hotels are located downtown or nearby, and all can be reached on foot.

Hotel Amarú *($; pb, hw, ☎, tv, ⊗; Calle 15 No. 8-49, ☎35 13 83, 35 13 84 or 35 13 85, ⌐33 87 40)* is a small hotel with a family atmosphere, located in a renovated building a stone's throw from downtown. The 22 rooms are clean and provide a good price/quality ratio for small budgets.

Hotel Cosmos *($; pb, hw, ☎, tv; Calle 15 No. 8-21, ☎33 14 22, 35 64 97 or 34 94 34)* is another small hotel not far from downtown with a family atmosphere. It has about 15 clean and comfortable rooms. You cannot ask for more at this price!

Finca de café

Hotel Monaco *($; pb, hw, ☎, tv, ⊗, mb, ℜ; Carrera 9a No. 15-39, ☎39 09 01, 39 09 02 or 39 09 03, ⇒33 09 08)* doesn't look like much from the outside, but it's an excellent hotel with 120 clean, adequately furnished, and very inexpensive rooms. In addition, weekend guests can use the facilities of the owners' relaxing country inn located just minutes from downtown, which includes a swimming pool, a bar and a restaurant. Staff are attentive.

The **Hotel Ejecutivo** *($$; pb, hw, ☎, tv, mb, ⊗, ⦿, ℜ; Calle 7a No. 16-61, ☎25 82 92 or 25 82 96, ⇒34 37 41)* is Pereira's best hotel when it comes to price/quality ratio. It is located on the third floor of a small shopping centre on one of the town's busiest streets. There are 30 rooms in this renovated building. Guests are warmly greeted by smiling staff.

The **Hotel Soratama** *($$$$; pb, hw, ☎, tv, mb, ⊗, ⦿, ℜ; Calle 7a No. 19-20, ☎35 13 83, 35 13 84 or 35 13 85, ⇒33 87 40)* has a dozen or so floors and is located near the business district. Its 77 rooms are unimaginatively furnished, but comfortable. The Soratama offers a weekend package which includes the room, an American-style breakfast, and a welcome cocktail for two people, all for as little as 80,000 pesos.

The **Meliá** *($$$$$; pb, hw, ≡, mb, ☎, tv, ⦿, ≈, ℜ; Av. Circunvalar or Carrera 13 No. 15-73, ☎35 07 70 or 35 39 70, ⇒35 06 75)* belongs to the international chain of the same name and is Pereira's largest hotel. Located a short distance from downtown (less than 10 minutes on foot), the hotel provides first class service in a modern building of about a dozen floors. The vast lobby opens onto the street on one side and a shopping centre with expensive boutiques on the other. The reception is rather cold, and the staff snooty. The rooms are large and tastefully furnished, with all the usual comforts of large luxury hotels. Most of the rooms open out onto interior balconies on each floor, providing a view of the hotel. Huge windows reveal Pereira in all its glory at sunrise or sunset. This hotel will appeal to wealthy clients or travellers on expense accounts, although it also offers package deals.

 RESTAURANTS

Downtown Pereira has many restaurants, and the only real difficulty is in deciding which one to choose. For fast food, the rotisseries are the place to go: try **Zar Pollo La 14** *($-$$; Carrera 8 No. 14-62, ☎25 25 53)*, **Zar La Bolívar** *($-$$; corner Carrera 7 and Calle 28, ☎35 79 13)* or

Zar La Lorena *($-$$; Calle 21b No. 16b-61, ☎33 36 15)*, open every day from 10am to 10pm.

Typical Colombian food is less expensive in the market area *(between Calles 18 and 21 and between Carreras 9a and 10)*. The **Posada Paisa** *($-$$$; every day 11am to 9pm; Av. 30 de Agosto No. 48-40, ☎36 35 88)* is also worth a try.

For international cuisine, go to **Dos Castillas** *($$-$$$$; every day 11am to 10pm, Av. Circunvalar or Carrera 13 No. 15-73, ☎35 07 70)*, the Meliá hotel's restaurant, which, like the hotel, offers first-class service and cuisine. Located on the second floor near the pool, it serves meat and fish dishes as well as different kinds of pastas.

For seafood, head to **Aristi** *($$$; Carrera 7a No. 31 49)* or **El Rincón Costeño** *($$$; Carrera 14 No. 25-057)*.

ENTERTAINMENT

Pereira and the department of Risaralda organize a number of interesting cultural and social events. Among them are:

Aniversario del Departemento de Risaralda, February 1;

Semana Santa, in April;

Festival Nacional de Bambuco, a music festival, in November;

Agroferia, in December.

SHOPPING

As in other parts of Columbia, handicrafts play an important role in the day-to-day life of *Risaraldenses*, since the items are functional as well as decorative. Clothing, leather goods and pottery can be purchased in the following boutiques:

Sindamanoy, Calle 23 No. 7-78, ☎25 08 06;
Mi Pequeña Artesania, Km 4, via Armenia, ☎35 52 54;
El Turista, Calle 23 No. 7-20, ☎33 91 99.

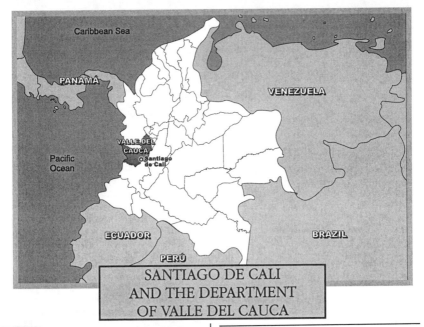

SANTIAGO DE CALI
AND THE DEPARTMENT
OF VALLE DEL CAUCA

The department of Valle del Cauca was part of the department of Cauca until 1863, when it split off and established its own capital, Santiago de Cali. Valle del Cauca is situated in mid-western Colombia and has a population of 3.5 million in an area of 22,140 square kilometres. It is renowned for the fertility of its soil and its various distinct climates. Valle del Cauca is Colombia's breadbasket, extending on either side of Río Cauca, for which the department is named. It is bordered to the north by the departments of Chocó, Risaralda, and Quindío, to the south by the departments of Cauca and Huila, to the east by Tolima and Quindío, and to the west by Chocó and the Pacific Ocean. It is a region of geographic contrasts, simultaneously embracing two snow-capped mountain ranges, the central and eastern cordilleras, and the sweltering equatorial climate of the Pacific, where dense forests crowd the coast. The department comprises 41 municipalities. Visitors should check with local tourism associations, travel agencies and even hotels before heading to this part of the country, since guerrilla groups apparently inhabit the area's mountainous countryside. Only Santiago de Cali, Tuluá, Guadalajara de Buga and Buenaventura are covered in this chapter, since they are considered safe and may be visited without worry.

Santiago de Cali

Cali is Colombia's "City of Women". Beautiful women. This claim is made by all of the city's promotional material – and turns out to be true!

The city stretches languorously between the wide-open arms of the two cordilleras, and basks in an outrageously sunny climate that makes its ample charms shine: enchanting colonial and contemporary buildings; long, shady avenues; patios overflowing with flowers and all sorts of people enjoying an afternoon of life's pleasures. Later in the evening, the city begins to stir to the rhythms of a seductive salsa that continues into the wee hours of the morning.

If Bogotá is Colombia's New York, Cali is, without exaggeration, the country's California (the pun is unintentional). It has the same climate, the same grandiose landscape, the same unconventional atmosphere, the same studied nonchalance and passion for the arts (especially music), the same tinge of madness reigning on the terraces of restaurants and bars, the same search for originality and distinction and, of course, the same carefree but structured philosophy that account for California's longstanding reputation as the hippest place in the United States. In Colombia, Cali fits this bill!

A Brief History

The city's full name is Santiago de Cali. It extends over more than 560 square kilometres and enjoys a steady climate with temperatures hovering between 23°C and 25°C. Founded two years before Bogotá, on July 25, 1536, by Sebastián de Belalcázar (see p 28), a lieutenant of Francisco Pizzaro, Cali immediately embarked on a course of development that was considered rapid for the era. Its astounding growth was sparked by the fertility of the soil in the region, which favoured the growth of sugarcane. Black slaves were imported from Cartagena de Indias specifically to harvest this crop. The modern *Caleño* population reflects this aspect of the city's past, since there is a significant proportion of people of mixed ethnicity. With close to two million residents in all, Cali is the second-largest city in Colombia after Bogotá.

Cali Today

The international capital of Salsa music, Santiago de Cali is in many ways the image of a beautiful European city: the lifestyle, culture, cuisine, sense of history, and, above all, the vision of the future are very similar. The city is full of vestiges of its colonial past, but simultaneously displays modern architecture that attests to its development and its aspirations. Cali is preparing to ring in the new millennium with gusto, by building a subway system scheduled to open at the beginning of the year 2000.

Cali today is the very picture of progress and success. The cleanup of Río Cali, which runs through the city, the modernization of the municipal administration, economic renewal, new construction projects, and the creation of social programs are some of the challenges that lay ahead for *Caleños*, who want to maintain their city's current level of growth and the quality of life it offers.

Tuluá

Tuluá is a small town like any other. It is divided by a busy road, an *autopista*, from which it looks like a desolate, dusty expanse of service stations and garages with long lines of cars and trucks in front of them. The road is also lined up with blaring advertisements for restaurants and hotels. This first impression is

misleading, however. Tuluá is also a pleasant, peaceful little town and wandering its quiet streets is a more than pleasant experience.

A Brief History

Tuluá is situated 105 kilometres north of Cali, in the centre of the department, on the river that is its namesake. Local people are not exactly sure when the town was founded. In fact, there is no legal document to formally prove that it ever was. However, historians have adopted the year 1639 as a reference point, because of a letter found in the historical archives of Guadalajara de Buga signed by Don Juan de Lemus y Aguirre, a rich landowner who was requesting permission to open a road to cross the land between Río Tuluá and Río Morales. Since the discovery of this letter, Señor Lemus y Aguirre and those involved in this project have been considered the founders of Tuluá. The town was given official status as a municipality in 1872.

Guadalajara de Buga

Legend has it that in 1570 El Señor de Los Milagros (Christ of the Miracles) appeared to an indigenous woman on the shores of Río Guadalajara, which runs through Buga. Because of this vision, Buga has become one of the most visited cities in ultra-Catholic Latin America, and has a clearly religious leaning, evident in its many churches. In 1959, Ciudad Señora de Guadalajara de Buga was recognized as a national monument.

A Brief History

Originally founded as Nueva Jeréz de los Caballeros in 1555 by Giraldo Gil de Estupiñán – who was later assassinated by Pijaos – Guadalajara de Buga did not officially become a municipality until 1857. It had actually been established on four successive occasions before this time, including one attempt in 1557 by *El Capitán* Rodrigo Díez de Fuenmayor, who gave the city its present name. Despite having been razed by the Pijaos, who refused to allow their territory to be invaded, Buga was finally incorporated in 1570.

Situated 75 kilometres from Cali in a livestock farming region, Buga is now an immense religious site permeated with a sense of the

sacred that coexists with the banality of daily life. The atmosphere is so heavy with spirituality that visitors have the impression they should keep silent when walking through its streets. Or at least bare their heads as a sign of respect.

The restaurants and hotels in this holy town are full of pilgrims, and some establishments have even transformed their lobby bars into chapels. The names of these enterprises leave no doubt as to their vocation: Hotel Los Angeles, Hotel Cristo Rey, Casa del Peregrino, and so on.

Guadalajara de Buga Today

Buga's 100,000 residents are perfectly adapted to their city's role as a holy place, and the architecture of their homes, hotels, churches and public spaces attest to this. The eclecticism of Art Deco, which first appeared here in 1924 with the inauguration of the Parque de Bolívar and Teatro Municipal, designed by architect Enrique Figueroa, is as prominent as colonial architecture.

Most of the city's plazas turn into veritable outdoor markets of religious knickknacks during the day. Hundreds of stands compete for the

attention of passers-by, with such items as hologram pictures of Christ that move their arms in a blessing gesture, Virgins with halos that light up, scapulars that guarantee entry into heaven or your money back, and life-size plaster lawn ornaments of the saints and collections of icons representing the entire gallery of saints. There are prayers for sale that guarantee direct ascendence to heaven with no bureaucratic hassle. There are candles, clothing, vases and liturgical books. For miracles, see the specialty shop across the street. Everything to edify the pious or to buy back a poor sinner's soul. In all honesty, it must be admitted that this merchandise – which can seem ridiculous in the eyes of some – often includes fine handmade crafts. It is particularly coveted by the elderly, who represent a large proportion of tourists to Buga, along with religious congregations. It would be redundant to note that Guadalajara de Buga is a safe city where tourists can walk alone day or night without fear. It would take a backhanded miracle for a crime to be committed here.

Salsa

Afro-Caribbean music made its first appearance in the Americas in the early days of the 16th-century Age of Discovery, with the large-scale arrival of black slaves from Africa. The daily drama of slavery was expressed through the simplicity and syncopated rhythms of African percussion instruments, roughly made from rudimentary materials in the holds of slave ships, and instruments already being used by indigenous Americans. It was influenced by several sources and pursued diverse courses, spreading to every island in the Caribbean and even to the southern United States. No precise records of this phenomenon exist, but it is known that salsa, which literally means "sauce", is but one piece of this great musical mosaic, another being Latin jazz. Salsa is an evolution and an amalgamation of different genres including *son*, *guajira*, *guaguancó*, *danzón*, conga, *guaracha*, mambo, bolero, rumba and cha-cha: rhythms and styles born in the alleys and suburbs of Havana, Cuba, and San Juan, Puerto Rico, airs that had their heyday in the United States in the early 1920s, especially in New Orleans. Several American musicians of the time travelled to Cuba often (especially during Prohibition, from 1919 to 1933), to play in the music halls and bars of Havana. They brought back with them this new musical influence, and the be-bop of Dizzy Gillespie, among others, was greatly inspired by Latin rhythms.

Salsa in the United States

Although salsa was inspired by Cuban rhythms, it was born in New York in the 1960s. Before the 1959 victory of Fidel Castro over the dictatorship of Fulgencio Batistá, several Cubans had already left their island to take refuge in the United States, especially in Florida and New York. New York's poor neighbourhoods were crowded with a huge population of immigrants from Puerto Rico, a Spanish colony that passed into the hands of the United States in 1898, who arrived in a steady wave of immigration over the years. Within a few years of the Cuban revolution, New York had the largest Latin American population in North America. It is no surprise that a new musical tradition, a fresh rhythm, a sensual dance, and a cohesive style should arise from the concentrated mix of these two cultural influences with those already fashionable in the American metropolis: jazz, rhythm and blues, and the early beats of rock and roll.

The *pachanga*, derived from the fading cha-cha, appeared at the end of the 1950s, and in the early 1960s some variations on *son* became popular in the United States. But the rupture in U.S.-Cuban relations abruptly curtailed the connection between Latin American musicians in the U.S. and their main source of inspiration. They turned to the energy of black music and musicians and the mix – or the sauce – that resulted from the supercharged blend of Latin music, soul and young rock and roll. This change in direction gave birth to *bugalú*, or boogaloo, from which arose salsa. This music, particularly influenced by musicians like Tito Puente (*¿Oye! Como Va?*, a song covered by Carlos Santana in the 1970s), characterized by the use of percussion instruments such as drums, congas, cowbells and kettledrums accented with brass instruments like trombone and trumpet, and easily conquered the world, especially after the release of the film *Salsa* in 1973. The movie featured the Fania All Stars playing pieces from an album entitled *Hommy* that was recorded in 1972 as a response to the rock-opera *Tommy*. Today, salsa is experiencing a world-wide revival, although purists would say that it has been contaminated by disco. Nevertheless, the genre is seducing a new generation of youth, especially with the notable influence of the group Miami Sound Machine and soloist Gloria Estefán, who offers up a sizzling brand of salsa. Perhaps less known but more authentic, *salsero* Yuri Buenaventura, whose real name is Yuri Bedova, a fisherman's son from Buenaventura (hence his stage name), recently completed an international tour to promote his record *Herencia Africa* (African Heritage), recorded in Bogotá, which pays homage to the black population of Colombia's Pacific coast. The record includes an interpretation of *Ne Me Quitte Pas*, by Jacques Brel, and caused a sensation in Europe.

Salsa in Colombia

Although Caribbean music reached Colombia in the early 1930s, salsa was only introduced later in a series of concerts by the band of Richi Ray and Bobby Cruz in February 1968 in Barranquilla. In December of the same year, the band also played in Cali and its surroundings, including Buenaventura, which has the largest black and mulatto population in the country. Salsa gained a firm foothold in the country when it won over the reticent crowds of Medellín and Bogotá, who found the music vulgar at first. This was accomplished by Cartagena's greatest *salsero*, Joe Arroyo, 14-time winner of the Congo trophy at the Carnaval de Barranquilla, who played in Bogotá on the occasion of his 25th anniversary in the music business. Although Baranquilla claims the title of capital of salsa, musicians and fans prefer Cali, largely because of the beauty of the *Caleñas*, who dance to the rhythm with such verve.

Buenaventura

Santiago de Cali is situated at about 1,000 metres above sea level. Thus, in order to reach Buenaventura which is right on the seaside and about 125 kilometres west of Cali, travellers must cross the entire width of the eastern cordillera on the Autopista Cali-Buenaventura, one of the most beautiful roads in all of Colombia, before descending to the coast. The road snakes through lost valleys, where little villages appear suddenly around bends in the haze of stagnant pockets of mist, then it climbs to unimaginable heights above lush green crenellated mountains. It runs through six tunnels piercing the mountainsides, including one that is half a kilometre long.

Not everyone will appreciate Buenaventura. Despite what one might expect, this port town is at a disadvantage because of its geographic location on the Pacific coast. Firstly, Buenaventura is not on the ocean but rather on a bay, Bahía de Buenaventura, which is only visible if you are right on the shore. Furthermore, the bay itself is disappointing, and looks like an immense black, muddy marsh full of the detritus of the sea at low tide. Not a pretty sight. It is, however, a natural phenomenon and no one can do anything about it.

A Brief History

Buenaventura is the country's main port, and 60 percent of all of the nation's imports and exports pass through it. The city was founded on July 14, 1540, the feast day of San Buenaventura, by Don Juan Ladrilleros, who came to America with Vasco Núñez de Balboa, the discoverer of the Pacific, under the orders of Pascual de Andagoya. The city first developed on the island of Cascajal, which was populated by the Buscajáes at the time. Then, following the discovery of silver mines and the presence of abundant gold in the waterways of the region, the Spanish had thousands of African slaves brought from Cartagena de Indias to work these deposits.

These natural riches were soon exhausted, and the Spanish dispersed leaving the black slaves behind. Their descendants form the population of modern Buenaventura, which now has about 250,000 residents.

Toward 1878, Cuban engineer Francisco J. Cisnero built a bridge, Puente El Piñal, linking the island of Cascajal to the mainland, where Buenaventura continued to develop. The city was completely destroyed by fire in 1881, and another blaze again destroyed the southern part of the city in 1892. Still later, in 1931, the entire business district burned down. Gradually, the city rebuilt itself.

Buenaventura Today

Buenaventura has undergone several transformations in recent decades, the most important of which is doubtless the paving of the streets, which is about 80 percent complete now. As well, parks, green spaces and playgrounds have been established to improve the quality of life for the citizens.

It is impossible to swim in Buenaventura itself, and the humid heat can be a major nuisance for some visitors. Nonetheless, Buenaventura is the favourite vacation destination of many *Vallecaucanos*, who enjoy visiting nearby beaches. From the tourist dock, the Muelle Turístico *(corner of Calle 1a and Carrera 2)*,

SANTIAGO DE CALI

there are *lanchas*, or motorboats, to the many beaches in the area. A new Muelle Turístico is under construction less than 100 metres from the present one. The new dock is being built with concrete at water level. The wharf in use at the time of our visit was not particularly safe. It was made of wood – planks with holes in them that were not always properly affixed – on piles about five metres above the water, without guardrails. As for the *lanchas* used for passenger transportation, they provide a questionable level of comfort, and also carry merchandise. Life jackets are provided, and given these conditions, it is advisable to wear them.

The beach of Ladrilleros is located about 20 minutes on foot from the beach of Juanchaco, which itself is 45 minutes by boat from Buenaventura *(24,000 pesos, round-trip)*. These are fishing villages built along one dirt road – Juanchaco stretches over nearly five kilometres – and comprising rudimentary little *tiendas* where visitors can eat, drink or sleep in hammocks. From Juanchaco, you can take a *lancha* via the mouth of Río San Juan to visit a small indigenous community of Cholos and Wuaunanás people, who still live according to their time-honoured traditions.

La Bocana *(15,000 pesos, round-trip)* is 25 minutes by *lancha* from Buenaventura. This is another *pueblito* with a series of *tiendas* stuck together in a row, along with a few hotels frequented by vacationing *Caleños*.

Only 15 minutes from Buenaventura, Cangrejos *(7,000 pesos, round-trip)*, offers only a beach and a private club (see p 262) where you can spend the night in one of 12 motel-type *cabañas* for 35,000 double occupancy, including full board. The place is peaceful and quiet, and serves excellent cuisine – *cangrejo* means "crayfish." A magnificent sunset on the Pacific is also part of the package!

None of these beaches is particularly attractive by the usual standards. The sand is black and the Pacific's strong tides dump a lot of flotsam on the shore. This debris, which often consists of trash like plastic bags and tin cans, sticks out of the mud at low tide. *Vallecaucanos* are not put off by this, though. To the contrary, in fact – they find these spots ideal for letting loose on weekends. *Farniente* soon takes hold here in all its splendour, and anything and everything is a pretext for a party. Music is omnipresent from one *tienda* to the next, especially reggae, salsa and other styles that are popular in Colombia and elsewhere. Beer,

rum and *aguardiente* flow freely, heating things up and keeping dancers grooving day and night.

Food and lodgings are not a problem here, since every *tienda* is a restaurant-inn. Naturally, the freshest fish and seafood in the department are to be found here, caught the same day by local fishermen who haven't been converted to the tourism industry. For example, I dined on crayfish at a wooden table set on a small patio in the sand shaded by palm trees. How many crayfish? Five! How much did it cost? 5,000 pesos! Less than US$5. What more? The owner suggested with a broad grin that crayfish is an infallible aphrodisiac. When I responded that I have no need of a stimulant in that area, she repeated my statement to her neighbours who laughed and danced, slapping their thigh and winking their eyes lustily, all the while enjoying themselves thoroughly. It's a party alright!

FINDING YOUR WAY AROUND

On Foot

Santiago de Cali

Cali's *calles* run north-south and their numbers increase from west to east. *Carreras* run east-west and their numbers increase from north to south. *Avenidas* run both ways, but are also numbered.

Tuluá

Tuluá's *calles* run north-south and their numbers increase from west to east. The *carreras* run east-west and their numbers increase from north to south.

Guadalajara de Buga

The *calles* of Buga run east-west and their numbers increase from south to north. The *carreras* run east-west and their numbers increase from east to west.

Fries

Fries were in all likelihood a staple in Colombia long before Christopher Columbus arrived, before Belgium became famous for its french fries, or Italians decided to eat them cold in salads. The indigenous people of Colombia possessed all of the ingredients to cook up good fries – potatoes, corn oil and salt – and they were already frying pans, especially on the seaside where fried fish was a staple. The Andean potato was not imported to Europe by the Spanish until 1534, and it did not make its first appearance in France until 200 years later, when it was introduced by agronomist Antoine Augustin Parmentier in Sablons, Neuilly, on the orders of Louis XVI, who wanted to use it to quell a famine that was ravaging the country's population. Good fries can be found throughout Colombia, but, like elsewhere, they are better in some places than in others.

Here is one way to make fried potatoes that, although not exactly a Colombian tradition, will satisfy your taste. Scrub one large potato (or two medium potatoes) per person under running water, to avoid having to peel them, and cut them into two-centimetre thick strips. Soak in ice water in the refrigerator for a few hours to leach out excess starch. Once they are dried, plunge them, along with two or three (or more) unpeeled garlic cloves, into simmering corn or olive oil and let them cook over medium heat for 20 minutes. Take out the garlic cloves and increase the heat to maximum. The potatoes will immediately begin to change colour. Stop cooking when they are golden or browned to taste (brown is about 10 minutes). This method keeps the fries tender on the inside and makes them pleasantly crunchy on the outside. Serve with salt and the garlic cloves (peeled), which become creamy like butter when cooked this way. Belgians eat their fries with plain or garlic mayonnaise. For a different flavour, try them sprinkled with lime juice and generous quantities of fresh-ground pepper.

SANTIAGO DE CALI

Buenaventura

Buenaventura's *calles* generally run east-west and their numbers increase from south to north. The *carreras* generally run north-south and their numbers increase from west to east.

By Plane

Santiago de Cali

The **Palmaseca international airport**, also called Alfonso Bonilla Aragón, is located 15 kilometres northwest of Cali *(Autopista Cali-Palmira, ☎442 26 24)*. You can reach it by taking the minibus marked *"Aeropuerto"*, at the left end of Terminal de Transportes, on the second floor.

Here is the schedule for direct Avianca flights to international destinations:

Mexico City, Mexico, Sat 6am with stopover, Tue, Thu, Fri 7:29am with stopover.
Miami, Florida, every day 8:40am with stopover
New York, New York, Fri 2:05pm with stopover.

Here is the schedule for Avianca flights to other Colombian cities:

Barranquilla, every day 8:40am, Mon to Wed and Fri and Sat 1:30pm with stopover, Fri 2:05pm; 232,000 pesos.
Bogotá, Mon to Sat 6:24am; Mon to Wed, Fri, Sun 7:29am; Mon to Sat 8:01am; every day 9:25am; Mon to Fri and Sun 10:29am; every day 11:45am, 12:27pm, 2:01pm and 3:31pm; Mon to Fri and Sun 5:29pm; every day 6pm and 6:33pm; Mon to Fri and Sun 7:35pm; every day 10pm; 129,000 pesos.
Cartagena, every day 1:30pm; Thu, Sun 1:30pm with stopover; 232,000 pesos.
Medellín, every day 6:45am, 1:30pm and 6pm; 131,000 pesos.
Pasto, every day 6:30am and 3:24pm, 127,000 pesos.
San Andrés, every day 8:30am.
Santa Marta, every day 6:45am with stopover.
Tumaco, every day 9am.

Most national airlines as well as some international ones serve this airport. Here are their addresses:

Aces, Avenida 8n No. 24an-07, ☎668 09 09.
AeroRepública, Calle 25n No.6n-42, ☎660 40 50.

Aires, Avenida 6n No. 20n-73, ☎660 47 77.
Avianca, Avenida 4n No. 17n-78, ☎667 69 19.
Intercontinental de Aviación, Calle 10 No. 3-23, ☎880 70 65.
SAM, Avenida 4n No. 17n-78, ☎667 69 19.
American Airlines, Calle 10 No. 4-47, ☎884 26 00.
Copa, Avenida 4n No. 23n-49, ☎660 02 24.

Buenaventura

The Buenaventura airport is located about 15 kilometres outside the city and can only be reached by taxi, which costs at least 5,000 pesos. Only one airline flies to Bogotá and Cali:

Satena, Calle 1a No. 2a-39, ☎242 31 89 or 242 38 25.

By Bus

Santiago de Cali

The Cali **Terminal de Transportes** *(Calle 30n No. 2an 29,* ☎*668 36 55)* is a new building with all the services, including restaurants that serve very good, affordable fare, a place to store luggage, and even showers, on the second floor. Ticket offices of the different bus lines including Espreso Palmira, Espreso Bolivariano and Flota Magdalena, which regularly travel to all of the destinations in Colombia including the airports, Bogotá (12 h), Medellín (10 h), Popayán (2.5 h), Tuluá (1.5 h), Guadalajara de Buga (1 h) and Buenaventura (3 h). Arrivals are on the first floor near the taxistand, and departures leave from the second floor.

Tuluá

Tuluá's **Terminal de Transportes** *(Carrera 20, between Calle 26 and Calle 27)* is at the entrance to the town.

Guadalajara de Buga

Buga's **Terminal de Transportes** *(on Carrera 19, between Calle 5 and Calle 6)* is across from the old train station, where the buses park.

Buenaventura

Buenaventura's **Terminal de Transportes** *(Carrera 5, at the ends of Calle 7a and Calle 7b)* is in a new building about 500 metres from downtown. There are departures for Cali and Buga every hour, beginning at dawn.

Public Transportation

Santiago de Cali

Buses of all sizes, shapes and classes run through Cali. The fare is between 350 and 450 pesos. Travellers must know where to wait, though. Since most tourist attractions are downtown, it is easy to travel from one to another on foot, especially because the downtown area is relatively safe, even at night.

By Taxi

Santiago de Cali

Santiago de Cali's taxis are ochre yellow and identified *Servicio Público*. They have meters, but fares rarely exceed 1,000 pesos. Taxis can also be hired for 8,000 pesos per hour. They can be hailed in the street or at hotel entrances, or summoned by telephone, since they are equipped with radios.

Coopetriunfo, ☎558 12 60
Sindiunión, ☎855 55 55
Tax Emperado, ☎881 06 45 or 881 07 99
Tax Libre, ☎444 44 44
Taxi Valcali, ☎443 00 00

Tuluá

Tuluá's taxis are ochre yellow and identified *Servicio Público*. They do not have meters, but most trips cost less than 1,000 pesos.

Guadalajara de Buga

Buga's taxis are also ochre yellow and identified *Servicio Público*. They do not have meters, but most trips cost less than 1,000 pesos.

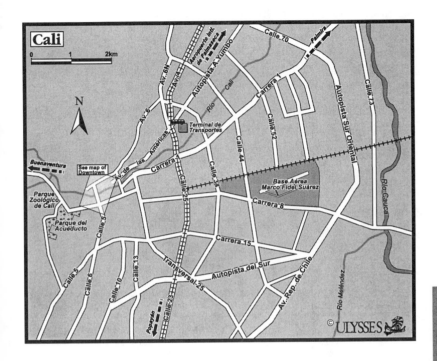

Buenaventura

Buenaventura's are ochre yellow and identified *Servicio Público*. They do not have meters, but trips rarely cost more than 1,000 pesos, except at night.

Renting a Car

Cali is ridiculously congested at rush hour and traffic is heavy throughout the day, so it is preferable to rent a car only for day trips to the other towns in the department. For example, the trip to Buenaventura offers memorable landscapes along Autopista Cali-Buenaventura, which crosses the entire eastern cordillera from east to west, winding up and down along the mountainsides for about 125 kilometres, and passing through six tunnels. Traffic is slow because trucks have to inch up the steep hills, but be extremely cautious when passing.

Rentamovil, Avenida 1a Norte No. 3n-71, ☎661 01 03 or 661 30 42.

Hertz, Avenida Colombia No. 2-272, in the Inter-Continental hotel at the end of the lobby on the left, ☎882 24 28 or 882 32 25 ext. 221.

 PRACTICAL INFORMATION

Area Code: 2

Mail

Mail service is provided by **Avianca**, Avenida 4n No. 17n-78.

Tourist Information

Santiago de Cali

Corporación Regional de Turismo del Valle (CORTUVALLE) *(Mon to Fri 8am to noon and 2pm to 6pm, Avenida 4n No. 4n-20, ☎660 50 00).*

Fondo Mixto de Promoción del Valle del Cauca *(Mon to Fri 8am to noon and 2pm to 6pm, Calle 8 No. 3-14, 13th floor, ☎882 32 71, ext. 300).*

Subsecretaría de comercio y Turismo *(Mon to Fri 8am to noon and 2pm to 6pm, Calle 19n No. 2n-29, 39th floor, ☎667 20 06).*

Oddly, none of these tourist organizations showed any particular eagerness to provide information on Cali and its surroundings, and none had a map of Cali to offer.

Guadalajara de Buga

Oficina de Turismo (TURISBUGA S.A.) *(Carrera 14 No. 5-53, suite 507, ☎28 04 46, ⌐28 00 93).*

Buenaventura

Oficina de Turismo *(Mon to Fri 8am to noon and 2pm to 6pm, Calle 1 No. 1-26, ☎224 44 15).*

Money and Banking

Santiago de Cali

Banks are open from Monday to Friday from 8am to noon and 2pm to 4pm, some to 4:30pm. It is easy to get cash 24 hours a day by using automatic teller machines (ATMs), which can be found throughout the department. To exchange travellers cheques or foreign currency in Cali, go to **Banco Industrial Colombiano** (BIC) *(Carrera 6 No. 10-46, between Calle 10 and Calle 11, ☎882 25 63).*

Tuluá, Guadalajara de Buga and Buenaventura

There are automatic teller machines in Tuluá, Guadalajara de Buga and Buenaventura, but it is not possible to exchange traveller's cheques or foreign currency in these towns. It is best to change enough money in Cali beforehand to last you until you return to Cali.

Tours

Travel agencies organize various tours in the department of Valle del Cauca, departing from Santiago de Cali. Here is a sampler:

Aventura Pacífica, a 12-hour tour that includes ground transportation from your hotel at 6am to Buenaventura, boat transportation to the beaches, lunch, insurance, the return trip, etc. Price: 70,000 pesos per person for 12 passengers.

Juanchaco, a 24-hour tour that includes ground transportation, boat fare, lodging, supper and breakfast, insurance, etc. Price: 90,000 pesos per person and 40,000 pesos per additional day.

Viva Cali, a six-hour tour that leaves the hotels at 7am and includes transportation and admission to the various sights of interest in the city. Cost: 50,000 pesos, minimum five people.

Ruta Panorámica, a 10-hour tour that includes ground transportation from hotels at 8am, lunch, a tour of Lago Calima, Basílica del Señor de los Milagros and Capilla El Overo. Cost: 75,000 pesos per person, minimum two people. Groups of more than 20 pay about 35,000 pesos per person.

Information is available at the following travel agencies:

Santiago de Cali

Comercializadora Turística del Valle del Cauca S.A., Calle 20n No. 8n-40, ☎668 72 32 or 668 85 04, ⌐668 86 77
Comercializadora Turística, Avenida 6n No. 6n-43, ☎667 11 02 or 660 12 55
Tierra Mar Aire, Calle 22n No. 5bn-53, ☎667 67 67
Turiscali, Calle 24n No. 5n-29, ☎661 51 46

Tuluá

Turisvalle, Calle 26 No. 25-64, ☎24 44 01

Guadalajara de Buga

Casa del Turismo, Carrera 12 No. 5-74, ☎27 11 00, 28 05 62 or 28 02 36

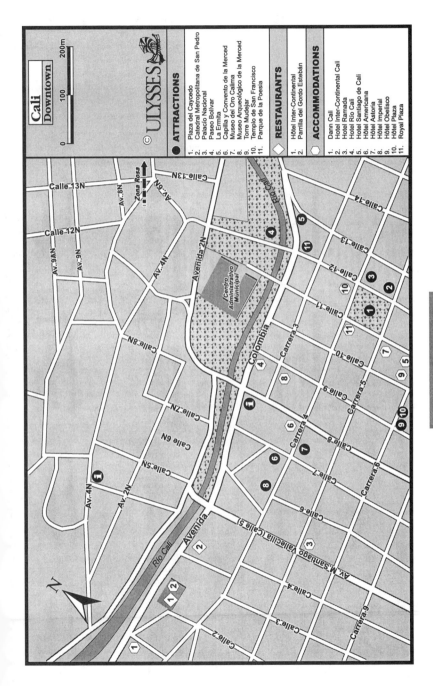

SANTIAGO DE CALI

Viajes Guadalajara, Carrera 14 No. 5-47, ☎28 07 32 or 28 07 31, ⌐36 16 23

Buenaventura

Promotore Cascajal, Carrera 1 No. 1a-88, ☎224 11 58
Viajes Balboa, Carrera 1 No. 2a-39, ☎241 80 67 or 242 38 25
Pacífico Tours, Calle 2a No. 4-17, ☎242 55 28, ⌐242 24 34
Yubarta Tours, Muelle Turístico, ☎243 41 57, ⌐243 35 70
Embarcaciones de Turismo, Muelle Turístico, ☎242 36 96 or 242 46 20, which also offers sport and commercial scuba diving trips.

EXPLORING

Santiago de Cali ★★★

Despite the presence of the drug cartel and the threat of guerrillas who are apparently active in the nearby mountains, Cali is the most pleasant city in Colombia, not only because of its climate, but also because of the European atmosphere that permeates its avenues, parks and the patios of its bars and restaurants. The laid-back welcome offered by *Caleños* is another plus. All of Cali's attractions are located downtown or on the periphery of downtown and can be visited on foot. Thus, you don't have to take the bus, even to go to the Zona Rosa, which is more of a *ruta rosa* here, since it stretches along only one avenue, Avenida Sexta Norte (6n).

Plaza del Caycedo ★★★ *(between Carrera 4a and Carrera 5a, between Calle 11 and Calle 12)* is the best-known and most popular square in Cali. It is the city's core, as well as its historic centre. It was called Plaza de la Constitución until 1813, when it was renamed Plaza Caycedo, after one of the leaders of the independence movement who came from Cali, Joaquín Caycedo y Cuero. Among the sights along its periphery are Catedral Metropolitana, Palacio Nacional and office buildings.

Catedral Metropolitana de San Pedro ★★ *(Calle 11 No. 5-53, ☎881 13 78)* is an example of the transposition of neoclassicism to the Americas. Erected in 1539 on Plaza de Caycedo, it was not actually inaugurated until

1841. After several renovations, necessitated by the ravages of successive earthquakes and other disasters such as fire, it has been greatly modified from its original design. Work was still underway at the time of my visit.

Palacio Nacional ★★ *(Carrera 4, between Calle 12 and Calle 13)* is a building inspired by French neoclassicism. It is a beautiful edifice which, along with the cathedral, sets the tone and the atmosphere of Plaza Caycedo. It is the work of *Bogotano* engineers Paulo Emilio Paéz and Giovanni Lignarolo, who imported the cement and the stone from Europe. The Palacio was inaugurated June 29, 1933, although its construction was begun February 15, 1926.

Paseo Bolívar ★★★ *(between Avenida 2 and Carrera 1 and between Calle 8 and Calle 12)* is another very popular part of Cali and the site of the municipal administration. Among its sights are a bronze likeness of Simón Bolívar (1992) by Italian sculptor Pietro Tenerani; a Carrara-marble statue of by Catalan sculptor Carlos Perea dedicated to writer Jorge Isaacs and representing Efraín and María, two of the author's characters from *La Obra de María*, which has been translated into five languages; and the brick Ortíz bridge, construction of which began in 1834 under the direction of Fray Francisco Ortíz. It is said that eggshell and bull's blood were mixed into the bricks. This magnificent arched bridge, which once was used for car traffic, is now reserved for pedestrians. It links downtown to Paseo Bolívar, which runs along Avenida Rosa (6n). Adjacent to the bridge is a very beautiful park, Parque de la Retreta, which was donated to the city by Banco de Occidente on the occasion of Cali's 450th anniversary in 1986.

La Ermita ★★★ *(Carrera or Avenida 1, corner of Calle 13, ☎881 85 53)* is without a doubt the most sensational church in Cali, and locals consider it their national and international symbol. Not only is it impossible to miss since it is directly across Paseo Bolívar, but its unique, extravagant, Gothic style, expressed in blue-tinted stone, is inspired by the cathedral of Köln (Cologne), Germany. The original construction dates from 1602, but it was destroyed by an earthquake in 1925. Señora Micaela Borrero raised funds from the *Caleña* community for the reconstruction, which began in October 1926 under the direction of architect and civil engineer Paulo Emilio Páez. On April 21, 1942, it was dedicated to Nuestra Señora de los Dolores by the apostolic nuncio Excelentísimo Señor Luis Adriano Díaz. Its alta is the work of Italian sculptor Alido Tazzioli. The only item spared by the earthquake was an effigy of Señor de la Caña, a native work representing Christ with a crown of thorns and a sugarcane, one of *Caleños* most important icons.

Capilla y Convento de la Merced ★★★ *(Carrera 3 No. 6-40, ☎880 47 37)* is located on the very square where Cali's first mass was celebrated, led by Fray Santos de Añasco, on the occasion of the founding of the town on July 25, 1536. The material used to produce the bricks with which the complex is built is a mixture of earth, water from the Río Cali, eggshells, lime and bull's blood, in undetermined proportions, which has resisted bad weather now for almost 500 years. Inside there is an icon of the Virgen de las Mercedes (the Virgin of Mercy) in 15th-century dress.

Museo del Oro Calima ★★★ *(Mon to Fri 8am to noon and 2pm to 6pm; Calle 7 No. 4-69, ☎883 43 53 ext. 263 or 269)* is set on the second floor of the Banco de la República building. A visit to this museum is a must if you want to become familiar with the lives of pre-Columbian natives. Many rooms display gold pieces and the jewels of the indigenous peoples, as well as urns and religious objects from the Calima culture.

Museo Arqueológico de la Merced ★★★ *(Mon to Fri 8:30am to 12:30pm and 2pm to 6pm; Carrera 4 No. 6-59, ☎881 32 29 or 880 42 31)* presents an interesting collection of pre-Columbian archaeological pieces from the Tolima, Quimbaya, Calima, Tierradentro, San Agustín, Tumaco and Nariño cultures. The colonial building that houses the museum is an important part of Cali's architectural heritage. Its restoration in 1976 was the work of architect José Luis Giraldo. His work is accessible to visitors (the entire design of the old monastery and Giraldo's plans are displayed along with explanations of the necessary modifications he made) for the sake of public education. The floors, walls and finishing touches, as well as the doors and windows, demonstrate the building's evolution to its present form.

The Torre Mudejar ★★★ *(Carrera 6, corner of Calle 9)* is a red-brick, four-storey square belltower that reaches a height of over 30 metres, and is one of the best examples of Mudéjar architecture in South America. Built in 1772 as an addition to the church of San Francisco, this belltower is as impressive today as it was in the era when it served to summon *Caleños* to mass or to warn them of some threatening event.

Templo de San Francisco ★★★ *(Carrera 6, between Calle 9 and Calle 10, ☎884 24 57)* was erected between 1803 and 1807, but the interior decoration of this immense neoclassical church, by Italian architect Mauricio Ramelli, was not added until 1926. Its marble alter, inlaid with precious wood and gold, was imported from Spain.

Parque de la Poesia ★ *(Avenida Colombia, corner of Calle 12)* is a tiny park adorned with about 10 realistic, life-size bronzes of poets and philosophers posed as though talking amongst each other and – why not? – with passers-by.

Just outside downtown (to return, you must ask a taxi driver to pick you up at a specific time or take the bus from the stop at the entrance), **Parque Zoológico de Cali** ★★★ *(2,500 pesos; every day 9am to 5pm; corner of Carrera 2a Oeste and Calle 14, Barrio Santa Teresita, ☎883 31 79 or 883 31 80, ☎883 02 62)* is one of the most beautiful zoos in Colombia. It is an eight-hectare lot transected by the Río Cali, which is spanned by a bridge. Set on both shores of the river, the zoo displays more than 800 animals, including 32 species of reptiles, 83 species of birds and 53 species of mammals. There are rhinoceroses, zebras, lions, dromedaries, antelopes, tiger, jaguars, monkeys, crocodiles, and more. In addition to providing these animals with a home, the zoo is engaged in an educational mission and offers special tours and programs for children and school groups.

SANTIAGO DE CALI

Tuluá ★

Despite first impressions, Tuluá proves to be a charming little city if you stay overnight. It has a population of nearly 130,000 inhabitants, and, although it offers no tourist attractions in particular, it does have a shady **Plaza Bolívar** *(corner of Calle 27 and Carrera 27)*, a varied downtown area, and a colourful **market** *(between Carrera 22 and Carrera 23 and Calle 27 and Calle 28)* overflowing with vegetables, especially potatoes, and fruit harvested from surrounding fields. It also offers attractive terraces, superb restaurants and two parks.

Parque Carlos Sarmiento Lora ★★★ *(Tue to Sat 10am to 5pm, Sun and holidays 10am to*

Torre Mudejar

6pm; *La Variante, Entrada Sur,* ☎*224 16 77 or 224 48 53)* is famous as one of the most beautiful municipal parks in Colombia. Among other facilities there are Olympic-size swimming pools, wading pools for children, soccer (*fútbol*) fields, volleyball and basketball courts, many picnic areas along the shores of Río Tuluá and restaurants set under tall trees that provide shade all day long. This is an ideal place for a family outing.

Parque de la Guadua ("Bamboo Park") ★★★ *(Avenida Cali, Barrio El Principe),* also known as Parque Principe, is another very beautiful shady park that offers something for the whole family, from water sports and ball games – soccer, volleyball, basketball – to fishing in its streams, and picnic areas.

Guadalajara de Buga ★★★

The main industry in Guadalajara de Buga is pilgrimage tourism. The town has many churches, all of which are worth visiting for their architecture and decoration, if not simply to witness the devotion they inspire in great numbers of spiritual sojourners.

Basílica del Señor de los Milagros ★★★ *(Carrera 14 between Calle 3 and Calle 4),* in a Doric Roman style, is a church with two steeples that was built between 1892 and 1902. Cristo Milagroso was first venerated in an hermitage founded between 1573 and 1576 on land donated by Señor Rodrigo Díez de Fuenmayor, but work on the present basilica was not begun until August 7, 1892. Construction took 15 years and cost an astronomical

sum for the period. It was the work of three Redemptorist brothers: Brother Juan Stiehle designed the plans, Brother Sylvestre (José Bindner) managed the construction, and Brother Urbano (Francisco Meyer) made the 120,000 bricks with the help of the entire *Bugeño* community.

The belltowers are 45 metres tall and the French five-bell carillon is reputed to have the best resonance of any in Colombia. Its clock, also French, has been keeping time for the population of Buga since March 18, 1909.

The high altar, the secondary altars and the confessionals were all created by Hernand Herrera y Ramón Molina and designed by Brother Sylvestre. There are eight altars in all including one dedicated to the Virgen de Carmen, which features an allegorical representation of purgatory with human figures, and another to Santa Teresa del Niño Jesús, which incorporates a statue of Santa Rosa de Lima, another of Santa Teresa de Ávila, and an imposing effigy of Santa Teresa del Niño Jesús. The high altar displays 10 niches and four small towers decorated with androgynous cherub and images of the Dolorosa, San Juan, Santa Elena, the Verónica, Santa Bárbara and María Magdalena. The retable is decorated with sculpture of the resurrection, and the sacristy is integrated into the high altar. There are an impressive number of stained-glass windows throughout the church. They are French-made and represent various moments in the lives of Señor de los Milagros (The Miraculous Christ), the Virgin and other saints. Under the high altar, a crypt is visible, containing the remains of the Redemptorist missionaries who helped build the church.

An anthro-
pomorphic
statue at
the Parque
Arqueológico
de San
Augustín.

La guadua, one
of the species
of palm trees
that grow in the
Quindío region.

The western cordillera dominates the landscape along the Pacific coast.

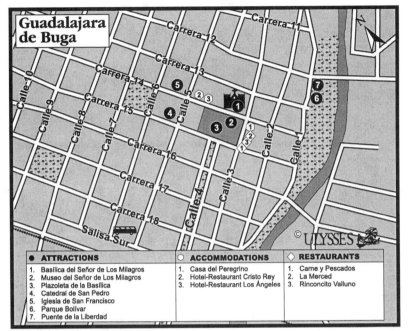

ATTRACTIONS
1. Basílica del Señor de Los Milagros
2. Museo del Señor de Los Milagros
3. Plazoleta de la Basílica
4. Catedral de San Pedro
5. Iglesia de San Francisco
6. Parque Bolívar
7. Puente de la Libertad

ACCOMMODATIONS
1. Casa del Peregrino
2. Hotel-Restaurant Cristo Rey
3. Hotel-Restaurant Los Ángeles

RESTAURANTS
1. Carne y Pescados
2. La Merced
3. Rinconcito Valluno

Museo del Señor de los Milagros ★ *(Mon to Sat 9:30am to 1pm and 2pm to 4:30pm, Sun and holidays 9am to 5:30pm; Carrera 14 No. 3-37,* ☎*28 28 23 or 28 01 60)* is a small museum dedicated to the Basílica del Señor de los Milagros across from it. It exhibits, among other things, religious objects, sacerdotal robes and murals recounting the story of Señor de los Milagros.

Like most of the *plazas* in the city, **Plazoleta de la Basílica** *(across from Basílica del Señor de los Milagros, Calle 4, between Carrera 14 and Carrera 15)* turns into an outdoor religious shopping mall every day. Hundreds of stands compete for the attention of passers-by, with mechanical figures of Christ that make a blessing gesture, the Virgin with a light-up halo, scapulars that guarantee entry into heaven or your money back, and life-size plaster lawn ornaments representing the saints.

Catedral de San Pedro ★★★ *(Carrera 15, between Calle 5 and Calle 6)* was initially built by the Jesuits in 1573. The church was partially destroyed by the earthquake of 1766, and rebuilt in 1775 with the financial assistance of

the king of Spain. The cathedral is now considered an important part of Buga's colonial heritage.

Iglesia de San Francisco ★★ *(Carrera 14, between Calle 5 and Calle 6)* was erected in 1745 by the Jesuit brother Simón Schnherr to serve as a chapel dedicated to Jesús Nazareno. In 1870 its façade, the only part of the church damaged by the earthquake of 1766, was rebuilt.

Parque de Bolívar ★★ *(Carrera 12, at the corner of Calle 1)* was designed in 1924 by architect Enrique Figueroa. It includes an admirable replica of the statue called *Libertador*, by sculptor Tenerani, which stands in Bogotá's Plaza Mayor.

Puente de la Libertad *(Carrera 12, between Calle 1 and Calle 3)* was built from 1897 to 1898 under the aegis of the governor of the department of Cauca at the time, Manuel Antonio Sanclemente, who later became president of the Republic.

Basílica del Señor de los Milagros

Buenaventura ★★

Buenaventura does not offer many tourist attractions aside from its beaches, which are not even very appealing by most standards. However, the atmosphere that permeates this area is worth the trip in itself. From June to October, you can also spot migrating whales here.

Calle 1 ★★★ *(between Carrera 1a and 5)* is one of the prettiest avenues in Buenaventura, a sort of *ruta rosa*, one could say, that is less than one kilometre long. It offers views of the bay across Parque Colpuertos, and is lined with hotels, restaurants and charming patios. This is where *Bonaverenses* come in the evening to meet and enjoy refreshments. A stop to see the craftspeople who sell jewellery and leather clothing on the sidewalk at the corner of Carrera 3a is a must.

The hotel **Estación** ★★★ *(Calle 2a No. 1a-8, ☎243 40 70, ⊷243 41 18)* is one of the city's historic monuments (see p 262). Its construction dates from 1928, an era when turn-of-the-century romanticism was still exerting an influence. It is the work of *Bogotano* engineer Paulo Emilio Páez, who is also credited with the Palacio Nacional (see p 254) and the reconstruction of La Ermita (see p 254), both found in Cali. For a long time the hotel was owned by Ferrocarrils Nacionales, División Pacífico, the national railroad company, which, along with

its location directly across from the old, abandoned train station, explains the name "Estación". In short order, the hotel became the centre of Buenaventura's social and commercial life, and is still known for this role today. At the beginning of the century, Buenaventura was the port of entry for most visitors to the country. It was an era of great splendour and prosperity. With its typically European elegance, reflecting a style also common in California, the hotel organized balls with orchestras, concerts and fashion shows. Some guests say that you can still hear strains of the waltzes of imperial Vienna wafting through the hotel. Following the decline of the railroad, the hotel gradually lost its glamour and the quality of service deteriorated. However, in 1979 a conglomerate made up of the Federación Nacional de Cafetero, Hoteles Estelar, which manages the Estación, Cortuvalle, and the Corporación Nacional de Turismo was formed to revive the Estación. Today, the hotel reflects all of the splendour of the Belle Époque, with its long white staircases decorated with ornate banisters; its wide white balconies adorned with columns and intricate balustrades; its restaurants with views of the ocean; its spacious, tastefully decorated rooms; its inviting pool; and the whole atmosphere that pervades its sitting rooms and the open-design lobby. Together, these features create the impression of a decor specially designed for the needs of the film *Fitzcarraldo* (1982), by German director Werner Herzog, which is set in this part of the world at the turn of the cen-

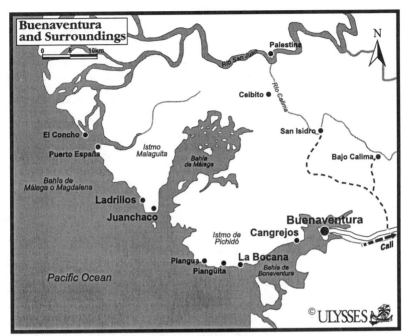

Buenaventura and Surroundings

SANTIAGO DE CALI

tury, the heyday of the billionaire rubber barons.

Parque Colpuertos ★★★ *(on Buenaventura Bay, Calle 1a between Carreras 1a and Carrera 3a)* is a very beautiful park that has gradually become part of *Bonaverenses*'s daily routine. It exhibits a bronze sculpture of José Prudencio Padilla, the hero of the war of independence, who defeated the Spanish in a naval battle on Lake Maracaïbo on July 24, 1823. The park also encloses a lighthouse which may be visited *(500 pesos)* and which offers an impressive view of the city and Buenaventura Bay – after you climb up its 75 steps. The park also comprises an open-air theatre, and on Sundays, clowns and other children's performers entertain while vendors offer all sorts of victuals cooked up on the grill. At the far end of the park, at the entrance to the Muelle Turístico, there are some paved playing courts for *balonpesado*, a ball game invented in Colombia (see p 260).

Palacio Nacional ★ *(Carrera 3a, corner of Calle 3a)* was built in 1934 and vaguely recalls the Art Deco style of the top of the Empire State Building in New York. The yellow terracotta building now houses the seat of the upper council of justice.

Diagonally across from the Palacio Nacional, **Catedral San Buenaventura ★** *(Calle 6, across from Carrera 3)* is a large red stone Gothic building with three belltowers, the nave of which is practically open to the outdoors. It includes an admirable, rather spectacular stained-glass window at the entrance on the right.

 ACCOMMODATIONS

Be especially careful when choosing accommodations in this region so as not to end up in a brothel. This is true not only in Cali, but also in Buenaventura, which is a port city. This is not, however, a problem in Guadalajara de Buga.

Santiago de Cali

The **Plaza** *($; pb, hw, ⊗, ☎, tv, ▣, ℜ; Carrera 6a No.10-29, ☎882 25 60)* is a budget hotel that has the advantage of a central, downtown location. With 41 clean, adequately furnished rooms, it offers good value for the money. A good gauge of this hotel's quality is that it is owned by Klonis Hoteles, a company that

El Balonpesado

Balonpesado is played in a 15-metre-by-28-metre rectangle, at both ends of which there are two circles 1.5 metres in circumference in which the goals are scored.

There are 10 players per team, 5 on the court and 5 "on the bench". The object is to try to get possession of the ball, which resembles a volleyball.

Balonpesado is played in two 25-minute periods, with a 4-minute break between. Thus, the winner is decided in about an hour.

To begin, the five players on each team form two lines facing each other and the ball is placed on a scrimmage line. The referee blows a whistle and the game begins. Whoever gets the ball runs in any direction, trying to shake off his rivals with his hands and also trying to pass the ball to his teammates. The opposing team tries to take the ball and can do so by holding the player with the ball by the hand or arm or even by the belt. Tripping is not permitted. A direct goal is scored when a player, without knocking anybody over, succeeds in getting the ball in the circle of the opposing team's zone, either by rolling it or throwing it. An indirect goal is scored when a player enters the circle carrying the ball, or when the ball is thrown by one player and caught by a teammate in the opposing team's zone.

Invented by Professor Roberto Lozano in Buenaventura on March 27, 1973, *balonpesado* is now played all over Colombia and even occasionally outside the country. Games have been organized in Cuba, Germany, Mexico and even in the former USSR.

operates six hotels in downtown Cali and is known to strive to maintain its good reputation.

Hotel Ramada *($-$$; pb, hw, ≈, mb, ☎, tv, ▣, ℜ; Calle 5 No. 5-025, between Carrera 5 and Carrera 6, ☎881 01 67 or 884 49 07, ⊸881 17 48)* is a small, new, five-storey hotel near the Inter-Continental, which offers 22 quality rooms at advantageous prices. It is also fun to dine on the hotel's rooftop terrace, which offers a magnificent view of the city. This, too, is an excellent value for the price.

🏊 **Hotel Río Cali** *($-$$; pb, hw, ≈, mb, ☎, tv, ▣, ℜ; Avenida Colombia No. 9-80, ☎880 31 56 or 880 31 57, ⊸880 31 58)* is an old, colonial four-storey hotel on the shore of Río Cali across from Paseo Bolívar. Its huge rooms are surprising because of their old-fashioned, respectable style. Because it is slightly out of fashion by today's standards, the hotel is not very busy, but it is perfectly satisfactory for budget travellers.

The **Royal Plaza** *($$; pb, hw, ⊗, ☎, tv, ℜ; Carrera 4 No. 11-69, ☎883 92 69, ⊸883 99 55)* is a 70-room hotel established in an imposing 10-storey building. The rooms, with European-style furnishings, are pleasant and very comfortable. The reception and ser-

vice are attentive. This hotel also belongs to Klonis Hoteles.

The **Astoria** *($$; pb, hw, ⊗, ☎, tv, ℜ; Calle 11 No. 5-16, ☎883 32 53, ⊸884 35 79)* is set in an eight-storey building that rounds off the corner of Calle 11 and Carrera 5. The 67 rooms are furnished with remarkable bronze beds that give them an unusual old-fashioned charm. Also part of the Klonis Hoteles chain.

The **Americana** *($$$; pb, hw, ≈, ☎, tv, mb, ℜ; Carrera 4 No. 8-73, ☎882 43 70, ⊸880 77 10)* is decidedly more modern than the other hotels in the Klonis Hoteles chain. Inside a downtown building of about 15 floors, the Americana offers comfortable rooms decorated with contemporary furniture.

The **Imperial** *($$$; pb, hw, ≈, ☎, tv, mb, ≈, ⊗, △, ℜ; Calle 9 No. 3-93, ☎889 95 71)* is another excellent Klonis hotel that occupies an eight-storey Art-Deco building. It has a rooftop pool with a magnificent view of downtown Cali. Its 51 rooms have European-style furniture and a modern decor.

Hotel Santiago de Cali *($$$-$$$$; pb, hw, ≈, mb, ☎, tv, ▣, ℜ, ⊘, ⊗, △, ; Carrera 6a No. 11-48, ☎889 19 51 or 889 19 52, ⊸880 97 51)* is housed in a six-storey downtown building with 85 comfortable rooms decorated with a certain refinement. Although it is not a five-star hotel, the Santiago de Cali offers the same services as top-class hotels at better rates. The service is friendly.

The **Obelisco** *($$$$; pb, hw, ≡, mb, ☎, tv, ▦, ℛ, ≈, ◌; Avenida Colombia No. 4o-59, ☎880 91 21, ⇢883 02 19)* is Klonis Hoteles' luxury model. In a recently completed building, the Obelisco offers 50 modern rooms, some of which have balconies. Also located downtown, this hotel mainly caters to businesspeople but will also meet the needs of tourists with moderate budgets.

The **Dann Cali** *($$$$$; pb, hw, ≡, mb, ☎, tv, ▦, ℛ, P; Avenida Colombia No. 1-40, ☎882 32 30, ⇢883 01 29)* is located across from the Inter-Continental on calle 2. This unremarkable, recently built hotel of about 10 storeys offers no surprises. Everything is adequate, except for the stiff reception at the front desk.

🏨 Hotel **Inter-Continental Cali** *($$$$$; pb, hw, ≡, mb, ☎, tv, ▦, ℛ, ⊘, ⊛, ◌, indoor P; Avenida Colombia No. 2-72, ☎882 32 25 or 881 21 86, ⇢889 10 89, www.interconti.com)* faces Río Cali, on the edge of downtown. One of the best hotels in Cali, the Inter-Continental is a nine-storey building that encloses 236 rooms, 60 *ejecutiva* suites and five *especiale* suites. Although the hotel is slightly sterile, like most hotels of this type, the staff at the reception, lobby and bar are exceptionally kind. The rooms are huge and pleasantly furnished. The hotel was renovated in 1996. There are four restaurants, a complete gym, a tennis court, a shopping mall and a casino on site. A choice hotel for travellers for whom money is no object.

Tuluá

There are a number of pleasant hotels in Tuluá's centre. Here are a couple:

🏨 Hotel **Juan María** *($$; pb, hw, ⊛, ☎, tv, ▦, ℛ; Carrera 28 No. 27-10, ☎24 45 62, ⇢24 35 55)* is set in a four-storey building across from Plaza Bolívar. It has 53 rooms and four comfortably furnished suites in a pleasant, peaceful atmosphere.

Hotel Principe *($$$; pb, hw, ≡, mb, ☎, tv, ▦, ℛ, ⊛; Carrera 24 No. 26-46, ☎25 81 11,* ⇢*25 87 66)* offers 39 rooms and six elegantly furnished suites in a new three-storey building right downtown. The reception is pleasant.

Guadalajara de Buga

All of Buga's hotels specialize in religious tourism, so they all have a quiet family atmosphere. Whether this appeals to you or not is a matter of taste, and perhaps faith.

Casa del Peregrino *($; pb, hw, ⊛, ☎, tv, ▦, ℛ; Calle 5a No. 14-45, Plazoleta de la Basílica, ☎20 03 08)* is a large three-storey colonial building with 79 rooms, some of which have balconies overlooking the street while others have verandas opening onto one of two interior courtyards, one of which is used as the dining room. The clientele comes here mainly for its proximity to the Basílica del Señor de los Milagros, less than 50 feet away, diagonally across from the hotel.

Hotel-Restaurant Cristo Rey *($; pb, ⊛, ☎, tv, ▦, ℛ; Carrera 14 No. 5-50, ☎27 28 06, 27 28 23 or 27 83 11)*, adjacent to the Los Angeles, is a 52-rooms hotel and is also just steps from the basilica. The rooms all open onto a pretty, flower-filled interior courtyard that is adorned with a remarkable fountain decorated with indigenous figurines.

Hotel-Restaurant Los Angeles *($; pb, hw, ⊛, tv, ▦, ℛ; Carrera 14 No. 4-34, ☎28 10 18 or 28 05 76)* houses a few rooms with private washrooms, but is mainly made up of common dormitories that can accommodate up to eight people. Set 20 metres from the basilica, this hotel mainly receives groups of pilgrims who spend as little as 8,000 pesos per night for beds in the dormitory rooms. The hotel also has its own little sanctuary right in the middle of the interior courtyard.

Buenaventura

All of the recommendable hotels in Buenaventura proper are located near Parque Colpuertos. This section also includes accommodations in Juanchaco, La Bocana and Cangrejos, small villages that can only be reached by boat.

The **Cascajal** *($; pb, ≡ or ⊛, ☎, tv, ▦; Calle 2a No. 1-10, ☎241 81 34, 241 80 88, 242 28 06* or 242 29 62, ≈241 40 78) is a small three-storey hotel less than 30 steps from the *ruta rosa*. It offers pleasant rooms at affordable prices. Because of Buenaventura's stifling heat and constant humidity it is a good idea to get air conditioning.

Gran Hotel Buenaventura *($$$; pb, hw, ≡, mb, ☎, tv, ▣, ℜ; Calle 1 No. 2a-71, ☎243 45 27 or 241 80 28, ≈243 48 46)* is a good hotel located right on Buenaventura's *ruta rosa*. The rooms are comfortable and the service is adequate.

🛏 **Hotel Estación** *($$$$-$$$$$; pb, hw, ≡, mb, ☎, tv, ▣, ℜ, ≈; Calle 2a No. 1a-8, ☎243 40 70, ≈243 41 18)* is one of the most spectacular hotels in all of Colombia (see p 258). It was built in 1928, in an era when turn-of-the-century romanticism was still in vogue. There are 71 large rooms and four suites comfortably furnished with pieces from the 1900s. The architecture and the decor of the Estación are reminiscent of the splendour of the Belle Époque, with its long white staircases with intricate banisters, its wide white balconies decorated with columns and ornate balustrades, its restaurants with views of the ocean, its huge, tastefully decorated rooms, its inviting pool and the whole atmosphere that permeates its sitting rooms and the open lobby. For this reason, the hotel is described as an attraction – it is actually Buenaventura's most interesting sight. Some of the front-desk staff speak English.

In Juanchaco, La Bocana and Cangrejos – Buenaventura's beaches – every *tienda* is a family business that does double-duty as a restaurant and hotel, and all are pretty much alike. The prices are more or less the same at every stand, ranging from 4,000 to 10,000 pesos. The hotels recommended below are a bit more expensive. They are housed in more solid structures and have telephone numbers in Buenaventura or on the premises so that you can confirm their rates, which are, as everywhere, subject to change without warning. It is also possible to make reservation before leaving on the boat from Buenaventura.

Juanchaco

🛏 The **Asturias** *($; pb, ⊛, ℜ; Avenida de la Playa, ☎246 02 04)* is a small, new, red brick

motel-style hotel with two floors. The service is friendly and attentive. The clean hotel gives the impression of being well-organized and managed by professionals. Guests feel at ease. The relaxed service amplifies this atmosphere.

Hotel Liliana *($; pb, ⊛, ℜ; Avenida de la Playa, ☎246 02 60)* is a small wooden hotel on two storeys with about 10 rooms, two of which have views of the sea. The family atmosphere at this unpretentious hotel will satisfy budget travellers.

La Bocana

Hotel Las Cabañas *($; pb, ≡, ⊛, ℜ, ≈; Avenida de la Playa, ☎242 26 44)* is a motel-style hotel, the main asset of which is its distance, slightly set back, from the hub of the beach. The hotel also offers excellent value.

🛏 **Centro Turístico La Bocana** *($$; pb, ≡, ⊛, ℜ, ≈; Avenida de la Playa, ☎92 24 62, 92 22 56, 92 22 57 or 92 22 58)* is the largest hotel in La Bocana with two swimming pools, a nightclub, a restaurant and conference rooms. Located at the western end of the beach, this resort comprises a series of semi-detached white and blue two-storey buildings with peaked roofs covered in round blue tile reminiscent of the smart little houses of Mediterranean Greece. All of its motel-style rooms have balconies with views of the sea or private terraces on the ground floor. They all open onto an immense yard in which there are swimming and wading pools. The reception is warm and the service relaxed.

Cangrejos

For 35,000 pesos double occupancy including full board, **Refugio Isla Cangrejos** *($$; pb, ⊛, ℜ, ≈; ☎241 71 57)* offers a night in one of a dozen *cabañas*, or cabins, spread out on a small hillside under the trees, all of which have views of the sea. The black mud beach, strewn with debris at low tide, leaves much to be desired, so guests who love to swim will be disappointed despite the wonderful welcome. They can use the pool, of course, but this is usually the last resort when you're right by the ocean.

RESTAURANTS

Santiago de Cali

For the best restaurants in Cali, go to the Zona Rosa, which is actually a *ruta rosa*: Avenida 6n between Calle 15 and Calle 29, from Paseo Bolívar to Chipichape, which is the old factory of Ferrocarrils Nacionales, now transformed into a huge shopping mall, probably the largest in all of South America. At Chipichape, pronounced "tchipi tchapé", and on either side of Avenida 6n, there are all sorts of restaurants serving all sorts of fare, most of them with patios. Therefore, there is ample selection for moderate or unlimited budgets. For tighter budgets, there are a good number of fast-food restaurants downtown. For more elaborate meals in this price range, there are the restaurants at the Terminal de Transportes, open 24 hours a day, where bus and taxi drivers eat. These last are all very good and affordable, offering *almuerzo*, a full meal with soup and a main dish, for under 5,000 pesos.

For more refined gastronomy try:

La Casa Roma *($-$$; every day 11am to midnight; Calle 5b No. 41-54, ☎553 47 21)* is a very charming Italian restaurant that offers pasta in all kinds of sauce.

La Cueva del Cangrejo *($-$$; every day 11am to midnight; Avenida Roosevelt No. 36b-18, ☎557 36 89)*, as its name suggests, serves the best crayfish in town. This restaurant specializes in fish and seafood and offers a pleasant atmosphere.

Mi Tierra *($-$$; every day 11am to midnight; Avenida 8n No. 10n-18, ☎668 28 86)* is a traditional Valle del Cauca restaurant. It serves country fare that consists of meat with beans, rice and mixed vegetables.

There are four restaurants at the Inter-Continental Cali: La Taberna, La Brasserie, La Pizzería and La Terraza. At **La Terraza** *($$-$$$$; every day 7am to 10pm; Avenida Colombia No. 2-72, ☎881 21 86)*, you will get to savour its excellent continental cuisine and enjoy its first-class service, all in a relaxed atmosphere. Set around the pool, La Terraza offers a fresh decor and tables decorated with flowers on tablecloths.

For regional fare in a unique setting, **Cali Viejo** *($$-$$$$; Mon to Sat noon to midnight, Sun noon to 5pm; Casona del Bosque Municipal, ☎883 31 77 or 888 17 89)* is a must. This restaurant on the banks of Río Cali, 200 metres from Parque Zoológico de Cali, specializes in regional Valle del Cauca cuisine. Set in an old colonial house, Cali Viejo offers dining in interior courtyards or on a pleasant patio decorated with flowers and green plants.

Parilla del Gordo Esteban *($$-$$$$; every day 11am to 3pm and 6pm to midnight; Avenida Colombia No. 4-08, ☎882 24 89 or 885 54 10)*, next door to the Inter-Continental Cali, serves grilled meat and fish in a sophisticated atmosphere. The Argentine owner, Esteban Fagandini Arrojo, is a culinary expert who has made grilled meat dishes his specialty. Diners get to choose a piece of beef or a trout directly from the grill. The service is friendly and attentive, as well as discreet.

Tuluá

There are a number of inexpensive places to eat around the market *(between Carrera 22 and 23 and Calle 27 and 28)*.

For more refined fare, the following restaurants are a must:

Restaurante y Pescadería Red Lobster *($$$; every day 10am to 10pm; Calle 35 No. 26-52, ☎224 17 61, ⌐225 77 47)* is, obviously, a seafood restaurant. Among other dishes, it offers crayfish for as little as 15,000 pesos. The restaurant is small and divided into three rooms attractively furnished with Spanish-style pieces. The owner speaks English.

El Montechelo *($$-$$$$; every day noon to 11pm, much later on weekends when the restaurant runs a nightclub; Carrera 27a No. 42-39, ☎224 41 78 or 224 85 63)* is a beautiful restaurant set under a roof of dried palm fronds with a flower-filled open-air dining room that also functions as a patio and nightclub on weekends. Local cuisine and grill dishes figure on the menu. The service is pleasant and relaxed.

Guadalajara de Buga

All of Buga's hotels have restaurants to serve their special clienteles, made up largely of pilgrims. There are also attractive patio-restaurants on Plazoleta de la Basílica *(Calle 4, between Carrera 14 and Carrera 16)*.

Rinconcito Valluno *($-$$; Mon to Fri 10am to midnight, Sat, Sun and holidays 10am to 2am; Calle 4 No. 15-61, ☎27 56 69)* specializes in local fare. Most diners choose to eat on the patio, which lets them watch tourists strolling on Plazoleta de la Basílica. The service is efficient.

Carne y Pescados *($-$$; Mon to Fri 10am to midnight, Sat, Sun and holidays 10am to 2am; Calle 4 No. 15-81, ☎28 15 13)* features grilled fish and seafood. Freshwater fish, such as trout, is the house specialty.

La Merced *($-$$; Mon to Fri 10am to midnight, Sat, Sun and holidays 10am to 2am; Calle 4 No. 15-87, ☎27 60 35)* is another restaurant-patio that focusses on traditional cuisine. Here, the best bet is the *almuerzo*, including chicken or beef soup, followed by a main course of chicken, pork or beef, accompanied by rice and a fresh vegetable salad.

Buenaventura

Across from Parque Colpuertos, on Calle 1a between Carrera 1a and Carrera 5, which is one of the prettiest boulevards in Buenaventura, there are about a dozen restaurants and charming patios, as well as some fast-food stands like **Rapido-Rapido** *($; every day 11am to 11pm; Calle 1a No. 1a-08, ☎242 43 44)*, which serves pizza, hamburgers, hot dogs *(perros calientes)* and fries on a very busy sidewalk terrace.

For more sophisticated cuisine, first choice is **Primo's** *($$; every day 11am to 11pm; Calle 1a No. 3-33, ☎242 31 09)*, a small seafood restaurant with an appealing atmosphere and friendly European-style service. The dining room opens out onto the sidewalk, which serves as a terrace. These streetside tables are great for taking in evening sea breezes, although the many passers-by may be a bit irksome. The seafood is recommended since it is always fresh. The garlic shrimp are excellent.

The best restaurant in Buenaventura is unquestionably that of the **Estación** *($$-$$$; every day 7am to midnight; Calle 2 No. 1a-08, ☎243 40 70)* (see p 262). Actually, there are four dining rooms here, but they have the same kitchen and menu: Las Gaviotas, Cafetería Paso a Nivel, La Pizzería and El Malecón. To please its entire clientele, every evening from 6pm the hotel serves pizza prepared on the lawn next to the pool with ingredients chosen by the guests and cooked indoors. On Thursdays, the chef concocts a *parilla* of meat and seafood on a grill set up on the lawn. Diners can choose from the tables in the dining room, where the full-blast air conditioning is a bit unpleasant, especially considering that there are tables set on a large balcony so that diners can enjoy the refreshing breeze blowing gently from the sea. Or they may choose a table on the lawn where they can enjoy the sunset. Meals are also served around the pool itself.

  ENTERTAINMENT

Santiago de Cali

To sample Cali's bars, terraces and fashionable nightclubs, visitors must head to the Zona Rosa, Avenida 6n *(between Calle 15 and Calle 29)* from Paseo Bolívar to Chipichape.

Buenaventura

Buenaventura's bars and popular terraces are on the *ruta rosa*, Calle 1a between Carrera 1a and Carrera 5.

Events

Some interesting social and cultural events in the Valle del Cauca are:

Muestra de Talleres de Bordado, an embroidery fair held in March in Cartago;

Festival Nacional de Intérpretes de la Canción "Mono Núñez", a music festival held in May in Ginebra;

Exposición Agropecuaria e Industrial, in Tuluá in June;

Fiestas de la Virgen de Carmen, in Buenaventura in July;

Festival de la Canción de Buga "Festi Buga", in Guadalajara de Buga in August;

Feria Internacional del Vino, in Cali in November;

Feria Internacional de la Caña de Azúcar, in Cali in December.

 SHOPPING

Cartago, a small city of about 100,000 residents in the department of Valle del Cauca, about 170 kilometres north of Cali, is known as the Colombian capital of embroidery. Exquisite examples of this art can be found in all of Cali's craft shops.

Artesanía La Caleñita, Carrera 24 No. 8-53, ☎559 21 36.
Artículo Tipico Calima, Calle 9 No. 29a-22, ☎556 54 66.
El Paraíso de las Artesanías, Carrera 28 No. 8-40, ☎514 08 61.
Galería Museo Dorado, Avenida 5a Norte No. 23dn-68, ☎667 69 26.
Los Balcones Colonial, Carrera 38 No. 10-04, ☎335 03 46.
Museo de Artesanías de Colombia, Calle 12 No. 1-16, ☎880 53 14.

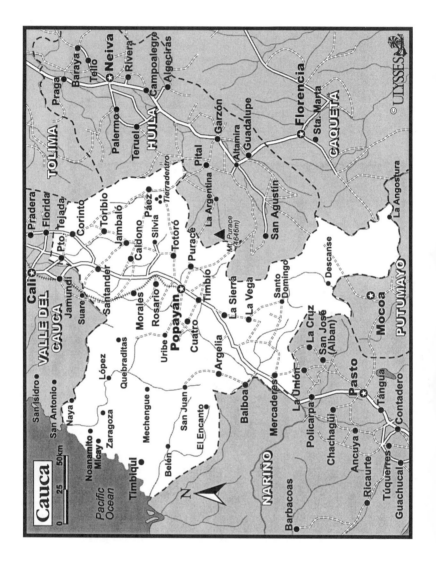

Cauca

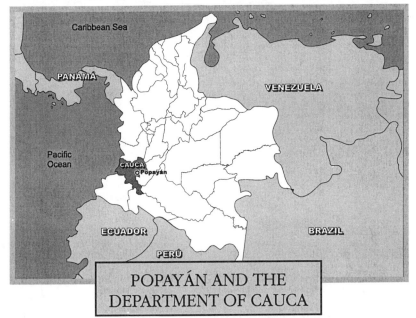

POPAYÁN AND THE
DEPARTMENT OF CAUCA

T he department of Cauca, in south-western Colombia, is certainly the most outstanding tourist attraction in the country. It offers a combination of history, archaeology, anthropology, culture and ecology that is unique in the world. Located on the Pacific Coast, south of the department of Valle de Cauca and north of the department of Nariño, its eastern neighbours, from north to south, are the departments of Tolima, Huila and Putumayo. With an area of 31,000 square kilometres, it is home to nearly 1,000,000 people.

There are 34 municipalities in El Cauca, including the capital, Popayán. The four major Colombian rivers, Río Cauca, Río Magdalena, Río Patía and Río Caquetá, all originate here. The department also contains one of the most spectacular mountains in the country, Mount Puracé, whose 4,600-metre-high peak is capped with snow throughout the year, even though the average temperature on the mountain is 20°C.

Popayán

Popayán, capital of the department of Cauca, is the ideal place from which to investigate the history, anthropology and archaeology of the extraordinary region that falls within the Popayán-Tierradentro-San Agustín triangle. It offers a peaceful city environment and a downtown area that has been proclaimed a national

heritage. Surprisingly, the accommodations and restaurants here are of better quality and are less expensive than those in other parts of the country.

A Brief History

On Christmas Eve in 1536, Captain Juan de Ampudia and his soldiers secured a strategic area in the region, readying it for the arrival of their leader, Sebastián Moyano de Belalcázar. It was Belalcázar who officially founded Popayán on January 13, 1537, under the authority of General Francisco Pizzaro, then governor of Perú. On August 15 of the same year, Belalcázar held a grand ceremonial mass in the public square and, in the name of Charles V, baptized the new colony Asunción de Popayán. The new town, situated on the route linking Cartagena de Indias to Quito, Ecuador and to Lima, Peru, immediately superceded Cali in terms of importance in Colombia's development. After the defeat of the Pijaos, Popayán became the seat of regional government. It was subject first to the authority of Quito, and later to that of Bogotá. During this period, many of the land-owning elite, or *caleños,* constructed private mansions here as secondary residences, taking advantage of the area's moderate climate. Thanks to an elevation of 1,700 metres above sea level, the temperature in the city is a pleasant 18°C.

According to some sources, the name Popayán means "in honour of the greatest cacique" (hereditary chief). Others believe it is derived from the Quechua word "pampayan": *pampa*, means "valley", and *yan*, means "river". Thus, Popayán would be a valley with a river running through it, in this case, the Río Cauca.

Popayán Today

Today, Popayán is an outstanding example of a typical old Colombian city: a veritable colonial gem, whose downtown area was almost completely reconstructed after a devastating earthquake on March 31, 1983. This was a slow and painstaking process, so as to ensure authenticity. There are no skyscrapers here. The mandated skyline of two-storey houses is breached only by church steeples; they rise as if to salute the city's glorious past. In the aftermath of the earthquake, it was decided that all reconstructed houses would be painted white and have red tile roofs. The wrought-iron balconies overlooking the narrow streets is mirrored in the old-fashioned lampposts that illuminate them. By day or by night, the overall effect of the scene is to transport the visitor back in time, to the period when the hooves of conquistadors' horses still clattered on the cobble stones.

Silvia

Silvia is a colonial *pueblito* with fewer than 5,000 inhabitants, some 70 kilometres from Popayán. At an altitude of 2,500 metres, the temperature varies between 14°C and 18°C. The village is lovely, with narrow streets separating simple little houses, many of which are white, with red tile roofs. But the principal attraction occurs on Tuesday morning (from dawn to 1pm) in the village square, when the *Guambianos* come down from the mountains at daybreak to set up their market stalls. From 6am on, they arrive in their *chivas* laden with fruit, vegetables, cheeses and poultry from their farms, as well as handcrafted clothing, pottery and jewellery. While the handicrafts are intriguing, it is the spectacle of setting up their stalls that really charms visitors. Arrive by 7am in order not to miss anything; it might be best to stay in Silvia on Monday night. The car ride from Popayán takes at least an hour and a half by way of a small asphalt road that snakes labouriously up to Silvia from Piendamo, on the Cali-Popayán highway. The landscape is magnificent as the sun rises in the mysterious Andes. Often, the mountaintops are hidden from view by the pale and chilly morning mist.

Market day at Silvia is special because of the large number of Guambianos who attend it. These Amerindians have kept their language and traditions intact despite their close contact with mainstream society. They wear traditional costume which, for women, is a long black skirt with pink trimmings. A royal blue mantle with fuchsia fringes is draped across their shoulders, and countless strands of white beads hang around their necks. A round, gray or black hat and brown or black leather boots complete the outfit.

The men also wear mantles over their shirts, skirts down to their ankles (in the same black and fuchsia colours of the women's skirts), round hats and brown or black leather boots.

San Agustín

San Agustín is widely recognized as the single most fascinating archaeological site in Latin America. It is situated some 110 kilometres southeast of Popayán, in the department of Huila. The road from Popayán crisscrosses the central cordillera and is unpaved and poorly maintained. It is an exhausting seven-hour trip by four-wheel drive vehicle – the most common means of transport used by travel agencies for these excursions. You can also take the bus from the Terminal de Transportes in Popayán, but the trip is just as uncomfortable.

About 10,000 people live this quiet city, and 20,000 more in the nearby suburbs. Centuries ago, a flourishing indigenous civilization existed in this region. Since nothing is known about the origins of this civilization or the reasons for its disappearance, archaeologists refer to it as San Agustín, for lack of a better name. Only vestiges remain of this formerly vast civilization – terraces, roads and foundations of villages spread over a mountainous 200-square-kilometre area at an altitude of 1,700 metres. However, an impressive number of sculptures and statues are displayed at the Parque Arqueológico, declared a world heritage historical and archaeological site by UNESCO in December 1995.

The Páez

Ramiro is a Páez Amerindian who works at the Plazuela hotel in which I stayed. The owner, Señora Yolanda Mosquera, had asked him to be my guide and driver for a day trip to Silvia. He had to be sure we were there by 7am, so that we wouldn't miss the arrival of the Guambianos at the Tuesday market. I don't speak Spanish very well, so he patiently translated and explained what was going on to me all day long.

The Páez lived in this region long before the arrival of the Spanish. Although the newcomers appropriated their land, the Páez are still a proud people. They have retained their culture, their language and many of their traditional costumes. However, they are gradually being forced to change their ways because of the systematic lack of comprehension on the part of the white majority. For example, the Páez have always maintained equilibrium between their needs and the renewal of natural resources, a concept that is almost completely ignored by white society.

Today, there are about 25,000 Páez living on 3,000 square kilometres in the mountains around Popayán, Tierradentro and San Agustín. They grow corn (maize), beans, manioc (yuca) and other fruits and vegetables that they sell at nearby markets. They have their own government, consisting of an annually elected council. They live in a hierarchical society in which those in power control the activities, divide communal labour and function as the judicial authority for the culture as a whole.

Their homes are constructed with bamboo and have thatched roofs. They vary in size and style, depending on the climate and availability of natural resources. The Páez are excellent craftspeople and make their own clothing, mainly from hemp. Until recently, they also fabricated most of domestic items, such as wooden spoons and terra cotta dishes.

They know nothing, or so they claim, about the statues, tombs and archaeological treasures discovered throughout the mountainous regions around San Agustín and Tierradentro.

These remains were first brought to light by Fray Juan de Santa Gertrudis who visited here in 1758. However, it was not until 1913 that the first studies were made by German archaeologist K.T. Preuss. Since then, other scholars have pursued more detailed studies and analyses of the area. The most prominent of these are José Pérz de Barradas in 1936, Gerardo Reichel-Dolamtoff in 1966 and Luis Dunque Gómez since 1943.

According to these experts, the region was a sacred burial ground for an indigenous people who sometimes travelled great distances in order to perform the religious ceremonies and inter their dead at this site. Most of the large, impressive statues represent the gods associated with burials. They were first discovered by the Spanish colonists cultivating their fields. Undoubtedly, some were destroyed, which led to the establishment of the current Parque Arqueológico. Researchers at the park are convinced that only about 60 percent of the statues still in existence have been recovered. Thus, farmers and residents in the region are constantly on the lookout for them. It is hoped that no more of this unique heritage will be lost.

Almost nothing is known about this civilization which dates back as far as 3,500 years BC. It has, however, been established that its disappearance coincided with the arrival of the first Spaniards in Colombia. The vast range of styles and quality of craftsmanship in the statues, from the very crude first renderings to the refined and sophisticated later works, leave no doubt as to the remarkable longevity of this civilization.

Tierradentro

The road from San Agustín to Tierradentro is a fairly straightforward drive, according to the map, and should take at least seven hours to travel. However, this in no way implies that the road is straight or even that it runs consistently in one direction. Like the one between San Agustín and Popayán, this road is unpaved and poorly maintained. It snakes through the Andes, with many deep ravines, lofty mountain peaks and tumultuous *ríos* surging to the next waterfall along the way. Breathtaking landscapes appear at every hairpin curve in the road, after every tortuous climb, after every hair-raising descent...

The region of Tierradentro is so named because of the difficulty involved in getting to it. Not only is it geographically strategic, but the indigenous people here also resisted the invading Spaniards with great tenacity. Hence the Spanish name for the area, *La Tierra Adentro* (literally, "far" or "interior" land), which dates from the earliest attempts to penetrate it. Tierradentro is 110 kilometres northeast of Popayán. A bus runs here from the Terminal de Transportes in Popayán. However, the journey is not a comfortable one by any means.

Today, the region's main town is San Andrés de Pisimbalá, a small community with fewer than 1,000 inhabitants, set in a valley surrounded by mountains that contain the most spectacular pre-Columbian tombs on the continent.

 FINDING YOUR WAY AROUND

Popayán

The *calles* in Popayán run east-west, with the numbers of the streets increasing from north to south. The *carreras* run north-south, with the numbers of the streets increasing from east to west.

By Plane

Aeropuerto Guillermo León Valencia *(take the road going north from the traffic circle on Autopista Norte a Cali, to the west of the Terminal,* ☎*23 13 79)* is located behind the Terminal de Transportes. Take a taxi if you have a lot of luggage. However, the airport is only a 15 minutes' walk from the downtown area. Also, buses marked "Ruta 2, Centro" go directly to the airport from the city centre. Here is the Avianca schedule for flights within Colombia:

Bogotá, Mon to Thu, Sat and Sun 4:14pm; 114,000 pesos.

Airline Companies

Avianca, Carrera 7 No. 5-77, ☎24 09 01
Intercontinental de Aviación, Carrera 7a No. 4-28, room 1b, ☎24 03 35
Satena, Calle 4a No. 7-39, ☎24 21 36

Inter-City Transportation

Popayán

The **Terminal de Transportes** *(Transv. 9a No. 4n-125,* ☎*83 54 25)* is a new building, less than 15 minutes from downtown on foot, though it is best to go by taxi. The same bus that goes to the airport ("Ruta 2, Centro") also runs to the Terminal. Many bus and minibus companies provide transportation to Cali, San Agustín and Tierradentro. Here are the phone numbers of the largest ones:

Expreso Palmira, ☎23 19 99;
Expreso Bolivariano, ☎23 29 27;
Flota Magdalena, ☎23 05 02;
Rapido Tolima, ☎23 38 92.

Silvia

Colectivos leave the Terminal de Transportes in Popayán for Silvia starting at 8am every day. In Silvia, the *colectivos* leave from the Parque Central.

San Agustín

Buses to San Agustín leave early every morning from the Terminal de Transportes in Popayán. The trip takes seven hours and is exhausting since the dirt road is poorly maintained. The Terminal de Transportes in San Agustín is on Calle 3 at the intersection with Carrera 11.

Tierradentro

Three buses run from San Andrés de Pisimbalá to Popayán every day. They leave from the centre of the village, near the church, at 7:30am, 12:30pm and 3pm.

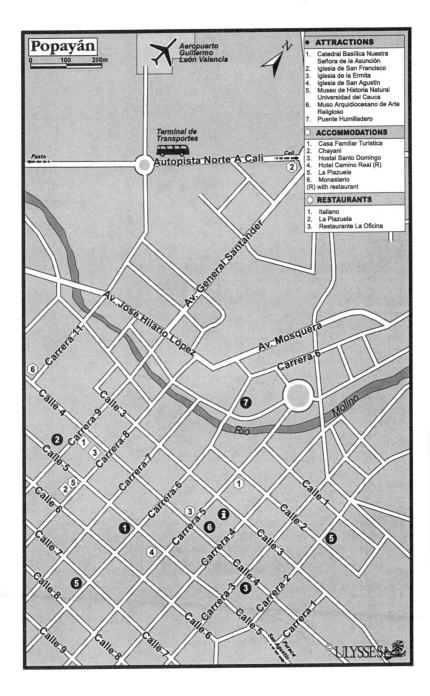

Popayán

0   100   200m

Aeropuerto Guillermo León Valencia

N

Terminal de Transportes

Pasto

Autopista Norte A Cali

Cali

Av. General Santander

Av. José Hilario López

Carrera 11

Av. Mosquera

Carrera 6

Calle 4

Calle 3

Carrera 9

Carrera 8

Carrera 7

Rio Molino

Calle 5

Calle 6

Carrera 6

Calle 1

Calle 7

Carrera 5

Calle 2

Calle 8

Carrera 4

Calle 3

Calle 4

Carrera 2

Calle 5

Carrera 3

Calle 6

Carrera 1

Calle 5

Calle 9

Calle 8

Calle 7

Paseo San Agustín

© ULYSSES

● ATTRACTIONS

1. Catedral Basílica Nuestra Señora de la Asunción
2. Iglesia de San Francisco
3. Iglesia de la Ermita
4. Iglesia de San Agustín
5. Museo de Historia Natural Universidad del Cauca
6. Muso Arquidiocesano de Arte Religioso
7. Puente Humilladero

○ ACCOMMODATIONS

1. Casa Familiar Turística
2. Chayani
3. Hostal Santo Domingo
4. Hotel Camino Real (R)
5. La Plazuela
6. Monasterio
(R) with restaurant

◇ RESTAURANTS

1. Italiano
2. La Plazuela
3. Restaurante La Oficina

By Taxi

Popayán

Taxis are yellow ochre and marked *Servicio Público*. Instead of metres, there is a fixed rate of 1,000 pesos. You can flag down a taxi on the street or summon one by telephone:

Servitaxi, ☎23 33 33;
Taxi Belalcázar, ☎23 11 11;
Taxi a domicilio, ☎23 99 99.

Silvia, San Agustín and Tierradentro

There is no taxi service in these three places.

Public Transportation

Popayán

City buses go everywhere in Popayán regularly *(350 pesos)*. However, all the points of interest in the town itself are within walking distance.

San Agustín

There is no public transportation in either Silvia or Tierradentro. There are minibuses in San Agustín that usually go to the Parque Arqueológico *(250 pesos)*.

 PRACTICAL INFORMATION

Area Codes

Department of Cauca: 28
Department of Huila: 88

Mail

Popayán

Mail service is provided at the **Avianca** office, Carrera 7 No. 5-77.

Tourist Information

Popayán

Oficina de Turismo, Calle 3 No. 4-70, ☎24 22 51, ⌐24 23 29.
Fondo de Promoción Turística del Cauca, Calle 3 No. 4-70, ☎24 04 68.

Banks

Popayán

Banks in Popayán do not cash traveller's cheques. It is best to cash cheques or exchange currency in Cali before coming here. However, the ATMs accept all credit cards. Also, **Almacén Salvador Duque** *(Calle 5a No. 6-25, between Carreras 5a and 6a, ☎24 17 00)* will cash American traveller's cheques and exchange American currency. This store is known for its reasonable exchange rates.

Silvia, San Agustín and Tierradentro

It is impossible to exchange currency or cash traveller's cheques in these three places. Be sure to plan ahead for this.

Excursions

Many organized excursions are available through travel agencies in the areas of Popayán, Silvia, San Agustín and Tierradentro.

Enquire at the following travel agencies:

Popayán

Lucia Nates Turismo, Calle 4 No. 8-79, ☎24 22 22.
Lunapaz Ecoturismo, Carrera 7 No. 6-23, office 201, ☎24 35 47.
Viajes Puracé, Calle 5 No. 6-83, ☎24 30 58.
Viajes Popayán, Carrera 7 No. 5-19, ☎24 41 05.
Regional Sur Andian de Parques, Carrera 9n No. 18n-143, ☎/⌐23 99 32.

Silvia

Operador de Turismo de Silvia, Carrera 2 No. 14-66, ☎25 14 84.

San Agustín

Lucio Moreno Bravo Múños, Calle 4 No. 12-64, ☎37 30 73, ⌨37 32 14.
Cooperativa de Transporte Turístico COO-TRANSTUR, Calle 5 No. 15-47, ☎37 30 19.

Tierradentro

Jaime Calderón Devia, Carretera Principale, No. 56, ☎25 29 09.

 EXPLORING

Popayán ★★★

Popayán is the ideal tourist town. The downtown area is a veritable history book; all its buildings are like works of art in an outdoor exhibition. The churches, hotels and residences are lovingly polished gems. Even the banks, which are such glaring eyesores in the rest of Colombia, are modestly enclosed in colonial buildings and identified only by a small plaque that can barely be seen from the street. Sometimes, the ATMs lie immediately behind a colonial wood door with a bronze or wrought iron doorknob. Others are screened from view by an elaborately worked, colonial-style wrought iron grill.

All commercial and public buildings are painted white including the churches, chapels and convents. A picture perfect! The downtown area is simply charming, and safe for pedestrians day or night.

Popayán's churches are its main tourist attractions. They are not all equally splendid, but each has enough charm of its own that it should not be missed.

The **Catedral Basílica Nuestra Señora de la Asunción** ★★★ *(corner of Calle 5 and Carrera 6)* was built in 1906. The town's first cathedral was constructed with rudimentary materials in 1558, but did not withstand the effects of the weather, particularly the rain. In 1575, the townspeople decided to build a "real" cathedral out of tile and brick, which would give them a more respectable image. On February 2, 1736, a powerful earthquake destroyed most of the city's churches and damaged the cathedral beyond repair. It was demolished, and so the Iglesia de la Ermita (see further below) served as the *Payaneses'* cathedral for a time. A third cathedral was begun in 1819, designed by the Academia de San Fernando in Spain, but was not completed until 1906. Then, on March 31, 1983, its was severely damaged in another earthquake, along with the other buildings in Popayán. Since then, it has been painstakingly reconstructed. A mixture of Romanesque and baroque styles, it contains a marble statue of Nuestra Señora de la Asunción.

The **Iglesia de San Francisco** ★★★ *(corner of Calle 4a and Carrera 9a)* dates from 1775 and was constructed over a 20-year period. It is considered the most beautiful church in the city. Its baroque façade is currently being restored.

The **Iglesia de la Ermita** ★★★ *(corner of Calle 5a and Carrera 2)* was built around 1602, and is the oldest church in Popayán. It withstood the earthquakes of 1736, 1817, 1827 and 1906, and served as the temporary cathedral for the *Payaneses* while their "true" cathedral (see further above) was being built. The baroque retable, crowned by winged vultures above the high altar, is the church's most prized feature. However, the Stations of the Cross are also remarkable as they comprise the oldest frescoes in Popayán. The Jesús Nazareno and the Santa Rosalía are also superb. Although the 1983 earthquake badly damaged the walls, most of the religious objects were not harmed. This is why the *Payaneses* are especially devoted to the Ermita.

The **Iglesia de San Agustín** ★★ *(corner of Calle 7a and Carrera 6)* is a Romanesque church with a Mudejar steeple. Its many frescoes are attractive, but it is the statue of Christ kneeling on a globe that is the main attraction.

The **Museo de Historia Natural Universidad del Cauca** ★★ *(every day 8am to 11am and 2pm to 5pm; Carrera 2a No. 1a-25, ☎23 41 15)* was founded by professor Carlos Lehmán in 1936 as a centre for animal protection and research. Today, it displays the largest collection of stuffed animals in Colombia, if not in all of South America. There are ocelots, pumas, crocodiles and a few exotic creatures, such as a polar bear. There are also collections of insects, birds and snakes. The single most impressive exhibit is probably the condor with a wingspan of nearly two metres. Also, there is a 10-metre-long anaconda devouring an adult wolf whose fangs are bared in a vain attempt to bite its attacker. Another section focuses on the geology, palaeontology, ethnography and archaeology of the region's indigenous cultures. A tour of this museum is an absolute must!

The **Museo Arquidiocesano de Arte Religioso** ★★★ *(every day 9am to 12pm and 2pm to 6pm; Calle 4a No. 4-56, ☎24 27 59)* was created in 1977 to protect, preserve and restore the numerous works of religious art in the city of Popayán and elsewhere in the department of Cauca.

The museum was inaugurated on September 21, 1979 in the 18th-century former residence of the Arboleda family, and was restored by architect Marcelino Pérz de Arroyo. The museum was badly damaged during the 1983 earthquake, and the artwork was restored and temporarily housed by the Banco de la República. Today, the museum displays sculptures, paintings and gold objects in nine different exhibition halls that present an eloquent retrospective of the 16th, 17th and 18th centuries.

The **Puente Humilladero** ★ *(Carrera 6, near Calle 2)* has a very interesting architectural structure in the baroque style. Twelve supporting arches sustain this 240-metre-long, 5.6-metre-wide bridge, which dates from 1868 and spans a little valley that runs right through the centre of Popayán.

Silvia ★

In addition to the spectacular Tuesday morning market day and the village itself, tourists can visit the **Museo de Artesanías del Mundo** ★ *(every day, at the convenience of customers, since the museum is situated in an inn, see p 279; Carrera 2 No. 14-19, ☎25 10 34)*. The museum specializes in handicrafts from around the world. It is a rather small collection, but displays several works from China, Japan, North Africa and Mexico, among other places.

Horses can be rented near the Turismo Silvia hotel (see p 279) for an excursion to a little Amerindian community in the Andes, called La Campaña. It is about a half-hour away by car,

and not much longer by horseback, since the dirt road is not easily navigable, even by four-wheel drive.

San Agustín ★★★

Parque Arqueológico San Agustín ★★★ *(5,000 pesos; every day 9am to 4pm; less than 2 km west of San Agustín)* can be explored on foot in under an hour. It is a gigantic indigenous cemetery with 130 gravestones, some isolated and others in groups, that were sculpted in different periods from 3,000 BC to the beginning of the colonial period. However, it is a totally different experience to explore this place with a guide whose explanations convey the true significance of these unique statues. The best of these, who speaks French, English and German, in addition to Spanish, is the Bureau Nacional de Turísmo's professional guide, No. 018: Lucio Moreno Bravo Muños (see p 273). A native of San Agustín, his interest in the site dates back to his childhood, and he speaks about it with a passion that makes his personal attachment to the place obvious. It costs 50,000 pesos for a group of ten people to hire him, or about US$5 per person. At such a low price, tips are also accepted.

The statues themselves are sculpted from volcanic rock and are strikingly anthropomorphic. Some have angry expressions, intended to inspire fear in the enemies. Others look serene and are meant to appease. The heads of some are gigantic, up to half the size of the statue, with deeply carved features and thick lips with teeth protruding like a jaguar's. According to specialists, the disproportionate size of the head and the amount of detail on it, compared to the rather perfunctory treatment of the much smaller body, indicates that the indigenous people of the time placed much greater importance on the intellect than on the physical body. There are also zoomorphic figures that represent sacred animals, such as the condor and the frog. The park is divided into four main sections *(mesitas)*, three supplementary sections and a statuary garden. *Mesitas* A and B, C and D contain burial mounds that served as temples, with groupings of statues, many of which are surmounted by a tombstone. Most have enormous heads and tiny legs. There are also animal figures and half-animal, half-human ones. The most astonishing work at Mesita B is a stele with carvings of human heads from top to bottom. Often, smaller warrior statues are

grouped around large ones, which are believed to represent immortal guardians for the large stones that represent the great caciques.

After crossing a bamboo forest containing an enormous frog sculpted from rock, you will arrive at a large work called *Fuente de Lavapatas*. This is a complex labyrinth of canals in the forms of serpents, lizards and salamanders, with human faces. These channel a stream into three pools of varying sizes at different heights. It is an extraordinary example of the architectural ingenuity that this civilization attained, using the natural elements in their surroundings: in this case, the stone and the water of rapids. Archaeologists presume that this site was used for ritual bathing and other sacred ceremonies.

The Cerro de Lavapatas is a plateau that rises about 50 metres higher than the rest of the area. It is believed to be a burial ground for children. More importantly, it provided a strategic vantage point as a lookout to defend the territory, or to plot an offensive foray from. The site has remained essentially unchanged; and the uninterrupted view of the area for kilometres around is magnificent.

The last site, the Bosque de las Estatuas, was recently installed. This garden contains 35 monolithic sculptures surrounded by trees. They have been classified according to style by anthropologist Reichel-Dolmatoff: archaic, naturalistic, expressionist or abstract. First discovered by local farmers in the nearby fields, they have been assembled here to be better preserved. One of them has been defaced by of a contemporary graffiti artist. The aerosol paint is indelible and can not be removed without risk of damaging the soft, porous stone of the sculpture.

A minibus leaves for the park from downtown San Agustín every 15 minutes. There are more than 15 additional sites similar to this one within 35-kilometre radius from San Agustín. The aforementioned sites are the closest and most interesting. There are more than 500 statues to be seen outside the Parque Arqueológico, notably at El Tablón, La Pelota, La Chaquira, Obando y El Jabón, Altos de las Piedras, Alto de las Guacas y El Mortiño, Quebradillas, Quichana, La Parada and Naranjos y La Vaderos. These can be visited on foot, by hiking several kilometres. It is also possible to rent horses in San Agustín for such an excursion.

POPAYÁN

The **Museo Precolombiano Villa Real** ★ *(1,500 pesos; every day 8am to 12pm and 2pm to 7pm; Calle 5a No.12-35, ☎37 34 79 or 37 33 44)* is the headquarters of the Instituto Colombiano de Antropología Muestra Arqueológica. This small museum is housed in a former residence whose rooms have been transformed into exhibit halls. The museum operates in conjunction with the government, which protects the archaeological objects, as they are part of the public domain.

Tierradentro ★★★

In addition to the little community of San Andrés de Pisimbalá, a picture-perfect town lost in the Andes, the primary reason for going to Tierradentro, Department of Cauca, is to see the underground tombs scattered on the mountain. Along with San Agustín, Tierradentro is one of the largest pre-Columbian archaeological finds of the century. There are tombs of differing sizes, quality and depths, in groups of 10 to 60 or more, at about a dozen sites.

Parque Arqueológico de Tierradentro ★★★ *(1,000 pesos; every day 8am to 6pm; at the edge of the pueblo, San Andrés de Pisimbalá)* consists of four separate archaeological sites in the surrounding mountains: Segovia, El Duende, Alto de San Andrés and El Aguacate. The tour is on horseback. The guide, Jaime Calderón, will have the horses saddled and ready for a quick getaway at around 1pm. The horses valiantly climb the steep trail, with the mountain on one side and the cliff on the other. The scenery is simply unreal! The horses are used to the journey, so no particular riding expertise is required. The horses pick out their own path along the trail, which allows the brave riders to take more photographs! After about 20 minutes, the guide ties up the horses' reins and leads the group into an area enclosed by a wooden fence: Segovia. There are 28 well-preserved underground tombs accessed by ancient spiral staircases carved out of the rock. Some of the tombs are lit up, while others are visited with a flashlight. It is forbidden to take pictures in the tombs, since flash can damage the colours in the cenotaphs, some of which are decorated with very intricate motifs.

Several tombs are shallow, just a few metres deep, but others are up to seven metres below ground. These are funeral chambers, or ossuaries, the largest of which is three metres high, eight metres wide and five metres deep. They have five or six niches that are supported by two or three columns. Some of the most spectacular have red, white and black geometric motifs, painted in indelible colours that the Amerindians extracted from native plants, including berries and fruit from local shrubs and trees. (Later, the guide demonstrated this process by pulverizing the fruit of one of these trees, while trying very hard to keep the dye from staining his clothing. In fact, he had a hard time removing it from his hands!). There are also anthropomorphic designs, hieroglyphs and petroglyphs representing animals, humans or mythic gods, whose meanings are yet unknown. One can imagine, however, that these Amerindians, who vanished more than three thousand years ago, meant to communicate the timeless message of hope for immortality. In a way, they have achieved their goal, for here we are, the guide and I, very much alive, absorbing the message of their art transmitted over the millennia.

The sarcophagi housed funeral urns that contained the remains of the deceased. The deceased person's weapons and other objects that might be useful in the afterlife were placed into the tombs as well, according to the social rank of the deceased. Today, these urns and other artifacts are kept in different museums in order to preserve them. Many are on display at the museum in Tierradentro, at the entrance to the Parque Arqueológico.

At tomb number 8, a moment of silence is observed in memory of Alvaro Chávez Mendoza, the archaeologist who discovered it. Professor Mendoza died in Bogota in 1976, but his ashes have been kept here since 1994 in an urn placed inside this, the deepest and most elaborately decorated grotto. The professor specified in his will that he wished to symbolically unite contemporary man with this ancient civilization and its many marvels.

Once again we mount our horses for the 20-minute climb to El Duende, a site which is not as well preserved, but still interesting. At an altitude of more than 2,000 metres, the Andes become increasingly awesome, and our horses seem to materialize magically from the clouds below. This plateau affords a unique panorama, not only of the point of departure at the entrance to the Parque Arqueológico at the far end of the valley, but also of other burial grounds on distant mountainsides in all directions.

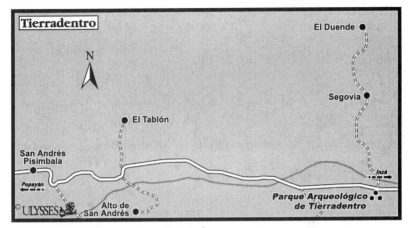

Later, we stop at the terrace of a little *tienda*, located behind the church in the heart of the *pueblo*, **San Andrés de Pisimbalá**. The houses of the *pueblo* are scattered along a single dirt road, the Carretera Principale, which stretches at least two kilometres. People travel mostly on horseback here. An almost mystical calm descends at nightfall, and at the same time a light mist, like a halo, confers a beatific dignity to the countryside. This does not prevent us from ordering cold beer, which we enjoy on the small terrace with only two tables.

The little **Iglesia de San Andrés de Pisimbalá** ★★★ *(in the heart of the village)*, with its thatched roof and whitewashed walls, is a real gem, dating back some 350 years. Its small belltower, only two metres high, is topped by a thatched roof. The ceiling of the spartan interior is supported by hand-hewn wooden beams. The furniture is also hand carved by machete and dates from early colonial times. The statue of San Andrés, primitively sculpted by an unknown artist, rests on a wooden pedestal with handles, so that it can be carried through the streets during religious festivals. To visit the church, obtain the keys from the elderly lady drying her coffee beans on the left side of the village square. On a shelf in the *tiende* where one buys beer, a single dusty bottle of Barton & Guestier white wine rests on a shelf, lost in the heights of the Andes. Later, we savour the contents of the bottle, after cooling it in the freezer at our guide's home. Like most other homes in Tierradentro, it is sometimes transformed into a restaurant to meet the needs of visitors since the hotel's restaurant is not always open. The guide, Jaime Calderón (see p 273), considers

his services worth 20,000 pesos per person for a four-hour excursion on horseback to the principal sites. Unfortunately, he speaks only Spanish. However, his exhaustive commentary helps one to understand and appreciate the surreal scene, especially since the terms he uses are easily understood in English.

The **Museo Tierradentro** ★★ *(daily from 7am to 11am and 1pm to 5pm; at the entrance to the pueblo San Andrés de Pisimbalá)* exhibits artifacts of the indigenous Páez culture on two floors. There is an admirable miniature model village depecting the lifestyles of this civilization (see p 269) as well as funeral urns and objects from the burial sites in surrounding mountains.

Other sites to visit in Tierradentro are El Tablón (different from the El Tablón of San Agustín), Alto de San Andrés and El Aguacate. You can go on foot or hire a guide and horses (see p 273)

Parque Nacional Puracé ★

The Parque Nacional Puracé is a national reserve inaugurated in 1968 and covering some 850 square kilometres in the central cordillera. It is the source of the Colombia's network of natural waterways, since four of the country's principal rivers originate here: the Río Magdalena, the Río Cauca, the Río Patía and the Río Caquetá. Sixty kilometres from Popayán are hot springs amid the flora and fauna particular to this area of steep, snow-capped mountains that can reach heights of up to

Iglesia de San Andrés de Pisimbalá

4,800 metres. These include the well-known Pan de Azúcar (sugar loaf).

Mont Puracé is 4,646 metres high and has erupted frequently, notably in 1831, 1881 and 1927. Indigenous people and rural inhabitants suffered the most from this volcano, since many were forced to leave their homes on its slopes between 1849 and 1852. However, the strongest eruption occurred in May 1889, when rocks and lava were spewed more than 30 kilometres from the crater. The last eruption was accompanied by an earthquake which claimed the lives of 17 students of the Universidad de Cauca on May 26, 1949.

Parque Puracé has two types of hot springs. Those of the Río Vinagre are acidic and sulfurous, while those in the region of San Andrés de Pisimbalá are saline and sulfurous. There is a very diversified fauna, with 22 species of mammals including pumas and deer. More than 246 species of birds live in four different biodomes: the tropical rain forest, the Andean montane, the alpine-like *páramo* and the boreal forest. A strange meteorological phenomenon also occurs here: when Popayán is in the rainy or winter season, *inverno* (beginning in December), Parque Puracé, a mere 40 kilometres away, is in the dry, or summer, season, the *verano*. Certain nectar-producing flowers that attract hummingbirds blossom in the summer season, and these tiny birds invade the region by the thousands.

ACCOMMODATIONS

Popayán

All the hotels in Popayán are in colonial buildings and offer excellent value in terms of quality for the price.

The **Casa Familiar Turística** *($; pb, hw; Carrera 5 No. 2-11, ☎24 48 53)* is the same type of hotel as the Miramar in Santa Marta (see p 144), and has a similar, if not identical clientele, who probably heard of the Casa Familial while staying at Miramar. Budget travellers of all ages come here from throughout Europe and the Americas, and chat and compare notes in an atmosphere reminiscent of the seventies. They also exchange tips and information about other destinations in Colombia. The Casa Familiar Turística has 11 rooms, none of which are private. A bed in a dormitory goes for 5,000 pesos. Hot water showers, a fully equipped kitchen and small dining room are at the guests' disposal. For 2,000 pesos, the owner herself will prepare an American-style breakfast. The establishment is known for being safe and quiet. Music is not permitted after 11pm.

The **Chayani** *($$; pb, hw, mb, ☎, tv, ▨, ℜ; Carrera 9a No. 17n-38, ☎23 01 54 or 23 01 55)* is probably the only recently built hotel in Popayán. It is located on a traffic circle on the Autopista Norte a Cali, just outside the city. The rooms are clean and adequately furnished, and the welcome is warm. It should be noted, however, that better quality accommodations are available in the downtown area at the same rates, notably at La Plazuela and the Hostal Santa Domingo.

Hotel Camino Real *($$-$$$; pb, hw, mb, ☎, tv, ▣, ℜ; Calle 5a No. 5-59, ☎24 15 46, 24 13 54, 24 06 85 or 24 12 54, ⊷24 08 16)* offers 27 rooms and one suite in a monastic atmosphere. The two-storey white building is right on the street and flower boxes adorn each of the seven windows. The rooms are pleasant and offer every comfort. Since Popayán is a quiet town, one can choose a room facing the street without forfeiting a good night's sleep.

Like some other hotels in Popayán, **La Plazuela** *($$-$$$; pb, hw, mb, ☎, tv, ▣, ℜ; Calle 5a No. 8-13, ☎24 10 84 or 24 26 64, ⊷24 09 12)* is a former family dwelling. You will feel as though you are stepping back in time as soon as you set foot in the entrance hall and reception area, which are decorated with colonial furniture. However, La Plazuela offers every modern comfort in its 30 large rooms, including four with balconies that face an interior courtyard with arches, columns, pilasters and a beautiful fountain. The spacious, high-ceilinged rooms are tastefully furnished in a colonial style, as well as functionally and conveniently arranged. La Plazuela is owned by Señora Yolanda Mosquera T., a descendant of the former four-term President of the Republic, Tomás Cipriano de Mosquera, a native of Popayán (born in 1798, died in Coconuco in 1878). Señora Mosquera is very sociable. A stay at La Plazuela is certain to please. The front desk personnel speak English.

Hostal Santo Domingo *($$-$$$; pb, hw, mb, ☎, tv, ▣, ℜ; Calle 4a No. 5-14, ☎24 06 76 or 24 16 07, ⊷24 05 42)* is a former private hotel designed for the Guzmán family in the 18th century by Marcelo Pérez de Arroyo, the best-known architect of the period. In the early part of the 19th century, the building was divided into two residences. After the earthquake of 1983, which partially destroyed the structure, it was entirely renovated and transformed into a *hostal*, a hotel for transients and short-term guests. Today, the rooms are pleasant and the dining room is tastefully decorated. All the furniture is colonial-style and belongs to the family. The rooms overlook a courtyard filled with geraniums, azaleas and other plants that are indigenous to the region. The owner, Señora María Helena Ayerbe de Guzmán, greets the guests herself. The staff speaks English.

The **Monasterio** *($$$$; pb, hw, ≈, mb, ☎, tv, ▣, ℜ, ≈; Calle 4a between Carreras 10a and 11a, ☎24 21 91, ⊷24 40 65)* is in a former monastery that has been completely renovated and now has a hundred or so rooms on two storeys. The spacious rooms have antique but functional furniture and face a courtyard and patio decorated with flowers, green plants and a fountain. Crossing the courtyard, which is surrounded by a gleaming white colonnade that contrasts with the red-tiled roof, is an area with tables and deck chairs around a huge pool. Of course, there is nothing monastic about the Monasterio! It is an ideal place for relaxation, and the personnel provide excellent service.

Silvia

It is a good idea to spend the night in Silvia if you want to get the most out of the Guambianos' market day at 6am on Tuesday mornings.

The **Casa Turística de Silva** *($; pb, hw, ▣, ℜ; Carrera 2 No. 14-39, ☎25 10 34)* claims to be the Swiss chalet of the Andes, and rightly so. This is an old colonial two-storey wooden house with a magnificent flower-filled courtyard. Some of the 30 rooms, aligned motel-fashion along a veranda, overlook the yard with its lovely lawn. These rooms are popular because of their view of the Alps... er... Andes, where an old white abandoned chapel is perched. The atmosphere is very friendly. The complex includes both a restaurant with a terrace on the veranda (see p 280) and the Museo de Artesanías del Mundo (see p 274).

Hotel Cali *($; pb, hw, ℜ; Carrera 2 No. 9-70, Parque Central, ☎25 10 99)* is a family-style establishment for budget-conscious travellers. Located in the heart of the village where all the action is, the hotel is perfectly situated near the site of the colourful Tuesday market. This old colonial house has nine rooms, all facing onto a courtyard which has been transformed into a restaurant (see p 280).

Hotel de Turismo Silvia *($-$$; pb, hw, ▣, ℜ; Carrera 2 No.11-18, ☎25 10 76 or 25 12 53)* is also a family-style place and belongs to the CONFANDI (Caja de Compensacíon Familiar del Valle del Cauca). Thus, the atmosphere is relaxed, with game rooms, television rooms, a park and organized activities for the whole family. Needless to say, children are welcome.

POPAYÁN

San Agustín

San Agustín has several inexpensive hotels on Calle 5a, notably the **Residencias Náñez** *($; pb, hw; Calle 5a No. 15-78, ☎37 30 87)*.

The **Hotel Yalconia** *($$; pb, hw, mb, ☎, tv, ◙, ℜ, ≈; Carretera al Parque Arqueológico, ☎37 30 13 or 37 30 01, ⌐37 30 01)* is the best hotel in San Agustín, with 36 clean well-furnished rooms. All basic comforts are provided at affordable prices. The atmosphere, however, is not particularly welcoming and the service is lax, except in the dining room (see p 281).

Tierradentro

In Tierradentro, almost all homes welcome tourists for one or more nights at negligible cost. Some homes are stylish *Residencias*. Try the **Residencias y Resaturante Pisimbalá** *($; pb, ℜ; 200 m from the entrance to Parque Arqueológico, ☎25 29 21)*, which offers full room and board for 15,000 pesos.

El Refugio *($; pb, hw, mb, ☎, tv, ◙, ℜ, ≈; 200 m from Museo Arqueológico, ☎324 22 51 or 24 04 68, ⌐24 23 29)* is a typical hotel-motel-style establishment with about 30 rooms that are comfortable and well-appointed for the price. This is without doubt the best hotel in Tierradentro. However, during our visit the pool was not in operation and the dining room was closed. The manager assured us that everything is totally functional during the peak season, from December to March.

✖ RESTAURANTS

Popayán

All the hotels in downtown Popoyán have restaurants of international caliber that offer local cuisine as well as Italian, French and American food.

 Restaurante La Oficina *($$; every day 11am to 11pm; Calle 4 No.8-01, ☎24 03 80)* is a typical Colombian-style restaurant known

for its generous portions. The staff is friendly and welcoming. The best time for a quiet meal is 8pm, when the restaurant is less busy.

 The International Press Federation for Gastronomy, Viniculture and Tourism has awarded its Certificate of Merit to the restaurant at the hotel **Camino Real** *($$-$$$; every day 7am to 10:30; Calle 5 No. 5-59, ☎24 12 54, 24 15 46, 24 06 85, 24 29 09 or 24 35 95)*. International and French Cuisine are served, and the wine list has been carefully selected. The dining room has a monastic decor and an air of quiet refinement, with white flowered tablecloths. Prices are reasonable, considering the quality offered. Delicious, juicy steaks are one of the popular items on the menu.

 Italiano *($$-$$$; every day 11am to 12am; Calle 4 No. 8-63, ☎24 06 07)* serves Italian food, of course, but also specializes in Swiss cuisine. You can choose from pasta, pizzas, lasagna, cheese and meat fondues, as well as à la carte items such as sandwiches or an excellent steak with fries. This is a small two-storey establishment with a mezzanine, managed by a French-speaking Swiss. The eclectic clientele includes *Payanese* students and intellectuals as well as tourists, especially those from the Casa Familiar Turística (see p 279).

 The restaurant at the hotel **La Plazuela** *($$-$$$$; every day 7am to 10:30pm, Calle 5 No. 8-13, ☎24 10 84 or 24 10 71)* is situated in a courtyard behind the hotel. The restaurant, with its plush atmosphere, colonial furnishings and attractively decorated tables, also provides excellent service. The cuisine is local as well as international and the chef presents a varied daily menu including pasta and other specialties. The *spaghetti carbonara* served *al dente* proved to be excellent. The service is quick, efficient and discreet.

Silvia

 The restaurant at the **Hotel Cali** *($; every day 7am to 9pm; Carrera 2 No. 9-70, Parque Central, ☎25 10 99)* serves typical Colombian cuisine and features a daily special, such as soup followed by a meat dish, accompanied by manioc, plantains, rice and beans.

 The restaurant at the **Casa Turística** *($$; every day 7am to 9pm; Carrera 2 No. 14-39,*

☎24 03 80) is located on a wooden balcony in the hotel courtyard and has a magnificent view of the Andes. This is probably the prettiest restaurant in Silvia. The cuisine is Colombian and international, and the decor is unique.

San Agustín

The **Arturo Pizzería** *($; every day 11:30am to 8pm; Calle 5a No. 15-58, on the way to the Parque Arqueológico, ☎37 35 85)* is a small, simple Italian restaurant where you can choose from a variety of pizzas, including vegetarian.

Brahama *($; every day 11:30 to 8pm; Calle 5a No. 15-11, on the way to the Parque Arqueológico, ☎37 32 26)* serves typical local food in the courtyard of a colonial residence where a television has been installed. Vegetarian and salad dishes are also available, but the television...!

Facing the Hotel Yalconia, **La Brasa** *($; every day 11:30 to 6pm; Carretera al Parque Arqueológico, ☎37 36 79)* is situated on an enclosed terrace and serves *churrascos*, a mixed grill cooked over charcoal. Chicken is the featured dish, but beef, sausages and blood pudding are also on the menu. The owner tends to the barbecue and his wife and daughter look after the service. This is a family enterprise with a pleasant atmosphere.

The restaurant at the **Hotel Yalconia** *($$-$$$; every day 7am to 10pm; Carretera al Parque Arqueológico, ☎37 30 13 or 37 30 01, ≈37 30 01)* is probably the best in San Agustín. International cuisine is served in a tastefully furnished dining room with white tablecloths and floral decorations. Panoramic windows open onto the pool and provide a magnificent view of the mountains beyond. The wine list includes French and Chilean vintages. Grilled foods are the specialty of the chef. The service here, in contrast to the chilly reception at the front desk (see p 280), is friendly and professional.

Tierradentro

Nearly all the homes in Tierradentro become restaurants and hotels with the seasonal influx of tourists.

El 56 *($; Carretera Principale)* is the home address of guide Jaime Calderón Devia, who turns his kitchen into a restaurant according to the needs of his clients. His wife cooks while his daughter waits on the only table – the family table – which seats only four people at a time. The house specialty is *sopa de verduras*, a vegetable soup made with chicken broth. A complete meal costs no more than 5,000 pesos, but you must purchase your own wine at the little *tienda* across the street, 50 metres to the left.

ENTERTAINMENT

Cultural Activities

The departments of Cauca and Huila organize social and cultural events that will likely be of interest to tourists. Here are a few:

Temporada de Taurina, January, Popayán;

Semana Santa, March or April, Popayán;

Mercado Nacional de Artesanías, April, Popayán

Feria de Verano, a summer fair, August, Silvia;

Semana Cultural Integral, October, San Agustín.

SHOPPING

Handicrafts

Given the isolation of certain areas in the departments of Cauca and Huila, and the interest in indigenous communities that have preserved many of their customs and traditional lifestyles, this region is a paradise for handicraft shopping. You can find clothing, leatherwork, gold jewellery, household items, reproductions of archaeological artifacts (mainly in

POPAYÁN

San Agustín), and more. A wide choice of handmade articles is available at the following shops:

Popayán

Oficina de Turismo, Calle 3 No. 4-70, ☎24 22 51;
Pubenza, Calle 4 No. 5-20, ☎24 00 83.

Silvia

In Silvia, many of the stalls in the **Guambiano market** sell products for daily use and handicrafts created by these local native people: woolen clothing (sweaters, scarves, gloves), leather goods, jewellery, etc.

Museo de Artesanías del Mundo, Carrera 2 No. 14-19, ☎25 10 34.

San Agustín

In San Agustín, there are a dozen or so craftspeople who specialize in the reproduction of artifacts and will even replicate specific objects for tourists. Most are on Calle 5a, while some exceptional ones are at **Darwin**, No.16-02, **Artesañas Taller José**, No.15-46, **Cerámicas El Timaco**, No. 15-30, **Artesañas y Raplicas Précolombianas Andaquí**, No. 15-07.

Tierradentro

In Tierradentro, locally made handicrafts are for sale pretty much everywhere. Guides can provide specific names and addresses.

LETICIA AND THE DEPARTMENT OF AMAZONAS

Who hasn't dreamt of crossing a primal forest, machete in hand, warding off tigers, jaguars, snakes and venomous spiders, to the incessant chattering of parrots and monkeys high up in the trees above? Or of navigating the Amazon – the second-longest river in the world – at the helm of a fragile pirogue, battling strong currents, crocodiles, giant anacondas and voracious piranhas, and braving the humidity and mosquitoes, as well as cannibal headhunters armed with curare-poisoned arrows? The conquistadors did, and were the first to enter Amazonia in 1541, led by Francisco de Orellana. Upon hearing Indian tales of a population of women warriors, each of whom was more ferocious than 10 men, living at the mouth of the river, they christened this enormous land and the great river they discovered Amazonas, thus drawing a parallel with the formidable female warriors – the Amazons – who, according to Greek myths, lived on the shores of the Thermodon and cut off their right breast to better draw their bow. What's more, the indigenous population used the quechua word *amaçunu*, meaning "crash of water," to designate a tidal bore at the mouth of the Amazon in Brazil, which reached heights of four to five metres. Today, this immense territory of 6,430,000 square kilometres encompasses seven countries: Brazil, Guyana, Bolivia, Peru, Ecuador, Venezuela, and Colombia.

Amazonia

The Amazonian basin is irrigated by a complex system of tributaries and canals. Numerous Indian groups, some of which are still sheltered from the modern world, are scattered across all seven countries along with small clusters of settlers, established here and there in the scant plains. Amazonia has a unique biological diversity and a tremendous capacity for photosynthesis, acting as the planet's lungs by regulating its oxygen levels. However, the basin is constantly threatened by deforestation and mining as well as by the populations of the seven countries hoping to use it for livestock breeding and agriculture purposes. All such activities sadly result in systematic tree cutting and the destruction of the rain forest on a massive scale.

Amazonas

Roughly one third of Colombia's territory lies in the Amazonian basin. This 400,000-square-kilometre area rises between 100 and 600 metres above sea level and is mostly covered by a dense and impenetrable primal forest. It is divided into six departments: Putumayo, Caquetá, Guaviare, Guanía, Vaupés, and Amazonas. The latter, with a surface area of 109,655 square kilometres and a population of approximately 60,000 inhabitants, became a department in 1991 following the redrafting of the Colombian constitution. Today,

Freshwater Dolphins

Two types of dolphins swim in the waters of the Amazonian lakes. The first, known as the "Bugeo", is a pink dolphin whose scientific name is *Inia geoffrensis*. It can grow to a length of 2.7 metres and weigh up to 180 kilos. Other than its characteristic pale pink colour, this dolphin is distinguishable by its snout, small eyes and short dorsal fin. It feeds on three to four kilos of fish per day.

The second Amazonian dolphin is the grey dolphin, or "Tucuxi", which scientists refer to as the *Sotalia fluviatilis* and which resembles the sea dolphin in weight, colour and shape. It measures up to 1.6 metres in length and weighs as much as 60 kilos, and consumes over 5 kilos of fish per day.

Amazonas is bordered by the departments of Caquetá, Vaupés and Putumayo to the north, by Peru to the south and west, and by Brazil to the east. Averaging temperatures of 27°C and a humidity of over 90 percent, Amazonas is fed by four great rivers: the Río Putumayo, the Río Caquetá, the Río Apaporis and the Río Amazonas, although only 130 kilometres of the latter's 6,520 kilometres flow through Colombia, in accordance with a treaty signed in 1930 by Colombia, Brazil and Peru following border conflicts.

The Amazonas economy revolves around agriculture (corn, manioc, plantains, rice) and livestock breeding, with freshwater fishing also playing an important role. Over the years, tourism has become one of its growing industries, especially in Leticia, which is reputed for the diversity of its flora. In addition to palm trees and myriad medicinal plants, the land is rich in cedar, rosewood and the "Victoria Regia", named after the Queen of England, a huge water lily that often spans two metres in diameter and floats in stagnant waters. Its small white and red flowers contrast with the green rubbery texture of the plant.

Tourists also seek out the region's unique fauna: tigers, jaguars, monkeys, crocodiles, and snakes, including the anaconda, or *eunecte*, a reptile that grows to lengths of 10 metres and lives in swamplands. However, is it mainly the pink and grey dolphins of the Amazon that draw tourists, many of whom also dream of capturing a piranha.

Leticia

Located on the northern shore of the Amazon, Leticia, the capital of Amazonas, is the only city in the department with the infrastructure to accommodate mass tourism.

A Brief History

Leticia was founded as San Antonio on April 25, 1867 by Captain Benigno Bustamente. The city belonged to Peru until it was yielded to Colombia through a treaty signed in 1930, thus becoming Leticia.

Leticia Today

With a population of 27,000 inhabitants, small and charming Leticia doesn't seem to fit in with the rest of Colombia, or, to say the least, has adopted a different lifestyle. Leticia is the self-proclaimed world capital of tranquility, which is no exaggeration. Although it is lost in the depths of Amazonia, this city, which is the size of a village and can be toured in less than half an hour, plays an essential role in bridging the gap between the modern world and the delicate ecology of the rainforest. For instance, there are 10 small motorcycles for every car in Leticia. Traffic is never heavy, and no one drives over 20 kilometres per hour. Taxis are used only to get from the hotel to the airport. Upon setting foot in Leticia, visitors are always greeted warmly by the locals and instantly find themselves in a serene environment that contrasts sharply with the hustle and bustle of the rest of Colombia.

Except in the city's hotels and restaurants, all the recommendations and warnings concerning water and general heath (see p 57) – especially regarding mosquitoes – must be observed in Leticia, especially when venturing off into the Amazon, the region's main attraction.

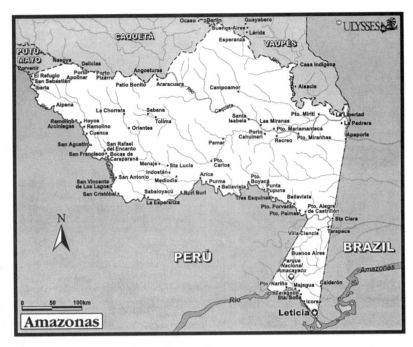

FINDING YOUR WAY AROUND

In Leticia, *calles* run east-west and addresses increase from south to north. *Carreras*, on the other hand, run north-south and addresses increase from east to west.

By Plane

The **Aeropuerto Vásquez Cobo** is situated 1.5 kilometres north of the city, at the end of the avenue of the same name. A tourist tax (*6,000 pesos*) is collected from all foreigners arriving in Leticia. This money is used to develop tourist infrastructure and to preserve and maintain existing sites. Airport officials search all bags upon arrivals and departures, as if you were entering a foreign country. Because there is no border crossing between Leticia in Colombia and Tabatinga in Brazil, custom formalities are performed in the airports of the two cities. There is no bus from the airport to Leticia, and the only means of getting downtown is by taxi (*2,000 pesos*).

Three airlines service the area. Avianca flies twice a week from Bogotá, on Saturday at 1pm and on Tuesday at 5:15pm. AeroRepublica has daily flights, and Satena, a cargo company, sometimes accepts passengers. All three airlines have offices in Leticia:

Avianca, Carrera 11 No. 7-58
Satena, Carrera 11 No. 12-22
AeroRepublica, Carrera 11

The other airport in the vicinity, located in the Brazilian town of Tabatinga, provides domestic flights. Tabatinga is a 20-minute drive from Leticia, and there is no border crossing between the two cities. A shuttle bus leaves downtown Leticia every five minutes for Tabatinga, stopping downtown and at the airport.

Public Transport

The only buses in Leticia drive along the round-trip route to Tabatinga and back. Touring the city on foot is easy, however, as the most interesting sites are in the centre of town.

LETICIA

Renting a Car or a Motorcycle

It is not possible to rent a car in Leticia, as the preferred means of transportation is the motorcycle. Motorcycles (opt for a scooter with automatic transmission) can be rented at the places listed below, open daily from 7am to 8pm. Prices are comparable from one rental agency to the next: 5,000 pesos/hour, 30,000 pesos/day, 45,000 pesos/24 hours, and 80,000 pesos for five days.

Motos Memo, Calle 8 No. 6-47
Motos Alex, Calle 8 No. 7-63
Turismo Leticia, Calle 8 No. 7-70
Moto Tour, Carrera 9 No. 8-08
Papillon, Av. Internal No. 3-13

 PRACTICAL INFORMATION

Area code: 8

Mail

Mail service is provided by the offices of **Avianca**, Carrera 11 No. 7-58.

Banks

Banks are open daily from 8am to 1pm, and to 2pm on Fridays. However, banks in Leticia do not cash cheques or change money. American currency can be changed in shops on Calle 8, west of Carrera 11, toward the river. Shops only accept American dollars as there is no market for other currencies. You should negotiate the exchange rate and shop around for the best one. If you are using a bank card (ATM), the Banco de Bogotá, at the corner of Calle 7 and Carrera 10, accepts MasterCard and cards of affiliated institutions.

Tourist Information

Secretaría Departemental de Turismo y Fronteras, Mon to Fri, from 7am to 12pm, and 2pm to 5:45pm. Carrera 11 No. 11-35, ☎27505.

Excursions

Leticia is a good starting point for excursions in the vicinity and expeditions up or down the Amazon River, depending on your schedule and budget. Excursions can last one or two days, a week or even more.

The following list outlines the typical kinds of excursions that are offered. Prices are based on groups of five people. If you are travelling alone, reserve as soon as possible with a travel agency so that it has time to gather a sufficient number of people, thus allowing you to benefit from a group price.

Lagos Yahuarcacas: admire the Victoria Regia water lilies, 30,000 pesos;

Comunidad de Los Huitotos: visit a Huitoto Indian community, 43,000 pesos including lunch;

Benjamin Constant: visit the Brazilian village located on the other bank of the Amazon, 50,000 pesos including the *almuerzo típico brasilero* for lunch;

Isla de Los Micos: tour the island of monkeys, 50,000 pesos including a visit to a Ticuna community;

Bellavisia: tour this part of Peru, 65,000 pesos, including the Peruvian *almuerzo*;

Puerto Nariño: tour this little fishing port, the Lagos de Tarapoto, home of the pink dolphin, and the Parque Amacayacu, a wildlife reserve, 80,000 pesos including lunch.

The following are useful addresses of travel agencies, the most recommended being that of the Anaconda Hotel:

Anaconda Tours, Carrera 11 No. 7-34, in the lobby of the Hotel Anaconda, ☎27119, 27891 or 27274; in Bogotá, Carrera 14 No. 77-46 2nd floor, ☎218 01 25, 218 46 79, 611 32 19 or 256 09 10, ≈611 23 58

Amaturs, Carrera 11 No. 7-34, also in the lobby of the Hotel Anaconda, ☎27018; in Bogotá, Calle 85 No. 16-28, suite 203 ☎256 11 35, 257 22 00 or 257 03 35 ≈218 21 13, amaturs@impsat.net.co

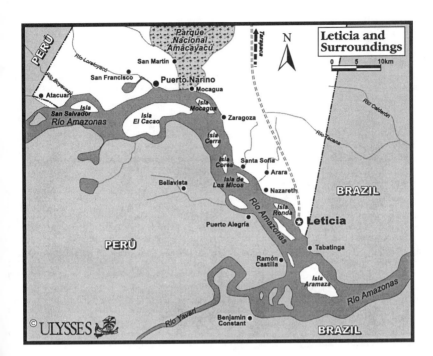

Turamazonas, Carrera 11 facing Calle 6, in the lobby of Parador Ticuna Hotel, ☎27243, ☎27273.

Independent guides on the street also offer excursions or expeditions that they claim to be more focussed on ecology and closer to nature. You must discuss prices and get a clear understanding of what is included: transportation, entrance fees to sites, lodging if necessary, lunch, etc. One of the guides speaks English: he hands out photocopied flyers advertising fishing excursions for piranhas or *pirarucu*, the large freshwater fish found only in the Amazon. **Expedition Tony El Mowgli**, Calle 9, No. 8-62, ☎83301.

 EXPLORING

Leticia

The most spectacular attraction in Leticia – and probably in the entire country – is an **expedition on the Amazon ★★★**. The boat leaves the pier early in the morning. Walk west down Calle 8,

as the sun rises and the many shops slowly awaken in the already unbearable heat and humidity. You soon see the river in all its grandeur, over two kilometres wide and with a large island in the middle. To prevent flooding caused by the frequent elevations in water levels, the shoreline is covered in sandbags that form a wall nearly three metres high. Wooden footbridges cross over the sandbags and lead to floating restaurants to which motor boats, small yachts and long pirogues that seat 30 or more passengers are moored.

The boat leaves the dock and slowly heads north toward Puerto Nariño. In less than 10 minutes, you enter the Lagos Yahuarcacas, a series of lakes fed by the Amazon. The lush vegetation is stunning, especially the profusion of "Victoria Regia", the grandiose water lily of Amazonia.

The captain then returns to the river. The water is brownish in colour, and the current is strong, five or six, or maybe ten knots. After passing the island facing Leticia, the boat accelerates and the captain cheerfully steers the craft between dead trees and other debris of the forest. He obviously has experience with this difficult course. Along the way, you come

LETICIA

Native Communities

The Ticunas

The Ticuna Indians inhabit a sizable portion of the southern part of Amazonas. The larger communities are located near Leticia, in Nazareth, which is on the northern shore of the Amazon, in Arara by the Río Quebrada and in Puerto Nariño, by the Río Loretoyacu. There is also a Ticuna community along the Leticia-Tarapacá route.

The women weave baskets and clothes, while the men produce plant-derived materials that are used to create the masks worn during the *pelazón* ritual, which is celebrated around Leticia. The *pelazón* is a dance that introduces a young girl entering womanhood to the community. It is celebrated when a young girl begins her menstrual cycle. The girl, painted in black and adorned with plumage and shells representing fertility, is surrounded by other tribeswomen and courted by the men who form a circle around them.

The Huitotos

The Huitoto nation lives in the region between the Río Caqueta and the Río Putumayo. Another large community is located near Leticia, between Kilometres 7 and 11 of the Carretera Leticia-Tarapacá.

The Huitoto civilization was nearly eradicated at the turn of the century, when the golden age of rubber production was in its heyday. Today, government agencies and other interest groups focus on rebuilding and valorizing this native culture.

Huitoto community prayer houses, called *maloca*, sit on four major piles that represent the four natural elements: earth, water, air and fire. A main entrance is used during the day, whereas another is used at night.

The Huitotos smoke tobacco and chew coca leaves.

The Yucunas

This native group lives in the northern region of the Department of Amazonas, on the banks of the Río Mírítí-Panamá. Neighbouring groups include the Matapis, Tinimukas and Letuamas.

Yucuna community dwellings are built in a circular fashion with two large triangular openings in their upper parts.

Their religious rituals call for masks and colourful plumage.

across fishermen in pirogues fishing for *bagre* (catfish). Curiously, when alone, fishermen sit at the bow of their fragile boat to paddle while the back of the boat barely grazes the water.

The shores of the great river are deserted save for the occasional native Ticuna dwelling. Venturing out alone on these shores is dangerous as they are infested with crocodiles. Note that these creatures only become active at night, since the heat of the day literally prevents them from moving unless it is to defend themselves. Within 10 minutes, the boat lands on a small beach at the far end of which is a wooden hut with a thatched roof. You can admire more of the water lilies from a wooden bridge that spans a lagoon and leads to the private property.

Twenty minutes later, practically on the other shore of the Amazon, you arrive at the "island of monkeys", Isla de los Micos, which is 10 kilometres long and one kilometre wide. This island, officially called Isla Santa Sofia,

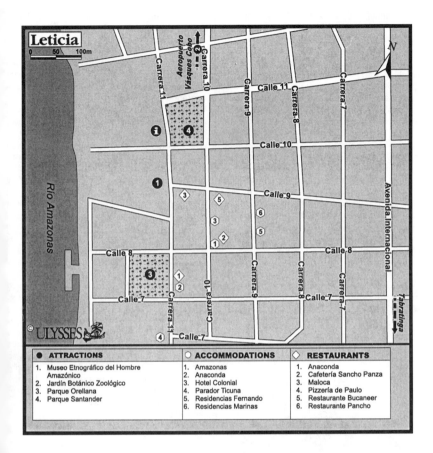

Leticia

0 50 100m

Aeropuerto Vásquez Cobo

Carrera 11
Carrera 10
Carrera 9
Carrera 8
Carrera 7

Calle 11
Calle 10
Calle 9
Calle 8
Calle 7

Avenida Internacional

Río Amazonas

Tabratinga

© ULYSSES

● ATTRACTIONS	○ ACCOMMODATIONS	◇ RESTAURANTS
1. Museo Etnográfico del Hombre Amazónico	1. Amazonas	1. Anaconda
2. Jardín Botánico Zoológico	2. Anaconda	2. Cafetería Sancho Panza
3. Parque Orellana	3. Hotel Colonial	3. Maloca
4. Parque Santander	4. Parador Ticuna	4. Pizzería de Paulo
	5. Residencias Fernando	5. Restaurante Bucaneer
	6. Residencias Marinas	6. Restaurante Pancho

populated with 20,000 monkeys that, until 1974, were shipped to laboratories around the world. The Colombian government then prohibited the exportation of these animals, and the island and its hotels were abandoned by their American owners. Hotels now belong to the Parador Ticuna Hotel in Leticia and are sometimes used to accommodate researchers. This stop not only gives you the chance to observe these curious little monkeys, who eat out of your hand, but also to admire the flora and fauna of the island, especially the many bird species.

The boat then cuts across the Amazon and follows a tributary of the river, the Río Amacayacu, where a Ticuna Indian community lives five kilometres from the mouth of the river. Some 350 people live in little huts that look like small country cottages. Electricity is produced by oil-powered generators and is only

available three hours a day, from 6pm to 9pm. The Ticuna trade fish and crafts for sugar, salt, vegetables, and oil. To protect themselves from the sun and mosquitoes, they coat their skin with a plant extract.

The captain now heads for the Río Loretoyacu, another tributary of the Amazon. On the shores of its black waters is the town of Puerto Nariño, where you will stop for lunch. Next it's full speed ahead to the Lagos de Tarapoto, 15 kilometres away, to catch sight of a strange animal, the pink dolphin of Amazonia, the only freshwater dolphin on earth. The motor is shut, silence fills the air, and then the sound of unusual breathing is heard. A dolphin suddenly surfaces, spurts air from its blowholes and dives again to the depths of the river in search of food.

LETICIA

The **Museo Etnográphico del Hombre Amazónico** ★★★ *(Mon to Fri, 8am to 12pm and 2pm to 7pm, Sat 9am to 12pm; Carrera 11, between Calles 9 and 10, ☎27729 or 27783)*, inaugurated by the Banco de la República in 1988, features a comprehensive ethnographical collection on the *Ticuna, Huitoto* and *Yucuna* Amazonian groups, which look over 50 years for Franciscan and Capuchin missionaries living in the region to compile.

The exposition introduces visitors to the unique geography of Amazonia before showcasing a series of objects dating from pre-Columbian times to the modern era, profiling the decades of rubber exploitation at the turn of the century, a devastating epoch for the indigenous population who were forced into slavery.

Another room examines the daily life and religious rituals of today's Indians.

The museum's extensive library includes more than 3,000 works dedicated to the indigenous ways of life, a unique source of information for researchers and specialists of all kinds.

Puma

The **Jardin Botànico Zoològico** ★ *(1,000 pesos; every day 7am to 12pm and 2pm to 5:30pm; Av. Vásquez Cobo, immediately upon leaving the airport)* lets you observe Amazonian animals in their natural habitat. Monkeys, pumas, crocodiles, and a variety of other animals from the region live in the zoo, not to mention an eight-metre anaconda.

The **Parque Orellana** ★★ *(Carrera 11, between Calles 7 and 8)* is considered to be the town's centre. Townspeople gather in the park in the evenings, between 5 and 7pm, to enjoy the cooler air brought by the end of the day. Food

merchants fill the alleys, and on weekends the sounds of concerts held in the open-air theatre float through the air.

Although the **Parque Santander** ★ *(Carrera 11, between Calles 10 and 11)* is a pretty park with a bronze statue of Francisco de Paula Santander, its main attraction occurs around 5pm when thousands of birds suddenly flock into the park and perch in the trees. Noisier birds are hard to imagine! These cacophonous little parrots, called *loritos*, sound like a high pitched siren, making it literally impossible to converse under a tree. Groups of these birds fly away only to return more in number a few minutes later. Strangely, these birds do not frequent the Parque Orellana, only two streets south.

Tabatinga ★

Tabatinga is a border town in Brazil from which you can fly to other destinations in the country. Less than a 20-minute drive from Leticia, there is no border crossing between the two cities. A shuttle bus leaves downtown Leticia *(Carrera 10, corner of Calle 8)*, every five minutes *(450 pesos)* from 6am to 7pm, and heads to the terminal in Tabatinga, on the Brazilian shore of the Amazon, stopping downtown and at the Tabatinga airport. Time enough to sip a coffee, Brazilian of course, before returning to Leticia, all in less than an hour.

Puerto Nariño ★★

Situated 90 kilometres from Leticia, in the heart of the rainforest, Puerto Nariño has a population of 5,000 and is the second largest city in the Amazonas department. No four wheel drives, cars or motorcycles disturb this little community, paved with stone sidewalks. The only way to access this town is by water. Boats land directly on the beach or alongside a small wooden dock where children swim without worrying about the crocodiles who hesitate to approach as they are a favourite dish of the locals. A shuttle boat links Leticia and Puerto Nariño *(5,000 pesos)*; departure from Leticia are at 8am and 10am, departure from Puerto Nariño are at 12pm and 2pm.

The village extends to the outer limits of the forest some 200 m above the beach, leaving the vast parcel of land separating the beach and the edge of town vacant. In Puerto Nariño, for reasons of economy and following the wishes of the locals, electricity, produced by oil-powered generators, is only available at certain times of the day from 11am to 1pm, and from 5pm to 2am.

Parrots

Puerto Nariño could also lay claim as the capital of world peace if it weren't for the mosquitoes that wage war on humans and animals, especially at dusk. A handful of hotels provide exceptional comfort despite being located in the bush. Quaint restaurants at the entrance of the village prepare delicious fresh fish caught in the Amazon and its tributaries.

 ACCOMMODATIONS

Leticia

You'll find good hotels in Leticia. For more comfort, choose a hotel with air-conditioned rooms as the heat and humidity become stifling as soon as the sun rises.

Residencias Marinas *($; pb, ⊗; Carrera 9 No. 9-29, ☎27309 or 27303)* is a little family-style hotel with 19 spotless rooms. For small budgets.

Residencias Fernando *($; pb, ⊗; Carrera 9 No. 8-80, ☎27372),* also for small budgets, is situated in front of the Residencias Marinas and is of comparable quality. Relaxed atmosphere.

Hotel Colonial *($$; bp, hw, ℜ, ≡; Carrera 10 No. 7-08, ☎27164)* is a charming old hotel situated a stone's throw from downtown. The modestly furnished rooms are clean. The welcome is satisfactory.

The **Amazonas** *($$$; pb, hw, tv, ☎, mb, ≡, ≈, ℜ; Calle 8 No. 10-32, ☎28025, ⊷28027)* is a recently renovated two-storey colonial building with 22 rooms. Its architecture, decor and furnishings give it an Amazonian ambiance.

The **Parador Ticuna** *($$$; pb, hw, tv, ☎, mb, ≡, ≈, ℜ; Carrera 11 No. 6-11, ☎27243, ⊷27273)* is worth the detour. Situated in a wooded area, a few steps from the centre of town, this one-storey hotel looks like a motel with its rooms that open onto a lovely courtyard landscaped with trees and around the pool. The loft-like rooms are spacious and have a screened veranda. The safari-style furniture blends in perfectly with the ambiance. The hotel's exceptional open-air bamboo lobby, decorated with flowers and pieces of local art, also has a safari flair. Reception is friendly. The Parador Ticuna can organize stays of one or more days on the Isla de los Micos. Information can be obtained at the reception desk or at the Turamazonas travel agency located in the lobby (see p 287).

The **Anaconda Hotel** *($$$$$; pb, tv, ☎, mb, ≡, ≈, ℜ; Carrera 11 No. 7-34, ☎27119, 27891 or 27274, ⊷27005)* is unquestionably the best hotel in Leticia. This four-storey building of nondescript decor has a lobby and reception desk that look more like a shopping centre than the entrance of a grand hotel. It is the meeting place of all Leticians, who feel very much at home here, from the bank manager and local *aguardiente* distributor to the independent tour organizer. Rooms are adequately furnished. To get a breathtaking view of the sun setting on the Amazon, reserve a room in the front, with a balcony, preferably on the 4th floor. The hotel has a large pool surrounded by tables and chairs as well as deck chairs. There is a bar on the same terrace as the restaurant.

Puerto Nariño

The few hotels in Puerto Nariño offer varying degrees of comfort and electricity is only available at certain times of the day. However, if you are looking for a complete change of scenery, try the following:

To experience a real bush expedition, stay at the **Brisas del Amazonas** *($; ⊗; no address but situated to the left of the village as you* step off the dock; you can reserve in Leticia, Carrera 8, No. 9-90, ☎/☎27424, or in Bogotá, Calle 59, No. 9-63, room 247-59, ☎211 13 59, ☞211 11 05), a two-storey log cabin on piles, complete with a thatched roof and a relaxed atmosphere. The hotel offers 12 rooms, no private bathrooms, and an open-air room where you can sleep in a hammock, protected by a mosquito net of course. There is no air conditioning but the hotel is shaded by trees and remains relatively cool even during the hottest times of the day. Reception is very friendly and can organize excursions to fit the tastes and budgets of their guests.

 RESTAURANTS

Leticia

As in most of Colombia, one eats well in and around Leticia. Restaurants offering good food at affordable prices are found on Carrera 10. The **Cafetería Sancho Panza** *($; every day, 12pm to 2am; No. 8-72)*, **Restaurante Pancho** *($; every day, 12pm to 2am; No. 8-68)* and **Restaurante Bucaneer** *($; every day, 12pm to 2am; No. 8-10c)* serve typical food, notably the noontime *almuerzo*, a complete meal including soup and main course.

Enjoy breakfast on the small terrace of **Pizzería de Paula** *($; corner Calle 8 and Carrera 10)*. American-style breakfasts, omelets as well as pizzas and hamburgers are served.

For a more upscale dining, opt instead for one of the following:

 Enjoy grilled fish and meat dishes in the open-air dining room of the **Maloca** *($-$$; every day, 8am to 2am; Calle No. 9-87)*. This huge hut, topped with a thatched roof, recreates the large prayer room traditionally used by the Huitotos.

The **Anaconda** *($$-$$$; every day, 7am to 10pm; Carrera 11 No. 7-34, ☎ 217119, 27891 or 27274)*, the restaurant of the hotel

of the same name (see p 291), seats its guests in an air-conditioned dining room overlooking the pool. If you prefer to dine outdoors, you can sit on the terrace next to the pool. Continental cuisine, fish and juicy steaks are served, accompanied by French or Chilean wine.

  ENTERTAINMENT

Special Events

Several interesting events are organized in the Department of Amazonas, especially around Leticia:

Elección and Coronación of Miss Amazonas Colombia: in Leticia, April;
Cupleaños de Leticia: the city celebrates the anniversary of its foundation with military parades and flower exhibitions, April 25;
Festival de la Confraternidad Amazónica: the Amazonian countries compete in sports and cultural events in Leticia, July 15 to 20;
La Piraña de Oro: piranha-fishing competition in Puerto Nariño, more specifically in the Lagos de Tarapoto, August 15 to 21;
Pirarucú de Oro: Amazonian music festival drawing musicians from neighbouring countries in Leticia, November;
Desfile de Muñecos Viejos: a mini-carnival of puppets marks the end of the year, December 31.

SHOPPING

Amazonas is the ideal place for buying eclectic and unique souvenirs such as a machete or a blowgun with darts. Blowguns must be packed in your checked luggage as it is doubtful that they be allowed aboard a plane, regardless of their craftsmanship. Tamer gift ideas include carpets, tree bark dolls, feather-adorned Indian headdresses, woven bags, wicker baskets and other common native objects. Go on an excursion to shop for souvenirs since there is no actual crafts shop in Leticia.

GLOSSARY

GREETINGS

Goodbye	*adiós, hasta luego*
Good afternoon and good evening	*buenas tardes*
Hi (casual)	*hola*
Good morning	*buenos días*
Good night	*buenas noches*
Thank-you	*gracias*
Please	*por favor*
You are welcome	*de nada*
Excuse me	*perdone/a*
My name is...	*mi nombre es...*
What is your name?	*¿cómo se llama usted?*
yes	*no*
no	*sí*
Do you speak English?	*¿habla usted inglés?*
Slower, please	*más despacio, por favor*
I am sorry, I don't speak Spanish	*Lo siento, no hablo español*
I am a tourist	*Soy turista*
single (m/f)	*soltero/a*
divorced (m/f)	*divorciado/a*
married (m/f)	*casado/a*
friend (m/f)	*amigo/a*
child (m/f)	*niño/a*
husband, wife	*esposo/a*
mother	*madre*
father	*padre*
brother, sister	*hermano/a*
I am hungry	*tengo hambre*
I am ill	*estoy enfermo/a*
I am thirsty	*tengo sed*

DIRECTIONS

beside	*al lado de*
to the right	*a la derecha*
to the left	*a la izquierda*
here	*aquí*
there	*allí*
into, inside	*dentro*
outside	*fuera*
behind	*detrás*
in front of	*delante*
between	*entre*
far from	*lejos de*
Where is ... ?	*¿dónde está ... ?*
To get to ...?	*¿para ir a...?*
near	*cerca de*
straight ahead	*todo recto*

MONEY

money	*dinero / plata*
credit card	*tarjeta de crédito*
exchange	*cambio*
traveller's cheque	*cheque de viaje*

I don't have any money	*no tengo dinero*
The bill, please	*la cuenta, por favor*

SHOPPING

store	*tienda*
market	*mercado*
open	*abierto/a*
closed	*cerrado/a*
How much is this?	*¿cuánto es?*
I would like...	*yo quisiera...*
batteries	*pilas*
cameras	*cámaras*
cosmetics and perfumes	*cosméticos y perfumes*
cotton	*algodón*
eyeglasses	*lentes, gafas*
film	*película*
handbag	*bolsa*
hat	*sombrero*
jewellery	*joyería*
leather	*cuero, piel*
local crafts	*artesanía*
magazines	*revistas*
newpapers	*periódicos*
pants	*pantalones*
sandals	*sandalias*
shirt	*camisa*
shoes	*zapatos*
skirt	*falda*
sun screen products	*productos solares*
T-shirt	*camiseta*
wool	*lana*

MISCELLANEOUS

a little	*poco*
a lot	*mucho*
good (m/f)	*bueno/a*
bad (m/f)	*malo/a*
beautiful (m/f)	*hermoso/a*
ugly	*feo*
big	*grande*
small (m/f)	*pequeño/a*
cold (m/f)	*frío/a*
hot	*caliente*
dark (m/f)	*oscuro/a*
light (colour)	*claro*
do not touch	*no tocar*
expensive (m/f)	*caro/a*
cheap (m/f)	*barato/a*
less	*menos*
more	*más*
new (m/f)	*nuevo/a*
old (m/f)	*viejo/a*
What is this?	*¿qué es esto?*
when?	*¿cuando?*
where?	*¿dónde?*

TIME

in the afternoon, early evening	*por la tarde*
at night	*por la noche*
in the daytime	*por el día*
in the morning	*por la mañana*
now	*ahora*
today	*hoy*
yesterday	*ayer*
tomorrow	*mañana*
What time is it?	*¿qué hora es?*
hour	*hora*
Sunday	*domingo*
Monday	*lunes*
Tuesday	*martes*
Wednesday	*miércoles*
Thursday	*jueves*
Friday	*viernes*
Saturday	*sábado*

ACTIVITIES

beach	*playa*
museum or gallery	*museo*
scuba diving	*buceo*
to swim	*bañarse*
to walk around	*pasear*
hiking	*caminata*
trail	*pista, sendero*
cycling	*ciclismo*
fishing	*pesca*

TRANSPORTATION

arrival	*llegada*
departure	*salida*
cancelled (m/f)	*anulado/a*
one way ticket	*ida*
return	*regreso*
round trip	*ida y vuelta*
schedule	*horario*
north	*norte*
south	*sur*
east	*este*
west	*oeste*
airplane	*avión*
airport	*aeropuerto*
bicycle	*bicicleta*
boat	*barco*
bus	*bus*
bus stop	*parada*
bus terminal	*terminal*
train	*tren*
train crossing	*crucero ferrocarril*
station	*estación*
neighbourhood	*barrio*
collective taxi	*colectivo*
corner	*esquina*
express	*rápido*
safe	*seguro/a*
be careful	*cuidado*

car	*coche, carro*
To rent a car	*alquilar un auto*
gas	*gasolina*
gas station	*gasolinera*
no parking	*no estacionar*
no passing	*no adelantar*
parking	*parqueo*
pedestrian	*peaton*
road closed, no through traffic	*no hay paso*
slow down	*reduzca velocidad*
speed limit	*velocidad permitida*
stop	*alto*
stop! (an order)	*pare*
traffic light	*semáforo*

ACCOMMODATION

double, for two people	*doble*
single, for one person	*sencillo*
double bed	*cama matrimonial*
cot	*camita*
with private bathroom	*con baño privado*
hot water	*agua caliente*
breakfast	*desayuno*
air conditioning	*aire acondicionado*
fan	*ventilador, abanico*
pool	*piscina, alberca*
room	*habitación*

INDEX

ORDER FORM

ULYSSES TRAVEL GUIDES

☐ Atlantic Canada	$24.95 CAN $17.95 US	☐ Lisbon	$18.95 CAN $13.95 US
☐ Bahamas	$24.95 CAN $17.95 US	☐ Louisiana	$29.95 CAN $21.95 US
☐ Beaches of Maine	$12.95 CAN $9.95 US	☐ Martinique	$24.95 CAN $17.95 US
☐ Bed & Breakfasts in Québec	$13.95 CAN $10.95 US	☐ Montréal	$19.95 CAN $14.95 US
☐ Belize	$16.95 CAN $12.95 US	☐ New Orleans	$17.95 CAN $12.95 US
☐ Calgary	$17.95 CAN $12.95 US	☐ New York City	$19.95 CAN $14.95 US
☐ Canada	$29.95 CAN $21.95 US	☐ Nicaragua	$24.95 CAN $16.95 US
☐ Chicago	$19.95 CAN $14.95 US	☐ Ontario	$27.95 CAN $19.95US
☐ Chile	$27.95 CAN $17.95 US	☐ Ottawa	$17.95 CAN $12.95 US
☐ Colombia	$29.95 CAN $21.95 US	☐ Panamá	$24.95 CAN $17.95 US
☐ Costa Rica	$27.95 CAN $19.95 US	☐ Peru	$27.95 CAN $19.95 US
☐ Cuba	$24.95 CAN $17.95 US	☐ Portugal	$24.95 CAN $16.95 US
☐ Dominican Republic	$24.95 CAN $17.95 US	☐ Provence - Côte d'Azur	$29.95 CAN $21.95US
☐ Ecuador and Galapagos Islands	$24.95 CAN $17.95 US	☐ Québec	$29.95 CAN $21.95 US
☐ El Salvador	$22.95 CAN $14.95 US	☐ Québec and Ontario with Via	$9.95 CAN $7.95 US
☐ Guadeloupe	$24.95 CAN $17.95 US	☐ Toronto	$18.95 CAN $13.95 US
☐ Guatemala	$24.95 CAN $17.95 US	☐ Vancouver	$17.95 CAN $12.95 US
☐ Honduras	$24.95 CAN $17.95 US	☐ Washington D.C.	$18.95 CAN $13.95 US
☐ Jamaica	$24.95 CAN $17.95 US	☐ Western Canada	$29.95 CAN $21.95 US

ULYSSES DUE SOUTH

☐ Acapulco	$14.95 CAN $9.95 US	☐ Cartagena (Colombia)	$12.95 CAN $9.95 US
☐ Belize	$16.95 CAN $12.95 US	☐ Cancun Cozumel	$17.95 CAN $12.95 US

ULYSSES DUE SOUTH

☐ Puerto Vallarta	$14.95 CAN $9.95 US	☐ St. Martin and St. Barts	$16.95 CAN $12.95 US

ULYSSES GREEN ESCAPES

☐ Cycling in France . . . . $22.95 CAN
$16.95 US

☐ Cycling in Ontario . . . . $22.95 CAN
$16.95 US

☐ Hiking in the . . . . $19.95 CAN
Northeastern U.S. $13.95 US

☐ Hiking in Québec . . . . $19.95 CAN
$13.95 US

ULYSSES CONVERSATION GUIDES

☐ French for Better Travel . . . . . $9.95 CAN
$6.95 US

☐ Spanish for Better Travel . . . . $9.95 CAN
$6.95 US

ULYSSES TRAVEL JOURNAL

☐ Ulysses Travel Journal . . . $9.95 CAN
(Blue, Red, Green, Yellow, Sextant)
$7.95 US

☐ Ulysses Travel Journal . . . $14.95 CAN
80 Days $9.95 US

TITLE	QUANTITY	PRICE	TOTAL

Name _____	Sub-total	
Address _____	Postage & Handling	$8.00*
_____	Sub-total	
_____		
Payment : ☐ Money Order ☐ Visa ☐ MasterCard	G.S.T. in Canada 7%	
Card Number _____		
Signature _____	TOTAL	

ULYSSES TRAVEL PUBLICATIONS
4176 St-Denis,
Montréal, Québec, H2W 2M5
(514) 843-9447 fax (514) 843-9448
www.ulysses.ca
*$15 for overseas orders

U.S. ORDERS: **GLOBE PEQUOT PRESS**
P.O. Box 833, 6 Business Park Road,
Old Saybrook, CT 06475-0833
1-800-243-0495 fax 1-800-820-2329
www.globe-pequot.com